POSTCOLONIAL CHALLENGES IN EDUCATION

Studies in the
Postmodern Theory of Education

Joe L. Kincheloe and Shirley R. Steinberg
General Editors

Vol. 369

PETER LANG
New York • Washington, D.C./Baltimore • Bern
Frankfurt am Main • Berlin • Brussels • Vienna • Oxford

POSTCOLONIAL CHALLENGES IN EDUCATION

Edited by ROLAND SINTOS COLOMA

PETER LANG
New York • Washington, D.C./Baltimore • Bern
Frankfurt am Main • Berlin • Brussels • Vienna • Oxford

Library of Congress Cataloging-in-Publication Data

Postcolonial challenges in education /
edited by Roland Sintos Coloma.
p. cm. — (Counterpoints: studies in the postmodern
theory of education; vol. 369)
Includes bibliographical references.
1. Education—Philosophy. 2. Education—Methodology.
3. Postcolonialism. 4. Education and globalization.
I. Coloma, Roland Sintos.
LB14.7.P665   370.1—dc22   2009030271
ISBN 978-1-4331-0650-7 (hardcover)
ISBN 978-1-4331-0649-1 (paperback)
ISSN 1058-1634

Bibliographic information published by **Die Deutsche Bibliothek**.
Die Deutsche Bibliothek lists this publication in the "Deutsche
Nationalbibliografie"; detailed bibliographic data is available
on the Internet at http://dnb.ddb.de/.

Cover image: Filipino schoolchildren, circa early 1960s.
Used courtesy of David Warren and the Scarboro Foreign Mission society.

© 2009 Peter Lang Publishing, Inc., New York
29 Broadway, 18th floor, New York, NY 10006
www.peterlang.com

All rights reserved.
Reprint or reproduction, even partially, in all forms such as microfilm,
xerography, microfiche, microcard, and offset strictly prohibited.

to Edward W. Said and Gloria E. Anzaldúa
for paving the way

to the Lakeside Collective
for walking with me

Contents

Interventions

Chapter One   3
Palimpsest Histories and Catachrestic Interventions
Roland Sintos Coloma, Alexander Means, and Anna Kim

Chapter Two   23
Education and the New Imperialism
Leon Tikly

Chapter Three   46
Postcolonialism and Globalization in Education
Fazal Rizvi

Chapter Four   55
Diaspora and the Anthropology of Latino Education: Challenges, Affinities, and Intersections
Sofia A. Villenas

Curriculum

Chapter Five   67
Decolonization and Education: Locating Pedagogy and Self at the Interstices in Global Times
Nina Asher

Chapter Six   78
Nā Wāhine Mana: A Postcolonial Reading of Classroom Discourse on the Imperial Rescue of Oppressed Hawaiian Women
Julie Kaomea

Chapter Seven   100
Postcolonial Technologies of Power: Standardized Testing and Representing Diverse Young Children
Radhika Viruru

Chapter Eight 119
Post-apartheid Dilemmas: Black Teachers Theorizing Social Justice
Sharon Subreenduth

CULTURAL STUDIES

Chapter Nine 139
The Future in the Present: The Status of Sport and Intellectual Labor in C.L.R. James' *Beyond a Boundary* and His Other Works
Cameron McCarthy

Chapter Ten 161
Multicultural and Creole Contemporaries: Postcolonial Artists and Postcolonial Cities
Rinaldo Walcott

Chapter Eleven 178
Border Crossing with M.I.A. and Transnational Girlhood Studies
Lisa Weems

Chapter Twelve 195
Postcolonial Studies as Re-education: Learning from J. M. Coetzee's *Disgrace*
Aparna Mishra Tarc

GENDER AND SEXUALITY

Chapter Thirteen 217
Decolonizing the Flesh: The Body, Pedagogy, and Inequality
Antonia Darder

Chapter Fourteen 233
Postcolonial Subjects, Black Feminism, and the Intersectionality of Race and Gender in Higher Education
Heidi Safia Mirza

Chapter Fifteen   249
Dis/locating Oriental Citizen-Subject Makings: A Postcolonial Reading of Korean/Asian American Women's Narratives
Jeong-eun Rhee

Chapter Sixteen   268
Putting Queer to Work: Examining Empire and Education
Roland Sintos Coloma

METHODOLOGIES

Chapter Seventeen   289
Postcolonial Technoscience, Toleration and Anti-imperialism, and Education and Psychology
Bernadette Baker

Chapter Eighteen   309
The Contradictions of Negotiating Legitimacy at Home/Field
Binaya Subedi

Chapter Nineteen   326
The Noninnocence of Recognition: Subjects and Agency in Education
Stephanie Lynn Daza

Chapter Twenty   344
Mediating Globalization: The Non-resident Indian Student in an Era of "India Poised"
Aliya Rahman

AFTERWORD

Southern Theory **and Its Dynamics for Postcolonial Education**   365
Anne Hickling-Hudson

Acknowledgments   377

Contributors   379

PART ONE

Interventions

CHAPTER 1

Palimpsest Histories and Catachrestic Interventions

ROLAND SINTOS COLOMA, ALEXANDER MEANS, AND ANNA KIM

The twenty-first century opened with primal scenes of empire. On September 11, 2001, the United States and the rest of the world witnessed the fall of the World Trade Center in New York City, another plane crash into the Pentagon, and a failed attempt to wreck havoc to Washington, D.C. Since Wall Street, New York City, the Pentagon, and Washington, D.C. represent, respectively, the financial, cultural, military, and political centers of the United States, Germany's *Suddeutsche Zeitung* newspaper referred to the hijacks and crashes as "Terrorist attack[ing] the heart of America."

The mo(u)rning-after headlines of major newspapers around the world reveal the immediate ways in which these scenes were construed in the United States and beyond. Attack and war, in various languages, underpinned the grammar to describe what had taken place, which served to fuel, justify, and enact the subsequent U.S. governmental and military responses. The newspaper front pages blared with "U.S. Attacked" (*New York Times*, United States), "Attack on America" (*Times of India*, India), and "Attaco all'America" (*la Repubblica*, Italy). 9/11 became "A day of infamy" (*Globe and Mail*, Canada) and "¡Día de terror!" (*El Universal*, Colombia). The attacks on the United States were deemed as "A declaration of war" (*Guardian*, United Kingdom) or, simply yet provocatively, "War" (*O Dia*, Brazil). The global impact of 9/11 was best captured by two headlines from different parts of the world: "The United States hit, the world seized with dread" from the French *Le Monde* and "The Day that Shook the World" from New Zealand's *Waikato Times*. September 11, 2001 has certainly taken on "an aura of history, an apocalyptic moment, a turning point in the history of America and its relationship to the world"

(Denzin & Lincoln, 2003, p. xiii).

9/11, however, was not, and is not, a single event. The visuality of the towers' fall as well as the empathetic focus on the incalculable human death and suffering, ensuing loss and mourning, however, relayed repeatedly by television and cable networks, in newspapers and magazines, and in the Internet, became a simulacrum that risked decoupling what happened in the United States from a broader history of U.S. violence, complicity, and responsibility. What 9/11 signifies and evokes cannot and must not be divorced from the history, legacy, and continuity of U.S. imperialism. Indeed, as "the world's last significant remaining colonial power" (Young, 2001, p. 3), the United States has played and continues to play a crucial role in domestic and global affairs for an assortment of reasons, through multiple means, and with various effects.

Raising the specter of U.S. imperialism in the early and mid-1900s, scholars such as W.E.B. DuBois (1907, 1920) and William Appleman Williams (1959, 1980) interrogated the discursive and material conditions of "foreign peoples at home and abroad" and asserted that U.S. imperialism is tied intimately to its project of nation-building (Jacobson, 2001; Kaplan, 2005). Extending earlier theoretical and empirical examinations of empire, a critical mass of Americanists and transnationalists emerged in the 1990s not only to challenge disciplinary orthodoxies and received understandings, but also to generate fresh analytics for what may be considered as the new field of U.S. empire studies (Kaplan & Pease, 1993; Lewis & Mills, 2003; Stoler, 2006). The new vanguards, wielding innovative interpretive and methodological techniques from the humanities and social sciences and from the vantage points of ethnic, feminist, queer, and cultural studies, have set their analytical gaze upon the continental conquest and expansion of the United States, its overseas occupations, and deterritorialized domination.

Histories as Under Erasure and Overwritten

"Why do they hate us?" was incessantly asked by many in the United States in the aftermath of 9/11. To respond to this question is to necessarily narrate and invoke the complex and multilayered history and legacy of U.S. imperialism that critical scholars, educators, and activists are pursuing and grappling to understand. By way of an answer, in a word: *palimpsest*.

According to the *Oxford English Dictionary*, a palimpsest is "a parchment or other writing surface on which the original text has been effaced or partially erased, and then overwritten by another." For scholars, educators, and activists, the concept of palimpsest is particularly relevant to comprehend the discursive, material, and psychical linkages of history and the present since, despite effacements, the sedimentation of previous texts remains. It is also "a useful way of understanding the developing complexity of culture, as previous 'inscriptions' are erased and overwritten, yet remain as traces within present consciousness" (Ashcroft, Griffiths, & Tiffin, 2001, p. 176). The consequence of writing, erasing, and writing-over is a layering of history:

> While the "layering" effect of history has been mediated by each successive period, "erasing" what has gone before, all present experience contains ineradicable traces of the past that remain part of the constitution of the present. Teasing out such vestigial features left over from the past is an important part of understanding the nature of the present. (p. 174)

In other words, to make sense of 9/11, imperialism, and antagonism toward the United States is to dig into the layers of history and investigate the vestigial features in the present.

Commenting on Freud's use of "mystic writing-pad" as an analogy of palimpsest for discursive intertextuality and psychical historicity, Derrida (1978) points out that

> the *depth* of the Mystic Pad is simultaneously a depth without bottom, an infinite allusion, a perfectly superficial exteriority: a stratification of surfaces each of whose relation to itself, each of whose interior, is but the implication of another similarly exposed surface. It joins the two empirical certainties by which we are constituted: infinite depth in the implication of meaning, in the unlimited envelopment of the present, and, simultaneously, the pellicular essence of being, the absolute absence of any foundation. (p. 224)

Spivak (1976) suggests that "the relationship between the reinscribed text and the so-called original text is not that of patency and latency, but rather the relationship between two palimpsest" (p. lxxv), thereby elaborating on Derrida's point of the absence of any origin and the deferral of finalities.

Palimpsest as a metaphor and metonym grapples with the history and legacy of imperialism of the United States and other colonial nations. Young (2001) defines imperialism as "the exercise of power either through direct conquest or (latterly) through political and economic influence" from metropolitan centers that ultimately results to domination "through facilitating institutions and ideologies" (p. 27). Colonialism, on the other hand, is the "material condition of the political rule of subjugated peoples" by U.S. and other imperialist powers (ibid.; Cooper, 2005). Young proffers three "key foundational models of the different forms of colonialism and imperialism"— French, British, and American—to categorize and schematize their ideologies and operations (p. 31).

French imperialism was undergirded by "*mission civilisatrice*, whose task was to bring the benefits of French culture, religion and language to the unenlightened races of the earth" (p. 30). Essentially a system of benevolent assimilation, it derived from "an Enlightenment belief in a common liberty, equality and fraternity for humankind" (ibid.). Young notes the paradox in this model: its policy of equality for all rested on the assumption of the subjugated's inferiority that drove the uniform imposition of imperialist cultures and institutions as the most advanced expressions of civilization.

The British operated two forms of imperialism that were enacted not due to a desire to assimilate the colonized, like the French, but because of a racialized duty to address the "white man's burden." The two forms were (1) "the politically liberal Anglo-Saxon colonization of suitable, allegedly empty, parts of the globe"; and (2) "the autocratic or 'paternalist' rule of subject races for purposes of economic exploitation, justified by notions of cultural and racial superiority, with only limited forms of internal or local assembly" (p. 40). The British imperialist duty produced two intertwined imperatives: "first to exploit for the benefit of others ('the civilized world') the available raw materials that would otherwise be left unused, and then to extend the culture of civilization to the society being exploited" (ibid.). In this model of imperialism, despotic rule was intertwined with and as moral responsibility.

Finally, the United States practiced two phases of imperialism that initially drew from the French and British models. From the 1890s to the First World War, the "high point" of "jingoist imperialism," the United States "shifted its policy from the acquisition and assimilation of contiguous territory through a militarized form of settler expansion, to one of direct acquisition and control of colonies overseas" (p. 42). The latter phase, starting after the Second World War, which characterized the U.S. model of imperialism, was primarily compelled by economic motives that "preferred forms of indirect rule and influence to direct colonial control" (ibid.).

After giving nominal political independence to many colonized countries in Africa, Asia, and the Americas after the Second World War, the U.S. and European imperialist nations retained economic control and influence over them, generating the current prevailing system of domination otherwise known as neocolonialism. "Neocolonialism denotes a continuing economic hegemony" (p. 45) in which the putatively autonomous nation-states work under the dictates of and are put in a position to depend on their former colonial masters and new global power brokers, such as the World Bank, the International Monetary Fund, the World Trade Organization, the Organisation for Economic Co-operation and Development, and the International Trade Security and Facilitation programs, which are constituted and controlled by them. Under neocolonialism, "national sovereignty is effectively a fiction" (p. 46).

Palimpsest can also be used to narrate the history, legacy, and continuity of anticolonial resistance. Whether through national liberation movements, global activisms, or everyday individual or collective "weapons of the weak," the colonized have worked and continue to work against imperialist subjugation and imposition (Cabral, 1970; Khagram, Sikkink, & Riker, 2002; Scott, 1987). For instance, in 1804 Haiti became the first independent and black-led nation in the Caribbean whose sovereignty was won through successful slave rebellions. Its independence was garnered, in large part, due to earlier guerilla campaigns and military victories of Toussaint L'Ouverture, recounted by C.L.R. James in *The Black Jacobins* (James, 1938/1989).

In 1955 the Bandung Conference brought together 29 African and Asian nations constituting over half of the world's population. It was convened to oppose the neocolonialisms of the United States, Soviet Union, and other imperialist powers as well as the polarizing alignments of the Cold War. It also aimed to forge solidarity among peoples of color around the world on the basis of self-determination, anti-imperialism, and reciprocal international relations, resulting in the adoption of the Declaration on Promotion of World Peace and Cooperation. The historical events and global implications of Bandung were covered by African American writer Richard Wright (1956/1995) and Filipino diplomat Carlos P. Romulo (1956), who became the first Asian president of the United Nations General Assembly in 1949, only a few years after his own country's independence from the United States.

In 2007 the United Nations adopted the Declaration on the Rights of Indigenous Peoples, after more than 20 years of advocacy by the Working Group on Indigenous Populations. Although this Declaration passed by an overwhelming majority, it must be noted that four countries—the United States, Canada, Australia, and New Zealand—voted negatively. The anticolonial struggles persist for indigenous communities, clearly illuminated in the intellectual and political work, for instance, of Hawaiian Haunani-Kay Trask (1993) and Maori Linda Tahuwai Smith (1999). For native and Aboriginal communities, anti-imperialism and decolonization are an ongoing fight for sovereignty, survival, and preservation (Green, 2007; Stewart-Harawira, 2005).

Interventions as Working Within and Against

For colonized and postcolonial subjects working within and against imperialism, Young (2001) argues that they "inhabit the conceptual, cultural and ideological legacy of colonialism inherent in the very structures and institutions that formed the conditions of decolonization" (p. 418). In Spivak's word: *catachresis*—"a space that the postcolonial does not want, but has no option, to inhabit" (ibid.). Spivak (1993) suggests that

> One might, then, look at the larger third world as diversely postcolonial, making catachrestic claims.... The political claims over which battles are being fought are to nationhood, sovereignty, citizenship, secularism. Those claims are catachrestic claims in the sense that the so-called adequate narratives of the concept-metaphors were supposedly not written in the spaces that have decolonized themselves, but rather in the spaces of the colonizers. (p. 13)

As a way to intentionally wrest, displace, and misappropriate meaning from a referent or its proper name, catachresis offers a way to rework and expand terms and knowledge. Furthermore, in regard to national identity and agency in postcolonial spaces, Spivak contends that "the persistently critical voice must be raised ... as a strategic use of essentialism—in other words this is the crucial scene of the usefulness of catachresis" (p. 162). Such is the position that she has taken in response to the terror of 9/11 and its aftermaths: "there is no response to war.... Yet one cannot remain silent. Out of the imperative or compulsion to speak, then, two questions: What are some already existing responses? And, how [to] respond in the face of the impossibility of response?" (Spivak, 2004, p. 81).

How, then, do we as scholars, educators, and activists respond in the face of impossibility? In the face of violence, complicity, and responsibility? On what grounds do we make our catachrestic claims? In the ongoing realities and aftermaths of colonialism and imperialism?

Postcolonial theory offers some directions and possibilities. As an intellectual, political, and pedagogical project, postcolonial theory, according to Young (2001), has three fundamental tasks:

> First, investigating the extent to which not only European [and U.S.] history but also European [and U.S.] culture and knowledge was part of, and instrumental in, the practice of colonization and its continuing aftermath. Second, identifying fully the means and causes of continuing international deprivation and exploitation, and analysing their epistemological and psychological effects. Third, transforming

those epistemologies into new forms of cultural and political production that operate outside the protocols of metropolitan traditions and enable successful resistance to, and transformation of, the degradation and material injustice to which disempowered peoples and societies remain subjected. (p. 69)

In a somewhat similar vein, Hardt and Negri (2000) offer two potential approaches:

the first is *critical and deconstructive*, aiming to subvert the hegemonic languages and social structures and thereby reveal an alternative ontological basis that resides in the creative and productive practices of the multitude; the second is *constructive and ethico-political*, seeking to lead the processes of the production of subjectivity toward the constitution of an effective social, political alternative, a new constituent power. (p. 47, original italics)

Ultimately the postcolonial project is, in itself, catachrestic. Prakash (1994) in "Subaltern Studies as Postcolonial Criticism" maintains that postcolonial work draws from "a catachrestic combination of Marxism, poststructuralism, Gramsci and Foucault, the modern West and India, archival research and textual criticism" (p. 1490). Kaomea (2003) further adds, "my theoretical framework and interpretive methods are intentionally eclectic, mingling, combining, and synthesizing theories and techniques from disparate disciplines and paradigms.... I do not have the luxury of attaching myself to any one theoretical perspective but instead 'make do' as an interpretive handyman or *bricoleur*.... moving within and between sometimes competing or seemingly incompatible interpretive perspectives and paradigms" (p. 16). The multipronged and hybrid arsenals mobilized by postcolonialists are both the resources and effects of their catachrestic interventions.

Postcolonial Challenges in Education traces the palimpsest histories of imperialism and colonialism and puts to work the catachrestic interventions of anti-imperialism and decolonization. Although the concept *postcolonial* is fraught with multiple and competing definitions, it is mobilized here to attend to the discourses, structures, and relations of colonialism, neocolonialism, and anticolonialism in various temporal contexts within and across the geographies of metropoles and peripheries. The book tracks the operations and effects of colonialism during and after territorial occupation as well as the ways in which colonized individuals and multitudes navigate within and resist imperialist subjugation. It considers the realm of *education* to include not only the components of elementary, secondary, and tertiary schooling, such as curriculum, pedagogy, and policy, but also the corollary techniques of cultural and knowledge production, subject formation, and community/nation building. Education is therefore construed to address both formal schooling and, more broadly, the construction, circulation, consumption, and contestation of knowledge through processes of teaching and learning.

The book is primarily positioned as a set of theoretical and empirical *challenges* to two fields of scholarship. It challenges (1) the inadequate attention to issues of education in studies of imperialism and colonialism and (2) the relative absence of empire as a category of analysis in studies of education. Thirty years after the publication of Edward W. Said's *Orientalism* (1978) and twenty years after Gloria E. Anzaldúa's *Borderlands* (1987), two foundational texts in the field of postcolonial studies in the global north academe, there has been relatively limited research on the role of education in colonialism. *Postcolonial Challenges in Education* engages and extends postcolonial studies by foregrounding the centrality of education in imperialism since education has served as "a massive cannon in the artillery of empire ... [through] a domination by consent [that] is achieved through what is taught to the colonised, how it is taught, and the subsequent emplacement of the educated subject as part of the continuing imperial apparatus" (Ashcroft, Griffiths, & Tiffin, 1995, p. 425). A rigorous examination of the discursive, material, and psychical relationships between empire and education is direly needed, since "Education is perhaps the most insidious and in some ways the most cryptic of colonialist survivals" (ibid.).

Instead of representing education as exclusively and uniformly reprehensible, the contributors in this edited volume depict it as a double-edged sword that wields power for subjugation and oppression as well as for subversive revolution and self-determination. It is precisely the nuanced insights from inquiries on the complexities and contradictions of education as a root of and route for oppression and subversion that theorists and researchers of education offer as part of their significant contribution to postcolonial scholarship on power, resistance, and agency.

Although this book marks, and consequently serves as a corrective to, the lack of attention to educational topics in postcolonial studies, it also indexes the need for and the relevance of empire as an integral category of analysis in educational research. Ten years have passed since the publication of Cameron McCarthy's *The Uses of Culture* (1997) and John Willinsky's *Learning to Divide the World* (1998), two groundbreaking projects in education that considerably engage the theories and methodologies of postcolonial studies. In spite of such well-regarded projects that have paved ground for rigorous engagements, the use of empire as a category of analysis has not been fully developed in studies of education. Whereas several disciplinary and interdisciplinary fields, including history, literature, anthropology, geography, ethnic studies, women's studies, and cultural studies, have extensively developed lines of inquiries and critiques regarding colonialism and imperialism within the past 20 years, the field of education in general has not.

The contributors in this volume, all of whom are affiliated with departments or faculties of education, thereby represent a growing critical mass of education scholars who challenge many of the foundational narratives, epistemologies, and methodologies in academe and in education in particular. The book ushers in a collective of dissident voices that unabashedly aim to contest and intervene in the current local-global order.

Toward these ends, *Postcolonial Challenges in Education* brings to bear cutting-edge theoretical formulations and empirical research in examinations of empire and education. It draws from a wide arsenal of interpretive frameworks, ranging from historical materialism, poststructuralism, and psychoanalysis to critical race, feminist, and queer perspectives. Both disciplinary and interdisciplinary, it is also situated within and at the intersections of education, sociology, anthropology, history, philosophy, geography, and literary studies as well as area and diaspora studies, ethnic and indigenous studies, women's and gender studies, sexuality and queer studies, and cultural studies. Its spatial scope encompasses the metropoles and the territories with varying units and scales of analysis at the local, national, regional, and transnational levels. For example, the authors attend to the dynamics of the global city of Mumbai, India, the post-apartheid nation-state of South Africa, the regional archipelagos of the Caribbean, and the transnational connections between Korea and the United States. Methodologically, the authors utilize the traditions of archival research, ethnographic participant-observation, interview and oral history, document and text analysis as well as the relatively newer approaches of autoethnography, discourse analysis, and media studies. Consequently the book's depth and breadth offer a rich, nuanced, and innovative treatment of empire and education that is unprecedented and unparalleled to this date.

Book Sections and Chapters

The book is divided into five parts—Interventions, Curriculum, Cultural Studies, Gender and Sexuality, and Methodologies—and concludes with an Afterword. Individually and collectively, the contributors engage with the key debates and dilemmas in postcolonial and educational studies as well as map out theoretical, empirical, and political agendas for the twenty-first century.

Part One: Interventions

This section set the stage as overarching frames for the entire volume. The chapters offer various assessments of the state of the field, outlining the temporalities and geographies of imperialism, and bridging the foundational and emerging projects of postcolonial education studies. They argue for the "turn to empire" in educational studies to address the colonial vestiges in the current local-global order, and foreground the generative insights of mobilizing the catachrestic techniques of innovative theories, methodologies, and politics.

Leon Tikly in "Education and the New Imperialism" calls for the rethinking of global governmentality that accounts for a new form of imperialism that has emerged alongside older forms of classic and settler colonialism. Interrogating the discourses of the World Bank and other multilateral development agencies, he delineates the prevailing rationalities that underpin the language and structure of educational policies and practices especially toward low-income, formerly colonized nations. Such discourses render populations into economic and political docility serving dominant global interests with education functioning as a disciplinary technology. To counter these trends, Tikly also outlines anti-imperialist critical formulations of knowledge and development that forward a more emancipatory and collectivist agenda.

Emphasizing the strategic use of a combined material and discursive analysis, Fazal Rizvi in "Postcolonialism and Globalization in Education" highlights the need to ground the significant changes happening at local and global levels within historical and political contexts. In his critique of the universalism and functionalism of globalization theories, he notes their failure to historicize economic relations and to locate people's situatedness and positionality. Rizvi posits postcolonial theory as a relevant complement that attends to the cultural dimensions and deterritorialized circuits of knowledge and power that shape the contours and operations of imperialism and globalization.

In "Diaspora and the Anthropology of Latino Education: Challenges, Affinities, and Intersections," Sofia Villenas brings into conversation the theoretical categories of immigrant and diaspora, especially as they pertain to the conditions of Latino/as in the United States. She traces the scholarly genealogy of Latino/a educational anthropology, and finds resonance in the intellectual and political project that the concept of diaspora brings to denaturalizing nation, migration, and identity. Their juxtaposition also sutures the cultural border crossing taking place between Mexico, the rest of Latin America, and the United States, and articulates the hybrid cosmopolitan subjectivities and practices that rupture geographies and generations.

Part Two: Curriculum

Under imperialism, curriculum instructs teachers and students to uphold an onto-epistemological view aligned with the dominant world order. The chapters in this section track the lingering effects of colonialism within educational systems and pedagogical texts across geographic and psychic borders. Education is confronted as a tool of empire to destabilize historical and contemporary curricular, pedagogical, and testing practices that work to erase and distort the discursive representations and material conditions of marginalized communities.

In "Decolonization and Education: Locating Pedagogy and Self at the Interstices in Global Times," Nina Asher mobilizes critical self-reflexive analysis to unpack her situatedness as a scholar and teacher educator as well as her geographic and intellectual border crossing. Aiming to enact a decolonizing praxis, she draws on autobiography to understand the self in relation to the social and the effects of difference along the lines of race, class, gender, language, and culture in relation to self-constituting and pedagogical practices. Asher argues that by attending to the sites of interstices where hybridity and uncertainty reside, both teacher educators and preservice teachers can interrogate the nexus of privilege and oppression in their journey toward becoming social justice advocates.

In "Nā Wāhine Mana: A Postcolonial Reading of Classroom Discourse on the Imperial Rescue of Oppressed Hawaiian Women," Julie Kaomea deconstructs curriculum and classroom discourses to unsettle the myth that colonialism liberated indigenous women from primitive and patriarchal conditions and to interrogate how this myth continues and is reinforced in schools in the contemporary period. She juxtaposes traditional Hawaiian and Foucaultian methods of genealogy to provide a counternarrative of powerful native women, including goddesses, sovereign queens, high priestesses, and commoners, in order to contest the prevailing Eurocentric telos of progress and increased civilization through colonial pedagogy. Kaomea points instead to Euro-American forms of government and Christian domestication as culprits in the undermining of Hawaiian women's autonomy in public and private spheres.

Radhika Viruru in "Postcolonial Technologies of Power: Standardized Testing and Representing Diverse Young Children" examines the reading passages of the third and fourth grade standardized tests in 11 U.S. states from

2001 to 2004. While much has been written on the promises and perils of the No Child Left Behind Act, little attention has been given to the medium through which students are being tested. Through document and textual analysis, Viruru reveals that the content of standardized tests is rife with imperialist and racist values, messages, and representations, particularly in regard to people of color as well as nonmainstream locations and materials in the United States and beyond. That such problematic test content is provided as a legitimate form of knowledge to be memorized and assessed makes it psychically and culturally detrimental and dangerous for all students.

Sharon Subreenduth in "Post-apartheid Dilemmas: Black Teachers Theorizing Social Justice" foregrounds the narratives of black educators who lived through the apartheid regime in South Africa and are now teaching with a post-apartheid curriculum that aims to redress the history and legacy of segregation, inequity, and oppression. Using texts from written essays and focus group conversations of a two-year international exchange program, she highlights the predicaments and aspirations that the educators individually and collectively face in light of their ardent commitments as advocates of educational, political, and sociocultural transformation. While racial, economic, and geographical disparities continue to haunt the present, their will for a better future for themselves and their students propels them to persevere.

Part Three: Cultural Studies

This section explores representation, power, and culture by illuminating the production of intellectual and cultural goods within the circuits of globalization. Through critical readings of postcolonial writers, artists, and intellectuals, the chapters offer fresh perspectives for theorizing agency and contestation within the realms of sports, literature, and music. They perform the crucial work of connecting material and symbolic struggles of race, class, gender, and sexuality, while foregrounding the role of culture in a postcolonial to come.

In "The Future in the Present: The Status of Sport and Intellectual Labor in C.L.R. James' *Beyond a Boundary* and His Other Works," Cameron McCarthy suggests that James' meditations on Caribbean sports belie a contextual and relational methodological sensibility in which popular culture becomes a key text for understanding social and political change within the shifting postcolonial geography. James located in cricket a popular text and a set of cosmopolitan practices where boundaries between intellectual labor and the labor of sport break down. In McCarthy's reading of James' work, professional cricket players, many of whom derived from abject classes, represented an intellectual vanguard through which racial and class anxieties were challenged and aspirations for Caribbean independence were publicly expressed.

In "Multicultural and Creole Contemporaries: Postcolonial Artists and Postcolonial Cities," Rinaldo Walcott seeks to rethink both the city and multiculturalism as sites of imagination and ethical responsibility in the post-9/11 historical moment. Against the xenophobia and ethnocentrism that have largely eroded the state multicultural compromise, he argues that more vibrant and hopeful visions of a postcolonial space and humanity are being articulated through the aesthetic scripts of theorists and artists, such as Stuart Hall and Dionne Brand. He aims to reframe multiculturalism as a new ethnopolitical urban sociality in which a nonessential creole-ness that is attentive to new possibilities for solidarity and in which a postcolonial city and human yet to come become the new grammar of understanding and living.

Lisa Weems in "Border Crossing with M.I.A. and Transnational Girlhood Studies" emplots Sri Lankan British hip-hop artist M.I.A. to trouble normalized representations of white, middle-class, heterosexual girls so that the subjectivities and resistances of third world and diasporic girls might be located within global capitalism and imperialism. She explores M.I.A.'s vivid lyrical imagery to highlight the complex positions that postcolonial and racialized girls take to assert themselves in global spaces. As war, corporate profiteering, sexualized violence, and colonial vestiges continue to shape the horizons of "freedom" for girls of color, Weems calls for the rethinking of both postcolonial studies and transnational girlhood studies to account for their complicated embodiment of identity and assertion of agency.

Aparna Mishra Tarc contends in "Postcolonial Studies as Reeducation: Learning from J. M. Coetzee's *Disgrace*" that, in light of immense global changes where past forms of domination and violence anxiously mingle with contemporary forms of oppression, historical remembrance is a crucial pedagogy for learning, un-learning, and being with others. Through textual analysis of a novel set in post-apartheid South Africa, she suggests that we need to establish material and psychological links to the past so as to orient the future toward more empathetic and nonviolent human relations. Mishra Tarc argues that literature has the potential not only to bring into relief the horror of injustice, but also to harness its affective and pedagogical power for a reparative solidarity movement.

Part Four: Gender and Sexuality

Feminist and queer theories from intersectional, critical race, diasporic, and transnational perspectives are brought to bear in order to shed light on embodied epistemologies and sexual politics in highly contested sites like higher education and research. Insisting on the necessity of gender and sexuality as relevant analytical categories in inquiries regarding empire and education as well as race, space, and research, the chapters in this section map the constructions and effects of subversive subjectivities and knowledges that contest the patriarchal and heteronormative ones that often remain unmarked yet dominate educational policies, programs, and practices.

Marking the absence of the body in postcolonial and educational research, Antonia Darder in "Decolonizing the Flesh: The Body, Pedagogy, Inequality" offers a much needed corrective by putting the body at the center of teaching. She is critical of the overemphasis on the psychological understanding of the self that downplays or omits the lived experiences of disenfranchised students. Although colonialism has historically inscribed within its educational project the body's subjugation, Darder counters with possibilities of resistance when bodies are made not in service of docility but for critical empowerment. If we are to fulfill the emancipatory potential of school and society, she urges us to engage with the physical, emotional, and material conditions that are embedded in the process of living and learning.

Heidi Safia Mirza in "Postcolonial Subjects, Black Feminism, and the Intersectionality of Race and Gender in Higher Education" marks another absence, in this case, the bodies and experiences of diasporic black and ethnicized women in higher education in the United Kingdom. She contends that their in/visibility is materially and discursively structured by the failure to use an intersectional analytical approach that accounts for multidimensional marginality along the lines of gender, race, class, and other social divisions. Mirza's archival discovery of a pioneering Indian female law student and Indian women suffragettes in the late nineteenth century uncovers marginalized histories that link contemporary black and postcolonial feminist struggles with their buried pasts.

In "Dis/locating Oriental Citizen-Subject Makings: A Postcolonial Reading of Korean/Asian American Women's Narratives," Jeong-eun Rhee draws on the narratives of four women to investigate subject formation as an effect of the intertwined projects of United States nation and empire building. Set against the broader historical backdrops of U.S. colonialism in Korea and Korean immigration to the United States, the constitution and self-making of Asian American women enable Rhee to chart their various identities and life trajectories that reveal the workings of U.S. imperialism and orientalism. Pushing to expand the discourses of minority lives and experiences beyond a U.S. domestic regime, she posits a transnational frame to rework histories under erasure and open possibilities for subjugated voices and positions.

In "Putting Queer to Work: Examining Empire and Education," Roland Sintos Coloma offers three queer approaches to underscore the relevance of sexuality as an analytical category in studies of colonialism and schooling. Drawing on his archival research about the Philippines under U.S. rule, he scrutinizes major intellectual and political themes, such as exclusion, normalization, subject position, and agency via the interpretive frames of within, through, and beyond the rubric of sexuality. Coloma questions the compulsory heteronormativity even in putatively critical projects like nationalism, feminism, antiracism, and decolonization, and calls for the exploration and actualization of revolutionary alliances across multiple differences.

Part Five: Methodologies

Grappling with tensions in postpositivist and posthumanist inquiries, this section examines the emergence and limits of academic boundaries, transnational subjectivities, and the messy and ethically fraught mediations between researcher and researched in fieldwork. The task of decolonizing research praxis in the interest of anti-imperialist commitments requires more than a simple reflexive assessment of techniques and methods. It demands a deliberate agenda aimed at transforming discourses and structures as well as underlying taken-for-granted processes of research.

Bernadette Baker offers a historical philosophical perspective on disciplinary foundations and their limits and possibilities for anti-imperialist research in "Postcolonial Technoscience, Toleration and Anti-imperialism, and Education and Psychology." After engaging the recent debates in postcolonial technoscience by marking its onto-epistemological aporia, she turns to William James, a nineteenth-century Harvard psychologist and anti-imperialist, to explore how the act of comparison became a formal principle of knowledge production. Raising the specter of logocentrism in scholarly and imperialist frames, Baker contends that, at the inception of modern disciplinary fields, human perception was linked to a discursive alignment of power and authority, an alignment whose vestiges remain to this day.

Binaya Subedi in "The Contradictions of Negotiating Legitimacy at Home/Field" analyzes reflexively the ethical negotiations made by scholars with hybrid Western and non-Western identities when undertaking research in communities that they affiliate with. Examining his position as a "halfie" insider/outsider during his ethnographic fieldwork in Nepal, he demonstrates how scholars with heterogeneous identities at times find themselves complicit with hegemonic discourses, and offers revealing insights for responsibly navigating research dilemmas. Subedi provides useful reflexive strategies that are attuned to the asymmetrical distinctions between the class, gender, and ethnic identities of the researcher and the researched in transnational spaces.

In "The Noninnocence of Recognition: Subject and Agency in Education," Stephanie Daza revisits her previous formulation about her ethnographic fieldwork in Colombia and rethinks the humanist investments in subject authenticity and research. Addressing the tensions in self-identification and interpellation as a brown queer mother, she argues that a noninnocent recognition destabilizes the discursive fictions that locate legibility in a knowing or knowable subject and, in the process, thrusts open possibilities for being recognized otherwise. Locating in posthumanism paradoxically the hope of being human that acknowledges the impossibilities of subject authenticity, Daza contends that noninnocent recognition allows for a more robust vision of agency in research praxis and in broader social relations.

In "Mediating Globalization: The Non-resident Indian Student in an Era of 'India Poised,'" Aliya Rahman grapples with India's drive for both national liberation and global economic power. She examines how NRI university students in the United States understand their role and position in this movement and finds that, while they embody both past oppressions and national aspirations, they do not imagine themselves as participating in transformational processes. Instead, they tend to view their NRI status as bestowing them with greater freedom to pursue economic and social choices as global liberal citizens. Rahman's analysis challenges the pursuit of anticolonial work when national and individual narratives of emancipation are written through scripts that do not attend to past and present forms of imperialism.

Afterword

To close and comment on the book, Anne Hickling-Hudson underscores the urgency and necessity of engaging the theoretical, empirical, political, and educational insights "from below" in her Afterword, "*Southern Theory* and Its Dynamics for Postcolonial Education." She points out that drawing from and working through indigenous, African, Asian, and Latin American thinkers and ideas not only deconstructs and displaces the prevailing Eurocentric hegemony in intellectual and pedagogical projects, but also significantly positions them as theories from which we can learn as scholars, educators, and activists. By foregrounding the work from the global South, Hickling-Hudson does not advocate for a mere reversal whereby marginalized conceptualizations now occupy a place of privilege and dominance; rather, such a move calls into question the ontologies, epistemologies, and methodologies of knowledge construction and circulation that fail to account the technologies and effects of power. She locates *Postcolonial Challenges in Education* both within the growing critical mass of interventionist projects in the field of education as well as within counterhegemonic productions that contest the historical and contemporary local-global order.

Of Ruptures, Synergies, and Possibilities

This chapter began by suggesting that the attacks on September 11, 2001, and their subsequent international fallout were and continue to be inextricably shaped by the broader history of imperialism. Such a statement should not be misconstrued as an attempt to dismiss the ruptural characteristics of the event or to replace one narrative of origin (e.g., "clash of civilizations" or "jihad versus mcworld") with another. Rather, this framing seeks to foreground the noninnocence of the United States in its history of military, cultural, and economic imperialism in order to claim that 9/11 and its effects can only be grasped within a multilayered and reflexive historical critique.

For theoretical clarity, we introduce the notion of palimpsest and mark its usefulness for tracing the histories, legacies, and continuities of colonialism and imperialism as well as anticolonial resistance within the present. As a conceptual lens, palimpsest situates historical legibility as determinate upon residual and emergent material, social, and psychical elements. These elements combine and recombine in processes that erase, overlay, and reconstitute the boundaries of the visible, the sayable, and the knowable. As the chapters in this volume make evident, a fundamental precondition for the productive synergy between postcolonial perspectives and the field of education is recognition of the myriad ways in which they are each embedded and implicated in the palimpsest process of legibility. Mobilizing Spivak's notion of catachresis, we describe postcolonial inquiry as an im/possible task because it is self-consciously aware of its intimacy with the institutional structures and onto-epistemologies it attempts to critique, subvert, and transform. Yet the unwanted but obligatory space of catachresis also has contributed to the dynamism of postcolonial analytics and methodologies and the transgressive knowledge and praxis they have made thinkable and actionable, a dynamism and transgressiveness that the field of education desperately needs.

As we rapidly approach the second decade of the twenty-first century, what productive tensions, analytics, and problematics might emerge through continued synergy between postcolonial and educational studies? Brought together in this volume are a series of challenges that forward a relational and interdisciplinary conversation and research agenda for postcolonial educational studies. While the two fields of inquiry are deeply imbricated, their intimate ties and productive potentials have largely remained underexplored. As we take stock of the rapidly moving cascade of events that mark our present moment, the chapters assembled have outlined a number of directions for future research. Such fresh perspectives could not be more urgent.

Since 9/11, seemingly tectonic shifts have occurred on the global stage portending further uncertainty for the world's most vulnerable and marginalized populations. Despite the bloody, illegal, and costly failures of recent U.S. foreign policies, the global War on Terror continues, along with U.S. commitments to grotesque military expenditures and the permanence of its some 737 military bases around the world (Johnson, 2007). Moreover, the greedy and reckless deregulatory regimes and financial abstractions of neoliberalism have brought the global economy to the brink of collapse, affecting, as it always does, those least responsible, that is, the poor, women, children, and racialized populations. Such conditions provide the chaotic stage from which regional, national, and religious tensions have historically erupted, often in catastrophic acts of violence like those recently witnessed in Mumbai, an event hastily dubbed as "India's 9/11" by the global media. It is necessary to note, however, that the current moment is not one of total domination or despair. While it remains to be seen what impact it will have on U.S. domestic and foreign policy, the unprecedented catastrophe of the Bush administration has paved the way for the election of Barack Obama, the first African American president of the United States. Moreover, throughout the global south and north vast numbers of the world's people have taken to the streets and to the polls in recent years in order to speak out against the excesses of neoliberal capitalism and in favor of economic, social, and environmental justice.

What are the prospects for decolonizing, anticolonial, and justice-oriented educational projects in a time of such uncertainty and change? The insecurities that plague the current moment make commitments to transformative research and pedagogical movements against empire a central task for promoting local and global equity, peace, and sustainability. To revisit Spivak's notion of catachresis, *Postcolonial Challenges in Education* aims to provide a series of interventions, tools, and perspectives for engaging the im/possibilities of response in order to make legible transformative modes of praxis. By tracking and calling into question the historical and contemporary layers of various forms of oppression, postcolonial interventions in education seek to unlock myriad channels of critical intellectual and ethicopolitical agency in order to enliven hope and possibility for as yet unwritten futures.

References

Anzaldúa, G. (1987). *Borderlands: The new mestiza = la frontera.* San Francisco, CA: Spinsters/Aunt Lute.
Ashcroft, B., Griffiths, G., & Tiffin, H. (1995). *The post-colonial studies reader.* London: Routledge.
Ashcroft, B., Griffiths, G., & Tiffin, H. (2001). *Post-colonial studies: The key concepts.* London: Routledge.
Cabral, A. (1970). *Revolution in Guinea: Selected texts.* New York: Monthly Review.
Cooper, F. (2005). *Colonialism in question: Theory, knowledge, history.* Berkeley: University of California Press.
Denzin, N. K., & Lincoln, Y. S. (2003). Introduction: 9/11 in American culture. In N. K. Denzin & Y. S. Lincoln (Eds.), *9/11 in American culture* (pp. xiii-xvii). Lanham, MD: Altamira.
Derrida, J. (1978). Freud and the scene of writing. *Writing and difference* (Alan Bass, trans.) (pp. 196-231). Chicago, IL: University of Chicago Press.
DuBois, W.E.B. (1907). *The souls of black folk.* Chicago, IL: A. C. McClurg.
DuBois, W.E.B. (1920). *Darkwater: Voices from within the veil.* New York: Harcourt, Brace and Howe.
Green, J. (Ed.). (2007). *Making space for indigenous feminism.* London: Zed.
Hardt, M., & Negri, A. (2000). *Empire.* Cambridge, MA: Harvard University Press.
Jacobson, M. F. (2001). *Barbarian virtues: The United States encounters foreign peoples at home and abroad.* New York: Farrar, Straus and Giroux.
James, C.L.R. (1938/1989). *The black Jacobins: Toussaint L'Ouverture and the San Domingo revolution.* New York: Vintage.
Johnson, C. (2007). *Nemesis: The last days of the American republic.* New York: Henry Holt.
Kaomea, J. (2003). Reading erasures and making the familiar strange: Defamiliarizing methods for research in formerly colonized and historically oppressed communities. *Educational Researcher, 32*(2), 14-23.
Kaplan, A. (2005). *The anarchy of empire in the making of U.S. culture.* Cambridge, MA: Harvard University Press.
Kaplan, A., & Pease, D. E. (Eds.). (1993). *Cultures of United States imperialism.* Durham, NC: Duke University Press.
Khagram, S., Sikkink, K., & Riker, J. V. (Eds.). (2002). *Restructuring world politics: Transnational social movements, networks, and norms.* Minneapolis: University of Minnesota Press.
Lewis, R., & Mills, S. (Eds.). (2003). *Feminist postcolonial theory.* New York: Taylor and Francis.
McCarthy, C. (1997). *The uses of culture: Education and the limits of ethnic affiliation.* New York: Routledge.
Prakash, G. (1994). Subaltern studies as postcolonial criticism. *American Historical Review, 99*(5), 1475-1490.
Romulo, C. P. (1956). *The meaning of Bandung.* Chapel Hill: University of North Carolina Press.
Said, E. W. (1978). *Orientalism.* New York: Pantheon.
Scott, J. C. (1987). *Weapons of the weak: Everyday forms of peasant resistance.* New Haven, CT: Yale University Press.
Smith. L. T. (1999). *Decolonizing methodologies: Research and indigenous peoples.* London: Zed.
Spivak, G. C. (1976). Translator's preface. In J. Derrida, *Of grammatology* (G. C. Spivak, trans.)

(pp. ix–lxxxviii). Baltimore, MD: Johns Hopkins University Press.
Spivak, G. C. (1993). *Outside in the teaching machine*. New York: Routledge.
Spivak, G. C. (2004). Terror: A speech after 9-11. *boundary 2, 31*(2), 81–111.
Stewart-Harawira, M. (2005). *The new imperial order: Indigenous responses to globalization*. London: Zed.
Stoler, A. L. (Ed.). (2006). *Haunted by empire: Geographies of intimacy in North American history*. Durham, NC: Duke University Press.
Trask, H-K. (1993). *From a native daughter: Colonialism and sovereignty in Hawai'i*. Monroe, ME: Common Courage.
Williams, W. A. (1959). *The tragedy of American diplomacy*. New York: World.
Williams, W. A. (1980). *Empire as a way of life*. New York: Oxford University Press.
Willinsky, J. (1998). *Learning to divide the world: Education at empire's end*. Minneapolis: University of Minnesota Press.
Wright, R. (1956/1995). *The color curtain: A report on the Bandung conference*. Jackson: University Press of Mississippi.
Young, R. J. C. (2001). *Postcolonialism: An historical introduction*. Oxford, UK: Blackwell.

CHAPTER 2

Education and the New Imperialism

LEON TIKLY

Postcolonial theory is a critical idiom used to analyze the legacy of European colonialism and uncover the oppositional discourses of those who have struggled against its lingering effects. It will be used to argue that what we are currently witnessing on a global scale is the emergence of a new form of imperialism whose purpose is to incorporate populations within the former "second" and "third worlds" into a regime of global government. Central to the new imperialism is education that has become a key aspect for the World Bank and other multilateral agencies in their vision of "development."

This chapter will commence with an account of how the new imperialism can be interpreted. The first step is to understand it as a discursive phenomenon by extending Foucault's (1991) notion of governmentality to critique dominant forms of rationality or ways of thinking about global governance. The next part will consider the concept of "development" in the discourses of the World Bank and other agencies that have roots in the dominant rationalities that provide the language and motivation for education policy and practice. It will argue that discourses around education and development have the effect of rendering populations economically useful and politically docile in relation to dominant global interests. It will conclude by setting out ways to challenge dominant discourses and create spaces for historically marginalized knowledges and ways of understanding education and development.

Understanding the New Imperialism

Said (1993) defines imperialism to mean "the practice, theory, and the attitudes of a dominating metropolitan center ruling a distant territory" (p. 8). It is a process distinct from colonialism that is the "implanting of settlements on a distant territory" (p. 8). Although imperialism is not reducible to colonialism, colonialism has provided in the past a principal means by which imperialist interests have been realized.

The term "new imperialism" is increasingly used within the popular literature by both supporters (Cooper, 2002; Johnson, 2003; Pfaff, 1995) and critics (Ali, 2003; Lewis, 2002; Pilger, 2003) of the United States as an imperialist power in world affairs since the end of the Second World War up to and including the recent occupation of Iraq. Within the more academic literature, Harvey (2003) characterizes the new imperialism as "a contradictory fusion of the politics of state and empire" (p. 26). By the former, Harvey refers to the "political, diplomatic and military strategies invoked and used by a state (or some collection of states) operating as a political power block as it struggles to assert its interests and to achieve its goals in the world at large." By the latter, he refers to "the ways that economic power flows across and through continuous space, towards or away from territorial entities (such as states or regional power blocks)" (ibid.). This latter form of power is associated with the actions and interests of transnational corporations (TNCs), the workings of global financial markets, the development of new forms of production based on new technologies, and the globalization of the labor market.

These two aspects of the new imperialism are often in a relationship of tension and contradiction with one another. They provide alternative but intertwined logics for understanding the actions of powerful nations. Whereas the political/strategic aspect is based on power that is largely territorialized and subject to political influences at a range of levels (the nation-state, the region, the province, etc.), the economic aspect is more diffuse, defies territorial boundaries, and is much harder for nation-states to control.[1] The diffuse economic aspect of the new imperialism in Harvey's work bears some similarities to Hardt and Negri's (2001) analysis of Empire, a term they use to denote the spread of Western capitalism and culture around the world. In Hardt and Negri's work, Empire also has a discursive basis, which will be explored in the second part of the chapter.

The new imperialism emerged within the broader context of contemporary globalization, although none of the recent literature explicitly talks of a new imperialism per se (see, for example, Amin, 1997; Hall, 1996; Hoogvelt, 1997; Santos, 2002). What these accounts have in common is that they describe an increase and qualitative change in the nature of global flows and networks in the economic, political, cultural, military, and environmental spheres in the post-Second World War period. They describe a "reterritorialization" of the way power operates within these spheres that has involved a repositioning of the nation-state and the emergence of global and regional structures of political and economic governance and regulation. They also emphasize the growing inequalities both within and between countries and the identification of clear "winners" and "losers" in the process.

Among the "winners" are the United States and its Western allies, some countries in the Pacific Rim, and others in Asia and eastern Europe. Among the "losers" are the majority of low-income countries that were subject to colonialism under European powers. However, globalization has been uneven in its effects *within* countries. There has been a growing polarization within rich and poor states with pockets of the so-called fourth world appearing in the slums and ghettos of Western nations and indigenous elites from the global periphery benefiting from integration into the global economy (Amin, 1997).

Although the new world order is premised on Western hegemony, the post-Second World War period has marked a decisive break with previous forms of European imperialism (Hardt & Negri, 2001; Harvey, 2003). It is a move away from "illiberal" forms of control by Western countries over non-Western ones, including forms of direct violence and coercion under classical and settler colonialism and more subtle forms of domination and control through neocolonialism (Altbach & Kelly, 1978). Along Nkrumah's (1965) original analysis of neocolonialism, the new imperialism is based on a notional recognition of the sovereignty of former colonized nations. The term "notional" is used because, as recent events in the Middle East and Africa serve to demonstrate, military intervention and illiberal occupation in the name of "global security" can override the principle of national sovereignty.

The new imperialism also involves the incorporation of the economies of formerly colonized nations into the emerging global economy albeit as part of the global periphery. This incorporation serves as a basis to continue to extract surplus value through imposing trade liberalization measures with the object of opening up new markets in low-income countries for Western goods and services; the emergence of a system of global economic regulation in which the more powerful nations have been able to determine terms of trade in goods and services; locating manufacturing production wherever in the peripheral global economy production costs are lowest; and imposing a system of debt peonage on low-income countries that has served to "oil the wheels" of the global financial markets (Hoogvelt, 1997). To a limited extent, some low-income countries have found a niche within the global economy linked to an indigenously determined growth path by developing specialist areas of manufacturing or services. This has led to the "success" of the so-called Asian Tigers as well as some provinces in China and states in India. Integration into the global economy for these regions, however, has had contradictory effects for poverty and inequality (Townsend & Gordon, 2002). Continued Western dominance is also evident in the ongoing dependency of Asian Tigers on Western-based TNCs and Western forms of knowledge and innovation (O'Hearn, 1999).

The new imperialism differs, however, from the older analysis of neocolonialism in two important respects.[2] The first relates to the changing context of Western domination and the development of contemporary globalization, which was in its infancy when Nkrumah made his original formulation. In this respect, dominant global economic interests are to a lesser extent identified with nation-states or even with elites in nation-states, but are increasingly *transnational* in their composition (Robinson & Harris, 2000). This emerging class is tied to TNCs and to global financial firms and funds, and exerts an inordinate influence over national policy agendas in high-, middle- and, especially, low-income countries (Hoogvelt, 1997; Khor, 2002). For example, an increasing number of policies are determined by transnational bodies such as the World Trade Organization (WTO) and, to a lesser extent, the Organisation for Economic Co-operation and Development (OECD) and the United Nations (UN). While the WTO and the Bretton Woods institutions have historically served to promote the empowerment of the market, most UN agencies operate under the belief that public intervention is necessary to ensure basic needs and human rights. Low-income countries are often caught between the policy imperatives of these global organizations in contradictory ways, including in the sphere of education and training (Mundy, 1998).

The second way in which the new imperialism is distinctive from neocolonialism is in the way in which it is analyzed and understood. Whereas critiques have often adopted structuralist forms, the new imperialism has coincided with the poststructuralist and culturalist turn in the social sciences. Indeed, it is in relation to the cultural/scientific sphere that the distinctiveness of the new imperialism can be marked from previous forms. Many commentators have described how classical and settler colonialism were legitimated in relation to a virulent biological racism with origins in the eighteenth-century eugenics movement (Gould, 1997; Stoler, 1995). The post-independence period has coincided with a gradual discrediting of "race" as a meaningful category to explain difference and to legitimize inequality. "Race" has been superseded, although not entirely replaced, by an emphasis on culture within Western societies as the category for explaining difference and conflict and for legitimizing inequality.

The Discursive Basis of the New Imperialism

Since the latter half of the twentieth century, the new imperialism has emerged as an aspect of Western discourse around "development" manifesting in the rationalities and programs of the World Bank and, to a lesser extent, other multilateral development agencies. Since education has been considered a key aspect of development, it is against this analysis that a discussion of education's role in relation to the new imperialism can be better understood.

In response to possible objections that an emphasis on the discursive level detracts from challenging dominant economic, political, and military interests that are shaping our world, it is worth making three brief points. First, the discursive terrain provides a necessary starting point for those interested in social critique and transformative action because it is within this terrain that shared understandings about the nature and implications of economic, political, and cultural change are constructed and contested. This is to acknowledge, for example, the perspectives and concerns of feminists, indigenous groups, and new social movements as they attempt to grapple with the implications of globalization and change. It means extending analysis beyond the economic and political to embrace issues of culture and identity and to address profound questions about the nature of knowledge itself. Second, Foucault's (1997) understanding of discourse is concerned with more than the way identities and social realities are constructed in language. Rather they encompass a range of social practices that constitute individuals and populations as subjects. In Foucault's work, this includes a consideration of forms of authority and exclusion, an analysis of the operations of the technologies of power, of the apparatuses of surveillance and governmentality. It is these attributes that have made his ideas popular among anticolonial and antiimperialist scholars (Young, 2001). Third, education provides a key site for discursive struggle over social realities. Discourses about the nature of social reality and of human nature itself, including those about education and development, provide the final recourse in relation to which hegemony and counterhegemony are constructed and contested.

Global Governmentality

Discourses about "development" can be construed as an aspect of global governmentality (Tikly, 2003b). Governmentality involves the extension of a particular Western liberal view of how populations ought to be governed in those parts of the world that were previously subject to "illiberal" rule under classical and settler colonialism. On the one hand, it involves making these populations "economically useful" for global capitalism and the spread of capitalist markets. On the other, it entails managing the risks posed to emerging global markets through social intervention and aid. In reality, this does not mean that the poor and marginalized in low-income countries have been treated in the same terms as those benefiting from globalization. Rather, the way that Western interests manifest in relation to the non-West is through the perpetuation of a cultural bias that serves the interests of Western hegemony.

The emergence of global governmentality is exemplified by shifts in the thinking of multilateral development agencies associated with the Washington and post-Washington consensus. Foucault began to analyze before his death the emergence of what his followers describe as "advanced liberal governance" (Dean, 1999; Harris, 1999; Rose, 1996). This form of governance can be understood as a response to economic globalization and the shift from Fordist to flexible forms of production, thereby redefining the relationship between state and society. Just as liberal governmentality, as it emerged in eighteenth-century Europe, was informed by the development of neoclassical economics, advanced liberal government is underpinned by the development of neoliberal economic theories since the Second World War.[3] Neoliberal theories challenge the notion of society as a basis for governmental activity and intervention, including a critique of the welfare state and the notion of society itself. Neoliberalism reached its apotheosis under the administrations of Thatcher in the UK and Reagan in the United States.

Neoliberalism provided the basis for the "Washington consensus" that emerged in the wake of the oil shock in the 1970s (Fine, 2001; Gore, 2000; Stiglitz, 2002), and provided a normative action framework for major multilateral and donor agencies in their dealings with Africa and other parts of the "developing" world. The consensus was based on encouraging low-income countries to adopt policies of trade liberalization, export-led growth, and the creation of conditions favorable to attract foreign direct investment, including cuts in government expenditure, the use of user fees in public services, and an end to price controls for basic commodities. The consensus was accompanied by governmental techniques that translate the rationality into practice (i.e., structural adjustment programs and conditional lending). These techniques are based on the assumption that economic growth is principally linked to the development of individual entrepreneurialism and the extension of the market into the social sphere (e.g., by transferring costs for services to households).

Recently there have been important shifts in the nature of advanced liberal governance across the globe, for instance, in the emergence of the "post-Washington consensus." It has been recognized by the World Bank, including its former chief economist Joseph Stiglitz (2002), that the blind faith in untrammeled market forces as a way out of poverty in low-income countries has, to some extent, been counterproductive. Poverty under structural adjustment programs is acknowledged by the World Bank to have increased in some cases rather than decreased (Gore, 2000). Emerging as a central plank of the post–Washington consensus is a belief in the importance of "social capital" as a necessary corollary of "human capital"—a belief in the importance of social solidarity as a necessary condition for prosperity and growth. This returns to a central problematic of the Western liberal state from the eighteenth century onward, which was concerned with securing economic prosperity while offsetting threats to accumulation by intervening in the social sphere. Behind the World Bank discourses on education is a shifting articulation of a *plurality of rationalities* of government, including neoliberal rationalities that underpin the new imperialism.

"Development" and the New Imperialism

The spread of Western ways of thinking about government has been accompanied by a redefinition of the West's relationship to the low-income world through the notion of "development." This section examines the emergence of this concept as a basis for locating changing discourses concerning education and training. Its focus will be on the World Bank as the leading global institution in determining social policy. Of particular interest will be the changing "discursive repertoire"[4] of multilateral agencies around the theme of "education and development." The organizing concepts include a consideration of "development" along with the "object" of its discourse, such as "poverty reduction" and "gender equity." Discussion will turn to key concepts that mark out education's role in the development of human and social capital. It will show how, taken as a whole, these concepts operate to construct individual and group identities in relation to the new imperialism as well as versions of social reality that serve to legitimize it. It will be argued that these concepts serve to place non-Western inhabitants of low-income regions discursively within the economic and political terrains.

The concepts of "development" and "underdevelopment" and the birth of the "development age" coincided with the end of the Second World War and the ferment of post-war reconstruction in Europe. The development age was "officially" consecrated with point four of U.S. President Truman's inaugural address (Escobar, 1995; Fagerlind & Saha, 1989). A number of scholars demonstrate the European and Eurocentric nature of the development discourse, and counterpose it with other worldviews from different cultural traditions based on alternative assumptions about the nature of social change (Sardar, 1999). For Rist (1997) the notion of "development" is part of the Western "religion of modernity" and for Tucker (1999) "the central myth of western society." In both cases, the unshakable Western view of progress and social change has roots in the European enlightenment. They show how "development," along with "progress" and "civilization," has been used in Western modernist thought to legitimize such disparate projects as liberalism, Marxism, fascism, and imperialism. It also is implicated in struggles against racism, colonialism, and slavery. "Development" is thus a central organizing principle in the Western episteme including the discourses of anticolonial activists who, given the hegemony of the development discourse, have been obliged to struggle within its boundaries. "Development," however, has changed over time in relation to what it is meant to signify.

Truman's speech represented in discursive terms a break or disjuncture in the way that "development" was understood. The binary of developed and underdeveloped provided a mechanism to reinscribe the old north-south relationship that had been formed in relation to the colonizer/colonized opposition. Whereas development in the past had been a "natural" phenomenon, in the new worldview development took on a transitive meaning, something that could be performed by one actor or region over another. Whereas colonizers and colonized had belonged previously to two different universes, the new binary represented a step in the reinvention of the "third world" (Escobar, 1995). Furthermore, whereas classical colonialism was premised on the view that, although the "natives" could be "civilized" to some degree, they could never achieve equality with the West, in development discourse it became possible for underdeveloped regions and populations to evolve into developed ones. This did not mean, however, that the previously colonized were seen as cultural "equals" with the West. As Rist (1997) puts it,

> From 1949 onwards, often without realising it, more than two billion inhabitants of the planet found themselves changing their name, being "officially" regarded as they appeared in the eyes of others, called upon to deepen their westernization by repudiating their own values. No longer African, Latin American or Asian (not to speak of Bambara, Shona, Berber, Quechua, Aymara, Balinese or Mongol), they were now simply "underdeveloped." (p. 79)

The discursive move to the development paradigm was critical for emerging post-war U.S. hegemony since it provided a means to discredit European colonialism, to bring within the orbit of U.S. political influence a range of leaders of national liberation movements, and to gain access to new markets.

At an epistemological level, the development paradigm was accompanied by the growth of development studies as a field. Although this field is multidisciplinary in nature, the key subdiscipline has always been development economics and its offshoot, development planning. Hardly surprisingly, it was the development economists who had a profound impact on the forms of technical assistance in education and other spheres offered by the World Bank from the 1960s onward. From the perspective of governmentality theory, the significance of the emergence of development studies was that it allowed for the incorporation of knowledge about populations in the former colonies into a global archive of reports and statistics held by development agencies including the World Bank. This has provided for the "normalization" of the low-income, postcolonial world in relation to development discourses, and has served as a mechanism to know and control these populations through the application of governmental technologies (i.e., policies, technical assistance programs, projects, etc.).

Economics, including development economics, is profoundly a *cultural* discourse (Escobar, 1995). It must be noted that economics as a distinct discipline emerged in a particular historical and cultural conjuncture in eighteenth-century Europe and was tied intimately with the birth of liberal governmentality and of the nation-state. In this respect, the separation of the economic from other areas of social, political, and cultural life is not a feature of all cultural traditions. Sardar (1999) cites the examples of *tazkiyah* in Islamic economics, based on achieving a dynamic equilibrium between the infrastructure and the rest of society, and *kongsi* in Chinese philosophy that links the development of new enterprises and the quest for new resources to a notion of brotherhood or partnership, whose aim is to protect economic gains and resist outside aggressors. Zaoual (1997) describes how the African exchange system is an "inextricable mixture of economic, social, affective, symbolic, mythic facts, explicit or implicit" (p. 32). In these examples, the economic is linked to cultural realities, and the *collective* rather than the individual nature of economic agents is emphasized. Moreover, Western economics is tied to the emergence of a specific subject, *homo economicus*, the individual economic agent unfettered by the state, free to pursue his/her own economic interests. This individualistic model is in contrast to the models of economic/social actors in many non-Western traditions. Development economics, far from being culturally "neutral," shows a distinct cultural bias from its inception.

In the post–Second World War period, the rise of development studies provided a means by which issues could be presented largely as a *technical* question of utilization of scientific knowledge, growth of productivity, and expansion of foreign trade, and thereby removed from the political realm. "By defining 'underdevelopment' as a lack rather than the result of historical circumstances, and by treating the 'underdeveloped' simply as poor without seeking the reasons for their destitution, 'development policy' made of growth and aid (conceived in technocratic, quantitative terms) the only possible answer" (Rist, 1997, p. 79). These concepts were accepted by leaders of newly independent states because they became a means to assert their claim to benefit from the aid that accompanied development and to affirm the legal equality that was refused to them under colonialism. The raising of GNP also became globally accepted as the number one imperative in relation to "development." Linked to this imperative was a theory of evolutionary modernization that was, in the context of the cold war, counterposed to the Marxist revolutionary model. Although modernization theory was criticized for equating modernization unapologetically with Westernization, it provided a rationale for educational expansion through the influences of thinkers such as Rostow, Perou, and Seers on World Bank discourses.

The discursive limits of the developed/underdeveloped binary within development studies were stretched through various challenges during the 1970s and 1980s. In disciplinary terms, the challenges came from the elaboration of neo-Marxist dependency theory and the discourses of self-reliance from Julius Nyerere and other members of the nonaligned movement, which culminated in proposals made by the nonaligned movement for a new international economic order (NIEO) in 1974. Although the proposals appeared radical at the time and led to demands for a redistribution of income between north and south, neither dependency theory, self-reliance, nor the NIEO contested the basic premises of the development paradigm, namely a belief in modernization and progress achieved through increased economic growth (Rist, 1997).

They led, however, to a recasting of the developed/underdeveloped binary in new terms. Walter Rodney's (1972) *How Europe Underdeveloped Africa*, for example, challenged the hegemonic conception of underdevelopment being a "natural" phenomenon, and can be seen as part of a growing recognition of the euphemistic and racist use of the term "underdeveloped." This awareness led to its replacement with the equally euphemistic "developed/developing" binary, which persists to the present day.

In addition, the 1970s and 1980s witnessed an upsurge in feminist activism against male domination and oppression within the field of development politics. The feminist concerns were first given voice in a series of UN conferences during the 1970s; the UN Decade for the Advancement of Women (1976-1985); the World Plan of Action; and the First World Survey on the Role of Women in Development. Various redefinitions of the development problematic emerged during this era, including neo-Marxist accounts and accounts that stressed patriarchy as the "cause" of underdevelopment. The dominant account, however, went under the "Women in Development" umbrella, which sought to broaden the liberal conception of development as modernization in order to highlight women's rights and recognize the place that women occupy in relation to development and underdevelopment.

Taken together, the various strands in feminist development discourse had the effect of widening the object of development discourse in multilateral agencies, first within the UN and then the World Bank, to include a concern not just with poverty reduction but also with gender equity. Like the goal of poverty reduction, it is necessary to differentiate between the discursive effects and the material realities, in which women's position in relation to poverty and oppression has barely improved (Saunders, 2002). Unfortunately, dominant feminist discourses have reinforced a homogenous worldview by imposing a Western conception of women's empowerment based on the notions of individual rights, sex equality, and universal sisterhood. Although such a view may be supported by elites in many low-income, non-Western countries, it connects neither with the unique forms of oppression and power relationships experienced by many women in low-income contexts, nor with alternative, more collectively oriented, and indigenous forms of struggle organized around a view of basic needs as "rights" (Parpart, 2002; Wangari, 2002). These struggles were, ironically, often against the effects of "development projects" that had "flooded their land, destroyed their forests, separated children from parents and grandparents, divided men from women, and ridiculed their religions, philosophies and ways of life" (Simmons, 1997, p. 249).

In relation to World Bank discourses, it was disciplinary rather than political rationales that most influenced the development of programs and technologies targeted at women. A persuasive economic rationale in the World Bank and other development agencies is the notion that women's productivity is often "wasted" because it mostly flows through informal channels, unaccounted for and unexploited by the world market. This leads the World Bank to assert that "no country can afford to under-utilize and under-equip more than half of its resources" (in Simmons, 1997, p. 245). For the Bank, women's productive capabilities are to be developed as a means to integrate them more effectively into national and foreign markets. The remedy to their poverty is to make them central to development projects and planning through "gender mainstreaming."

World Bank discourses also have been concerned with women's roles as nurturers, as providers of welfare, and with women's reproductive capabilities. This is linked to a concern with overpopulation as a major factor in poverty. Since the 1970s, there has been an emergence of various programs and technologies of governance at a global level, under the auspices of the World Bank and other development agencies, targeting the fertility of women in low-income contexts. Such concerns do not compare the consumption patterns between populations in low- and high-income contexts (Wangari, 2002). In the context of new imperialism, they illustrate a resurgence of biopolitical racism that uses cultural differences to explain social problems and obscures the role of the West in relation to issues such as high fertility rates and the spread of diseases such as HIV. The discourses also avoid dealing with the effects of high levels of consumption by Western populations and the effects of economic globalization on poverty and the environment.

In addition, the 1970s saw the emergence of a new way of conceiving the causes of poverty through the elaboration of neoliberal economic principles and the Washington consensus. This recast the liberal *homo economicus* as a free economic agent invested with basic rights and civic duties. It valorized entrepreneurialism as the basis for growth and change through the actions of individuals rather than through state intervention. The neoliberal experiment was not only Eurocentric, but also failed as a development project to stimulate growth and reduce poverty. The critics of pure neoliberalism and the Washington consensus from the field of development studies argued that the "failure" of neoliberal "solutions" lies in the need for state intervention to rectify market imperfections (Colclough & Manor, 1991; Stiglitz, 2002). Such critiques led to a reappraisal of the Washington consensus and the emergence of the post-Washington consensus (Fine, 2001; Gore, 2000).

What these critiques do not acknowledge is that the failure of the neoliberal model, like that of the classical liberal model, may lie in *cultural* as well as economic explanations, for neoliberalism remains premised on a Western, individualistic understanding of human nature. Asking poor people in rural areas in the low-income world to become more "entrepreneurial" and to take responsibility on an individual or family basis to pay user fees for basic services like education and health means going against more traditional, collective forms of social action in these areas (Ndoye, 1997). Recognizing this situation along with the success of Asian models of growth and development has led the recent emphasis by the World Bank on social capital as a necessary corollary of human capital.

Putnam (1993) defines social capital as "trust, norms and networks, that can improve the efficiency of society by facilitating coordinated action" (p. 167). With the emphasis on "the social" in the post-Washington consensus, the idea of social capital became the "missing link" in development economics. Fine (2001) and Harriss (2001) reveal how the idea of social capital has allowed economists associated with the World Bank to "colonize" a sphere of social reality that was previously the domain of other disciplines. In this colonization, the social is reduced to a technical question of measuring the number of different kinds of associations at a local level and quantifying the extent of "social characteristics," such as compassion, altruism, respect, and tolerance. Correlations are made between the existence of these phenomena and poverty reduction, and the conclusion is drawn that social capital in these terms assists poverty alleviation and economic prosperity. Ethnicity can play a "good" or "bad" role in relation to social capital formation in that ethnic bonds can lead to intergenerational prosperity or to ethnic conflict. Critics of social capital theory have highlighted not only the methodological difficulties of measuring social capital, but also the depoliticization of social and cultural relations by not considering the sociohistorical contexts of interactions and the power relations based on class, gender, ethnicity, and so on. For these critics, the concept of social capital has developed in a way as to lay the blame for poverty at the feet of communities for not having enough social capital.

A further difficulty in the use of social capital is the way that non-Western cultures and identities become "essentialized" as being relatively "fixed" in nature with little change over time. This is reflected in the extent to which differences within ethnic groups based on class and gender are barely acknowledged and in the lack of attention given to shifting ethnic relations (Bates, 1999). There is also a clear connection between social capital as developed in the U.S. academy and World Bank discourses and modernization theory of the 1950s and 1960s, a relationship acknowledged in some of the discourses (Fukuyama, 2001). As in modernization theory, the attributes of non-Western groups with respect to their social interactions and cultural norms and values can be compared against the template of more "developed" communities where social capital is claimed to exist. Within the U.S. literature, this template is often derived from the social realities and institutions of white, middle-class America. Furthermore, the basic unit of analysis in many studies of social capital is the household, despite the fact that it is a highly problematic and culturally specific concept.

Education and the New Imperialism

Studies of the policy processes and changing priorities of the World Bank in the field of education already exist (Ilon, 1996; Jones, 1992; Mundy, 1998). Where the current analysis differs from previous ones is the emphasis on the discursive basis of World Bank policy and its relationship to the new imperialism. It is not being suggested that the World Bank represents a monolithic "whole" in terms of underlying views of education and development. As previous studies have shown, the Bank is a vehicle for a number of competing views and debates around education and development that have shifted over the years and have been hotly contested. However, at the level of governance the Bank remains overdetermined by the interests of specific national and transnational interests, which delimit what is possible in terms of the Bank's operational activities (Stiglitz, 2002).

A necessary starting point is to understand how education policy, as developed at the global level by the World Bank and other multilateral agencies, relates to the analysis of global governmentality. Distinctions have been made between *political rationalities* (ways of thinking about the dimensions and practices of government); *programs of government* (which use theories and particular ways of doing to translate political rationalities into actual measures that affect populations); and *technologies of government* (techniques, procedures, and strategies used to put political rationalities and programs into effect) (Harris, 1999; Rose & Miller, 1992). Education policies, such as those promulgated by the World Bank, can be seen as acting at the interface between programs and technologies of government. In other words, education policies take the form of political programs of government and attempt to use technologies of government to implement them that is consistent with the underlying rationality of government.

Colonial Education as a Basis for the New Imperialism

Modern forms of education with their roots in Western cultures and civilizations have been implicated in and provide a common thread between European imperialism and colonialism and the new imperialism. First, formal educational institutions have provided a key disciplinary institution within classical and settler colonialism. They provided a basis for the exercise of the pastoral power of colonial missionaries who often controlled formal schooling. By reinforcing and legitimizing the trusteeship status of the colonial master through a particular interpretation of the Bible, they helped to forge the colonized as colonial subjects rather than equal citizens. The imperative of schooling, however, often clashed with a more "modernist" economic imperative, which prepared through the inculcation of basic skills, dispositions, and attitudes the indigenous workers intended largely to staff the colonial administrations. For the indigenous elites who progressed beyond basic education, colonial schooling was also "disciplinary" because it inculcated them into a "colonization of the mind" (Nandy, 1997; Ngugi, 1981). Second, the effect of schooling was to produce bifurcation, a split in the loyalties and identities of the colonized (Fanon, 1970). Third, the spread of the Western episteme based on Eurocentric conceptions of human nature and social reality led to the development of oppositional discourses, albeit couched within Western discursive frameworks of liberalism or Marxism.

Following independence, formal education continued to operate as a disciplinary technology. Education remained in missionary hands, although as schooling came under government control, it was used by elites as a tool for transforming colonial subjects into new kinds of postcolonial identities linked to alternative forms of sovereignty. In some instances, the receivers of formal education remained as subjects of illiberal sovereignty under dictatorial and oppressive regimes or under one party rule. In other cases, they were constituted as citizens of an emerging liberal state. Postcolonial education was not disciplinary in the sense that it sought to forge postcolonial subjectivities in relation to new political imperatives and identities. It was disciplinary in that it extended the modernist, economic imperative of schooling through the gradual expansion of formal education at all levels. The belief in the modernist view of the role of formal schooling was a precondition for the subsequent spread of global governmentality.

Education and the Development Problematic

Education has had a significant role to play in relation to the development project and its focus on economic growth and poverty reduction. From the perspective of the United Nations and the nonaligned movement, education was viewed as a basic human right and its extension was a means for expanding global citizenship. Of particular relevance was how education was constructed, following the groundbreaking work of Theodore Schultz regarding the question of raising "human capital." Human capital theory remains a central tenet of World Bank thinking on education and proves to be a flexible and resilient discursive resource (Fagerlind & Saha, 1989; Little, 2003; Rose, 2002).

In the post-war period and until the late 1970s, human capital was primarily considered in terms of its contribution to raising GNP (Ilon, 1996). The World Bank and the other agencies hence supported projects to expand the skills base of low-income countries in order to provide necessary human capital to kick-start the industrialization process. Human capital was conceived largely as a "technical" question of inculcating the skills required for economic competitiveness and growth. As such, human capital theory contributed to the depoliticization of development discourse by removing reference to the role of education in reproducing social inequality. In human capital discourses, skills were conceived as discrete competencies acquired by individuals, with little attention to the social nature of skills (i.e., team work, communication, etc.) and the cultural context of skills acquisition. In contrast, more recent studies emphasize the dimensions of skills formation to understand different paths adopted by various countries and regions (Tikly, Crossley, Dachi, Lowe, Garrett, & Mukabaranga, 2003). Human capital theory also has a distinctive cultural bias. In the 1960s and 1970s, the development of human capital through education was seen as an important means to promote "modernization" through the institutionalization of Western education (Fagerlind & Saha, 1989).

Due to the failure of the human capital/modernization coupling to promote growth and reduce poverty, attention shifted during the 1980s to the role of human capital in determining resource allocation and social rates of return to different levels of education (Psacharopoulos, 1983). Primary education was seen as a principal means to eradicate poverty because of its relatively high social rates of return to gross domestic product (GDP) and growth. Human capital theory thus became linked to structural adjustment lending and the increased use of development targets by multilateral agencies.

This new role for education serves to reinforce the new imperialism by further limiting the capacity of low-income countries to determine their educational agendas. Dependency and incapacity are reinforced through the disciplinary mechanisms of poverty conditional lending, poverty reduction strategies, and international target setting. The overemphasis on primary education at the expense of other levels of education removes the indigenous capacity for research and innovation, two important aspects if countries are to link education to indigenously determined priorities (Tikly, 2003a; Tikly et al., 2003). However, given the continued hegemony of Western textbooks, materials, and resources, it is likely that a Eurocentric kind of education will continue in the schooling of most of the world's children.

How social capital is conceived in the educational sphere is through forms of educational participation and representation that are Western in origin and emphasis. A critical reading of the "good governance" agenda of the World Bank suggests a homogenous (read: Western) view of what governance means in practice. In contrast, indigenous forms of educational provision and community participation in decision making predated and sometimes survived despite colonialism and neocolonialism. This was evident in the early forms of *Harambee* in Kenya and in the forms of school governance during liberation struggles in South Africa (Tikly, 1994).

As Cornwell (1998) argues in the African context, while the state must transform itself to become more accountable to ordinary people and their needs, it is problematic to assume that this ought to happen along the lines prescribed by the West. It ought to involve "the creation of voluntary neighborhood governments and rural grassroots movements that produce alternative institutions of decision-making, drawing on customary notions of justice, fairness and political obligation" (p. 14). Cheru (2002) identifies a series of grassroots, civil society organizations, such as peasants' organizations, informal economy and self-help associations, the human rights movement, trade unions, and religious organizations, which could lead a form of "democracy from below." Mobilizing civil society also allows rural people to build on the "indigenous," whatever they consider important in their lives, whatever they regard as an authentic expression of themselves (Ake, 1988). Indeed, there is popular support for education in many poorer communities, and both formal and nonformal education, particularly in rural areas, has often emerged as a result of mass community efforts. It is these efforts that are in danger of being atomized by the neoliberal emphasis on user fees and individual entrepreneurialism and undermined by continued dependency on the West (Rose, 2002; Sayed, 1999).

Conclusion: Education and the New Anti-imperialism?

An enduring feature of anti-imperialist and anticolonial struggle has been the ability of activists and intellectuals to critique imperialist practices theoretically and politically. They often have provided a resource for critical social thought within the Western episteme, as evidenced by Foucault's formative experiences with anticolonial struggle in Tunisia (Young, 2001). Another enduring feature is to go beyond critique and engage with the possibilities of a more progressive alternative to imperialism and colonialism.

The question remains, however, as to whether there can be an alternative to the "regime of truth" that operates around the education and development problematic and whether alternative visions of the future, education, and even "development" are possible. After all, as Mudimbe (1988) reminds us, even in the most Afrocentric perspectives on change, the Western epistemological order remains as both context and referent. Indeed, it will not have escaped the attention of the reader that the present chapter, like so much "postcolonial" scholarship, is also written largely within a Western frame of reference, whatever its intentions or commitments! For critics of the new imperialism, this poses a dilemma: is it possible to conceive of a critical social theory and epistemology on which an alternative to Western hegemony can be built, and what ought to be the role of education in this endeavor?

To some extent, this is not a new problem within the social sciences. It is a problem of how to go beyond the existing order of knowledge while working within its frameworks. For some critics, this means abandoning the "development" problematic entirely. Against this kind of nihilism is another view contending that such an abandonment is a betrayal of the poor and marginalized. As Tucker (1999) points out, "If we were to follow this logic, we would also need to abandon concepts such as socialism, cooperation and democracy because they have also been abused and manipulated for purposes of domination and exploitation" (p. 15). It is the poorest and most marginalized that have struggled hardest, both during colonialism and subsequently, to create educational opportunities for their children because they still perceive formal schooling as a way out of poverty and destitution.

At a theoretical level, Santos' (1999) work is particularly useful to begin to reconstruct a role for education. In what he describes as a postmodern critical theory (or, for our purposes, anti-imperialist critical theory), he points out that Foucault's great merit is "to show the opacities and silences produced by modern science, thus giving credibility to alternative 'regimes of truth,' for other ways of knowing that have been marginalized, suppressed and discredited by modern science" (p. 33). Part of this silencing is to obscure the nature and origins of Western science. To begin with, modern science as developed in the crucible of Enlightenment thought owes much to the Islamic world of scholarship. From its inception, it has had both emancipatory and regulatory dimensions. It was emancipatory when it brought the threatening chaos of natural forces under control in relation to an emerging liberal notion of freedom and equality. It was regulatory when it excluded and dominated large sections of humankind, including slaves, indigenous peoples, women, children, the poor, and others.

Santos' (1999) plea is for a reinvention of "knowledge as emancipation" based on the principle of solidarity and a commitment to praxis, combining new knowledge as emancipation with a commitment to meeting local needs.

Knowledge as emancipation calls for a move from monoculturalism toward multiculturalism based on the recognition of the "other" (indigenous and colonized peoples, women, rural dwellers, and others) as producers of knowledge. It means recognizing the silences, gaps, and omissions within and between hegemonic and counterhegemonic systems of knowledge in order to unearth alternative ways of knowing the world. Rather than posit one "knowledge as emancipation," it requires recognizing the multitude of voices of the marginalized and working toward a theory of translation, a hermeneutics that makes it possible for the needs, aspirations, and practices of a community to be understood by another. In addition, knowledge as emancipation involves developing greater awareness and links between the production of knowledge and its likely impact by contextualizing knowledge production rather than separating it as a technical area and by creating an ongoing critical and deconstructive approach toward forms of knowledge/power. Finally, Santos aims for emancipatory social action and to "inquire into the specific forms of socialization, education, and work that promote rebellious, or on the contrary, conformist, subjectivities" (p. 41).

Santos leads us to inquire as to what conditions are necessary for transforming education from a disciplinary technology to a potentially liberatory institution, based on knowledge as a means of emancipation from the new imperialism. As Sardar (1999) points out,

> Resistance to Eurocentrism, and hence development, can only come from non-Western concepts and categories. The non-Western cultures and civilizations have to reconstruct themselves, almost brick by brick, in accordance with their own world views and according to their own norms and values. This means that the non-West has to create a whole new body of knowledge, rediscover its lost and suppressed intellectual heritage, and shape a host of new disciplines. (p. 57)

The development of the Western episteme, which forms the basis for the structure and content of formal education around the world, took many centuries to evolve. The (re)creation of non-Western knowledges will not happen overnight, although Sardar (1999) notes that initiatives exist toward this end, for example, to create an Islamic economics. There is a role for educationalists in the West to support such initiatives and to take seriously the fruits of such endeavors.

Knowledge as emancipation also demands that educationalists critically engage with ideas such as the African renaissance that has implications for developing alternative forms of knowledge linked to African-driven "development" (Tikly, 2003a). Further, educationalists ought to consider the existing attempts to challenge Western globalization in the form of grassroots social movements in Latin America, Africa, Asia, and elsewhere. They represent an emerging form of "globalization from below" (Novelli, 2004), and each has a specific form of critical pedagogy that underpins the basis for knowledge as emancipation.

A key challenge for anti-imperialist activists and intellectuals must be to work away at the core assumptions within the Western episteme and in so doing to provide continuity and build on previous struggles. One aspect is to challenge the binaries of the development problematic by disrupting the use of terms such as "developed" and "developing" in our discourses and opening up for debate their normative basis. Educationalists also have a crucial role to play in questioning the hegemonic role of economics in determining educational programs and practices. It means exposing the Eurocentric assumptions and values of development economics. It also means that critical social science needs to "recolonize" the terrain currently occupied by development economics and to open up the black box of education and its links to issues of inequality and social change. For example, an important area that development economics ignores, with its narrow focus on targets and quantifiable indicators of quality, is the processes at the heart of education in low-income countries, namely curriculum and pedagogy. How can curricula and the way that they are delivered in different learning contexts be used to foster critical thought and social transformation? These are the issues that need to be addressed if education is to have a role in a new anti-imperialist politics.

Notes

1. The recent war in Iraq, according to Harvey (2003), in relation to complex and conflicting political and economic imperatives. He argues that, while the invasion of Iraq was important for securing U.S. economic interests because of the strategic significance of the Middle East region as the global oil spigot, it was more problematic in regard to securing the United States's hegemonic global status because of the deep international rifts that it caused.

2. The term "neo" means "new" in Nkrumah's formulation, although the term "new" is used here explicitly to signify qualitative differences between the "new imperialism" and "neocolonialism."

3. What has emerged are several *neoliberalisms* exemplified by the work of the German *Ordoliberalen*, the Chicago School, and the writings of Hayek (Dean, 1999). Each represents an advancement and critique of classical liberal thought, although not constituting a homogenous worldview.

4. Drawing on Foucault (1997), "discursive repertoire" implies a series of key concepts

(embedded within disciplinary discourses) that have the effect of producing the objects of which they speak (in this case, versions of social reality and individual/group subjectivities signifying "developed" or "educated").

References

Ake, C. (1988). Building on the indigenous. In P. Fruling (Ed.), *Recovery in Africa: A challenge for development cooperation in the 90s*. Stockholm: Swedish Ministry for Foreign Affairs.
Ali, T. (2003). *Bush in Babylon: The recolonisation of Iraq*. London: Verso.
Altbach, P., & Kelly, G. (1978). *Colonialism and education*. London: Longman.
Amin, S. (1997). *Capitalism in the age of globalization*. London: Zed.
Bates, R. (1999). Ethnicity, capital formation and conflict. Retrieved November 18, 2003, from http://www.worldbank.org/poverty/scapital/wkrppr/sciwp12.pdf
Cheru, F. (2002). *African renaissance: Roadmaps to the challenges of globalization*. London: Zed.
Colclough, C., & Manor, J. (1991). *States or markets?: Neo-liberalism and the development policy debate*. Oxford: Clarendon.
Cooper, R. (2002). The postmodern state. In M. Leonard (Ed.), *Re-ordering the world: The long term implications of September 11th* (pp. 11-21). London: Foreign Policy Centre.
Cornwell, R. (1998). African renaissance: Art of the state. *Indicator South Africa*, Winter, 9-14.
Dean, M. (1999). *Governmentality: Power and rule in modern society*. London: Sage.
Escobar, P. (1995). *Encountering development: The making and unmaking of the Third World*. Princeton, NJ: Princeton University Press.
Fagerlind, I., & Saha, L. (1989). *Education and national development: A comparative perspective*. Oxford: Pergamon.
Fanon, F. (1970). *Black skins, white masks*. London: Paladin.
Fine, B. (2001). *Social capital versus social theory: Political economy and social science at the turn of the millennium*. London: Routledge.
Foucault, M. (1991). Governmentality. In G. Burchell, C. Gordon, & P. Miller (Eds.), *The Foucault effect: Studies in governmentality* (pp. 87-104). Chicago, IL: University of Chicago Press.
Foucault, M. (1997). *The archaeology of knowledge*. London: Routledge.
Fukuyama, F. (2001). Social capital, civil society and development. *Third World Quarterly, 22*(1), 7-20.
Gore, C. (2000). The rise and fall of the Washington consensus as a paradigm for developing countries. *World Development, 28*(5), 789-804.
Gould, S. (1997). *The mismeasure of man*. London: Penguin.
Hall, S. (1996). When was the post-colonial?: Thinking at the limit. In I. Chamber & L. Curtis (Eds.), *The post-colonial question: Common skies, divided horizons*. London: Routledge.
Hardt, M., & Negri, A. (2001). *Empire*. London: Harvard University Press.
Harris, P. (1999). Public welfare and liberal governance. In A. Peterson, I. Barmes, J. Dudley, & P. Harris (Eds.), *Poststructuralism, citizenship and social policy* (pp. 25-64). London: Routledge.
Harriss, J. (2001). *De-politicizing development: The World Bank and social capital*. New Delhi: Left World.
Harvey, D. (2003). *The new imperialism*. Oxford: Oxford University Press.
Hoogvelt, A. (1997). *Globalization and the postcolonial world: The new political economy of development*. Basingstoke: Macmillan.

Ilon, L. (1996). The changing role of the World Bank: Education policy as global welfare. *Policy and Politics, 24*(4), 413-424.

Johnson, P. (2003). America's new empire for liberty. *Hoover Digest,* 4(Fall). Retrieved October 28, 2003, from http://www-hoover.stanford.edu/publications/digest/034/johnson.html

Jones, P. (1992). *World Bank financing of development: Lending, learning and development.* London: Routledge.

Khor, M. (2002). *Rethinking globalization: Critical issues and policy choices.* London: Zed.

Lewis, L. (2002, September 9). The African Union, Iraq and the new imperialism. *Global Black News.* Retrieved November 18, 2003, from http://www.globalblacknews.com/LesterLewis.html

Little, A. (2003). Motivating learning and the development of human capital. *Compare, 33*(4), 437-452.

Mudimbe, V. (1988). *The invention of Africa: Gnosis, philosophy and the order of knowledge.* London: Currey.

Mundy, K. (1998). Educational multilateralism and the world (dis)order. *Comparative Education Review, 42*(4), 448-478.

Nandy, A. (1997). Decolonizing the mind. In M. Rahema (Ed.), *The post-development reader* (pp. 168-178). London: Zed.

Ndoye, M. (1997). Globalization, endogenous development and education in Africa. *Prospects, 27,* 79-84.

Ngugi W. T. (1981). *Decolonizing the mind: The politics of language in African literature.* Oxford: James Currey & Heinemann.

Nkrumah, K. (1965). *Neo-colonialism: The last stage of imperialism.* London: Panaf.

Novelli, M. (2004). Globalisations, social movements, unionism and new internationalisms: The role of strategic learning in the transformation of the Municipal Workers Union of EMCALI. *Globalisation, Education and Societies, 2*(2), 154-169.

O'Hearn, D. (1999). Tigers and transnational corporations: Pathways from the periphery? In R. Munck & D. O'Hearn (Eds.), *Critical development theory* (pp. 113-134). London: Zed.

Parpart, J. (2002). Lessons from the field: Rethinking empowerment, gender and development from a post-(post-?) development perspective. In K. Saunders (Ed.), *Feminist post-development thought: Rethinking modernity, postcolonialism and representation* (pp. 41-56). London: Zed.

Pfaff, W. (1995). A new imperialism? *Foreign Affairs, 74*(1). Retrieved November 18, 2003, from http://www.foreignaffairs.org/1995/1.html

Pilger, J. (2003). *The new rulers of the world.* Australia: Pan Macmillan.

Psacharopoulos, G. (1983). *Returns to investment in education: A global update.* Washington, DC: World Bank.

Putnam, R. (1993). *Making democracy work: Civic traditions in modern Italy.* Princeton, NJ: Princeton University Press.

Rist, G. (1997). *The history of development: From western origins to global faith.* London: Zed.

Robinson, W., & Harris, J. (2000). Towards a global ruling class: Globalization and the transnational capitalist class. *Science and Society, 64*(1), 11-54.

Rodney, W. (1972). *How Europe underdeveloped Africa.* London: Bogle-L'Ouverture.

Rose, N. (1996). Governing "advanced" liberal democracies. In A. Barry, T. Osborne, & N. Rose (Eds.), *Foucault and political reason: Liberalism, neo-liberalism and rationalities of government* (pp. 37-64). London: University College London Press.

Rose, N., & Miller, P. (1992). Political power beyond the state: Problematics of government.

British Journal of Sociology, 43(2), 173-205.
Rose, P. (2002, July). Education and the Washington consensus: The triumph of human capital. Paper presented at Political Economy Research Centre, University of Sheffield.
Said, E. (1993). *Culture and imperialism*. London: Chatto and Windus.
Santos, B. d. S. (1999). On oppositional postmodernism. In R. Munck & D. O'Hearn (Eds.), *Critical development theory* (pp. 29-43). London: Zed.
Santos, B. d. S. (2002, August 22). The processes of globalization, *eurozine*. Retrieved November 18, 2003, from http://www.eurozine.com/article/2002-08-22-santos-en.html
Sardar, Z. (1999). Development and the locations of eurocentricism. In R. Munck & D. O'Hearn (Eds.), *Critical development theory* (pp. 44-62). London: Zed.
Saunders, K. (2002). Women, gender and development: The opening of a subfield. In K. Saunders (Ed.), *Feminist post-development thought: Rethinking modernity, post-colonialism and representation* (pp. 1-38). London: Zed.
Sayed, Y. (1999). Discourse of the policy of educational decentralisation in South Africa since 1994: An examination of the South African Schools Act. *Compare, 29*(2), 141-152.
Simmons, P. (1997). "Women in development": A threat to liberation. In M. Rahema & V. Bawtree (Eds.), *The post-development reader* (pp. 244-255). London: Zed.
Stiglitz, J. (2002). *Globalization and its discontents*. London: W. W. Norton.
Stoler, A. L. (1995). *Race and the education of desire*. London: Duke University Press.
Tikly, L. (1994). Education policy in South Africa since 1947. Ph.D. thesis, Glasgow University.
Tikly, L. (2003a). The African renaissance, NEPAD and skills formation: Policy tensions and priorities. *International Journal of Educational Development, 23*(5), 543-564.
Tikly, L. (2003b). Governmentality and the study of education policy in South Africa. *Journal of Education Policy, 39*(2), 161-174.
Tikly, L., Crossley, M., Dachi, H., Lowe, J., Garrett, R., & Mukabaranga, B. (2003). Globalization and skills for development in Rwanda and Tanzania: A policy report. *Policy Futures, 1*(2), 284-320.
Townsend, P. P., & Gordon, D. (Eds.). (2002). *World poverty: New policies to defeat an old enemy*. Bristol: Policy.
Tucker, V. (1999). The myth of development: A critique of a Eurocentric discourse. In R. Munck & D. O'Hearn (Eds.), *Critical development theory* (pp. 1-26). London, Zed.
Wangari, E. (2002). Reproductive technologies: A third world women's perspective. In K. Saunders (Ed.), *Feminist post-development thought: Rethinking modernity, post-colonialism and representation* (pp. 298-312). London: Zed.
Young, R. (2001). *Postcolonialism: An historical introduction*. Oxford: Blackwell.
Zaoual, H. (1997). The economy and symbolic sites of Africa. In M. Rahnema & V. Bawtree (Eds.), *The post-development reader* (pp. 30-39). London: Zed.

CHAPTER 3

Postcolonialism and Globalization in Education

FAZAL RIZVI

Education is deeply implicated in the processes of contemporary globalization. This much has become something of a mantra among education scholars, even if there is little agreement on the ways in which globalization relates to educational policy and practices. The lack of agreement is partly due to the fact that globalization is a highly contested concept employed to embrace a whole range of academic and popular discourses. It is a concept used to describe almost any and every aspect of contemporary life, from the complex contours of contemporary capitalism, to the declining power of the nation-state system, the rise of transnational organizations and corporations, the emergence of a global culture challenging local traditions, and the information and communications revolution enabling rapid circulation of ideas, money, and people. The term *globalization* appears to be quite useful in capturing some of the changes that have transformed the world over the past three decades. Yet, such is the all-encompassing nature of its use that its explanatory power has become increasingly questionable. It is not surprising, therefore, that the term's capacity to explain recent educational transformations is, at best, limited.

In this chapter, I argue that this is partly so because much of the recent theorization of globalization assumes it to be an objective self-evident entity, and does not attend sufficiently to the task of historicizing it, pointing to the hegemonic role it plays in organizing a particular way of interpreting the world. Globalization is often reified, ascribed a range of universal characteristics. Given this approach, education scholars have taken up the task of understanding its various forms and inferring its effects on education. In my view, this is a fundamentally misguided way of theorizing the relationship between globalization and education. A better way needs to focus on the politics of naming globalization and on understanding its salience in specific historical and political contexts. In this task, postcolonial theories can perform a valuable role, not least because they draw attention to the false universalism of globalization and show how contemporary social, political, economic, and cultural practices continue to be located within the processes of cultural domination through the imposition of imperialist structures of power.

The reification of globalization in educational literature is not hard to find both in neoliberal policy documents advocating reforms designed to meet the so-called imperatives of the emerging global knowledge economy and in the literature critical of these reforms. Apple (2000), for example, argues that "it is impossible to understand current educational policy in the United States without placing it in its global context" (p. 58). The problem with this formulation is that it makes no attempt to historicize the seemingly ubiquitous idea of "the global context." Globalization is assumed simply to exist, rather than being understood as part of a politics of naming. The debate is focused instead on different policy responses. In this way, there is remarkable commonality between writers who view globalization as unquestionably good, insisting that it brings only benefits to all, and critics for whom global tendencies necessarily have negative social, political, and economic outcomes.

When applied to developing countries, the hegemonic nature of the idea of the global context becomes more evident. Samoff (1999) shows how, through the global diffusion of Western ideas, thinking about education has become almost universal, dominated by a set of imperialist assumptions concerning economic progress, with notions of human capital and development becoming part of a broader discourse of capitalist triumphalism. In policy discourses, borrowed by or imposed on developing countries, the broader processes of economic, cultural, and political globalization are interpreted in similar ways, tending to steer national educational policies into the same neoliberal direction. Samoff maintains that "with few exceptions, the direction of influence is from European core to southern periphery" (p. 53). Institutional arrangements, disciplinary definitions and hierarchies, legitimizing publications, and institutional authority reside mostly within the core, with the periphery left simply to mimic the core's dominant discourses and practices.

This universalism is implicit in the widely held assertion that the processes of globalization are threatening the autonomy of national educational systems and the sovereignty of the nation-state as the ultimate rule in democratic societies, threatening to weaken education's links to the imperatives of a community, while making stronger its relationship to the requirements of the global economy. (Burbules & Torres, p. 9)

Although the modes of educational governance might be globally converging around the same underlying notions, the problem with this analysis is that it appears to assume a largely naturalized view of globalization that is both ahistorical and apolitical. An even stronger sense of this can be found in Currie and Newsom (1998), who suggest that the global convergence of educational policies is an outcome of the structural conditions under which they are developed and that these conditions are anchored in a global economy that shapes the policy options that nation-states have. Currie and Newsom speak of an unstoppable globalization and its tidal wave force, making the relationship between the global context and education appear natural and inevitable.

Although it is hard to deny that the changing global context has an effect on educational governance, what this construction fails to show is how this effect occurs and, more broadly, what is the nature of the relationship between the global context and educational change. Often, this relationship is assumed to be self-evident, and the notion of the context is not problematized. But, as Taylor, Rizvi, Lingard, and Henry (1997) point out, what counts as the context can be articulated in a variety of ways, and what is foregrounded as the global context is often ideologically constituted, the acceptance of which already predisposes analysis toward certain solutions. Many critical analyses of globalization are thus paradoxically complicit with the claims of its empirical reality and historical inevitability found in international business, global politics, and popular media.

Such complicity is common not only among education theorists but also in highly influential globalization theories that have sought to examine the changing structural conditions under which contemporary social life is now arranged. Indeed, globalization is a name that is given to the social, economic, and political processes that have, taken together, produced the characteristic conditions of contemporary existence. It refers to the ways in which distant parts of the world have become connected in a historically unprecedented manner, such that events in one part of the world are able to rapidly produce effects on distant localities. It is now possible to imagine the world as a single, global space linked by technological, economic, social, and cultural forces.

This general understanding of globalization is shared by most of its major theorists. For example, Giddens (1990) defines globalization as "the intensification of world-wide social relations which link distant localities in such a way that local happenings are shaped by events occurring many miles away" (p. 27). Harvey (1989) views it as "time-space compression" (p. 15), whereas Robertson (1992) characterizes it as "the compression of the world and the intensification of the consciousness of the world as a whole" (p. 19).

In her analysis of global cities, Sassen (1991) assumes a similar set of attributes to characterize globalization, including increased economic transgression of national boundaries, heightened capital mobility, shift from manufacturing to business and financial services, control of economic activity from a distance, and hierarchical organization of economic activity in a global system of accumulation, command, and movement of international capital. Underlying this characterization is a range of assumptions concerning the logic of global integration, which Sassen treats as foundational, adequate for understanding the changing nature of social life and cultural priorities in global cities throughout the world. In an analysis that is perhaps less foundational, Castells (1996) also speaks of the ways in which cultural and political meanings are under siege by global economic and technological restructuring. He represents late modernity as an "informational mode of development" through which global financial and informational linkages are accelerated, converting places into spaces and threatening to dominate local processes of cultural meanings. He argues that networks make up "the new social morphology of our societies, and the diffusion of networking logic substantially modifies the operation and outcomes in the processes of production, experience, power and culture" (p. 33).

Although these theories focus on different aspects of the logic of globalization, they share a set of epistemological and methodological assumptions. Writing about issues of urban politics, Smith (2001) points out that they each draw our attention disproportionally to the global economy, "reified as a pregiven thing, existing outside of thought," whose developmental logic not only "explains the development of cities but even determines the subjectivity of their inhabitants, without ever interrogating them about what they are up to" (p. 6). In explaining social change, these theories privilege economic over sociocultural and political processes. Smith adds that because such accounts of globalization give "scant attention to the discursive and material practices by which people create the regularized patterns that enable and constrain them, these discourses lack an effective theory of political agency, or any other kind of agency" (p. 11).

Many theories of globalization ultimately posit a functional theory of capital accumulation, with its superstructural conceptualization of "culture which radically separates economic from cultural practices and subordinates cultural dynamics to economic generalizations" (Smith, 2001, p. 11). There is an assumption that it is the time-space compression that *causes* people, independent of their historical and social location and their will, to experience a sense of insecurity that often expresses itself in various forms of identity politics. This approach renders a view of culture not as an ever-changing product of human practices but as an expression of the deeper logic of economic imperatives. Such a view fails to "come to terms with people's situatedness in the world—the situatedness of their knowledge as well as their unique positionality" (p. 17). It is largely devoid of historical actors, and elides the historicity of economic relations.

What such analysis suggests, then, is the need to understand contemporary ideological constructions of globalization historically, rather than as a set of naturalized economic processes operating in a reified fashion. Unless this is done, many neoliberal ideas that have become popular in recent years will continue to appear as a natural and inevitable response to the steering logic of economic globalization. It will be impossible to recognize the ideology of globalization as historically specific, which serves a set of particular interests on behalf of powerful social forces, namely, the transnational corporate and financial elite. It is significant that globalization will appear dissociated from its roots in the European projects of imperialism and colonialism, which continue to shape the lives of people within not only the developing but also the developed world, with a global geometry of power that is inherently unequal.

This observation suggests that the resources of postcolonial theory are potentially useful in the study of globalization and education, not least because there is a sense in which postcolonialism and globalization occupy roughly the same conceptual ground. Yet, there has in fact been very little written that takes up the position of postcolonial studies in relation to globalization. In an *Encyclopaedia of Postcolonial Studies* chapter, Szeman (2001) points out that this is partly due to the differences in their disciplinary origins (globalization in the social sciences and postcolonial theory in literary and cultural studies), but may have more to do with the fact that the animating concepts of postcolonial theory, such as place, identity, difference, nation, and modes of resistance, focus on the particular, and there remains a strong current of universalism in various constructions of globalization, especially as they appear to suggest the emergence of a single homogeneous planetary space. Furthermore, whereas the main impulse of postcolonial theory is deconstructive and liberatory, globalization "acts as a justification and as an ideological screen for the rapid, global spread of a pernicious neo-liberal capitalism intent on reversing the social gains of the past five decades and in introducing an economic rationality into the public sphere" (p. 211).

This is not to suggest that postcolonial theory has not also been criticized for its complicity with the new structures of imperialist power within the age of global capitalism (Hardt & Negri, 2000). It has been suggested by neo-Marxist scholars like Ahmad (1995) and Dirlik (1994) that insofar as postcolonial theory lacks a clear notion of a telos, it offers no way of critiquing global capitalism, and that its analysis travels along the same neocolonial, transnational routes as global capitalism. Dirlik even suggests that "postcoloniality is designed to *avoid* making sense of the current crisis and, in the process, to cover up the origins of postcolonial intellectuals in global capitalism of which they are not so much victims as beneficiaries" (p. 353, italics added). He argues that the postcolonial celebration of cultural Otherness and difference has assisted transnational capitalism to extend the market reach of its commodity products that represent themselves as culturally hybrid and responsive to the needs and desires of local customers. The question of how these desires are historically and politically produced is elided.

Although there is some truth to Dirlik's observations, his arguments appear a little overstated, not least because they suggest a kind of conspiracy theory. However, insofar as postcolonialism is tied to an uncompromising poststructuralism, Dirlik is perhaps correct in claiming that it does not provide any critical tools with which to understand the contemporary spread of global economic conditions. As During (2000) suggests, by deploying concepts like hybridity, ambivalence, and mimicry, which imply the incorporation of the colonized into colonizing cultures, postcolonialism has effectively become a reconciliatory rather than a critical, anticolonialist category. During argues that a more critical postcolonialism is needed if we are to understand how colonial assumptions remain embedded within the new discourses and practices of globalization, as expressed in the totalizing reach of increasingly flexible forms of capitalism that seek to intensify the convergence of local cultures and societies. But this needs to be done without losing sight of the historical specificity of the ways in which people engage with global relations of power that produce highly localized expressions of globalization.

One of the major achievements of postcolonialism has been its insistence on the cultural dimensions of imperialism and colonialism. It has argued that, far from being secondary to the economics of colonialism, culture must be seen as essential to the production and maintenance of colonial relations. If this is so, then, new analytical strategies are needed to help us understand the economic and cultural politics of colonial legacies without reducing one to another. Without such strategies, it may not be possible to fully describe various continuities and discontinuities between colonialism and globalization.

For people living in developing countries, it is not hard to identify the ways in which globalization is constituted to a large extent by the continuation and strengthening of Western imperialist relations in the period of decolonization and postcolonial nationalisms. Postcolonial histories have amply demonstrated the persistence of global inequalities and the threats to the continued existence of local cultures and traditions by the global consumerist culture anchored in the West. New information and communication technologies have enabled instantaneous circulation of information, ideas, and images, making it possible to conceive of the world as a single space shared by all of humanity. However, the routes of circulation have hardly been symmetrical and equal. On the contrary, the so-called global culture has by and large reproduced the colonial structures of inequalities, with the postcolonial elite playing a major role in their reproduction.

At the same time, there are major differences between the current phase of neo-imperialist globalization and earlier forms of imperialist power, located at clearly identifiable imperialist centers. Deterritorialized logic and circuits of power characterize contemporary globalization. One of the major insights of postcolonial theory has been its understanding of the dialectical relationship between the colonizers and the colonized. Scholars such as Said (1979) and Bhabha (1994) show persuasively how colonizers not only shape the culture and identities of the colonized but are in turn shaped by their encounter in a range of interesting and complex ways. Nor can the colonized be regarded simply as innocent bystanders in their encounters with the hegemonic processes of colonization. Postcolonialism refuses to treat the colonized as "cultural dupes," incapable of interpreting, accommodating, and resisting dominant discourses. And so it is with contemporary global relations, which involve negotiation of cultural messages, even if this occurs in spaces characterized by asymmetrical power relations. This suggests that relations between global and local are always complicated and ambiguous and require detailed ethnographic case-by-case analyses.

There are, thus, deep homologies between postcolonial studies and the critical study of globalization. As Szeman (2001) notes, "Both of these concepts exist at the intersection of imperialism, capitalism and modernity, and both deal with the effects and consequences of the unequal relations of power between different sites on the globe, as these are articulated economically, politically, and especially culturally" (pp. 215-216). Postcolonialism points to the inherent dangers in the analyses of contemporary cultural practices, which are overdetermined by global capitalism and regard globalization as historically inevitable. It views culture as pivotal to understanding the nature of contemporary reality characterized by the expansion of global cultural interconnections, which, even if they are powered by economic forces, need to be located in particular localities and interpreted through particular geometries of power, in the dialectic between the local and the global. As Jameson (1998) notes, the global present is defined by "the becoming cultural of the economic and the economic of the cultural" (p. 60).

To understand the relationship between globalization and education, we need to avoid the universalistic impulse at the core of many conceptions of globalization. Most education occurs at the local level, but localities have never been more connected to outside forces, a fact captured to some extent by the phrase "deterritorialization of culture and politics." However, these forces do not exist in a reified fashion, to be simply "read off" for their implications for educational policy and governance. They need to be understood historically as being linked to the imperialist origins of globalization, not in a uniform way but in ways that are specific to particular localities. It is only through this kind of complicated understanding that it will be possible for us to comprehend new modes of imperialist power and to devise ways of resisting it in and through education.

References

Ahmad, A. (1995). The politics of literary postcolonialism. *Race and Class, 36*(3), 3-19.
Apple, M. (2000). Between neoliberalism and neoconservatism: Education and conservativism in a global age. In N. Burbules & C. Torres (Eds.), *Globalization and education: Critical perspectives* (pp. 54-71). London: Routledge.
Bhabha, H. (1994). *The location of culture*. London: Routledge.
Burbules, N., & Torres, C. (Eds.). (2000). *Globalization and education: Critical perspectives*. London: Routledge.
Castells, M. (1996). *The rise of the network society*. Oxford, UK: Blackwell.
Currie, J., & Newsom, J. (Eds.). (1998). *Universities and globalization: Critical perspectives*. Thousand Oaks, CA: Sage.
Dirlik, A. (1994). The postcolonial aura: Third World criticism in the age of global capitalism. *Critical Inquiry, 20*, 348-367.
During, S. (2000). Postcolonialism and globalization: Towards a historicization of their interrelations. *Cultural Studies, 14*(3), 378-396.

Giddens, A. (1990). *Consequences of modernity.* Palo Alto, CA: Stanford University Press.
Hardt, M., & Negri, A. (2000). *Empire.* Cambridge, MA: Harvard University Press.
Harvey, D. (1989). *The condition of postmodernity.* Cambridge, MA: Blackwell.
Jameson, F. (1998). Notes on globalization as a philosophical issue. In F. Jameson & M. Miyoshi (Eds.), *The cultures of globalization* (pp. 3-24). Durham, NC: Duke University Press.
Robertson, R. (1992). *Globalization: Social theory and global culture.* London: Sage.
Said, E. W. (1979). *Orientalism.* London: Penguin.
Samoff, J. (1999). Institutionalizing international influence. In R. Arnove & C. Torres (Eds.), *Comparative education: The dialectic of the global and the local* (pp. 51-90). Lanham, MD: Rowman & Littlefield.
Sassen, S. (1991). *The global city: New York, London and Tokyo.* Princeton, NJ: Princeton University Press.
Smith, M. P. (2001). *Transnational urbanism: Locating globalization.* Oxford, UK: Blackwell.
Szeman, I. (2001). Globalization. In J. Hawley (Ed.), *Encyclopaedia of postcolonial studies* (pp. 210-222). Westport, CT: Greenwood.
Taylor, S., Rizvi, F., Lingard, B., & Henry, M. (1997). *Education policy and the politics of change.* London: Routledge.

CHAPTER 4

Diaspora and the Anthropology of Latino Education: Challenges, Affinities, and Intersections

SOFIA A. VILLENAS

The term *immigrant* in Latino/a and Chicano/a communities has long been contested. From the oft-cited mantra, "We did not cross the border, the border crossed us," to Latinos/as' participation in the spiritual transcontinental runs of the Peace and Dignity Journey uniting indigenous America, we are reminded of a hemispheric Amerindian sensibility of both place and movement as part of a millennium-old process. In this sense, Latinos/as have long challenged the ahistoricism of the category "immigrant" when we are inspired to think of ourselves as belonging to these Americas, despite the creation and maintenance of nation-state borders. Certainly, my own first conception of a "Latino Diaspora" in North Carolina had as much to do with resistance to the idea of "immigrant" and hence "not belonging," as with marking new patterns of Latino settlement. When I arrived in rural North Carolina from Los Angeles in the early 1990s, I confronted geographies of *Latinidad* beyond my imagination. My unfamiliarity and surprise at this unexpected geography for Mexicans and Central Americans, as well as my excitement for different possibilities (i.e., new identities, forms of leadership, education and community building) jolted me into a hyperawareness of language. I needed new words to mark movement and new settlement, but also belonging. Yet I have since only alluded to these first intuitive, and certainly southwest-oriented, conceptualizations regarding Latinos/as and diaspora.

In her provocative article, "The Difference that Diaspora Makes: Thinking through the Anthropology of Immigrant Education in the United States," Ritty Lukose (2007) offers a formidable challenge to anthropologists of education who work with "immigrant" or "diaspora" youths and families.

With respect to the diverse Latino communities, it seems to be the case that we have sparingly, if at all, used the word *diaspora* and explicitly engaged its most central tenets. As Lukose highlights, an engagement with diaspora studies allows for the interrogation rather than the assumption of the nation-state, and attention to youths' and parents' hybrid cultural practices that rupture geographies and generations. Lukose was gracious to take note of my work, particularly as my colleagues and I began to call attention to the educational experiences of the "New Latino Diaspora" in nontraditional sites of Latino settlement such as in North Carolina, Georgia, and Maine (Wortham, Murillo, & Hamann, 2002). She was also gracious to not offer up a much-needed critique of how I failed to clarify my own use of *diaspora* beyond my implicit intuitions, and to better develop a conceptual framework vis-à-vis the growing literature in diaspora studies. Further, I have most often used the term *immigrant* alongside *diaspora,* a category that, as Lukose insists, needs to be critically scrutinized as a powerful site for the production of U.S. national identity and dominant narratives of "immigrant America."

In this chapter, I write in affinity to Lukose's call for attention to the intersections between diaspora studies and the anthropology of immigrant education. I explore a few of the urgent challenges and questions presented to conversations on new Latino destinations, transnationalism, and Latino diversity. I highlight how Latino educational anthropology merges with the imperatives of diaspora studies to interrogate nation and center Latinos/as' hybrid cultural practices, despite our use of the "immigrant" category and our field's lack of an explicit, systematic connection to diaspora studies. In the end, I turn to affinities of diaspora in Latina third space feminisms for future direction.

Diaspora and New Latino Destinations

The work of diaspora studies and its concerns for centering cultural politics in a globalizing world is far from irrelevant at a time of post-September 11, 2001, nation fortification. Latino migrants continue to create lives and communities betwixt and between nations (Suárez-Orozco, 1998), even as the United States intensifies its "homeland security" with increased border patrolling, immigrations raids, deportations and unprecedented numbers of state- and local-level laws targeting unauthorized migrants (Preston, 2007). Yet it is precisely within the rapidly changing geographies of new Latino destinations that we witness in a heightened manner how Latinos/as are conscripted and actively work to be written into dominant narratives of "immigrant America" (Lukose, 2007). At the same time, Latinas/os remake identities and family lives as they "contend with, engage, identify themselves with and are identified through a subject position that is the category 'immigrant'" (p. 413). Lukose argues for attention to these processes and to spaces of education as key sites where the "work" of the figure of the immigrant to constitute U.S. national discourses of democracy and citizenship gets done. I recognize complementary questions here in Latino educational anthropology. For example, Murillo Jr. (2002) refers to the "disciplining" of Latinos/as on the "do's" and "don'ts" of living in small-town North Carolina, whereas I interrogated parenting and other adult classes as sites for the teaching of cultural assimilation (Villenas, 2001). The ongoing ethnographic research by Wortham, Allard, & Mortimer (2006) with the Mexican diaspora in Pennsylvania is another example of how this work of constituting a narrative of immigrant nation gets done. They have argued that, unlike nearby Hazelton with its notorious anti-immigrant measures, the suburban town of Marshall (a pseudonym) engages in a more welcoming response located in the town's strong identification in and narrative of its immigrant roots. Institutional agents such as educators, police, and social service workers mobilize the category of "immigrant" as a way to talk about their town and by extension the nation in terms of inclusion, fairness, equal opportunity, and democracy. As such, the immigrant narrative is a double-edged sword. Wortham and colleagues (2006) focus on discourses of Mexican identity circulating in Marshall that called up different dimensions of the immigrant narrative, from the hard-working immigrant working toward the American dream and the immigrant who is a drain on the economy, to a kind of "model minority" immigrant whose hard work does not translate to the realm of schooling.

However, much of our work on the different waves of the new Latino diaspora begins (albeit pragmatically, we might argue) with the terminology of "host" versus "newcomer" and "native" resident versus "immigrant," signaling Latinas/os as forever foreigners and nonresidents. No doubt, participating in the discourse of "immigrant America" and its constructs of assimilation might strategically facilitate cultural brokering and acts of advocacy vis-à-vis a powerful mainstream unfamiliar with Latino families. In a politically volatile climate around immigration, alliance building across different groups and political orientations is crucial for advocacy-oriented ethnography in new Latino diaspora communities. Yet as Lukose asks, how do we challenge and begin to denaturalize the nation-state and "assimilation" as the assumed horizon in the trajectories of Latino/a experiences and lives? In rapidly changing communities in which stereotypes and polarized relationships may not be so entrenched, might participatory action ethnography lend itself to dialogue at public forums addressing the diverse ways of doing community, family, and education? Such dialogues might provide openings for reworking terminologies of belonging and cultural citizenship rather than centering "assimilation." By historicizing migration and denaturalizing the "host" of mainstream United States, conversations may center instead on the community building efforts of Latino/as in transnational spaces.

Diasporic Transnationalism: Interrogating Two Nations

We are positioned for new imaginings in beginning to document the schooling experiences of transnational children in Mexico (Hamann, Zuñiga, & García, 2006) or the ways in which U.S.-born or -raised Mexican adults transform Mexican society and its educational system upon their return as teachers (Petrón, 2006). For example, we might begin to imagine schooling in transborder or hemispheric terms including collaborative transnational school reform efforts on both sides of the U.S.-Mexico border that respond to migrant children's realities (Hamann, 2003). Latino educational anthropology is also positioned to further develop conceptual lenses for understanding Latino hybrid cultural identities and practices that rupture geographies and generations. As Lukose emphasizes, we cannot assume that imaginings of the "homeland" are the purview of the first generation since succeeding generations of youth are also imagining place and "homeland." They are doing so not necessarily to connect to their parents but to construct youth identities in a globalizing world through the medium of popular culture and through understandings of family histories and experiences of gender, race, class, and sexuality in the United States and the "homeland." And neither is the "homeland" always imagined nor imagined in the same ways by the first generation of migrants.

Yet how do we do transnationalism with a diasporic sensibility such that we interrogate two nations instead of one? To reduce the discourse of migration to a contest between two nations and narrations, for instance, Mexico and the United States, is to severely limit the possibilities for reconceptualizing the subverted and reconfigured spaces between nations inhabited by the diaspora (Villenas & Foley, 2002). Educational historian Bernardo Gallegos (1998) writes that both "Mexico" and the "United States" serve as disabling discursive constructs of nation that erase indigenous identities and make invisible asymmetrical power relations around race, class, gender, language, and, I would add, sexuality. The struggles over competing narratives of nation and citizen are not new in Latin American thought (Mignolo, 2000; Quijano, 2000; Walsh, 2007), and are interrogated in recent educational ethnographies (Levinson, 2001; Luykx, 1999; Rockwell, 1998). However, the question remains, how do we pay attention to the ways in which both the United States and Mexico take hold of the subject on both sides of the border? How is the Latino diaspora actively recruited, and how it actively participates in but also reworks the dominant narratives of each nation-state—immigrant (in U.S. terms) and *mestizo* heteronormative Mexican national sojourner—are important lines of inquiry for considering education (K-12 and adult) and popular culture as key sites for this active "work."

Interrogating multiple nations also includes marking Latin American countries' differing relationships to the United States as the core of the capitalist world economy, and consequently examining Latino groups' diverse histories and experiences of oppression and racialization in the U.S. nation-state. Grosfoguel, Maldonado-Torres, and Saldivar (2005, p. 9) urge attention to how "colonial immigrants," those migrants who come from peripheral neocolonial locations in the capitalist world economy, are "racialized" at the time of arrival in similar ways to the "colonial/racial subjects of empire" (e.g., Puerto Ricans, African Americans, Chicana/os) that were already there for a longer time. They refer to the "Puertoricanization" of Dominicans in New York City, the "Chicanoization" of Salvadoreans in Los Angeles, the "African-americanization" of Haitians and Afro-Cuban *marielitos* in Miami. Hall's (2002) ambivalence toward a diaspora studies that elides dominant regimes of incorporation, including systems of racialization, is useful, even if it runs the risk of naturalizing nation. I would add that the dominant regimes of incorporation and racialization work across and within both the periphery and core of the world-capitalist economy. Latinas/os are conscripted and participate in dominant narratives of immigrant nation and mestizo/creole nationalisms (nonindigenous, non-Black) from Latin American countries with particular relationships and histories to the United States. In this way, both diaspora studies and Latino educational anthropology need to take great care with issues of racialization and power relations in transnationalism as we enter into more discussions with communities on the complexities of "Latino diaspora."

Diaspora as Difference and Diversity

Educational anthropology in conversation with Latino studies and diaspora studies needs to pay attention to how our use of *Latino diaspora* might run the risk of collapsing difference and homogenizing diverse experiences. In this vein, it is important to challenge the academic insularity of Latino group studies and explore the relationships and social integration between diverse groups or within hybrid Latino communities. For example, we need to ask about the role of Cubanos in Chicano/a Studies or Mexicanos in Puerto Rican Studies (Rodriguez, 2000), or how Afro- and Indo-Latinos feel excluded from discourses that equate Latinidad with "brownness" (as opposed to "blackness") and privilege whiteness (Grosfoguel et al., 2005). To the extent that Latino studies influences the work of Latino educational anthropology (and vice versa), it is fruitful to highlight the interconnections and eschew notions of originary "Latino cultures" coming together to form hybrid cultures, as Bhabha (1994) warns against. We also want to be careful in privileging a linear spatiotemporal narrative of a single originary culture and nation that ignores, for example, the diasporic character of pre-twentieth-century Puerto Rico or Mexico. Rather, we consider Latino diasporas as "living inside with a difference" (Clifford, 1994; Pérez, 1999) as we disperse and remake our cultural and linguistic practices over time and space in multiple and contradictory ways. For example, Kasinitz, Mollenkopf, and Waters (2002) use ethnography and mixed methods to explore how the experiences of the Latino diaspora's second generation in majority-minority immigrant gateways such as New York City further complicate the notion of "assimilation," whether linear, segmented, or otherwise. They highlight how immigrants and native minority youth are living difference in remarkably creative and, I would say, transdiasporic ways, creating a vibrant youth culture that is neither "immigrant" nor "middle American" but something new.

However, although Latino educational anthropology considers the hybrid cultural practices of second-generation youth (Miranda, 2003; Rolón-Dow, 2004; Valenzuela, 1999), we often do not do the same for the immigrant parent, assuming the first generation as the originators of a particular Latino culture. But parents, too, are figuring out their identities as mestizo, indigenous, or Afro-Latin American nationals (maybe becoming more indigenous Peruvian in the United States than in Peru), and as racialized, gendered, socially classed, and sexualized beings. They are figuring out their roles as parents in the diaspora and rightful residents across multiple geographies who engage in community building and socialization vis-à-vis their children and members of social networks. I found this to be the case with Latina mothers' efforts to construct strategic collective identities of hispanidad and their parenting practices that both reinvented and ruptured "tradition" (Villenas, 2001). In this vein, Vasquez, Pease-Alvarez, and Shannon (1994) and González (2001) have been influential by respectively highlighting how socialization ran both ways between Mexican parents and their children, thereby highlighting the changing identities of parents and emphasizing a borderlands perspective to contextualize Tucson Latinas' ways of bridging tradition and innovation. Latinas/os living in difference has certainly been part of the sensibilities of Latino educational anthropology.

Conclusion: Transformative Diasporic Subjects and Latina Feminist Inspirations

In this brief chapter, I have merely scratched the surface in articulating how the imperatives and concerns of Latino educational anthropology merge with those of diaspora studies. By exploring a few of the challenges and tensions, I hope to have highlighted the implicit dialogue and affinities between Latino educational anthropology and diaspora studies. In concluding this chapter, I locate the possibilities for diasporic Latina/o subjectivities in the canonical work of Chicana feminist Gloria Anzaldúa via feminist historian Emma Pérez's decolonial project. Pérez (1999) explains how Anzaldúa's *Borderlands* (1987) issued "a 'new' postnational project in which *la nueva mestiza*, the new mixed-race woman, is the privileged subject of an interstitial space that was formerly a nation and is now without borders, without boundaries" (p. 25). Pérez reads the new mestiza as the always gendered transformative diasporic subject who is "not only here and there, is not only Mexican or American, or Mexican American, or Chicano/a, but more, much more, is always recreating the unimagined, the unknown, where mobile third space identities thrive" (p. 79). Pérez insists that these modes of living diasporic subjectivities are not to be understated or overdetermined as assimilation and acculturation. Rather, we interrogate nation and re-read Latinas/os' agency and identities as acts of cultural survival, weaving through power and always recreating oneself in and through diasporic communities. I write this as a reminder of how Latina/Chicana and third space feminisms often remain elusive to an academic project that is always coming after to describe what is past tense to those who are creating the phenomena. Indeed these affinities offer hopeful pathways for the anthropology of Latino diaspora education.

References

Anzaldúa, G. (1987). *Borderlands/la frontera: The new mestiza*. San Francisco, CA: Aunt Lute.
Bhabha, H. K. (1994). *The location of culture*. New York: Routledge.
Clifford, J. (1994). Diasporas. *Cultural Anthropology, 9*(3), 302–308.

Gallegos, B. (1998). Remember the Alamo: Imperialism, memory, and postcolonial educational studies. *Educational Studies, 29*, 232-247.
González, N. (2001). *I am my language: Discourses of women and children in the borderlands*. Tucson: University of Arizona Press.
Grosfoguel, R., Maldonado-Torres, N., & Saldivar, J. D. (2005). Latin@s and the Euro-American menace: The decolonization of the U.S. empire in the twenty-first century. In R. Grosfoguel, N. Maldonado-Torres, & J. D. Saldivar (Eds.), *Latino/as in the world-system: Decolonization struggles in the 21st century U.S. empire* (pp. 3-27). Boulder, CO: Paradigm.
Hall, K. D. (2002). *Lives in translation: Sikh youth as British citizens*. Philadelphia: University of Pennsylvania Press.
Hamann, E. T. (2003). *The educational welcome of Latinos in the new South*. Westport, CT: Praeger.
Hamann, E. T., Zuñiga, V., & García, J. S. (2006). Pensando en Cynthia y su hermana: Educational implications of United States-Mexico transnationalism for children. *Journal of Latinos and Education, 5*(4), 253-274.
Kasinitz, P., Mollenkopf, J., & Waters, M. C. (2002). Becoming American/becoming New Yorkers: Immigrant incorporation in a majority minority city. *International Migration Review, 36*(4), 1020-1036.
Levinson, B. A. U. (2001). *We are all equal: Student culture and identity at a Mexican secondary school, 1988-1998*. Durham, NC: Duke University Press.
Luykx, A. (1999). *The citizen factory: Schooling and cultural production in Bolivia*. Albany: State University of New York Press.
Lukose, R. A. (2007). The difference that diaspora makes: Thinking through the anthropology of immigrant education in the United States. *Anthropology & Education Quarterly, 38*(4), 405-418.
Mignolo, W. (2000). *Local histories/Global designs: Coloniality, subaltern knowledges, and border thinking*. Princeton, NJ: Princeton University Press.
Miranda, M. K. (2003). *Homegirls in the public sphere*. Austin: University of Texas Press.
Murillo, Jr., E. G. (2002). How does it feel to be a problem?: "Disciplining" the transnational subject in the American South. In S. Wortham, E. G. Murillo, Jr., & E. T. Hamann (Eds.), *Education in the new Latino diaspora: Policy and the politics of identity* (pp. 215-240). Westport, CT: Ablex.
Pérez, E. (1999). *The decolonial imaginary: Writing Chicanas into history*. Bloomington: University of Indiana Press.
Petrón, M. A. (2006). I'm bien pocha: Transnational teachers of English in Mexico. Unpublished doctoral dissertation, University of Texas at Austin.
Preston, J. (2007, August 6). Immigration is at center of new laws around U.S. *New York Times*, p. 12.
Quijano, A. (2000). Coloniality of power, Eurocentrism, and Latin America. *Nepantla: Views from South, 1*(3), 533-580.
Rockwell, E. (1998). Ethnography and the commitment to public schooling: A review of research at the DIE. In G. L. Anderson & M. Montero-Sieburth (Eds.), *Educational qualitative research in Latin America: The struggle for a new paradigm* (pp. 3-34). New York: Garland.
Rodriguez, R. (2000). Chicano studies: As America's Latino diaspora evolves, so does the field. *Black Issues in Higher Education, 17*(16), 26-31.
Rolón-Dow, R. (2004). Seduced by images: Identity and schooling in the lives of Puerto Rican girls. *Anthropology and Education Quarterly, 35*(1), 8-29.

Suárez-Orozco, M. M. (1998). State terrors: Immigrants and refugees in the postnational space. In Y. Zou & E. T. Trueba (Eds.), *Ethnic identity and power: Cultural contexts of political action in school and society* (pp. 283-319). Albany: State University of New York Press.

Valenzuela, A. (1999). *Subtractive schooling: U.S. Mexican youth and the politics of caring.* Albany: State University of New York Press.

Vasquez, O., Pease-Alvarez, L., & Shannon, S. (1994). *Pushing boundaries: Language and culture in a Mexicano community.* New York: Cambridge University Press.

Villenas, S. (2001). Latina mothers and small-town racisms: Creating narratives of dignity and moral education in North Carolina. *Anthropology and Education Quarterly, 32*(1), 3-28.

Villenas, S., & Foley, D. E. (2002). Chicano/Latino critical ethnography of education: Cultural productions from *la frontera.* In R. R. Valencia (Ed.), *Chicano school failure and success: Past, present and future* (pp. 195-226). London: RoutledgeFalmer.

Walsh, C. (2007). Shifting the geopolitics of critical knowledge: Decolonial thought and cultural studies "Others" in the Andes. *Cultural Studies, 21*(2/3), 224-239.

Wortham, S., Allard, E., & Mortimer, K. (2006). Chronicles of change: Models of Mexican immigrant identity in suburban community narratives. Paper presented at the annual meeting of the American Anthropological Association, San Jose, CA, November 15-19.

Wortham, S., Murillo, Jr., E. G., & Hamann, E. T. (Eds.). (2002). *Education in the new Latino diaspora: Policy and the politics of identity.* Westport, CT: Ablex.

PART TWO

CURRICULUM

CHAPTER 5

Decolonization and Education: Locating Pedagogy and Self at the Interstices in Global Times

NINA ASHER

In a recent essay, Schubert (2008b) urges educators to "keep alive basic curriculum questions," such as "What has shaped us? How did we become what we are? ... Who do we want to become and how can we shape the journey to go there? How can we live together without continuing to destroy this planetary environment?" (p. 412). Such questions speak to sustaining citizenship and responsibility at the individual level as well as democracy at the systemic level. If we are to sustain citizenship, agency, and democracy, it is important that educators engage such curriculum questions consistently and thoughtfully in relation to specific micro and macro contexts in the twenty-first century. Even as connections across cultural and national borders are opening up due to digitization and globalization, inequities and barriers persist and, at times, are reified (Asher, 2009). Furthermore, we know that present-day forces of capitalism and globalization have roots in histories of colonialism. For instance, the exploitation of natural and human resources of colonized countries for economic gain was crucial to the colonial enterprise. According to Chow (2002), the forces of capitalism, racism, and cross-cultural ethnic relations operate even today to colonize racial and ethnic minorities, "keeping them in their place" (p. 95) in obvious and subtle ways.

This analysis is relevant to academic discourse and the field of education. Gandhi's (1998) incisive and troubling critique of postcolonial discourse illustrates this point. She writes:

> [T]here is little doubt that in its current mood postcolonial theory principally addresses the needs of the Western academy. It attempts to reform the intellectual

and epistemological exclusions of this academy, and enables non-Western critics located in the West to present their cultural inheritance as knowledge. This is, of course, a worthwhile project and, to an extent, its efforts have been rewarded. The Anglo-American humanities academy has gradually stretched its disciplinary boundaries to include hitherto submerged and occluded voices from the non-Western world. But, of course, what postcolonialism fails to recognise is that what counts as "marginal" in relation to the West has often been central and foundational in the non-West.... Despite its good intentions, then, postcolonialism continues to render non-Western knowledge and culture as "other" in relation to the normative "self" of Western epistemology and rationality. Rarely does it engage with the theoretical self-sufficiency of African, Indian, Korean, Chinese knowledge systems. (pp. ix-x)

Even as postcolonial discourse has gained currency, non-Western perspectives continue to remain marginal, serving as commodified representations of the "other." As historically silenced "voices of dissent" emerge (Schubert, 2008a, p. 392), they remain regulated by "market forces" within and beyond the academy.

Postcolonialists in the field of education, Hickling-Hudson, Matthews, and Woods (2004) note that "the aftermath of colonialism" (p. 3) pervades the metropolitan countries that built empires as well as their former colonies. It follows then that educational systems, curriculum, and teaching are shaped in context-specific ways by legacies of colonialism. For instance, about three years ago, while on a research trip to Mumbai, India, where I was born and grew up, I was stunned to read newspaper articles that talked of many Indian students who did not know who Mahatma Gandhi was. I wondered: Is this loss of history an indication that we are now "post-postcolonialism," or does it reflect the recolonization of the "East" succumbing to the lure of a "Western" global capitalism? Similarly, two summers ago, while teaching a master's level course on "Curriculum and Teaching in a Global Context" in Louisiana, United States, where I now live and work, I was stunned when my students informed me that they did not know anything about the Vietnam War, a war led and lost by the United States and that casts a long shadow over the collective U.S. consciousness. Again, I found myself wondering about the forces that work to erase history and reify seemingly unbridgeable divides between East and West, past and present, laborer and consumer, colonized and colonizer. Ironically, as the global north and south become closer and interdependent, it seems to get harder to cross borders and engage differences of culture, history, race, religion, and nation.

As a scholar located at the interstices between the U.S. South and South Asia, and at the intersections of postcolonial and feminist theories, here, I also engage perspectives from the field of critical geography to consider implications for decolonization and education. Critical geography informs and is informed by the recursive deconstruction of hierarchical social structures and practices within and across national borders in the contemporary context of global capitalism, neoliberalism, and consumerism (Blomley, 2006; Harvey, 2001). Indeed, Longhurst (2002) discusses the growing attention paid to the intersections of feminist geography and a range of critical theories in engaging questions of "diasporic identities, boundary crossings and local and global geographies" (p. 546). And, Sheppard and Nagar (2004) recommend that critical geography draw on feminist and postcolonial thought to "advance critical pedagogies" (p. 562) and that we engage "in collaborative work with one another and students, with educators in our local schools and communities, and with actors located in the global South who most directly experience the downside of neoliberal globalization" (p. 561).

To this end, I integrate self-reflexive analyses of my pedagogical practice "at the interstices" (Asher, 2005) into broad discussions of social theory, geography, and pedagogy. First, I situate myself by interrogating the challenges and contradictions of engaging in postcolonial research and writing as a South Asian situated in the "West." Then I discuss key issues pertaining to (de)colonization and education. In concluding, I examine the possibilities and limits of postcolonial approaches in addressing extant challenges in education. I argue that a dialogical process of conscientization (Freire, 1982) allows teachers and students to resist colonizing, consumeristic forces and offers ways of (re)claiming self and voice, place and history, as we work to connect across differences of race, nation, and culture in the twenty-first century.

Multiple Margins: Situating Self
Between the U.S. South and South Asia

One may say that the postcolonial self is always "other," always "elsewhere." That is, those of us who resist oppression and work to dismantle the effects of colonization are, in some ways, outside of the "mainstream." The academic who engages issues of marginality, the activist/educator who combats racism in the United States or caste-based oppression in India, the organization that works for women's rights or resists the hegemony of global capitalism become "outsiders." At the same time, we are implicated in the very systems we attempt to transform. As Pratt (1998) reminds us,

Crossing boundaries can have transformative effects or protect the status quo.... relations between place and identity are complex and variable. There is therefore a persistent need to examine the specificity of these processes, in time and place, and to resist overgeneralizing one set of relations or effects. There is a need to take seriously the historical geography of identity formation. (p. 45)

As an academic, a South Asian, and a "woman of color" in the United States, I find myself to be both "insider" and "outsider" (Asher, 2001, 2005, 2007). As I write and teach at the fluid intersections of postcolonialism, feminism, and curriculum theory, "East" and "West," I am at the margins as a "woman of color" and a South Asian in the United States, and at the center as a tenured, credentialed academic, earning a middle-class income. Many postcolonialists, including "expatriate" scholars such as myself, have acknowledged the irony of postcolonial scholarship emerging from academics situated in the "West" (Gandhi, 1998). Indeed, I struggle with my own implicatedness as a South Asian immigrant and a postcolonialist situated in the Western academy. While my work draws on critiques of colonialism and contributes to scholarship in education, I am aware that it does not draw on and represent the "self-sufficiency" of "Eastern" thought. I continue to wrestle with the contradiction of recreating the elision and bring self-reflexive scrutiny to bear on my work as it focuses on issues of representation, equity, justice, and transformation.

The notion that decolonization is an ongoing, recursive, self-reflexive process was brought into sharp relief when I went "home" to India in 2004. After giving a talk at a research center in Bangalore, I went to a local coffee shop and had a mind-bending experience. Walking in, I literally did a double-take. It was so much like one of the "American" coffee shops where I go to regularly "at home" in the United States with its big glass windows, modern furniture, and fancy coffee drinks with hybrid-sounding names that, for a few minutes, I could not believe I was in India. Yes, there was that twist in the double helix of postcolonialism and capitalism!

Reflecting on my culture shock, I realized that, despite my critical postcolonial consciousness, my initial response was an "othering" response. What has become "normal" in the urban, middle class, Indian context was a surprise for me, the expatriate Indian coming "home" from the "West" for a "visit." Despite my self-reflexivity, like Fanon's (1967) "black man" who returns to Martinique from France alienated from his "home" culture, I was out of touch with a twenty-first century India gone digital and capitalist.

As I have noted elsewhere, "The self, regardless of its location, is never exempt" (Asher, 2007, p. 72). Furthermore, being situated in the U.S. South, I encounter an additional layer of marginality. The U.S. South, characterized by racial segregation, poverty, and poor healthcare and education, has been historically "othered" and cast as "backward" in contrast to the "progressive" North (Anderson, 1988; Pinar, 1993).

Thus, my efforts to engage the struggles of decolonization by working through the effects of colonization in terms of educational theory, research, and practice are context-specific, recursive, and self-reflexive. They are shaped by complex and contradictory forces of race, culture, gender, class, and nation. As I engage differences in relation to the particularities of East and West, South Asia and the U.S. South, in the global context of capitalism and consumerism, I also see the similarities in their struggles to deconstruct the legacies and effects of oppression in school and society. I believe that such a nuanced perspective offers us the opportunity to participate in productive dialogue and to identify possibilities for building coalitions across different contexts to resist the hegemony of globalization.

Colonization and Education

Generally, colonization refers to the occupation and control of one nation by another, for example, India by England and Algeria by France. It goes hand in hand with economic exploitation through the colonizer's control of the land, material resources, and labor force of the nation under occupation (Chow, 2002; Fanon, 1967; Said, 1978). Colonialism also has shaped discourse, disciplinary knowledge, and language use. For instance, Chakrabarty (1995) notes that "'Europe' remains the sovereign theoretical subject of all histories, including the ones we call 'Indian,' 'Chinese,' 'Kenyan,' and so on" (p. 383), and that disciplinary areas like economics and history foster the growth of capitalism and nation states.

Postcolonialists note that education is deeply implicated in the project of colonialism: "conflicts rage over the educational implications of race, ethnicity, gender, and degrees of privilege, and not least, over the love-hate relationship between former colony and former colonizer" (Hickling-Hudson et al., 2004, p. 7). However, postcolonialism offers a "space for moving beyond the negative patterns that persist after colonialism began" (p. 2). Scholars have interrogated the pervasive Eurocentrism in education, the marginalization and loss of indigenous knowledges and epistemologies, the reproduction and internalization of colonialist structures and practices, and the resultant contradictions and contestations in curriculum and pedagogy. Hickling-Hudson (1998), a

Jamaican-born scholar in Australia, reveals how the intertwined identities of colonizer and colonized work to shape oppressive hierarchies in school and society, curriculum and teaching:

> The transculturation of the colonizing experience is irreversible: Caribbeans have absorbed and reworked African, Anglo and other elements in their West Indian identity; Australians are reworking the Anglo, Aboriginal and other elements in their identity. These hybrid postcolonials share many colonially rooted assumptions and practices, both between their societies, and within each society regardless of the conflict lines of class, ideology, and culture. Caribbeans discriminate against Creole-speaking peasants and labourers, disregarding their central role in building the society, as much as Australian society discriminates against Aborigines and selected other ethnic minorities. Australian educators have been able to promote through their teacher education structures a particular view of what kind of teacher preparation is desirable (as little emphasis as possible on all that contextual stuff about culture and ethnicity); Caribbean educators have been able to keep the Creole-speaking majorities out of high-status education by continuing to use European elitist structures that are contemptuous of folk literacy. They exclude Creole ways of knowing almost as much as Aboriginal ones are excluded in Australia. Education requires schooling in one type of essayist literacy, that of the Eurocentric middle class. (pp. 337–338)

We see how differences of race, class, language, and culture, intertwined with the internalization of the colonizer and the legacy of Eurocentrism in curriculum and teaching, work to reify, recreate, and transmit the effects of colonization within and across specific locales.

The editors of *The Post-colonial Studies Reader* (Ashcroft, Griffiths, & Tiffin, 1995) note that "Education becomes a technology of colonialist subjectification.... It establishes the locally English or British as normative through critical claims to 'universality' of the values embodied in English literary texts and it represents the colonized to themselves as inherently inferior beings" (p. 426). The technologies of teaching further reinforce this project. Linguistic devices of embodiment, such as learning the "English tongue" and texts "by heart," work to ensure, for instance, that recitation becomes a "ritual act of obedience, often performed by a child before an audience of admiring adults, who ... speaks as if s/he were the imperial speaker/master rather than the subjectified colonial so often represented in English poetry and prose" (ibid.).

Postcolonial educators remain implicated by their participation in systems of education that are rooted in Eurocentric, colonialist, and oppressive traditions. How then do we break out of recreating, recirculating, and transmitting colonizing educational structures and practices when we ourselves are enmeshed in the same? The question Fanon (1967) posed over 50 years ago remains: "How do we extricate ourselves?" (p. 10). In wrestling with this question as a teacher educator who teaches courses in multicultural education, I have borrowed from schoolteacher Bill Bigelow (2001), who has written about how he gets his students to connect with the "human lives behind the labels" by having them take a close and critical look at items, such as soccer balls and sneakers, that they use on a daily basis. Following Bigelow's example, I have asked my preservice students to look at items that they use daily and study the labels to see where they were manufactured. My students are typically young white women who come from small towns in Louisiana and are not used to thinking about global interdependence as relevant to their lives and teaching (Asher, 2005). As we embark on our study of multicultural education, I ask my students to become "vulnerable observers" (Behar, 1996) and begin by "researching" themselves. Pooling the collective "findings" of the class, we find that most items, such as clothing, shoes, and electronic goods, are manufactured outside of the United States. Year after year, the students are surprised at the very dailyness of their international interconnections.

Why is seeing such connections such a revelation? Such a moment of conscientization (Freire, 1982)? Should it not be the most obvious thing for consumers in a major capitalist country that they are implicated in relations of global interdependence? What system(at)ic forces are at work to keep them consuming? It seems that alienating forces distance the self from others as we consume goods produced by remote others "elsewhere." The history of colonization and its effects, including the erasure of such histories from official curriculum, continue to shape relations of power as well as patterns of production and consumption. The twist in the double helix of postcolonialism and capitalism is that the formerly colonized others also consume and reproduce "Western" cultural, material, and curricular artifacts "over there," even as they continue to supply labor, services, "ethnic goods," and "raw materials to "us" "over here." Witness, for instance, the widespread consumption, adaptation, and appropriation of U.S. popular culture in different parts of the world. Having my eyes opened wide by the coffee shop episode in Bangalore in 2004, I was *not* surprised when I encountered street vendors selling copies of Friedman's *Hot, Flat, and Crowded* in Mumbai in 2008. Miller's (2005) call to recognize the "necessary worldliness of curriculum studies" leads me, then, to ask: What are the implications for getting past such limiting binaries as "us" and "them," "here" and "elsewhere"?

Decolonizing Pedagogies, Self, and Other

In our efforts to enable ourselves and our students to expand our "constricted eye" (Pratt, 1984, p. 17) and emerge from fragmentation, alienation, and the lure of consumerism driven by a globalized capitalism, we can "choos[e] the margin" as a site of resistance and transformation (hooks, 1990). As we find ourselves constantly dislocated in multiple and unforeseen ways, perhaps we need to accept that our work toward decolonization emerges from and occurs in multiple, at times divergent, and inevitably interrelated locales. Our task includes resisting reimplication in the colonizing forces of being othered and participating in othering. It includes recognizing that each one of us is "at the interstices" of race, gender, culture, class, and nation in context-specific ways (Asher, 2005).

Feminist writers insist on engaging the affective and psychic aspects of the self in the process of decolonization (hooks, 1990; Trinh, 1989). Oliver (2004) suggests that we need to examine "our unconscious drives and affects that affect, even govern if not determine" our actions and values and to unlearn repression (p. xxiii). Otherwise "we risk the solidity that prevents fluid, living sublimation and idealization and leaves us with empty and meaningless principles in whose name we kill off otherness and those others who embody it for us" (p. xxiii). While it is my hope that my scholarship serves to inform curriculum and teaching, I continue to interrogate its possibilities and limits. Reflecting on my multicultural teacher education pedagogy, I wrote:

> But how much of this do my students take into their classrooms? What else can educational researchers and practitioners do to foster equity and justice? Perhaps we can draw strength from the progress we have made in recent decades—from Civil Rights, to school desegregation, to the development of such areas of study as ethnic studies, women's studies, multicultural education, and queer studies. At the same time, in the work we do on a daily basis—preparing teachers to teach in a context of increasing global interdependence—we continue to confront stereotypes and the presence of silencing forces. And, we also wrestle on a daily basis with the contradictions we encounter, given our implicatedness—individually and collectively—in systemic inequities of race, class, gender, and nation. Perhaps these are the very reasons for persevering in our individual efforts even as we consider what else we may do collectively. (Asher, 2007, p. 72)

We see evidence of writings that are transformative in the realm of practice. Witness, for instance, Peggy McIntosh's (2000) article "Unpacking the Knapsack of White Privilege" and Vivian Paley's (1979) classic *White Teacher*, where she presents candid analyses of her pedagogy and her evolving multicultural awareness. Publications from Rethinking Schools, such as *Rethinking Our Classrooms: Teaching for Equity and Justice* (Bigelow, Harvey, Karp, & Miller, 2001) and *Rethinking Globalization: Teaching for Justice in an Unjust World* (Bigelow & Peterson, 2002), draw on critical theory, history, and current events to inform practice.

The work of decolonization entails not only our self-reflexive efforts to work through mind-numbing alienation and essentializing divides, but also the commitment to transformation in social and educational contexts. Hickling-Hudson (1998) urges us "To reinterpret the binaries, to recognize that, bitter as the conflicts may be, both or all 'sides' carry in them elements of the belief system of the other. Recognizing this and acting on it may be a bridge for communication and the reworking of the areas of contention in a postcolonial way that can forge new answers" (p. 329). This vision is congruent with Ahmed's (1992) recommendation for a "dialectic of unity and difference" (p. 265) that engages both linguistic and cultural overlaps as well as competing conceptions of class and community. A critical, dialogical, self-reflexive pedagogy can draw on these recommendations productively and enable students to "learn through conflict" (Kumashiro, 2000). While such approaches do not guarantee the transformation of future teachers (Asher, 2005, 2007), they enable students to see that there is "no pure west and east" (Bulbeck, 1998, p. 6) and that identity, culture, and curriculum—including their own—are shaped by history, geography, and economics.

Furthermore, postcolonialism serves as a vehicle for making audible historically silenced voices and contributes to transforming the field of education. At the same time, postcolonial perspectives have been challenged and greeted with skepticism at conferences, in print, and in other academic contexts by both "insiders" and "outsiders." Those who doubt or are uninformed about the relevance of postcolonial theory to education might question the significance of such work. Even those who may be aware of and engaged in the ongoing work of decolonization of curriculum and teaching as well as self and other may challenge the use of the prefix "post," given the persistence of the effects of colonialism in the twenty-first century. I believe that if we can engage such contestations in sustained and self-reflexive ways, we can "break down the ... duality" (Anzaldúa, 1987, p. 80) and arrive at effective ways of meeting postcolonial challenges in education in global times.

References

Ahmed, A. (1992). *In theory: Classes, nations, literatures.* London: Verso.
Anderson, J. D. (1988). *The education of Blacks in the South, 1860–1935.* Chapel Hill: University of North Carolina Press.
Anzaldúa, G. (1987). *Borderlands/la frontera: The new mestiza.* San Francisco, CA: Spinsters/Aunt Lute.
Ashcroft, B., Griffiths, G., & Tiffin, H. (Eds.). (1995). *The post-colonial studies reader.* New York: Routledge.
Asher, N. (2001). Beyond "cool" and "hip": Engaging the question of research and writing as academic Self–woman of color Other. *International Journal of Qualitative Studies in Education, 14*(1), 1–12.
Asher, N. (2005). At the interstices: Engaging postcolonial and feminist perspectives for a multicultural education pedagogy in the South. *Teachers College Record, 107*(5), 1079–1106.
Asher, N. (2007). Made in the (multicultural) U.S.A.: Unpacking tensions of race, culture, gender, and sexuality in education. *Educational Researcher, 36*(2), 65–73.
Asher, N. (2009). Writing home/decolonizing text(s). *Discourse: Studies in the Cultural Politics of Education, 30*(1), 1-13.
Behar, R. (1996). *The vulnerable observer: Anthropology that breaks your heart.* Boston, MA: Beacon.
Bigelow, B. (2001). The human lives behind the labels. In B. Bigelow, B. Harvey, S. Karp, & L. Miller (Eds.), *Rethinking our classrooms: Teaching for equity and justice,* vol. 2 (pp. 91–99). Milwaukee, WI: Rethinking Schools.
Bigelow, B., Harvey, B., Karp, S., & Miller, L. (Eds.). (2001). *Rethinking our classrooms: Teaching for equity and justice,* vol. 2. Milwaukee, WI: Rethinking Schools.
Bigelow, B., & Peterson, B. (Eds.). (2002). *Rethinking globalization: Teaching for justice in an unjust world.* Milwaukee, WI: Rethinking Schools.
Blomley, N. (2006). Uncritical critical geography? *Progress in Human Geography, 30*(1), 87–94.
Bulbeck, C. (1998). *Re-orienting western feminisms: Women's diversity in a postcolonial world.* Cambridge: Cambridge University Press.
Chakrabarty, D. (1995). Postcoloniality and the artifice of history. In B. Ashcroft, G. Griffiths, & H. Tiffin (Eds.), *The post-colonial studies reader* (pp. 383–388). New York: Routledge.
Chow, R. (2002). *The protestant ethnic and the spirit of capitalism.* New York: Columbia University Press.
Fanon, F. (1967). *Black skin, white masks.* New York: Grove.
Freire, P. (1982). *Pedagogy of the oppressed.* New York: Continuum.
Gandhi, L. (1998). *Postcolonial theory: A critical introduction.* New York: Columbia University Press.
Harvey, D. (2001). *Spaces of capital: Towards a critical geography.* New York: Routledge.
Hickling-Hudson, A. (1998). When Marxist and postmodern theories won't do: The potential of postcolonial theory for educational analysis. *Discourse: Studies in the Cultural Politics of Education, 19*(3), 327–339.
Hickling-Hudson, A., Matthews, J., & Woods, A. (2004). Education, postcolonialism, and disruptions. In A. Hickling-Hudson, J. Matthews, & A. Woods (Eds.), *Disrupting preconceptions: Postcolonialism and education* (pp. 1–16). Flaxton, AU: Post Pressed.
hooks, b. (1990). *Yearning: Race, gender, and cultural politics.* Boston, MA: South End.
Kumashiro, K. K. (2000). Toward a theory of anti-oppressive education. *Review of Educational*

Research, 70(1), 25-53.
Longhurst, R. (2002). Geography and gender: A "critical" time? *Progress in Human Geography, 26* (4), 544-552.
McIntosh, P. (2000). White privilege: Unpacking the invisible knapsack. In J. Noel (Ed.), *Sources: Notable selections in multicultural education* (pp. 115-120). Guilford, CT: Dushkin McGraw-Hill.
Miller, J. (2005). *Sounds of silence breaking: Women, autobiography, curriculum.* New York: Peter Lang.
Oliver, K. (2004). *The colonization of psychic space: A psychoanalytic social theory of oppression.* Minneapolis: University of Minnesota Press.
Paley, V. (1979). *White teacher.* Cambridge, MA: Harvard University Press.
Pinar, W. F. (1993). Notes on understanding curriculum as racial text. In C. McCarthy & W. Crichlow (Eds.), *Race, identity, and representation in education* (pp. 60-70). New York: Routledge.
Pratt, G. (1998). Grids of difference: Place and identity formation. In R. Fincher & J. M. Jacobs (Eds.), *Cities of difference* (pp. 26-48). New York: Guilford.
Pratt, M. B. (1984). Identity: Skin, blood, heart. In E. Bulkin, M. B. Pratt, & B. Smith, *Yours in struggle: Three feminist perspectives on anti-Semitism and racism* (pp. 11-63). Brooklyn, NY: Long Haul.
Said, E. (1978). *Orientalism.* New York: Penguin.
Schubert, W. H. (2008a). Curriculum in theory: Introductory essay. In F. M. Connelly, M. F. He, & J. Phillion (Eds.), *The SAGE handbook of curriculum and instruction* (pp. 391-395). Thousand Oaks, CA: Sage.
Schubert, W. H. (2008b). Curriculum inquiry. In F. M. Connelly, M. F. He, & J. Phillion (Eds.), *The SAGE handbook of curriculum and instruction* (pp. 399-419). Thousand Oaks, CA: Sage.
Sheppard, E., & Nagar, R. (2004). From East-West to North-South. *Antipode, 36*(4), 557-563.
Trinh, T. M. (1989). *Woman, native, other: Writing postcoloniality and feminism.* Bloomington: Indiana University Press.

CHAPTER 6

Nā Wāhine Mana: A Postcolonial Reading of Classroom Discourse on the Imperial Rescue of Oppressed Hawaiian Women

JULIE KAOMEA

I open the chapter with a series of transcripts from classroom conversations that transpired during my visits to fourth-grade Hawaiian studies classes taught by predominantly non-Hawaiian teachers in Honolulu, Hawai'i. The conversations depict "precontact" Hawai'i as a dark, scary world with merciless rulers, senseless rules, and harsh, life or death consequences; a world where commoners had to submit to the oppressive *kapu* (tabu) system or risk being caught and clubbed to death or brutally strangled with a rope; where women were mistreated and abused by their men, subject to oppressive patriarchal conditions, and treated like beasts of burden. In this chapter, I focus on classroom conversations about the wretched conditions facing Native Hawaiian women.[1]

Consider the following transcript taken from a series of student presentations on early Hawaiian life. In Malia and Sarah's presentation on the *pu'uhonua* (place of refuge), the girls explain how women, children, and old people went to a place of refuge when the men were fighting in wars, and how others could go there if they broke a *kapu* (tabu or prohibition) and they did not want to get killed. They explain that in "old Hawai'i" there were many *kapu* and rules about what people, and particularly women, could not do:

> Sarah: If you were a woman you couldn't eat certain foods.
> Malia: You had to eat separate from the men and you couldn't cook ...
> Malia: If you got caught breaking a kapu they would kill you.
> Sarah: They would beat you to death with a club or strangle you with a rope.
> Malia and Sarah in unison: But if you could run to the pu'uhonua before they could catch you, you were safe and they couldn't kill you.

Their presentation was followed by Kim and Marcy's on Hawaiian *maka'āinana* (commoners) who, according to them, fought in battles for the chief, helped him build roads and temples, and worked in the chief's taro patches. Noticing the striking absence of Hawaiian women in Kim and Marcy's illustration, I struck up a conversation with the students to inquire about it following their presentation.

> Me: You did a great job on your picture. I was wondering, I noticed that in your picture all of the maka'āinana (commoners) were men. Were there women maka'āinana also?
>
> (Kim and Marcy look at each other for a second, intrigued by the question.)
>
> Marcy: No, I don't think so. There were just men. Because they had to fight in wars for their chiefs and do other things that I think women weren't allowed to do back then.
>
> Me: So you don't think there were any women maka'āinana (commoners)?
>
> Marcy: Well maybe, but not that many. If there were, then they mostly took care of the babies.

A recurrent theme throughout the students' Hawaiian studies reports was the oppressive conditions faced by early Hawaiian women. According to their presentations, there were many things that Hawaiian women "weren't allowed to do back then." They "couldn't eat certain foods," they "had to eat separate from the men," and they "couldn't cook." Their remarks resonate with a pervasive message in numerous classroom Hawaiian studies lessons that I have observed over the course of my research; that is, in precontact times Hawaiian women were held in low regard, overburdened with work, and subject to oppressive restrictions.

This message also was evident in other Hawaiian studies classroom lessons. For instance, consider the following excerpt from my field notes taken during another fourth-grade lesson on beating *kapa* (tapa cloth):

> As the children took turns beating and folding the kapa, their teacher discussed the craft's history. She explained that in ancient Hawai'i, kapa beating was strictly a job for women. "If you were a girl living in old Hawai'i," she said, "you would do this all day, every day—never stopping when you were tired, but working, working, working from morning until night. The only breaks you would ever get were the few days out of each month when you were considered impure and were banished to live in the community menstrual hut."

Similar messages are communicated through the students' Hawaiian studies textbook, which states multiple times that "Hawaiians thought women were not clean" (Dunford, 1980, pp. 65, 74), and through popular "Hawaiian" storybooks found on the classroom bookshelves.

One popular storybook in the classroom described above was a children's picture book entitled *The Woman in the Moon*. This illustrated book presents an embellished retelling of the traditional story of the goddess Hina. The book describes how Hina, the best tapa maker in the land, was driven to escape life in old Hawai'i to live on the moon because she was overworked by her people, mistreated by her spouse, and "tired of having so much of this natural world kapu, or forbidden, to her, simply because she is a woman" (Rattigan, 1996, book jacket). It goes on to explain that Hina's husband, Aikanaka-the-Wanderer, was usually gone hunting or fighting in faraway places. When he was home, he was lazy and complained about everything:

> Hina ... was weary of doing Aikanaka's work and of making so much tapa for the entire village. She also did not like living in a place where so many things were kapu, or forbidden for women. Because she was a woman, she was not allowed to eat fresh coconut, roast pork, or golden ripe bananas. She could not pray or eat with her husband or go with him on his adventures, like fishing for the deep-sea shark or hunting the wild forest boar. Hina longed for a place where such wonderful things in life were not kapu for her. She wanted a home where she did not have to work all the time. (pp. 9-11)

Eventually, Hina "looks for a better home" and rises above the restrictions placed on her by leaving her husband and the *kapu* of old Hawai'i to live on the moon where "her spirit was finally free" (p. 21).

While the book is popular with both teachers and children, I was personally dismayed by how this deceptively simple book had effectively disempowered a sacred Hawaiian goddess, portraying the female *akua* (god or goddess) who controls the moon, tides, and reefs as a feeble, weary, and overworked woman who flees to the moon to escape an abusive husband and an oppressive, misogynistic Hawaiian society. The author acknowledges at the back of the book that she used a bit of artistic license to support her personal "interpretation of the story." However, I believe that there is more at work than one author's use of artistic license. The familiar story of oppressed Hawaiian women that pervades Hawaiian studies curricula and popular children's picture books is a dominant discourse that has been and continues to be used to justify colonial interventions in indigenous societies today.

As Gayatri Spivak's (1985/1988) phrase "White men are saving brown women from brown men" (p. 296) so aptly suggests, the oppressive conditions faced by Native women has historically been used as a rallying cry by colonial forces looking to justify their overthrow of Native governments. According to the commentary of Lieutenant King (King & Douglas, 1784), who traveled with Cook and continued the captain's journals after his untimely death, early Hawaiians fell far short of other societies in "that best test of civilization, the respect paid to women." While King admits that he and his men did not observe any instance of personal ill-treatment toward Hawaiian women, he says it was nevertheless evident that they had "little regard . . . paid them." King expressed concern that in their domestic life Hawaiian women "appear(ed) to live almost entirely by themselves." "They (were) not only deprived of the privilege of eating with the men, but the best sorts of food (were) tabooed, or forbidden them" (p. 130). Similar remarks were made in missionary William Ellis' (1979) commentary on the "Severity of tabu relating to women." While Ellis condemned the *kapu* system as being oppressive to all Hawaiian commoners, he alleged that females were especially subject to its "humiliating and degrading force" (p. 281). Citing concerns with the oppressive restrictions that prevented Hawaiian women from cooking, eating with men, and partaking of certain foods, Ellis concludes that the only hope for the Hawaiian civilization was that Christianity would "elevate the degraded classes, especially the females, to the rank and influence for which they were designed," rendering their domestic society as "rational and happy," whereas under the *kapu* it was "abject and wretched" (p. 282).

While these discourses have been questioned in postcolonial Hawaiian scholarship as European colonial myths, which the colonizers carried with them to Hawai'i and which were more reflective of the tensions of eighteenth-century European society than of the precontact Hawaiian condition (Obeyesekere, 1992), they are rarely questioned in the general public and continue to influence the way in which children and teachers think and talk about Hawaiian society today. Despite their questionable origin, these discourses resonate with historical accounts of Hawai'i's postcontact period that emphasize progress toward "civilization" and improved conditions for Hawaiians, and particularly Hawaiian women, with the onset of colonization.

The classroom discussions of oppressed Hawaiian women sit alongside, or are articulated by, the presumably liberated conditions of contemporary Hawaiian women, a discourse of progress through colonization. In a lesson that compared the traditional Hawaiian *kapu* system with contemporary times, one teacher explained that in old Hawai'i if girls ate certain foods, they would be killed, but now, women can eat anything. Drawing from the State Hawaiian studies curriculum guide (Hawai'i Department of Education, 1984, p. 77), the teacher asked the children: "If you were a woman in early Hawai'i and were not allowed to eat *kālua* (baked) pig, how would you feel when you saw the pig being taken out of the *imu* (underground oven) and smelled the cooking?" The teacher proceeded to compare the gender roles of men and women in early Hawai'i alongside the gender roles of today. She explained that if women in early Hawai'i tried to do a man's job, like pound the *kalo* (taro root) into poi, which was *kapu* for women to do, they would be put to death. She asked if these gender restrictions still existed in contemporary times. Again, drawing from the Hawaiian studies curricular guide (Pescaia, 1981, p. 103), the teacher asked: "What about today? Can men become nurses? Can women become doctors? Can women become policewomen and men become beauticians?"

The implication is that, since colonization, Hawaiian women (and men) can eat anything that they wish and have unfettered access to any occupation. Let me state for the record that we have proportionately far more Hawaiian police officers and beauticians, than Hawaiian doctors and nurses, as Native Hawaiians continue to be underrepresented in professional and managerial positions and overrepresented in low paying service jobs and as inmates in prisons (Kana'iaupuni, Malone, & Ishibashi, 2005). Furthermore, while there are no longer religious *kapu* restricting Hawaiian women from eating *kālua* pig and other traditional Hawaiian foods, with the highest unemployment and poverty rates in the state, many Hawaiians are now restricted from eating these traditional foods because they have no land on which to grow them and cannot afford to buy them.

I scrutinize the notion that conditions for Hawaiian women improved postcontact and that the introduction of Christianity was a liberating force for Hawaiian women. I disrupt this dominant narrative of progress and increased civilization for Hawaiian women through colonization, and propose a counternarrative of traditionally powerful Hawaiian women, whose political and domestic autonomy were severely challenged and eroded with colonization and the imposition of Christianity.

Methodology

My method of analysis is a hybrid one that I call countergenealogy with roots in both Hawaiian tradition and Foucaultian genealogy.

Genealogy has always been important to Hawaiians, particularly to *ali'i* (chiefs). It was genealogy that determined the quality of any proposed sovereign. As Kamakau (1961) notes, often "the strife between ... chiefs took the form of denying each other's pure descent from a line of high chiefs .... Both sides ... had composers of *meles* [songs, chants, or poems] who chanted the names of ancestors, the high and godlike rank of their own chief, and the mean ancestry of the other" (pp. 152–153). Thus skilled genealogists who knew and could recite the names and deeds of a chief's ancestors were highly valued in traditional Hawaiian society. Consequently, we have genealogical chants like the Kumulipo ("Beginning-in-deep-darkness"), the sacred creation chant of a family of Hawaiian *ali'i* or ruling chiefs. Composed and translated entirely in the oral tradition, its two thousand lines trace the family's divine origin by genealogical pairs through great rulers, heroes, and primary gods, back to the first spark of life in the universe.

However, as Malo (1951) suggests, Hawaiian genealogies are not like the genealogy of Adam, which is one unbroken line without any stems. Due to multiple matings of male and female *ali'i*, and the bilateral determination of rank through both male and female lines, Hawaiian chiefly relations were multiplex and tangled, and their genealogies were susceptible to multiple readings. As Kamakau (1961) explains quite poetically, Hawaiian genealogies were "woven in and out" and "twisted into knots" (p. 86). Thus, Hawaiian *ali'i* could and did trace their relationships in a variety of ways, invoking particular ties, lines, and ancestors according to context and situational advantage.

For the most part, genealogies were recounted to verify the validity of, or smooth the relations between, ruling chiefs. It was the custom, when chiefs went to war with each other and both sides suffered reverses, for some expert in genealogies to suggest a conference to end the war, at which time they would recite the relevant genealogies in such a way as to reveal that the warring chiefs were related. However, just as ruling chiefs could justify their claims through a multiplicity of links, so could ambitious junior collaterals justify rebellion by recounting lesser-known lines of their genealogies that link them to high-ranking ancestors. Such is the story of the evil Hākau, son of the high chief Līloa, who was thought to be Līloa's uncontested heir, until it was revealed that Līloa had another son, 'Umi, a humble and generous young man raised by commoners. When journeying through Hamakua many years earlier, the high chief Līloa stopped to bathe in a stream where he met and seduced 'Umi's commoner mother, and left with her his loincloth, his necklace, and his club, as evidence of their encounter and proof that the child resulting from their encounter was his. As 'Umi grew older, and his mother revealed his chiefly genealogy, 'Umi took these tokens of proof back to the court of Līloa, where following their father's death, this new genealogical linkage was used to justify 'Umi's overthrow of the cruel and arrogant Hākau.

In cases of usurping a dominant ruler, the job of the *po'e kū'auhau* (genealogist) was to investigate local and lesser-known stories and fix upon the discontinuities or contradictions that would suggest an alternate reading to a widely accepted genealogy, revealing, for instance, the royal ancestry of a supposed commoner or the lowly origins of a reigning sovereign.

The commoner use of genealogy, which inspired the methodology of the chapter, is in many ways consistent with Foucault's (1977) genealogical method. Foucaultian genealogies are directed against great truths and grand theories or narratives. They turn away from the spectacular in favor of the discredited, the neglected, and a whole range of phenomena that have been denied a history. Foucault's genealogies focus on local, disqualified, illegitimate knowledge against the claims of a unitary body of theory. For Foucault, the process of genealogy involves an attack on the tyranny of "totalizing discourses" and a painstaking rediscovery of fragmented, subjugated, local, and specific knowledge (Foucault, 1980). Similarly, I apply countergenealogy to disrupt the dominant narrative of "white men saving brown women from brown men," and trace lesser-known lines of history to tell an alternative counterstory.

This method is applicable because it is useful to view the power of colonialism and colonial discourse as operating rhizomically rather than monolithically, like a root system that spreads across the ground rather than downward, and grows from several points rather than a single tap root (Kaomea, 2005). I argue that colonial ideologies are more variable, complex, and ambivalent than has been generally acknowledged, and that colonialism is not a unitary project but a fractured one, riddled with contradictions and exhausted as much by its own internal debates as by the resistance of the colonized.

For Hawai'i's postcontact period, the amount of English language "historical" evidence available is voluminous, but it is also overwhelmingly Euro- and androcentric. The historical accounts most often cited regarding Hawaiian women are largely from the perspective of male explorers, sailors, merchants, traders, and missionaries. From the visits of Captain James Cook in 1778 to the mid-nineteenth century whalers, Hawaiian women most frequently appear in the foreigners' historical records in terms of their sexual liaisons with foreign men, accounts that rarely, if ever, give any consideration to the Hawaiian women's motives and perspectives. Ralston (1989) argues that "Nowhere in the records of Hawai'i's past, pre- or post-contact, are the voices of Hawaiian women clearly and unequivocally heard" (p. 50). Since, there is "no direct evidence of their thoughts, motives, or experience," she contends, "this gap makes complete understanding of these women impossible."

I agree that in nineteenth-century Hawaiʻi, as elsewhere, Hawaiian and other women's public writings were small in volume relative to men's. However, following Silva (2004), I argue that throughout history Hawaiian women's voices are always present if we look (or listen) for them. Spivak (1985/1988) relates the various forms of covert communication that female subalterns are sometimes forced to engage in. She tells of a young woman who participated in the armed struggle for India's independence. The woman committed suicide but waited until she was menstruating to do so, so that her suicide could not be misinterpreted as brought on by an illegitimate pregnancy. While the subaltern woman was unable to speak overtly, her message was clear, and scholars like Spivak continue to recount and interpret the details of her death. Postcontact Hawaiian women engaged in veiled communications of other sorts. They composed and published eloquent poems and songs in Hawaiian language newspapers, many of which expressed anticolonial sentiments through hidden references and double meanings. They became the secret keepers of the knowledge of the missionary-outlawed hula, sewed the Hawaiian national flag into quilts taught to them by missionary women, signed petitions against U.S. annexation, and memorized and passed on *moʻolelo* (stories) of their strong female ancestors (Silva, 2004).

Although their communications are less voluminous and more difficult to find and decipher than those of male historians and colonial men, Hawaiian women did and continue to speak. Like the commoner Hawaiian genealogist, I seek out these less-cited voices, resurrect local, fragmented, and subjugated knowledge, and trace lesser-known lines of history to construct a countergenealogy of *nā wāhine mana*, or powerful Hawaiian women, who were descended from a culture with 20,000 divine female goddesses, prominent female *aliʻi*, and resilient commoner women who enjoyed relatively liberated positions in their families and communities, and stubbornly resisted the restrictive impositions of Christianity and U.S. domestication. Drawing from Native Hawaiian examples, I conclude with a challenge to educators and researchers across the globe to seek out similar countergenealogies in the teaching and writing of indigenous history and indigenous studies curricula.

The Countergenealogy

Mana Wahine and the Female Akua

As with great Hawaiian genealogies, this countergenealogy begins with the gods or *akua*. The genealogy suggested by classroom discussions cited earlier, places at the uppermost, originary position a feeble, disempowered Hina, a weary and overworked woman who flees to the moon to escape an abusive husband and an oppressive society where much is forbidden her because she is a woman. In contrast, the Hina of the Kumulipo genealogy is powerful. The Kumulipo is a genealogical and cosmological chant that recounts the genesis of living things on earth, including humankind. It links the chiefs to their ancestors, to the first humans, to animals, plants, and backward in time, to the gods and the beginning of the universe. While Hawaiian songs, poems, and stories, are often undervalued as historical sources, I contend that they are important to the construction of countergenealogies. Hawaiians understood that songs, poems, and stories had the potential for *kaona* or "hidden meanings," and used them to express and publish anticolonial sentiments that were difficult for the U.S. colonizers to decipher. In genealogical projects that aim for "an insurrection of subjugated knowledges" (Foucault, 1980, p. 81), attending to less-understood genres of resistance writing can yield insights unavailable from other sources.

In *Aloha Betrayed*, Noenoe Silva (2004) describes how the Kumulipo was preserved largely due to the efforts of Hawaiian women, and has functioned throughout history as an anticolonial counternarrative. After having been passed on orally through successive Hawaiian generations, in 1889 it was collected and transcribed by King Kalākaua's Board of Genealogy of Hawaiian Chiefs (headed by female president, Ke Kamāli'i Po'omaikelani) to validate King Kalākaua's claim to the throne in the face of encroaching foreigners. Several years after the Kumulipo was published by Kalākaua, Queen Lili'uokalani undertook her translation of it while imprisoned by the colonial oligarchy in 1896, and published it in 1897 to argue against U.S. annexation and military occupation of Hawai'i by demonstrating that Native Hawaiians are a people with a long history of residency and sovereignty in our islands.

According to the Kumulipo, the ancient Hawaiian world begins with Pō, the unfathomable and mysterious female night. Pō is the ultimate ancestor of all Hawaiian gods. She is the source of life, divinity, and ancestral wisdom. Hawaiian gods and goddess were created when Pō spontaneously gave birth by herself, without any male impregnating element, to a son and daughter, Kumulipo (male night) and Pō'ele (female night), who by their mating over a period of 8 days and nights created the world and 40,000 gods and goddesses (Kame'eleihiwa, 1999). The first child of Kumulipo and Pō'ele was the goddess Hina. The coral reefs were her body, and from the coral heads Hina gave birth to sea urchins, seaweeds, reef creatures, and their counterparts on the land: fresh water shrimp, mosses, and small ferns. In many parts of Polynesia, Hina is known as Hine, as in Hine-nui-te-pō, the Maori goddess of death, and

Hinetitama, the Maori goddess of the dawn. Hine is the shortened form of *Wahine* (Woman), a powerful source of new life, and a life-giving source of *mana* or spiritual power. Hence *mana wahine* (the sacred power of woman) is, in Hawai'i and throughout Polynesia, a force that men must never ignore, for in a world where genealogical ranking meant everything, the first ancestor is the most powerful (Kame'eleihiwa, 1999).

Women pray to Hina as the *akua* of reef fishing. They pray to her for permission to pick medicinal herbs in the forest. It is Hina who beats *kapa* (bark cloth) in the moon, and to whom women pray as they engage in the art of cloth making. It is Hina who gave birth to and nurtured the Pig-God Kamapua'a, who teaches men how to plant *kalo* (taro), as well as the great hero Maui. Hina empowered Maui to slow the sun in its race through the heavens so that she could dry her *kapa* properly. She inspired Maui to fish up land from the bottom of the ocean for new generations to live upon, to push up the sky so that people might walk upright, and to obtain the secret of fire from her sisters, the '*alae* (mudhen) birds. It is Hina (Woman) who gives birth to new life; it is Hina who controls the moon, tides, and reefs; it is Hina who has the secret of fire (Kame'eleihiwa, 1999).

This, I believe, is the Hina that should be taught in our classrooms as indicative of the power of the first Hawaiian female ancestor and the high regard with which Hawaiian women were traditionally held. While some historians contend that it is difficult to discern the relationship between "mythic, genealogical material" and patterns of everyday Hawaiian life (Ralston, 1989, p. 49), following Kame'eleihiwa (1999), I contend that this most sacred of Hawaiian genealogies stands as a clear indication, and a constant reinforcement, of the ancient paradigm through which Hawaiians viewed the world, including the regard given to Hawaiian women.

Of the 40,000 Hawaiian *akua* in the Kumulipo, at least half or 20,000 are female. These Hawaiian female deities are presented as strong, powerful, and intelligent with the ability to both create and destroy. In *Nā Wāhine Kapu: Divine Hawaiian Women*, Kame'eleihiwa (1999) suggests that female *akua* have inspired Hawaiian women throughout history, from the female supreme rulers of various islands and chiefesses of Kamehameha's kingdom, to strong female leaders of today. She explains:

> As Hawaiian women we are the intellectual as well as the physical descendants of our female ancestors, and in turn we will be ancestral inspiration for the generations to come .... Even where Hawaiian women have converted to Christianity, a religion that teaches female submission to male dominance, the inspiration of

strong female ancestors lingers in our subconscious Hawaiian memory. (p. 1)

Imagine the potential of a classroom genealogy of Hawaiian women where the powerful Hina of the Kumulipo, rather the disempowered Hina of the non-Hawaiian authored children's book, sits at the pinnacle. As Kameʻeleihiwa attests:

> It is the female Akua that empower Hawaiian women. They are our ancestors; they are our inspiration; they live in us. They are all we know of what it means to be female; they define our femininity, our sexuality, and our great capabilities. *Ua hānau ka pō*: the night gives birth. It is woman who creates the universe. (p. 3)

Aliʻi Wāhine and the *ʻAikapu*

Following the progression of Hawaiian genealogies, I move the discussion from Hawaiian gods to Hawaiian *aliʻi*. The students' Hawaiian studies textbooks, along with the classroom lessons that I observed during my research, would have one believe that precontact Hawaiian *aliʻi* were exclusively and invariably men. Throughout the students' Hawaiian studies reports and classroom textbooks (Dunford, 1980), every mention of precontact Hawaiian chiefs is accompanied by the male pronoun "he," and every illustration of a chief is likewise male. A closer look into Hawaiian history suggests otherwise. While Western historians often emphasize the part of precontact Hawaiian history in which males played a primary role, a look into less acknowledged histories reveals that precontact Hawaiian women functioned as supreme rulers and heads of state.[2]

In *Nā Wāhine Kapu*, Kameʻeleihiwa (1999) outlines a succession of powerful female Hawaiian rulers who are rarely acknowledged in Western historical accounts. Kameʻeleihiwa explains that, as early as A.D. 1375, Oʻahu was ruled by a *mōʻīwahine* or supreme female ruler. Kūkaniloko, the first female ruler of Oʻahu, was famous for her long and peaceful reign as an *akua* who walked the earth and brought prosperity to her people. Her daughter Kalanimanuʻia (c. 1400) followed her as Mōʻīwahine of Oʻahu, and Kalanimanuʻia's daughter, in turn, ruled the northern half of Oʻahu and fought her elder brothers for control of the island. Not long after, with the birth of Kaikilani-aliʻi-nuiwahine-opuna (c. 1475), Mōʻīwahine began ruling on the island of Hawaiʻi as well. Female high chiefs effectively ruled the island of Hawaiʻi from approximately 1550 to 1720, and with the appointment of Kamakahelei as Mōʻīwahine of Kauaʻi and Niʻihau (c. 1740-1795), supreme female rulers spread as far as the northern island kingdom.

Concessions of the existence of female Hawaiian *ali'i* are evident in missionary journals, if one looks for them. The missionaries arrived in Hawai'i with certain preconceptions of what they would find. They expected to find Hawaiian women in a degraded state, with low status and little regard given to them. A closer look at their journals suggests that the missionaries were surprised and shocked to discover the amount of power and respect that many Hawaiian women, including those of chiefly rank, enjoyed. In 1823, the leader of the mission (Bingham, 1981) admitted that "The females of rank at the islands, and even those without rank, have by some means, secured to themselves a high degree of attention and respect from their husbands and others" (p. 184). Similarly, in William Ellis' commentary on the Hawaiian government, he acknowledged that heredity, rank, and authority in Hawaiian politics were not confined to the male sex, but were also inherited by the females. He conceded that "according to tradition, several of the islands have been once or twice under the government of a queen" (Ellis, 1969, p. 412). Over a decade later, another missionary (Lyons, 1836) lamented that "Paul's injunctions are not observed on the Sandwich Islands. Women often usurp authority over the men and hold the reins of government over large districts."

At the same time that these acknowledgments of powerful female rulers are made by the missionaries, they are diminished by a companion discourse of the oppressive *'aikapu* (eating tabus), which regulated the actions of the female *ali'i* and commoners alike. The *'aikapu* was a system of rules that specified that men do all the cooking, that men and women eat separately, and that certain foods be *kapu* (prohibited) to women (Chun, 2006). While nineteenth-century missionaries and current day Hawaiian studies lessons suggest that the ancient *kapu* related to eating is evidence of early Hawaiian women's degraded status and oppression, Hawaiian scholar Lilikalā Kameʻeleihiwa (1992, 1999) and other postcolonial scholars of Polynesian women suggest that the *'aikapu* and restrictions related to menstruation are evidence of the early Hawaiian women's power.

In early anthropological work (Best, 1924) the emphasis was on the Polynesian women's inherent "polluting" nature, which was said to repel the gods and necessitate the restriction of women's activities. However, the restrictions on Polynesian women's activities have been reinterpreted in terms of a careful controlling of women's potency. Hanson (1982) suggests that Polynesian women, because of their reproductive capabilities, especially at menstruation and parturition, were considered to be close to the gods and spiritual realm and thus were viewed as potent forces requiring seclusion. Ralston (1987) contends that this revised view reveals the "misinterpretations and undervaluing of female power and participation" in earlier accounts of Polynesian women (p. 120).

Similarly, Kameʻeleihiwa (1992) argues that the ʻaikapu afforded many advantages to Hawaiian women, and did not make them inferior to men. She explains that, because of the ʻaikapu, men had to do all the cooking, build two separate eating houses, and prepare two separate food ovens. When a human sacrifice was required for the male akua Kū, only men could be sacrificed. Furthermore, she argues that the foods forbidden to women (pig, coconut, banana, and certain red fish, which were considered phallic symbols and physical forms of the major male akua) did not present any physical hardship, as there was plentiful protein and carbohydrates in other forms. Kameʻeleihiwa (1992) concludes:

> As a Hawaiian woman, I can frankly say that I would not mind if I never ate with a man. I can think of many more interesting things to do with men than to eat with them. And, if it meant that men would do all the cooking and that only men would be offered in sacrifice, I would ... agree to this law. I do not find the ʻaikapu demeaning. Instead, it seems likely to me that under this religion, men in traditional Hawaiʻi worked harder than men do in modern western society. Perhaps ... eating without men and forgoing certain foods was well worth the exchange of men doing their share of the work! (p. 36)

Kameʻeleihiwa (1999) goes on to explain that, according to Hawaiian tradition, it was only when the female akua Papahānaumoku agreed to the ʻaikapu that the new religion could proceed, and it was only when Hawaiian women aliʻi decided that the ʻaikapu was no longer serving their people, that these women aliʻi saw to its end. Drawing from the epic tradition of Papa and Wakea, Kameʻeleihiwa says that when Wakea (sky father) came to propose to Papahānaumoku (earth mother) the new ʻaikapu religion requested by the priest, Papahānaumoku questioned him about the details to make sure she had heard it right:

> We can imagine that she might have said, "You mean to tell me that if women give up eating these four foods (coconut, banana, pig and red fish), now and forevermore, men will do all of the cooking? Wakea answered, "Yes, that's right." She asked again, "And if women give up eating these four foods, only men will be sacrificed?" Again Wakea answered, "Yes." Then Papahānaumoku responded with the equivalent of "I'll take it!" (Kameʻeleihiwa, 1999, pp. 8-9)

Female sanction was necessary for the start of the ʻaikapu religion; likewise, the loss of female sanction brought about its end. As Kameʻeleihiwa (1999) explains, upon Kamehameha's death, it was his *wāhine*, Keōpūolani and Kaʻahumanu (the high chiefesses), who decided that they, and the entire *lāhui* (nation), would no longer follow the eating restrictions of their ancestors. Kameʻeleihiwa argues that this extraordinary action must be viewed in light of the inability of the old gods to stay the massive onslaught of foreign disease brought to Hawaiʻi with Western contact. Just as their divine female ancestor, Papahānaumoku, had first sanctioned the Sacred Eating religion, it was the responsibility of Keōpūolani and Kaʻahumanu to abolish the practice once it no longer seemed to serve their people's best interests.

Our classroom curricula and textbooks suggest that the coming of the Europeans helped to "liberate" the oppressed Hawaiian women by bringing about the abolition of the *ʻaikapu* restrictions on commensal eating between men and women. However, consistent with the writings of Gananath Obeyesekere (1992), this countergenealogy suggests that the European liberation of Hawaiian women is nothing more than a colonial myth. A look into less-cited aspects of Hawaiian history reveals that Hawaiian women were in many respects "much more liberated than their European counterparts" (p. 156). Ancient Hawaiian genealogies and cosmologies provided the traditional and spiritual basis for Hawaiian women to wield a substantial degree of power in both political and social realms, and early Hawaiian modes of government accorded *aliʻi nui* (high chiefs) places in government based on their genealogy and talent, regardless of whether they were male or female. It was through the imposition of Euro-American constitutions, laws, and churches that Hawaiian women were disempowered as their public voices and previous paths to power became limited, and their relegation to the private sphere, as in Europe and the United States, became hegemonic (Silva, 2004).

Commoner Misconceptions

In keeping with the progression of Hawaiian genealogies, I turn the discussion from the Hawaiian *aliʻi* to the commoners or *makaʻāinana*. The classroom Hawaiian studies lessons give us an image of commoner Hawaiian women who were mistreated and overworked by their people, endlessly beating *kapa* "all day, every day—never stopping when [they] were tired, but working, working, working from morning until night." These classroom teachings are consistent with the preconceptions that the missionaries had brought with them regarding the position of commoner women in traditional Hawaiian society. Based upon their limited knowledge of the prohibitions and constraints imposed on women's lives under the *kapu* system, the missionaries expected Hawaiian commoner women to be "servile, degraded and over-worked" and that an important part of their mission would be to liberate them and improve their lot to a "state of dignity" (Ralston, 1989, p. 60). A closer look at the missionary journals suggests that what they found upon their arrival in Hawai'i was quite contrary to their expectations.

Focusing on missionary journals and correspondence, missionary-controlled newspapers, and other mission documents, I demonstrate how the dominant colonial narratives concerning the project of "saving Hawaiian women" are replete with ambivalent and competing discourses that open up alternative readings. I also demonstrate how the voices of commoner Hawaiian women can be heard in these missionary journals, particularly in the accounts of missionary wives who were most closely involved in day-to-day interactions with Hawaiian women. I argue that a close reading of the missionary journals reveals a counternarrative of strong Hawaiian women who were not unduly oppressed by the traditional gendered division of labor, but instead enjoyed a good deal of freedom, and who good-naturedly resisted the U.S. missionaries' attempts to domesticate and "rescue" them.

While the missionaries expected to find the lives of the Hawaiian commoner women to be overburdened with work (Ralston, 1989), when they arrived in Hawai'i, the missionaries soon found that Hawaiian women were if anything disadvantaged by the usual division of labor that persisted prior to the mission period. In the foreword to William Ellis' *Polynesian Researches: Hawai'i*, Edouard R. L. Doty (1969) concludes that "at a time when European women were little more than chattels and slaves, women of Polynesia stood substantially on a social par with their men" (p. xii). As Kame'eleihiwa (1992, 1999) suggests, Hawaiian women's share in the productive labor was not onerous. Men undertook the bulk of heavy labor in building, fishing, and agriculture, and also cooked the meals. Women made mats and *kapa* (tapa cloth), collected shellfish, and were involved in the care of young children, a task that was shared with kin (Grimshaw, 1989). While the process of making *kapa* was a time-consuming task, it was a cooperative effort; no one person worked on the entire process alone (Jensen & Jensen, 2005). The men grew the *wauke* (paper mulberry) and delivered it to the women. The men also made the wooden mallets and bamboo stamps. The women, in turn, beat the bast into cloth, and used the tools and dyes made by the men to dye and print the *kapa*. The land and sea provided plentiful nutritious food, and the commoners were not driven to work to pursue personal wealth or accumulation. Thus they enjoyed a substantial amount of free time, which they spent in swimming, surfing, hula, storytelling, traditional sports, and other games of skill or chance (Grimshaw, 1989).

While the missionaries' preconceptions about the position of women in Hawaiian society proved illusory, nothing in the Hawaiians' situation appeared acceptable to the missionary wives who saw the reformation of Hawaiian women as their lifelong cause (Grimshaw, 1989). The missionaries found the influence and respect that Hawaiian women held in their families and communities to be unfitting and their "idleness" shocking. Thus the discourse of commoner Hawaiian women as beasts of burden and down-trodden slaves paradoxically sits alongside conflicting, but equally denigrating, accounts of idle Hawaiian women whom the missionaries portrayed as lazy, promiscuous, and lamentably unconcerned with promoting domestic comfort and harmony (Ellis, 1825/1979; Judd, 1928; Loomis, 1828).

The need for change in the lives of Hawaiian women was essential if they were to fit the model of Christian womanhood in which the missionaries so ardently believed. The missionaries had unshakeable views on the proper position of women in Christian society, on the appropriate sexual division of labor, and on female sexuality. The married Christian woman should be a docile, faithful wife and devoted mother, restricting her activities and influence to the circumscribed sphere of the nuclear household (Ralston, 1989). Thus the lives of commoner Hawaiian women became the focus of mission concern and active interference as the self-appointed evangelists set out to reform the chaotic Hawaiian family and singled out the Hawaiian wife and mother as the agent for "regeneration" (Grimshaw, 1989).

The regeneration of Hawaiian women was carried out through missionary documents, missionary-controlled newspapers, and the day-to-day work of missionary women. For instance, *A Word Related to Marriage*, a pamphlet prepared for mission purposes, outlined succinctly the roles and life patterns missionaries wanted Hawaiians to assume, with Hawaiian women leading a domestic-oriented existence based on a gendered division of labor in the United States mode:

> It is the husband's role to work out-doors—he farms and builds the home and prepares that which concerns the welfare of the body. The role of the wife is to maintain the husband's clothing and the food—the household chores—setting in place the sleeping quarters and all else that is within. (Clark, 1844, p. 5)

The wife was advised against deficiency in this area:

> It is wrong to neglect work and to leave the husband to keep the household. It is

right to remain within the house and to work without daydreaming, providing food, clothing and all that is essential for life together. (p. 5)

Government-sponsored, missionary-controlled newspapers, whose main purpose was to communicate laws and government policies, were used to proselytize, civilize, and admonish Hawaiian women to conform to Euro-American gender behavior. For instance, an article in an 1856 issue of *Ka Hae Hawaii* begins with a list of faults of Hawaiian women and provides a contrasting picture of "proper" womanly behavior:

> Hawaiian women have many failings ... [When] I look at the woman, her body is dirty, her hair is not well-kept, and the dress, not clean. It is the same with the house, it is dirty, and everything in the house is mixed up ... The woman's work is to care for the house until it is clean. This is perhaps the greatest fault, it is women just sitting; not working with the hands, just lying on the mat ... Women in civilized countries, who are well-taught, are not like that ... The body and the house of the civilized woman is clean, and her husband likes her a lot. The mind of the husband is not on other women because he has a good woman. (Cited and translated in Silva, 2004)

On a day-to-day basis, the task of reforming the Hawaiian women was the primary project of the mission wives. While the men of the mission undertook the dominant roles as preachers and teachers of men, the women were delegated a special obligation to female adults, thus providing "a more perfect system of mutual watchfulness over the different members and a more feasible mode of discipline" (Bingham, 1981, p. 365). The missionary wives led Hawaiian women in sex-segregated prayer meetings and Bible-reading groups. They instructed Hawaiian women in housekeeping, cooking (traditionally the males' responsibility), flower gardening, and other genteel occupations (Grimshaw, 1989). Believing that Hawaiian women did not have enough work to do, the missionaries taught Hawaiian women to sew and knit since this provided the clothing sorely needed by the whole population, and the clothes would generate further domestic occupation in mending, laundering, ironing, and sorting (Ralston, 1989).

So what did Hawaiian women think about all this? I suggest that if one listens closely, one can hear them speaking through the missionary journals and letters. Secondhand accounts of Hawaiian women's words and actions suggest that they were bemused by the puritanical drive of hardworking missionary women, resistant to relinquish the relative freedom of their current lifestyle, and not entirely convinced that they were the more oppressed. A young American, who was staying in Hawai'i for his health in the 1830s, described his missionary aunt's activities, and the Hawaiian women's response, in an ironical yet sympathetic fashion:

> My aunt could work, scold, preach, wash, bake, pray, catechize, make dresses, plant, pluck, drive stray pigs out the garden. There was nothing useful in this wilderness which she could not do. She exercised an influence from her energy and practical virtue which bordered on absolute authority. As I walked with her through the village, her presence operated as a civilizing tonic. True, the effect in many cases was transient. But the natives knew what she expected. As she appeared, tobacco pipes disappeared, idle games or gambling were slyly put by, Bible and hymn books brought conspicuously forward and the young girls hastily donned their chastest dresses and looks. (Restarick, 1924, pp. 50-51)

This characterization nicely captures both the single-minded effort of missionary women and the apparent conformity, but essentially evasive response, of Hawaiian women.

The reality of Hawaiian domestic life was far from the ideal projected by the Americans. The simply constructed Hawaiian houses with their sparse furnishings, together with the plainness of diet and dress, militated against the mission plan. The missionaries tried to persuade the Hawaiians to "live like human beings" in fenced-in Western-style, mud-walled cottages with separate sleeping places for children, home-built furniture, tables, chairs, and separate dishes and eating utensils. While the chiefs and a few of the better-off church families built Western-style houses, for the most part the Americans considered the Hawaiian's homes and diet unconducive to the performance of a day's domestic work by Hawaiian women. When the mission women went house-to-house visiting, it was usually only the sick, the lame, the blind, the maimed, or the old that they found at home—not a busy and welcoming Hawaiian housewife (Grimshaw, 1989). When Abigail Smith arrived at Kaluaaha in 1833, she was said to be driven to distraction by Hawaiian women who regularly came to observe her perform domestic chores. When the missionary wife begged the women to go home to their household duties and care for their children so she could get on with her tasks undisturbed, they asserted cheerfully that they had no duties, and continued unabashed to occupy her yard and doorway. On several occasions when Hawaiian women saw Americans ironing, they were said to have expressed with heartfelt sympathy, "I pity you" (Frear, 1934, p. 71).

While the classroom Hawaiian studies lessons cited earlier would have us believe that women in traditional Hawaiian society were mistreated and overworked until their liberation by U.S. missionaries, this countergenealogy suggests quite the contrary. I do not mean to imply that Hawaiians lived in a kind of Eden where they did not have to work, women included. Instead, I am arguing that the small, but telling, secondhand comments in missionary journals suggest that Hawaiian women had a keen understanding that living in a Western-style house requires endless housework and, when coupled with patriarchy, turns women into domestic servants in their own homes. Hawaiian women covertly and overtly resisted U.S. domestication, as they good-naturedly told mission wives: "We hear your advice but we forget it quickly" (Forbes, 1836).

Conclusion

In precontact Hawai'i, where genealogy determined the quality of a proposed sovereign, Hawaiian *ali'i* went to war with their genealogies and used counter-genealogies to displace, combat, or reconstruct dominant narratives and assert a counterreality. It is with similar intentions that I provide a countergenealogy of Nā Wāhine Mana, or powerful Hawaiian women.

Colonialism has often justified its "civilizing mission" by claiming that it was rescuing native women from oppressive patriarchal domination. This occurred in Hawai'i where the enduring colonial myth of "white men saving brown women from brown men" was used to legitimize past colonial oppressions of indigenous Hawaiian people, and continues to influence the way in which teachers, children, and the larger society think and talk about Native Hawaiians today. Through a deconstructive interrogation of elementary Hawaiian studies curricula and classroom conversations, I attempt to usurp the dominant curricular narrative of oppressed Hawaiian women who were liberated through colonization. I foreground a countergenealogy of powerful Hawaiian women who descended from a traditional Hawaiian culture with formidable female goddesses, influential female *ali'i*, and spirited commoner women, who held relatively liberated positions in their families and communities, and stubbornly resisted the restrictive impositions of Christianity and U.S. domestication.

Admittedly, issues of patriarchy and gender oppression are complex, and are difficult topics to discuss even as they apply to the current day. I, therefore, acknowledge the difficulty that classroom teachers might face in talking with contemporary boys and girls, both Hawaiian and non-Hawaiian, about sex roles and gender equality in precontact and colonial times. At the same time, I issue a plea to classroom teachers and curriculum writers for greater curricular consideration of the construction and employment of gender in the practices of imperialism and colonialism, and a more critical analysis of the colonialist deployment of feminist criteria to bolster the appeal of the "civilizing mission."

It is not just Hawaiian children who could benefit from a more critical perspective on Hawaiʻi's colonial history. The untruths and half-truths of our colonial history have harmed the descendants of the colonizer along with the colonized, albeit in different ways. As James Baldwin (1988) writes, "If I am not what I've been told I am, then it means that *you're* not what you thought you were *either*" (p. 8). He suggests that if the curriculum in schools were to be changed to include the historical perspectives of the colonized, "you would be liberating not only [the colonized], you'd be liberating white people who know nothing about their own history" (ibid.). If, in addition to studying the genealogy of powerful Hawaiian women outlined earlier, Hawaiʻi's school children were to consider the genealogy of the missionaries and other colonizers in Hawaiʻi, they would find that the missionary wives who sought to liberate Hawaiian commoner women came from a highly gender-unequal, gender-segregated society, with a Christian religion that was patriarchal.

On a larger scale, I propose that, in the teaching and writing of indigenous history and curricula across the globe, we need more countergenealogists to seek out and uncover indigenous voices and perspectives, and call into question the dominant colonial narratives that are prevalent in school history textbooks. One Hawaiian example that comes readily to mind is the work of contemporary Hawaiian scholar Noenoe Silva (2004), whose extensive study of anticolonial resistance in Hawaiian language newspapers uncovered an 1897 anti-annexation petition signed by 21,269 Hawaiians, which had been buried in the U.S. National Archives. This finding exploded the persistent and pernicious myth that Native Hawaiians passively accepted annexation by the United States and affirmed for Hawaiian school children of today that their ancestors had not stood idly and apathetically while their nation was taken from them, but instead had organized mass petition drives to demonstrate to the U.S. president and members of Congress that the great majority of Native Hawaiians were vehemently opposed to annexation. This countergenealogy has given Hawaiians, young and old, "permission" and inspiration from their ancestors to participate in our people's contemporary quest for national sovereignty.

According to Hawaiian tradition, in early Hawaiʻi there were genealogical experts who kept the histories and genealogies of chiefs and commoners alike. However, after ʻUmi's rebellion over his evil half-brother, Hākau, commoners were denied access to their genealogies (Kamakau, 1961). I propose that it is time that educators and researchers revive the role of the commoner countergenealogist and begin to reread indigenous historiography "against the grain" so that we might one day overthrow the "tyranny of globalizing discourses" (Foucault, 1980, p. 83) that currently reign in elementary and secondary school history classrooms.

Notes

1. Throughout the chapter I use the terms Hawaiian and Native Hawaiian to refer to the indigenous people of Hawai'i, the descendants of the aboriginal people who inhabited and exercised sovereignty in the Hawaiian islands for over 1,500 years prior to the 1778 arrival of Hawai'i's first European explorers.

2. It is interesting to note that while precontact women *ali'i* are ignored in elementary Hawaiian studies textbooks and trade books, postcontact women *ali'i*, such as Queen Lili'uokalani and Princess Pauahi, are honored. Perhaps, as my colleague Joseph Tobin suggests, this is because Queen Lili'uokalani and Princess Pauahi dressed in Western-style clothing and could be seen as products of Western contact and Christian influence.

References

Baldwin, J. (1963/1988). A talk to teachers. In R. Simonson & S. Walker (Eds.), *The graywolf annual five: Multi-cultural literacy* (pp. 3–12). Saint Paul, MN: Graywolf.

Best, E. (1924). *The Maori* (Vols. 1–2). Wellington, New Zealand: Polynesian Society.

Bingham, H. (1981). *A residence of twenty-one years in the Sandwich Islands*. Rutland, VT: Charles E. Tuttle Company.

Chun, M. (2006). *Kapu: Gender roles in traditional society*. Honolulu: University of Hawai'i Curriculum Research and Development Group.

Clark, E. (1844). *A word relating to marriage* (C. Silva, Trans.). Honolulu, HI: Mission.

Doty, E. (1969). Foreword. In W. Ellis (Ed.), *Polynesian researches: Hawaii* (pp. vi–xiv). Rutland, VT: Charles E. Tuttle.

Dunford, B. (1980). *The Hawaiians of old*. Honolulu, HI: Bess.

Ellis, W. (1969). *Polynesian researches: Hawaii*. Rutland, VT: Charles E. Tuttle.

Ellis, W. (1825/1979). *Journal of William Ellis, narrative of a tour of Hawaii*. Rutland, VT: Charles E. Tuttle.

Forbes, C. (1836, July 23). *Letter to American Board of Commissioners for Foreign Missions Archive*. Boston, MA: American Board of Commissioners for Foreign Missions.

Foucault, M. (1977). Nietzsche, genealogy, history. In D. F. Bouchard (Ed.), *Language, counter-memory, practice: Selected essays and interviews* (pp. 139–164). Ithaca, NY: Cornell University Press.

Foucault, M. (1980). *Power/knowledge: Selected interviews and other writings, 1972–1977*. New York: Pantheon.

Frear, M. (1934). *Lowell and Abigail: A realistic idyll*. New Haven, CT: Privately published.

Grimshaw, P. (1989). New England missionary wives, Hawaiian women and "the cult of true womanhood." In M. Jolly & M. Macintyre (Eds.), *Family and gender in the Pacific: Domestic contradictions and the colonial impact* (pp. 19-44). Cambridge: Cambridge University Press.

Hanson, F. (1982). Female pollution in Polynesia? *Journal of the Polynesian Society, 91*, 335-381.

Hawai'i Department of Education. (1984). *Hawaiian studies curriculum guide: Grade 5.* Honolulu, HI: Office of Instructional Services.

Jensen, L., & Jensen, N. (2005). *Nā kaikamahine ō Haumea (Daughters of Haumea): Women of ancient Hawai'i.* San Francisco, CA: Pueo.

Judd, L. (1928). *Honolulu: Sketches of the life social, political and religious in the Hawaiian Islands from 1828 to 1861.* Honolulu, HI: Honolulu Star Bulletin.

Kamakau, S. (1961). *Ruling chiefs of Hawaii.* Honolulu, HI: Kamehameha Schools.

Kame'eleihiwa, L. (1992). *Native lands and foreign desires.* Honolulu, HI: Bishop Museum.

Kame'eleihiwa, L. (1999). *Nā wāhine kapu: Divine Hawaiian women.* Honolulu, HI: 'Ai Pōhaku.

Kana'iaupuni, S., Malone, N., & Ishibashi, K. (2005). *Ka huaka'i: 2005 Native Hawaiian educational assessment.* Honolulu, HI: Kamehameha Schools Pauahi.

Kaomea, J. (2005). Indigenous studies in the elementary curriculum: A cautionary Hawaiian example. *Anthropology and Education Quarterly, 36*(1), 24-42.

King, J., & Douglas, J. (1784). *A voyage to the Pacific Ocean* (Vol. 3). London: Order of the Lords Commissioners of the Admiralty.

Loomis, M. (1828). *Journal of Maria S. Loomis 1819-1828.* Honolulu, HI: Hawaiian Mission Children's Society Library.

Lyons, L. (1836). *Hamakua station report 1836.* Honolulu, HI: Hawaiian Mission Children's Society Library.

Malo, D. (1951). *Hawaiian antiquities* (N. B. Emerson, Trans.). Honolulu, HI: Bishop Museum.

Obeyesekere, G. (1992). *The apotheosis of Captain Cook: European mythmaking in the Pacific.* Princeton, NJ: Princeton University Press.

Pescaia, M. (1981). *Early Hawaiian life: Instructional materials/resources for social studies (elementary).* Honolulu, HI: Department of Education.

Ralston, C. (1987). Introduction. *Journal of Pacific History, 22*(3), 115-122.

Ralston, C. (1989). Changes in the lives of ordinary women in early post-contact Hawai'i. In M. Jolly & M. Macintyre (Eds.), *Family and gender in the Pacific: Domestic contradictions and the colonial impact* (pp. 45-64). Cambridge: Cambridge University Press.

Rattigan, J. (1996). *The woman in the moon: A story from Hawai'i.* Boston, MA: Little, Brown.

Restarick, H. (1924). *Hawaii 1778-1920: From the viewpoint of a bishop.* Honolulu: HI: Paradise of the Pacific.

Silva, N. (2004). *Aloha betrayed: Native Hawaiian resistance to American colonialism.* Durham, NC: Duke University Press.

Spivak, G. (1985/1988). Can the subaltern speak? In C. Nelson & L. Grossberg (Eds.), *Marxism and the interpretation of culture* (pp. 271-313). Urbana: University of Illinois Press.

CHAPTER 7

Postcolonial Technologies of Power: Standardized Testing and Representing Diverse Young Children

RADHIKA VIRURU

The phrase "after 9/11, the world changed" has been reiterated, with different meanings and in different contexts, by various groups of people. Recognizing the fact that the people for whom the world has changed the most have probably neither access nor time to engage in dialogue about change, scholars are calling for a renewed commitment to work beyond the "Ivory Tower" and to take on the role of public intellectuals (Barsky & Ali, 2006). In postcolonial studies, there is a renewed focus on the technologies through which imperialist projects are carried out "abroad" or "at home," although the two are not so neatly divisible.

The unquestioned technology explored in this chapter is standardized testing in the United States. It invokes tremendous interest since it is upheld by both the right and the left as an "objective" assessment of how schools and students are performing (Kohn, 2000). However, a growing body of research views testing as the ultimate imposition of rampant scientism and corporate capitalism upon children and schools. The impetus for testing reflects a major corporate strategy used worldwide by big business (Park & Schwarz, 2005): to create a need and then try to fulfill it. In educational contexts, Kohn (1999) shows how many reports on public education are authored not by education professionals, but by business representatives, such as the Business Coalition for Education Reform, the Business Roundtable, the National Alliance of Business, and the Committee for Education Reform. Miyoshi (1993) contends that, whereas the "old" colonialism used nations, ethnicities, and races as its building blocks, the "new colonialism" works through transnational corporations. The new colonialism is harder to isolate and counter as it operates through multiple locations and through global networks. Martin (2004) comments that, in its search for new grounds, modern capitalist colonialism increasingly concentrates on the sphere of domestic life as an avenue for profit making: citizens are redefined as consumers and the home is transformed into a "command post for market manipulation" (p. 352). Similarly schools are targeted for such attention, especially through the imposition of standardized testing (Cannella & Viruru, 2004).

Critiques of standardized testing have focused on its effects, including the limited and narrow curricula that it has created in schools and how it has been tied to high stakes. Jobs, salaries, and in some cases the very existence of schools are tied to test score results. The effects on schools have been documented, such as the widespread teaching to the test and the elimination of recess and playtime (Kohn, 2000; Ohanian, 2002). The chapter aims to strengthen critique of standardized tests by exploring another part of testing that has not received much attention: What kind of material is actually on the tests? With focus on the skills covered by the tests and ensuring that students know them, little attention has been directed toward the medium through which skills are assessed.

In this chapter, first, I will elaborate on how standardized testing has been created as an imperialist project. Second, I will take an in-depth look at the technologies of power in the reading potions of standardized tests and how they contain colonialist images of people of color. With mandatory testing a reality in every state in the United States, test content should be scrutinized. My analysis suggests that standardized testing for young students is colonizing for three reasons: (1) how testing has been constructed represents corporate-driven rather than child-centered agendas; (2) the ideology of diversity represented in U.S. public policies, particularly standardized testing, is gravely limited; and (3) by mandating that children take tests but not regulating their content, racist and colonialist ideas are presented in legitimate forms. The logic of standardized tests seems to be that the content of reading passages is irrelevant since the tests are not about content, but more about testing comprehension. This kind of imperialist logic makes tests so dangerous.

Philosophical Perspectives

Standardized testing in its current avatar is perhaps more of an "American" preoccupation than a global concern.[1] I examine the construction of standardized testing as both cultural and imperialistic products. Recent postcolonial work focuses on the need to direct an anti-imperialist gaze upon U.S. policies around the world and within the United States. U.S. domestic policies are important to analyze because of their potential to impact the rest of the world and because they appear to be cloaked in a myth of what Park and Schwarz (2005) call "American exceptionalism ... that fetishizes the ideals of freedom and democracy and claims them as their own national property" (p. 153). The discourses that surround the constitution of public policies need to be deconstructed for their participation in the new imperialism: the kind of colonialism that has less to do with the conquest of lands and properties and more to do with constructing human beings with limited life trajectories and paths. Ducille (1996) argues that the rhetoric of U.S. imperialism is grounded on internal violence against racialized minority populations. Feldman (2004) notes that the United States is at war with more than terror; it also is engaged in "deterritorialized wars of public safety" (p. 330): wars that focus on achieving certain kinds of internal hegemony through the symbiosis of fear and other directed aggression.

An examination of standardized testing as an imperialist product cannot take place without recognizing the contexts within which it is constituted. U.S. troops are stationed in 19 countries around the world (Johnson, 2004). People in the United States constitute 6 percent of the world's population, but consume 25 percent of the world's resources. U.S. domestic policies have directed resources away from the most vulnerable communities as part of a larger plan for greater economic and territorial domination. The U.S. government also has defined its enemies in terms that enable the use of unconventional tactics and its self-appointment as defender of morality and ethics. For example, the United States considers itself as engaged in a war on "terror" (as opposed to terrorism), using the term "terror" to define specific populations who can be engaged and controlled in particular ways. Furthermore, U.S. imperialism is often justified as acceptable since it has, in its own eyes, achieved ideal domestic order (Kaplan & Pease, 1993). When trying to put world affairs in order, the contrast is made between the ideal form of the U.S. self and the untidy spaces where the United States is forced to intervene *noblesse oblige*. According to Trombold (2005), what the United States tries to impose upon the world is its own version of imperialist multiculturalism. It is within the framework of imperialist multiculturalism that we need to examine standardized testing.

Standardized testing foregrounds issues of "multiculturalism." The tests are defended as putting in place standards for all students, no matter what their background is, to allegedly ensure that everyone receives an equal education. The tests, however, end up defining students of color as the population with the highest risk of not meeting standards, thus reinforcing the labeling, tracking, and limited opportunities they are already subjected to. Donaldson (1992) shows how the U.S. "justice" system, which claims to be an instrument that assures freedom, is complicit in the marginalization and impoverishment of Native Americans. He suggests that much of the global power that the United States enjoys is based on the lands and resources usurped from Native Americans. As Park and Schwarz (2005) put it, "the discourse of nation is indeed complicit in the construction of the imperial imaginary in the way the nation does not include race per se, but rather racializes those included, unequally, in its constitution" (p. 157). Public figures, like Bork (1996), laud the Eurocentric U.S. culture as the best the world has to offer since the West was the originator of democracy and capitalism. Such rationalities are used to spread order around the world. For the U.S. civilizing mission to prosper, domestic cultural discourses have to be kept under control. I believe that the content of standardized tests is one of those discourses. The content analysis in the chapter indicates that standardized tests reflect limited forms of cultural knowledge and often present people of color in inadequate ways. If the United States aims to mold the world in its image, the content of standardized tests offers a close-up look of the image.

It could be argued that standardized tests, although mandated by the federal government, are actually written by testing companies. Although such an argument could absolve the government's responsibility, it does not stand up well to postcolonial contention regarding new forms of imperialism: "'privatization,' rather than limiting state power as is so often assumed, actually extends the web of state power when the state seeks to achieve its purposes by using 'private' actors" (Passavant, 2004, p. 381). In the post-9/11 world, the emphasis on smaller government does not always translate into less control over people's lives. Rather, states seek out other ways to achieve power (Osborne & Gaebler, 1992). This is undertaken, for instance, in the use of contract workers. The Department of Education reduced its workforce by 6 percent between 1984 and 1996, while increasing their contract labor force by 129 percent (Crenson & Ginsberg, 2002). The link between government and business was made obvious when, immediately after 9/11, President Bush encouraged people to spend money as a patriotic act. Standardized testing is an example of the conflation of interests between business and government.

Within contexts where government and business work closely together toward the same goals, Passavant (2004) interrogates how private spaces handle the issue of dissent. For example, suburban shopping malls have become the "public" space where people gather. But this space is not really public since it is privately owned and the right to freedom of speech is controlled. Currently "there is no First Amendment right to free speech in malls; claiming a right to free speech depends upon the laws of the state" (p. 394). I argue that standardized tests occupy a similar position in schools: they are public in the sense that all children have to take them, yet private in the sense that they are written by corporations, upon whom the public has no control. The right to free speech is also curtailed: students do not have the right to question what is on the test or to refuse to take it. The air of secrecy that governs the tests is legendary: few people are allowed to see them and very few states make them available for public scrutiny (Ohanian, 2002). Unfortunately, although the public seems to be aware of the problems with standardized tests, there has been little opposition to them. Dean (2004) describes this attitude as a "fetishistic disavowal," reflecting a standpoint of "I know but nevertheless I believe" (Žižek, 1991).

Critiques of Standardized Testing

Even though testing students as the only way to measure how students and schools are performing has received bipartisan political support, there are other sectors dissatisfied and challenging what is taking place in schools. As the most sweeping reform in recent U.S. educational history, the No Child Left Behind (NCLB) Act imposes standardized tests upon every student in public schools, starting in the third grade. Testing is spreading to earlier grade levels, with efforts to mandate testing as part of Head Start (Cannella & Viruru, 2004).

The official NCLB discourse on standardized testing projects great achievement and high expectations to end the "soft racism" of low expectations (Lee, 2006). President George W. Bush's foreword to the Act reads: "The quality of our public schools directly affects us all as parents, as students, and as citizens. Yet too many students are segregated by low expectations, illiteracy, and self-doubt. In a constantly changing world that is demanding increasingly complex skills from its workforce, children are literally being left behind" (http://www.whitehouse.gov/news/reports/no-child-left-behind.html). NCLB calls for increased accountability for student performance: "States, districts and schools that improve achievement will be rewarded. Failure will be sanctioned. Parents will know how well their child is learning, and that schools are held accountable for their effectiveness with annual state reading and math assessments in grades 3–8" (ibid.). Schools are deemed deficient if they are not preparing children with the requisite "complex skills" that big businesses demand.

Corporate agendas do not end there; they constitute a more complex web of power and control. In Chicago, for example, student expulsion rates in elementary and secondary schools have risen during the period of higher standards. Expelled children are directed to especially designed private programs, thus making expulsion a profit-generating enterprise (Meier, 2000). NCLB contributed to the demise of innovative programs, like one in Lynfield, Massachusetts, which ensured minority children to attend schools in affluent, mostly White communities. From the government's perspective, such programs did not help the school "raise its standards" (p. 4). These examples point out that the dominant focus on testing diverts attention away from how schools are denying equitable education to poor and minority children. Ayers (2000) notes the paradox in which the standards and tests that are supposed to promote equal opportunity for all students, in fact, have become avenues for the maintenance of inequity.

Kornhaber and Orfield (2001) point out three major assumptions that influence public policy on testing: (1) testing enhances economic productivity; (2) testing motivates students; and (3) testing improves teaching and learning. They present various data that dispel all three. One, the U.S. economy has performed better than European economies, even though the test scores of U.S. students have been lower. If we were to concede that test scores are predictors of future behavior, the connection between cognitive skills and economic productivity is not particularly evident (Levin, 2001). Test scores are not significant predictors of the qualities considered essential to job success, such as initiative, creativity, and reliability. Ferguson (2005) also comments on how discourses on economic productivity have changed over the years. At the end of the Second World War, modernization theories began to forward the notion that the more Western ideas, like industrial economy and technological reliance, spread across the world, the more likely the poor would overcome poverty and reap the benefits of modernity. Unfortunately modernity's "globalization" has not worked that way. For many, modernization has not brought benefits; instead it has brought the hollow knowledge that desired goods exist and are available, but not to them, sometimes resulting in violent efforts to seize what is desired (Mbembe, 2002). Those who enjoy privileges often police their privileges, using borders, walls, and other technologies of social exclusion. This resonates with critics of standardized testing who see it as a technology of social exclusion (Cannella & Viruru, 2004; Pena, 2006).

The second assumption in the widespread use of testing is that it motivates students to do better. According to Madaus and Clarke (2001), motivation is such a complex phenomena that making generalizations about it is an extremely risky process. Fordham and Ogbu (1986) underscore that cultural factors play a significant role in the area of motivation. Kornhaber and Orfield (2001) state that "common wisdom, as well as behavioral psychology, holds that normal thinking beings strive to gain rewards and avoid painful consequences" (p. 7).

The final assumption, that tests improve teaching and learning, is deemed fallacious since neither teaching nor learning operates in rational and constructive ways (Kornhaber & Orfield, 2001, p. 9). The research of McNeil and Valenzuela (2001) on standardized testing in Texas reveals that, especially for poor and minority students, the school curriculum has become more limited. Teachers, regardless of subject matter expertise, are expected to drill students on math, reading, and writing. Educational expenditures are significantly impacted as scarce instructional dollars are diverted from enhancing the curriculum to purchasing test preparation materials. A Harvard Civil Rights Project report on NCLB highlights similar findings: four years after the law was enacted, the students' achievement levels remained static or slightly deteriorated. In other words, the racial gap in educational achievement has not closed. Although the U.S. federal government allocates $412 million annually to testing, many states still have to generate additional funding to meet the testing requirements imposed on them (Lee, 2006). The report also indicates that, in low-performing schools, instruction has declined in nontested subject areas, and attracting and retaining highly qualified teachers has been very difficult. With the increased emphasis on testing, curriculum tends to suffer as "there often is a tendency to move into highly formulaic and rigidly programmed curriculum, boring to both students and teachers, and, worse yet, to spend time not on teaching their subjects but on drilling on testtaking strategies" (p. 7).

Examining Standardized Tests for Cultural Images

In light of these concerns, I undertook a detailed content analysis of the reading passages in the standardized tests of 11 states between the years 2001 and 2004.[2] Since standardized tests, as I argue, reflect imperialist agendas of controlling life paths and limiting human possibility, it is important to examine the actual tests in detail, with a particular focus on cultural images. Conventional wisdom might suggest that students, especially those in the third and fourth grades, are too young to pay attention to meta-messages. To them, it is argued, a reading passage is simply a reading passage, and they do not pay attention to its content or images. Research studies in early childhood education have contradicted this misconception (Cannella, 1997). My study also finds that imperialist ideologies have created colonizing structures such as standardized testing to regulate children's lives and their impact is enhanced through racially and culturally biased materials in the tests. The fact that students are presented with racist and colonialist messages should be a matter of grave concern to educators, parents, and policy makers.

Method

I conducted a qualitative content analysis on 94 reading passages taken from the third and fourth grade standardized tests of 11 states in the United States. Table 1 shows which state tests were included, for which grade levels, and for which years. I utilized what Hodder (2000) calls "mute evidence" or written texts and artifacts. Although mute evidence lacks the possibility of interaction with its creator and the insight of emic perspectives, it possesses the advantage of being more easily available and of being more "detached" from the contexts in which it was created. Furthermore the very muteness of the evidence can cause the interpreter to engage in "self-reappraisal" and does away with the need for member check.

Lincoln and Guba (1985) make distinctions between documents and records: documents are created for personal rather than official reasons with the opposite holding true for records. Documents may require more contextualized interpretations, given the nature of the situations under which they are created, whereas records "may have local uses that become very distant from officially sanctioned meanings" (Hodder, 2000, p. 156). The data analyzed in my study are considered records since they are created for a formal purpose. A disadvantage in using records is that access to them can be restricted by laws regarding privacy and confidentiality. This was a major issue that impacted the study since many states do not release publicly their standardized tests (Ohanian, 2002). States such as Texas, Georgia, and Virginia release all or most of the tests that students have taken in previous years and post them on their Web sites. Other states release only what they call "sample released test items," a few items that have appeared on previous state standardized tests. Thus the data for the study was collected through exhaustive searching of state department of education Web sites for full and partial releases of test items. A major factor that limited the data was the willingness of states to make tests available to the public. Consequently, from 11 states, a total of 94 passages were collected for analysis.

My content analysis was informed by Silverman (2004), who suggests that "researchers [need to] establish a set of categories and count the number of instances that [fall] into that category." Atkinson and Coffey (1995) cautions that when performing content analysis on mute evidence like records, they need to be construed as socially produced artifacts rather than being seen as "truths." Therefore the chapter attempts to link the selected reading passages to their contexts and to ask questions such as: What ideologies do the inclusion of the passages reflect? What messages do they give students when reading passages in the high-pressure situation of standardized tests?

Once the data was collected, I sorted them into what Lincoln and Guba (1985) call units. The unitizing of data began with the first sample passage and, as more and more samples were collected, they were similarly unitized. Since the data came from different sources, such as complete tests and sample items, each reading passage and its accompanying questions were treated as one unit. As data accumulated, I sorted these passages into "like piles" or the initial categories. Data were sorted and re-sorted, and categories emerged, were discarded, and re-emerged from the data.

Table 1: States from Which Tests Were Examined

States	Grades	Years	States	Grades	Years
Arkansas	4	2003	Pennsylvania	3	2003
Georgia	4	2000	South Carolina	3, 4	no year given
Maine	4	2002	Texas (TAAS)	3, 4	2002
Massachusetts	3	2002, 2003	Texas (TAKS)	3, 4	2003
New York	3	2001	Virginia	3	2000, 2002, 2003
Ohio	4	2002, 2003	Wyoming	4	2003

Emergent Patterns

The 94 reading passages can be categorized into fiction, nonfiction, or poetry groupings. The most cursory glance indicates that the perspectives of people of color are severely underrepresented in the standardized tests. The other patterns that emerged from analyzing the data include the treatment of difference; the creation of the "other" as menace; and the themes of rescue and salvation. Table 2 indicates how diversity is portrayed in these passages.

Table 2: Diversity in Standardized Test Reading Passages

Type of Item	Fiction	Nonfiction	Poetry
Total number	41	42	11
Items that include perspectives of people of color	16	6	0

Difference. Scholars believe that questioning the "different" categories used to describe people is a fundamental aspect of postcolonial theory. As Austin-Broos (1998) states,

> Difference is constructed rather than given. There is no simply natural differentiation of peoples in the world. Colonialism itself is the structuring of difference rather than simply a political act realised on a pre-given cultural field.... The proposal is to "interrogate" difference rather than to gaze Herder-like at the plenitude of God's creation, at the ontological range of humanity. (p. 300)

The modern intellect's claims to superiority come from its power to define and differentiate; thus, to simply accept the notion that the world is made up of "different" kinds of people is in some ways to accept the logic of colonialism (Gandhi, 1998). Said (1993) points out that many postcolonial nations have come to accept the idea of difference, claiming it as a sign of their own uniqueness and resulting in a form of reactionary politics in which difference is articulated in what Adorno calls "negative dialectics," an essentially defensive definition of culture. This kind of dialectics ultimately underscores the "binary oppositions and hierarchies" of colonial discourse (quoted in Gandhi, 1998, p. 109).

Stoler and Cooper (1997) offer an insightful analysis of the concept of difference by elaborating on the rigid forms of social division. They argue that even when difference is portrayed and constructed as monolithic and omnipotent, it always contains undercurrents of intermingling. Furthermore, competing strategies for acquiring and maintaining power are part of the operations of defining difference. This is not to underestimate the power of categories as they have allowed various forms of violence and have opened and closed possibilities in areas such as marriage, housing, and education. It is the questioning of difference that confounds formal colonization by positioning "contestation over the very categories of ruler and ruled at the heart of colonial politics" (p. 6). Recent work in postcolonial theory makes the point that difference is something that empires have had to work hard to define and maintain. Consequently, there is space for dialogue, action, and resistance regarding how "different" people could turn around the operations and discourses of empire.

Naming Difference. This study tracked how difference is portrayed in the reading passages of standardized tests. What is striking is that difference is not merely accepted; it is specifically named as if to make sure that it could not escape the student's attention. Out of the 16 fictional passages that include the perspectives of people of color, 5 have sub-titles that name the stories' geographical origin and focus. For example, a story about a spider and turtle is "a West African tale" (Virginia, 2003); one about a turtle flying south for the winter is "a Sioux legend" (Wyoming, 2003). All five passages identified as "non-European" are about animals. In the fictional passages about Euro-American characters, the racialized and geographical naming is not included. For example, a story about a wolf and a heron, taken from Aesop's fables, is not labeled according to its origin (Ohio, 2003).

Exoticizing Difference. Another aspect examined in the study is the depiction of the activities that children are engaged in. Their activities are markedly different along racial/ethnic lines. Of the 16 fictional passages that include perspectives of people of color, 10 of them are about children doing various things, such as dancing a Mexican folk dance (Ohio, 2003); playing double dutch jump rope (Ohio, 2003); visiting China and going to the market there (Texas, 2001); finding a special meeting place with friends (Texas, 2002); helping a girl from the wagon train (Texas, 2002); planning to play soccer (Texas, 2002); visiting Native American grandparents in Arizona, eating dinner, and making pottery (Texas, 2003); going to the museum and wishing one could be a paleontologist when grown up (Texas, 2003); playing traditional African drums (Texas, 2003); and gathering eggs (Virginia, 2003).

Out of the 25 fictional items that represent Euro-American perspectives, 19 of them describe children engaging in various activities, including helping grandfather learn how to read (Arkansas, 2003); learning about nutrition (Georgia, 2000); picking blackberries (Kentucky, 2004); growing peanuts in Georgia (Massachusetts, 2002); cleaning a neighbor's garage (Ohio, 2002); asking questions about family history (South Carolina, 2003); living on a farm and helping father get home safely during a dust storm (Texas, 2001); making ice cream (Texas, 2001); planning to take a weekend class on gardening (Texas, 2001); playing the piano and playing baseball (Texas, 2001); taking care of and playing with pets (Texas 2001, 2002); taking care of chickens on the farm (Texas, 2002); going to the airport (Texas, 2002); searching for sea turtle nests (Texas, 2002); visiting a television station (Texas, 2002); working on the family ranch (Texas, 2003); and having a picnic (Virginia, 2000).

The reading passages show children of color as engaged in "exotic" activities, such as playing the tribal drums while half naked or dancing folk dances in brightly colored costumes, whereas Euro-American children engage in "regular" activities such as playing with their pets. When children of color go somewhere, it is to exotic destinations such as China and a Native American village, whereas "regular" people go to places such as the airport or to Florida to look for sea turtles.

The Menacing Other. Feldman (2004) suggests that along with war on terror, the United States also is engaged in "securocratic wars of public safety," with an underlying message that "liberal" democracies are threatened by invisible and infiltrating dangers. Feldman outlines several strategies employed in these wars, including a "police concept of history." This type of history rewrites or remaps the world into secure idealized and orderly spaces that are threatened by their dichotomous other, the improper, and the transgressive. Human life is characterized by an orderly and visible "distribution of functions, profiles and positions within a society" (p. 333). In such a society, the non-events are considered normal since functions have been properly assigned to particular people and everyone is in her/his assigned place. Always lurking in the edges, however, is the menacing other—disorderly inhabitants (both animal and human) and unruly happenings—that require policing and control. The menace is portrayed in ways to make apparent that it can never be fully contained or apprehended. As a result, constant surveillance is required and new technologies of control must always be developed.

Drawing upon Feldman, my analysis indicates that the reading passages in many state standardized tests reflect imperialist ideologies. One passage is about the driver ants of Africa, described as the "most famous fighters" of all ants: "Most ants live in one place, but the driver ants are almost always on the move. They eat every insect and bird and small animal they can find. They will eat large animals and people who cannot get away. Even elephants run from an army of terrible driver ants." The last sentence reads: "So if you have a picnic in Africa, do not worry about these ants eating your sandwiches. Worry about them eating you" (Ohio, 2002, selection from "Insects Do the Strangest Things" by Leonora and Arthur Hornblow). A fourth grade passage is a fictional account of a child named Elizabeth who is traveling west on a wagon train in 1856 (Texas, 2002). When the train stops, her rooster goes missing and Elizabeth looks for it. Elizabeth meets a Native American girl named Sisika who helps her look. When they find the rooster, it is eating crickets, and Sisika tells Elizabeth that crickets are tasty: "my mother dries them and we make delicious cricket soup." Here, the image of the other is one who does not operate within the borders of the normal.

The only nonfictional passage on Native Americans, although some passages about Euro-Americans mention Native Americans as secondary characters, is entitled "Planting and Tending Crops" (Massachusetts, 2002). The first sentence of the passage summary reads: "Learning to farm in North America took the Native Americans many years." In other words, after thousands of years, Native Americans are still "learning" how to farm and have never mastered this technique. The passage gives details about the farming tools that Native Americans use: shells, the shoulder blade bone of a buffalo, and stone blades. The image shows a prehistoric people who have never acquired the sophistication to farm "properly." On the other hand, many passages about Euro-American adults and children in farms and ranches are portrayed as resourceful individuals. A passage about Daniel Boone narrates how Boone had some "exciting experiences" with Native Americans who came to "respect his skills as a hunter and woodsman" (South Carolina, 2003). The contrast between the orderly spaces of Euro-Americans where people do ordinary everyday activities like play the piano or make ice cream, and the unruly worlds outside of those boundaries (or within them before they were civilized) is evident.

In addition, the images of normal spaces are constructed through the inclusion of details. A remarkable feature that sets apart passages about European Americans from people of color is the use or omission of details in the descriptions of people and events. Precise details are given about one group and omitted about the other. The already few passages about people of color contain far fewer details, such as specific dates and places, in comparison to passages about Euro-Americans and their environments. In at least three nonfictional passages about people of color, details that easily could have been included are omitted. For example, the passage about African American scientist George Washington Carver does not include dates when he was born, even though it is about his childhood. In contrast, passages about Euro-Americans like politician and inventor Benjamin Franklin and hunter Daniel Boone mention the dates of their birth. The passage about Carver also is limited to a brief description of how he struggled to attend school, and makes no mention of his accomplishments later in life.

The passage about driver ants in Africa is remarkable for its lack of detail. It does not even mention where in Africa these ants are to be found. The sentence quoted earlier highlights the dangers of having a picnic in Africa, leaving a disturbing impression that the entire continent is overrun with them. On the other hand, passages about living creatures and their habitats in the Western world include more details, such as the various kinds of squirrels, how big spiders can be, and what to do if you found a gecko in your house.

Another passage about people of color that describes the environment focuses on Native American farming. It does not talk about specific dates and times (except to say that it took Native Americans thousands of years to learn how to farm), nor does it mention specific localities (although there is a reference to geographic regions). In contrast, descriptions in passages about Euro-Americans and their environments are full of details. For example, a passage describes the "Appalachian Trail": where the trail begins (Maine) and where it ends (Georgia), how long it is (2,167 miles), how much of it is in New York State (88.8 miles), and how many steps one will probably take per mile (2,300) (New York, 2001). The emphasis in Euro-American passages seems to be on details, including historical facts about cowboy boots (Texas, 2001) and how much garbage is produced every year (New York, 2001).

The only passages about people of color that include specific details are those about Mae Jemison, the first African American female astronaut, and the first African American polar explorers, Matthew Henson and Garrett Morgan. The passages about Jemison and Henson have actual photographs, but the passages about Carver and Morgan have sketches, even though their photographs are easily available. While there are passages about Euro-Americans with sketches, such as those of Jim Henson, the creator of the Muppets, and the anthropologist Jane Goodall, most of their passages include photographs, including one of President Theodore Roosevelt. The underlying message seems to be that people of color, unless they live in the United States and are engaged in the types of activities that are valued by the dominant culture, do not operate within the same dimensions of normalcy. Life outside the West is primitive, timeless, and without specific locations, and by implication populated by hulking and dangerous others who can threaten the safe spaces "we" live in.

Rescue Me. Pena (2006) characterizes the No Child Left Behind Act (NCLB) and its implementation as technologies that construct "children for the purpose of saving them" (p. 265). The language of "saving" children is reflected in multiple aspects of the legislation. Children, especially children of color, are defined as a collective who are far from desired levels of school performance and need saving from schools that are not performing up to par. According to Pena, NCLB is framed within language of salvation and redemption. Accountability, for example, has traditionally had a qualitative moral dimension, traceable to the work of Locke in 1690. Other features, such as ideas about choice and flexibility also carry such connotations. The version of salvation preached by NCLB is geared toward "fast tracking children to the final state of adulthood": acquiring the right kind of reading and math skills would prepare children to become the right kind of citizens and consumers. To receive salvation, children must perform in specific ways. Pena likens the emphasis on testing and re-testing to the insistence that there must be constant vigilance to stay in a state of grace. Even the title, no child left behind, invokes the promise of saving and being saved.

The metaphor of children of color being saved or rescued carries over in the reading passages of state standardized tests. The stories about European American characters portray them as individuals who solve problems in resourceful ways, whereas in the stories about people of color, they are rarely shown as either being presented with difficult situations or as finding solutions to them. They are depicted as individuals waiting for help or for change to come. Out of the 25 fictional passages about mostly Euro-Americans, 10 short stories are about resourceful and problem-solving children. For example, a child named Annie figures out a way to help her father come home in a dust storm (Texas, 2001). Although her father would be able to follow the fence around their land, Annie worries that he would not be able to find the way from there to the front door. She comes up with the idea of tying a rope from the door to the fence, which ends up helping her father come safely home. Another example includes a boy whose grandfather never learned how to read. The boy finds help for his grandfather, who ends up learning to read (Arkansas, 2003). Only one passage shows what happens when rules are broken. A child who is told not to enter the hen house does so and ends up letting all the chickens out. Her father helps her put them back inside.

In contrast, out of the 16 passages about people of color, only two show children as being able to find solutions to problems. In one story, a child named Kara Salazar is sent to gather eggs, but discovers that her basket has a hole in it. She ends up using her sweatshirt to line the basket so that the eggs do not fall out (Virginia, 2003). In the other story, three girls named Robin, Carmen, and LaShonda, who seem to be White, Hispanic, and Black from the illustration, want to find a special meeting place for their group called Friends Forever (Texas, 2003). Carmen comes up with the idea of a meeting place. After considering alternatives, something Robin says gives LaShonda the idea that they could use a patch of sunflowers as that place.

In stories about children of color, the children are shown mostly as passive beings to whom life happens. Many of the stories are concerned with descriptions rather than events. Two passages describe children returning to their origins, so to speak: a child named Mei Lin, who has lived in Texas all her life, visits her grandmother in China, and an unnamed child travels to Arizona to visit his Native American grandparents in a Hopi village (Texas, 2001). Both these passages contain details about physical things (e.g., how a mesa looks, what the houses are like, the vegetables in the market, and what they ate for dinner), but do not show the children engaging in purposeful actions. In a passage drawn from Gary Soto's children's book entitled "The Skirt," Miata is participating in a Mexican folk dance. The book's summary, which appears at the head of the page, states that Miata forgets her special skirt in the school bus and tries to get it back. However, the actual passage reproduced in the test is more concerned with descriptions of the skirt's pretty colors and how it looks when Miata twirls while wearing it (Ohio, 2003). Another passage, about the driver of an 18-wheeler named Tameka, consists entirely of descriptions: of the truck itself, of the log that Tameka must keep about what she does, of the truck's dashboard, and of a truck stop she visits along the way (Virginia, 2003). Similarly, there is a story about Lisa Vasquez who visits a museum of natural history (Texas, 2003). The story is mostly composed of details about the dinosaur bones that she sees there. The character appears to lack agency or power, and seems to be waiting to be given directions as to what to do.

Final Thoughts

As my analysis indicates, a distinct qualitative difference appears in the representations of European Americans and people of color in state standardized tests. European Americans tend to be depicted as "normal," engaging in routine everyday activities. People of color, on the other hand, are deemed "different," exotic, less resourceful, passive, and waiting for change to come. These dichotomous images need to be interrogated and challenged since these are the representations of difference that circulate within the United States and are exported around the world. There is a growing body of research regarding how standardized tests are failing children and schools. My analysis supports such findings, and adds that their effects do not stop there. In many ways, standardized tests are an encapsulated version of views about people, cultures, and difference that are being imposed around the world.

Notes

1. See Santos (2005) for postcolonial perspectives on the use of "American" to refer to citizens of the United States.
2. The standardized test items were retrieved on April 2004 from the following Web sites:
- Arkansas: http://arkedu.state.ar.us/actaap/pdf/G4%20RIB%200708.pdf
- Georgia: http://www.doe.k12.ga.us/_documents/curriculum/testing/op_form14.pdf
- Maine: http://mainegov-images.informe.org/education/mea/02MEAG4-ReleasedItems-C.pdf
- Massachusetts (two Web sites): http://www.doe.mass.edu/mcas/2002/release/g3read.pdf; http:// www.doe.mass.edu/mcas/2003/release/g3read.pdf
- New York: http://www.emsc.nysed.gov/3-8/ela-sample/home.htm
- Ohio: http://www.ode.state.oh.us/proficiency/previous_test/3rd_grade_Achv/default.asp
- Pennsylvania: http://www.pde.state.pa.us/a_and_t/cwp/view.asp?a=108&Q=73153&a_and_tNav=|670|&a_and_tNav=|
- South Carolina: http://www.sde.state.sc.us/new_site/offices/assessment//PACT/index.htm
- Texas: http://www.tea.state.tx.us/student.assessment/resources/release/taks/index.html
- Virginia (three Web sites):
http://www.pen.k12.va.us/VDOE/Assessment/release2000/grade3.pdf;
http://www.pen.k12.va.us/VDOE/Assessment/Release2003/VARIBs_ g3rdgwri-1.pdf;
http://www.pen.k12.va.us/VDOE/Assessment/Release2002/Grade3/VirgOnLine_Gr3_RdgWri_1-22.pdf
- Wyoming: http://www.k12.wy.us/SA/wycas/archive/TestResults/2003Release/03WY4ELA_V2.pdf

References

Atkinson, P., & Coffey A. (1995). Realism and its discontents: The crisis of cultural representation in ethnographic texts. In B. Adam & S. Allen (Eds.), *Theorising culture* (pp. 103–139). London, UK: University College London Press.

Austin-Broos, D. J. (1998). Falling through the savage slot: Postcolonial critique and the ethnographic task. *Australian Journal of Anthropology*, 9(3), 295–309.

Ayers, W. (2000). The standards fraud. In J. Cohen & J. Rogers (Eds.), *Will standards save public education?* Boston, MA: Beacon.

Barsky, R., & Ali, S. (2006). Introduction: Intellectuals who quest beyond the ivory tower. *AmeriQuests*, 3(2), 1–20.

Bork, R. H. (1996). Multiculturalism is bringing us to a barbarous epoch. *Chronicle of Higher Education*, 11 October, B7.

Cannella, G. S. (1997). *Deconstructing early childhood education: Social justice and revolution.* New York: Peter Lang.

Cannella, G. S., & Viruru, R. (2004). *Childhood and postcolonization: Power, education, and contemporary practice.* New York: Routledge.

Crenson, M., & Ginsberg, B. (2002). *Downsizing democracy: How America sidelined its citizens and privatized its public.* Baltimore, MD: Johns Hopkins University Press.

Dean, J. (2004). Secrecy since September 11. *Interventions: International Journal of Postcolonial Studies*, 6(3) 362–380.

Donaldson, L. E. (1992). *Decolonizing feminisms: Race, gender, and empire-building*. Chapel Hill, NC: University of North Carolina Press.

Ducille, A. (1996). *Skin trade*. Cambridge, MA: Harvard University Press.

Feldman, A. (2004). Securocratic wars of public safety: Globalized policing as scopic regime. *Interventions: International Journal of Postcolonial Studies, 6*(3), 330-350.

Ferguson, J. (2005). Decomposing modernity: History and hierarchy after-development. In A. Loomba, S. Kaul, M. Bunzl, A. Burton, & J. Esty (Eds.), *Post-colonial studies and beyond* (pp. 166-181). Durham, NC: Duke University Press.

Fordham, S., & Ogbu, J. U. (1986). Black students' school success: Coping with the burden of "acting white." *Urban Review, 18*(3), 176-206.

Gandhi, L. (1998). *Postcolonial theory: A critical introduction*. New York: Columbia University Press.

Hodder, I. (2000). The interpretation of documents and material culture. In N. K. Denzin & Y. S. Lincoln (Eds.), *Handbook of qualitative research*. Thousand Oaks, CA: Sage.

Johnson, C. (2004). *The sorrows of empire*. New York: Metropolitan Books.

Kaplan, A., & Pease, D. (1993). *Cultures of United States imperialism*. Durham, NC: Duke University Press.

Kohn, A. (1999). *The schools our children deserve: Moving beyond traditional classrooms and tougher standards*. Boston: Houghton Mifflin.

Kohn, A. (2000). *The case against standardized testing: Raising the scores, ruining the schools*. Portsmouth, NH: Heinemann.

Kornhaber, M. L., & Orfield, G. (2001). High stakes testing policies: Examining their assumptions and consequences. In G. Orfield & M. L. Kornhaber (Eds.), *Raising standards or raising barriers: Inequality and high stakes testing in public education* (pp. 1-18). New York: Century Foundation.

Lee, J. (2006). *Tracking achievement gaps and assessing the impact of NCLB on the gaps: An in-depth look into national and state reading and math outcome trends*. Cambridge, MA: Civil Rights Project at Harvard University.

Levin, B. (2001). *Reforming education: From origins to outcomes*. New York: RoutledgeFalmer.

Lincoln, Y. S., & Guba, E. (1985). *Naturalistic inquiry*. Thousand Oaks, CA: Sage.

Madaus, G., & Clarke, M. (2001). The adverse impact of high stakes testing on minority students: Evidence from one hundred years of test data. In G. Orfield & M. L. Kornhaber (Eds.), *Raising standards or raising barriers: Inequality and high stakes testing in public education* (pp. 85-106). New York: Century Foundation.

Martin, R. (2004). America as risk/securitizing the other. *Interventions: International Journal of Postcolonial Studies, 6*(3), 351-361.

Mbembe, A. (2002). African modes of self writing. *Public Culture, 14*(1), 239-273.

McNeil, L., & Valenzuela, A. (2001). *The harmful impact of the TAAS system of testing Texas: Beneath the accountability rhetoric*. New York: Century Foundation.

Meier, D. (2000). Educating a democracy. In J. Cohen & J. Rogers (Eds.), *Will standards save public education?* (pp. 3-34). Boston: Beacon.

Miyoshi, M. (1993). A borderless world: From colonialism to transnationalism and the decline of the nation-state. *Critical Inquiry, 19*(4), 726-751.

Ohanian, S. (2002). *What happened to recess and why are our children struggling in kindergarten?* New York: McGraw Hill.

Osborne, D., & Gaebler, T. (1992). *Reinventing government: How the entrepreneurial spirit is trans-*

forming the public sector. Reading, MA: Addison-Wesley.

Park, Y., & Schwarz, H. (2005). Extending American hegemony: Beyond empire. *Interventions: International Journal of Postcolonial Studies, 7*(2), 153–161.

Passavant, P. (2004). The governmentality of consumption. *Interventions: International Journal of Postcolonial Studies, 6*(3), 381–400.

Pena, K. (2006). No child left behind? The specters of almsgiving and atonement: A short genealogy of the saving grace of US education. In M. Bloch, D. Kennedy, T. Lightfoot, & D. Weyemberg (Eds.), *The child in the world/the world in the child: Education and the configuration of a universal modern and globalized childhood* (pp. 265–292). New York: Palgrave Macmillan.

Said, E. (1993). *Culture and imperialism.* London, UK: Chatto & Windus.

Santos, L. C. G. V. (2005). American, United Statian, US American, or gringo? *AmeriQuests, 2*(1), 1–9.

Silverman, D. (2004). *Doing qualitative research* (2nd ed.). Thousand Oaks, CA: Sage.

Stoler, A. L., & Cooper, F. (1997). Between metropole and colony: Rethinking a research agenda. In F. Cooper & A. L. Stoler (Eds.), *Tensions of empire: Colonial cultures in a bourgeois world* (pp. 1–58). Berkeley: University of California Press.

Trombold, J. (2005). Neo-Roosevelt, or why postcolonialism is premature. *Interventions: International Journal of Postcolonial Studies, 7*(2), 199–215.

Žižek, S. (1991). *For they know not what they do.* London: Verso.

CHAPTER 8

Post-apartheid Dilemmas: Black Teachers Theorizing Social Justice

SHARON SUBREENDUTH

The educational history of South Africa is intimately connected to the apartheid ideology of racial differentiation and discrimination because racial segregation was institutionalized and implemented in the educational system (Maylam, 2001).[1] Although the chapter addresses South Africa's contemporary educational situation, it intentionally engages with apartheid and post-apartheid ideology. Post-apartheid South Africa continues to be a deeply stratified nation that is marked by hierarchical access to knowledge, schooling, and learning (Motala & Pampallis, 2002). There is little chance for the maintenance of a democratic nation if deep stratification continues. I argue that the effects of apartheid remain so tightly woven in the mosaic of Black South African life that it threatens to remain a serious challenge to the possibilities of Curriculum 2005 (C2005) as a political and pedagogical project to create an equitable society.

Using Appadurai's (1991) notion of ethnoscapes, I foreground Black teacher voices in the deliberation and evaluation of Curriculum 2005. Their struggles and ambivalent experiences with it unravel the conundrum of what is "(their) nature of locality, as lived [educational] experience" in a dynamic and differentiated post-apartheid nation (Appadurai, 1991, p. 196). Their narratives interrogate and evaluate the decolonizing intentions of the African National Congress since it is the legitimate democratically elected government of the people. The analysis of such ethnoscapes can "generate new kinds of politics, new kinds of collective expression, and new needs for social [and educational] discipline and surveillance" within the complex reengineering of educational policy and legislation in post-apartheid South Africa (p. 198). By representing the lived particularities of their educational lives, I enact a practice of representation that "illuminates the power of large-scale, imagined life possibilities over specific life trajectories," thus offering "thickness with a difference" (p. 200).

By way of contextualizing and understanding these ethnoscapes, I offer a brief historical perspective of the role of education in apartheid South Africa, and then present the philosophy undergirding Curriculum 2005 as the vehicle for decolonization and transformation in post-apartheid South Africa. The Black teachers' examination of the role of Curriculum 2005 in enabling social justice, equity, and transformation is presented through their analysis of the role of education in the post-apartheid nation. Their articulations are elaborated through their vignettes and interrogations of educational encounters. I conclude with reflections on the teacher narratives and the ideological promises of Curriculum 2005.

Historical Context of Public Education in South Africa

The history of South Africa has been profoundly influenced, first, by Dutch and British colonization and, second, by the introduction of apartheid. While the respective external and internal forces of colonialism and apartheid impacted and added to the complexity of South African history, the collusion of colonialism and apartheid ensured the continuity of hegemonic White power and control (Subreenduth, 2006). The education of Black people in South Africa during Dutch, British, and National Party rule has a brutal and violent history. The colonial missionary zeal to Christianize the "heathen Kaffir" and educate them for menial labor violated indigenous principles of education and stripped Blacks of their human dignity, cultural roots, and history (Wilson & Ramphele, 1989). I use the term "indigenous" to reference native South Africans and their culture and practices. This is significantly different from my use of the term "Black" to reference the marginalized people of color in apartheid South Africa.[2] Starting in 1948, the National Party legitimized apartheid through the implementation of a number of legislative acts, such as the Race Classification Act and the Group Areas Act of 1950. It legislated inferior, segregated schools for Africans in 1953, Coloreds in 1963, and Indians in 1965 (Bassey, 1999). The implementation of Bantu education in 1953 ensured a legacy of separate and unequal education and interrupted the practice of an indigenous education in South Africa.[3]

The 1953 Bantu Education Act was enacted to serve the labor needs of the capitalist class and to reinforce ethnic divisions among Africans, with the intent to "retribalize," which would result in fragmenting communities and deterring the development of African nationalism (Kallaway, 1986).[4] While the physical separation of Black people was an important divide and conquer strategy of the apartheid regime, the educational systems for Bantus, Coloreds, and Indians were aimed at the minds of Black people. Bantu education became a pedagogy of labor to serve the privileged White population. This was a deliberate inferior form of education to train Blacks "exclusively for employment in menial, low-wage positions in a racially structured economy" (Nkabinde, 1997, p. 6). With the inferior education came the enforcement of subservience, most effectively meted out through rigorous curricula that served as sites of apartheid indoctrination. Bantu education served to advance the apartheid regime's "negative social engineering" and the long-term goal of denying Blacks "intellectual independence" in order to freeze any possibilities of economic, social, and political independence (p. 8). As a result of the 1953 Bantu Education Act, the apartheid regime had direct access to most young Black people. This made it easy to "institute control by inducing passivity in the students and by creating false ideas about Black history, identity and culture" (Mohamed, 1990, p. 259). Separation in education was to be a fundamental pillar of apartheid and maintained the structure of racial domination, rooted in the ideology of White supremacy and racial segregation (Christie & Gaganakis, 1989). Until the early 1970s, the apartheid regime was fairly successful in maintaining the status quo. With the 1976 Soweto uprising, the apartheid edifice started to crumble.[5] June 16, 1976, served as a warning signal that the "racist fantasies of the Vervoed-Vorster era were about to be blown away by the winds of change" (Alexander, 1990, p. 4).

The events of June 16 catapulted South Africa's youth and activists into two decades of unprecedented political and educational protest and action, resulting in South Africa's first democratic government in 1994. The Soweto uprising was a defining moment for Black youth in the struggle for equal education and national liberation. The resulting upsurge of student power demonstrated through the school boycotts of the 1970s and 1980s was a clear indication to the apartheid government that the schools, which were intended to propagate an "education for domestication," had become "Trojan horses" or the sites of struggle against such oppression (Kallaway, 1986, p. 20). The provision of apartheid education did not simply benefit the apartheid government at all times, and the colonized were not powerless, silenced, and passive. On the contrary, schools and schooling under apartheid were "systematically appropriated by the colonized people and have played an important historical role as sites of struggle" toward the struggle for national liberation (p. 10).

While South Africa's democratic curricula has unveiled and addressed the blatant intellectual and educational inequalities of the apartheid regime, the lack of institutional support, financial and teaching resources, teacher training, and the continued dependence on apartheid-era facilities and equipment, it has done little to impact the process of social reconstruction and transformation based on equity. In the post-apartheid democracy, the apartheid educational edifice continues to legitimize inequities and serve as a site of oppression for Black students and educators.

Working toward Social Justice and Equity

With a violent history rooted in the "demonic twin debacles of oppressive colonialism and apartheid" (Abdi, 2002, p. 108), the first democratic government began a number of projects and a series of legislation with the intention of transforming South Africa. Key to these projects of decolonization was the introduction of a unitary educational system and national curricula. In 1997 the South African Department of Education adopted the Outcomes Based Education (OBE) model and developed a framework called Curriculum 2005 (C2005).[6] C2005 was piloted in a number of schools in 1997, and in 1998 was phased into all of the grade levels. Central to the intention of C2005 is its role in promoting human rights, social and environmental justice with a particular emphasis on the issues of poverty, inequality, race, gender, age, disability, and sexual orientation. Multiple references to education for *all* in this document is a direct redress to the apartheid government's goal of education for *some*, suggesting that inclusivity of all contributes to achieving the goal of social justice, equity, and development. This is visible in the National Curriculum Statement:

> Social justice requires that those sections of the population previously disempowered by the lack of knowledge and skills should now be empowered by it. If social justice and equity are to be achieved, then curriculum needs to be structured and designed in such a way that all, and especially those with special needs, and least resources and skills, are empowered by it. (Department of Education, 2001, p. 3)

It is not my intention to analyze the statement above or C2005 per se. Instead, I intend to stage Black teachers' interpretations, dialogues, and workings within and against C2005 with particular attention to its ideological claim of transformation.

Background of the Study

The chapter stems from my larger study that explored the narratives of Black South African educators as they sought to redefine their pedagogy as critical agents in South Africa's journey through educational, political, and sociocultural transformation (Subreenduth, 2003a). The larger study investigated how teachers negotiated their practice within the tensions of identity, lived experience, liberatory struggles, and their notions of emancipatory teaching and learning. Attention to the social and historical contexts of classrooms, communities, and institutions as "complex intersections of cultural histories, multiple identities, institutional constraints and shifting power relations" was vital to the study (Kamler, 2001, p. 43).

Five South African educators participated in my research that was connected to a two-year funded project from 2001 to 2003. My qualitative study was framed within Smith's (1999) call for decolonizing methodologies that demand a reflexive research practice through an examination of issues of power, race, community, and of undertaking research within one's community and professional space. The study utilized interviews, focus group discussions, observations, and document analysis. The five teachers, two African males, two African females, and one Indian female only met each other as a result of their participation in the project. Lucky, an African male, has five years of teaching experience, and lives very close to his school that is located in a large township. All of his students are African and come from the township. Sabs is an African male whose school is located in a semirural area, and commutes from a nearby city. Although all of his students are African, 50 percent of the students come from two nearby townships, and the others are from neighboring farms. Gugu, an African female, teaches in a semirural secondary school that was considered a model during the apartheid era. She lives on the school site, while her students come from nearby farms. Thembile, an African female, teaches in a school located in an informal settlement. Her students, all of whom are African, live in the settlement. Layla, an Indian female, taught in a previously Indian school that now caters to 90 percent African students.

The primary focus of the chapter is to explore the transformative possibilities of the democratic curricular agenda in post-apartheid education through the narratives of Black teachers. I attempt to retell how they engaged with a number of critical issues related to C2005. Their narratives are represented through their descriptions of self as teacher that constructs how their individual identity formation and varied experiences may influence or dictate their teaching philosophy and practice. Through their vignettes, I trace their engagement with C2005 and their envisioned possibilities of a liberatory pedagogy that can counter the effects of apartheid. Their vignettes often interrogate the vicious legacy of apartheid as it continues to live within the educational, economic, and social structures of South Africa.

Narrating the Silenced within Dominant Educational Discourse

Even though South Africa's educational transformation is now entering its second decade, there are few published qualitative studies focusing on the perspectives of teachers with regard to post-apartheid curriculum and pedagogy. While there are critiques about South Africa's new educational ideology and curriculum (Kunnie, 2000; Motala & Pampallis, 2002; Satyo, 1999), what is missing are the voices of teachers. The voices of Black teachers in particular are resoundingly silent in the dominant discourse of educational transformation, educational policy, professional development, teaching and learning in South Africa. What are their perspectives of OBE and C2005? How do they conceptualize their teaching practice within this new framework? How do they negotiate their "new" roles within C2005? How do they empower students and themselves in environments that are still deeply embedded in the legacy of apartheid? Just as public education was a primary site for institutionalizing and perpetuating the social organization of apartheid, public education is now considered a primary site for creating equity and equality. Even though teacher narratives are situated closer to the initial implementation of the new post-apartheid curriculum, these questions remain critical for the current educational and historical juncture as South Africa reformulates apartheid structures to develop a more democratic teaching and learning environment and praxis. The chapter engages these questions through the narratives of Black teachers since they have a decisive role to play for the success and longevity of South Africa's democratic educational dispensation.

Theorizing a Transformative "Healing" Education

As part of the selection process to participate in the funded project, the teachers had to submit a short essay on "The role of education in addressing the needs of civil society in your local school and community." The following essay vignettes offer a glimpse of the teachers' visions of the role of education in South Africa's transformation, and serve to contextualize their later critiques of C2005. To capture the participants' desire for a transformative education, I offer them this space to envision South Africa in their own words.

My intention is not to use the data to support an analysis of their desires. I use their narratives "demonstrably, performatively" without the intervention of the researcher (Lather, 1992, p. 95). The lack of paraphrasing and analysis is not an avoidance of my "scientific" responsibility, but more an attempt to deconstruct the notion that the "researcher [is the] universal spokesperson who has privileged access to meaning" (p. 96). I attempt to limit my analysis, thereby leaving open (to the reader?) the role of "coanalyst" of the teachers' articulations (Erickson, 1986).

> Sabs: As educationalists we need to play an active role in healing the wounds left by institutionalized apartheid on civil society. Through education we can build a truly democratic society. The school curricula should be structured in such a way that they are able to address the immediate socioeconomic needs of the surrounding communities. For example, a school situated in a highly agricultural area should be able to produce learners who are ready to enter the field of commercial farming by the time they exit formal schooling. Education should be used as a tool to address the socioeconomic needs of more than five million South Africans who are presently living below the poverty line. Schools need to engage communities in establishing self-help projects [and] aim at inculcating a sense of ownership among communities.

> Thembile: Education is the key to success and better, brighter future. It is through education that we communicate. In our school poverty is the greatest problem that the society faces .... but our school is a place of learning and development. It is through education that we are able to reach out to ... people in our community [to address social issues like tuberculosis, poverty, etc.].

> Lucky: In urban community and schools educators are faced with children of the eighties, who come from the history of political violence, broken families and neglect ... these learners often feel isolated political, social, and economical. I strongly believe that educators with necessary training can play an important role in developing local schools and community.

> Layla: Public schools today have to respond to an ever-increasing diverse student population. Education plays a pivotal role in the lives of youth in modern day South Africa, as it is an effective tool to promote a multicultural and multiracial society. Through the powerful medium of education we are able to develop racial tolerance and equip students with the skills needed to coexist in an integrated work environment that a civil society demands. The school curriculum should thus expose students to a rich array of viewpoints, perspectives and experiences.

Gugu: Building a relationship between the school and other stakeholders such as parents, traditional leaders, businesses is very important. The school is the center for community activities [and we should] encourage ... parents ... to participate fully in the education of their children. Learners should also be part of the partnership in the school.

It is not surprising that Sabs and Thembile speak to the role of education in determining, impacting, and equalizing economic empowerment. They teach in schools and communities located in the midst of socioeconomic poverty and marginalization. However, economic disempowerment is not the only "wound" that education is expected to heal. Intrinsic to the teachers' vision of education in "healing the wounds institutionalized [by] apartheid" is their implication for an ideological shift from the apartheid view of schooling as technical and ahistorical to a sociopolitical perspective that focuses on the relationship between schooling and justice (Kunnie, 2000; Mzamane, 1990). The call for an ideological shift echoes the rhetoric of C2005 and the national political agenda of self-empowerment to achieve social justice:

Human rights and fundamental freedoms cannot simply be proclaimed, or legislated from on high. It is only when people themselves engage in social action to give meaning to the words enshrined in our constitution that human rights will become the living thread from which our social fabric is woven.... The organization of the people to act as their own liberators, to themselves transform the prescriptions of the Constitution into a living reality is the basis of this ongoing struggle. (Mbeki, 2002)

Lucky, whose formal education was interrupted as a result of his activism, raises a very crucial element in the government's attempt to equalize the playing field: What about the generation that was sacrificed in the name of freedom and liberation? What role will education and educators play in healing their scars? Layla's vision of education to create a harmonious multiracial and multicultural society is urgent, albeit utopian, for a society still scarred by apartheid's divisive practices. Gugu's desire for education to build strong partnerships with various communities also echoes the intentions of C2005. All five teachers craft compelling arguments that education has the possibility to be the potent nexus for political, economic, and social empowerment. Their arguments raise provocative considerations for possible interventions in South Africa's post-apartheid pedagogical model.

C2005 and Educational Policy: Enabling Transformation?

All five teachers seem to agree that despite the criticisms to C2005 and OBE, Curriculum 2005 offers opportunities for more "democratic teaching" than the apartheid curriculum. Yet, this curriculum is intended to offer more than just spaces for democratic practice; its goal is to provide a divided country the means for social transformation.

Burdened with apartheid inequities, the teachers are skeptical of how the new curriculum would bridge such inequities in their classrooms and professional collaborations. Although they do not discard its transformative possibilities, they argue that it continues to favor those who have been privileged and that its successful implementation is impeded in environments with limited resources, dismal facilities, and inadequate training. How is it possible, they inquired, for their students and themselves to compete equally with those who have classrooms and schools equipped with computers, running water, educational supplies, qualified teachers, extracurricular activities, economically supportive communities, smaller student-teacher ratios, financial resources for professional development, and innovative programming? Layla, the Indian educator, makes visible such inequities. Her school, though by no means privileged, offers more professional development opportunities for their teachers than other schools. The school where Gugu teaches is another example of students and teachers who continue to enjoy the limited structural privileges of having been a model township school during the apartheid regime. It was designed to be a showcase to the international community of how well apartheid in general, and education in particular, served the needs of the Black population, particularly the African population. Mostly staffed by White educators, these schools taught a Black elite that was disciplined to serve the apartheid state. Compared to typical township schools, they were well resourced in textbooks, educators, administrative staff, and extracurricular activities. Such continued privilege and marginalization make post-apartheid efforts to achieve equitable education for *all* a rather daunting task.

The "Bussinessification" and "Corporatization" of Schools

Unlike former White schools, Black schools are burdened by the social and economic constraints of the communities where the schools are located or from where students commute. The constraints, according to the teachers, are not adequately addressed by the government in its uniform mandates and expectations for *all* schools. Equality does not translate to equity, and the National Curriculum Statement's (NCS) idiom of "education for all" becomes a parody in the blatant distortion of its laudable intentions. The teachers are disconcerted about the government's threat to close down low performing schools, and have tense discussions about its implications. Governmental standardization within still divided, discriminatory, and disparate educational environments, they claim, maintains the apartheid status quo. In its attempt to equalize, the government has fallen into the Western archetype of aligning the function, organization, and "product" of schools to industry. The "corporatization" and "bussinessification" of education reflects a global capitalist trend (McLaren, 2003), and is contradictory to C2005's intention of disrupting apartheid divisions.

Lucky becomes emotionally charged during a discussion on governmental standardization. The comparison of schools to industry, he argues, is an unfair equalization of different and unequal structures. His analogy reveals his anger and frustration at the government's threat to close down "low" performing schools.

> [T]o me it is difficult to compare schools to industry because we are dealing with learners. We are not dealing with a tin of fish … where you see it is a reject you throw it away. But you have to understand the problem of the learner, the social and economic problems of the particular learner. Why is this learner not coping? … So now with the tin of fish if it is a reject you throw it away then you produce another tin. What we are approaching now [the government] say we must be like industry. If school is not producing it must close down.

Lucky insists that there is an urgent need to interrogate the possibilities of educational and social transformation and that policymakers can no longer view schools as objective and devoid of history, culture, and social conditions. Therefore, schools in democratic South Africa have to be viewed as sites that encompass economic, cultural, and social tensions that are inextricably tied to issues of power and control. Lucky's vignette suggests that the government's move is contrary to its educational intention of enabling equity. Due to the entrenched apartheid inequalities in education, wouldn't previously non-White schools automatically become "low performing" schools?

Lucky's insistence to address issues outside of curriculum is supported by Hlatshwayo (2000) and Jansen (1990) who state that curriculum change cannot be a substitute for social and structural change. They acknowledge that curriculum change cannot guarantee social change, but that schools can contribute to changes in society. Jansen (1990) argues that curriculum change is more a "reflector than a generator of social change or development," and emphasizes that it is a "significant component of social change to the extent that it encapsulates the knowledge of the people and reflects the aspirations of the nation" (p. 330). He cautions, similar to Lucky, that the optimal impact of curriculum change can only occur when it supports and is supported by broader social changes.

A Call for Responsibility and Accountability

Can the teachers' ambivalence to the possibilities of C2005 for social transformation speak to the government's call for patience? Is the expectation of radical structural and attitudinal changes within such a short time unrealistic? The teachers, although critical of the limitations of C2005, stress that educational change needs time to demonstrate its impact. They stress that such systemic change is a process rather than an event, therefore implying that the future holds more promise than the present. A discussion on the role of government to address racism within the educational and larger societal structures leads Lucky to state that racism is so pervasive in South Africa that it can overwhelm personal and group efforts and therefore requires governmental intervention (Subreenduth, 2003b).

While teachers place appropriate responsibility on the government, they also examine their accountability and responsibility within the system. They critique their own professionalism, those of their colleagues, and the role of teacher unions in the educational process of change. Sabs counters that teachers can make a significant impact, and advocates for self-reflection on the educators' role to eliminate racism. He challenges teachers to consider their role at what he calls the "micro-level":

> What I was talking about was looking at racism at a micro-level whereby you find that at the moment the sports people they are doing something there [about racism]. They have actually acknowledged the fact there is racism in sport and they are doing something to fight it. I wanted us to be specific with ourselves—to do an introspection on ourselves as teachers because as I am saying there needs to be fight against racism at the micro-level—where musicians come together and see what they can do ... the sports people ... now as teachers ... what can we do.

Lucky suggests a local teacher exchange that would allow teachers to spend time in schools that they would not have access to or that they would choose not to teach in. He offers this based on his participation in the project. He relays the acceptance that he received from his White male teacher partner in the United States, and questions whether such acceptance is possible in an ex-

White school in South Africa. His imagination for such possibilities is enthusiastic, but he tempers it with a seriousness that concerns all teachers. How would it be possible to be accepted and teach history in a White school? Lucky speaks again:

> [B]ut the problem is the stereotypes are still there. So there is a bridge to cross. I mean how can I go to [an ex-White school]? .... I am confident of myself, I can teach those [White] kids. I can teach them I am sure of that. But the problem is that the question of acceptance. The school that I am coming from, the results you see .... here [in the United States] I felt at home—we were accepted to Whites. Because at home I am only accepted to my people with my racial identity you see. So, that's my problem.

The concern for acceptance as professionals across schools is a shared problem since racist stereotypical attitudes are steeped in apartheid traditions of racial discrimination based on superiority and privilege. Similar to Ramphele's (1999) finding that the exclusionary practices and standards in South Africa's higher education are embedded in racism and prejudice, the teachers find the same happening in the K-12 educational setting. The continued exclusion of Black teachers from White schools and from higher administrative positions in Black schools echoes Ramphele's statement that the presence of Blacks in education is often assumed by many Whites as "testimony that standards of performance has fallen" (p. 151). Such racist notions, she explains, uses "standards as metaphors for exclusivity" (ibid.). Lucky's doubt of acceptance in and exclusion from such environments points to the continued colonial mentality that pervades South African education (Kunnie, 2000).

While Lucky articulates the embedded racism in education, he is also cognizant of the power and promise of time. I juxtapose Lucky's dialogues to establish the temporal complexities that teachers engage in and to disrupt any notion of a homogenous resistance or patronage of the new educational dispensations. He employs the metaphor of poison and disease to articulate the problem of attitudinal change in relation to educational and societal change. His metaphor puts into perspective the intensity and depth of apartheid's legacy and its offshoots, including racism, indoctrination, skepticism, and suspicion.

> But people especially must change—the attitudes of the teachers—because like say you give a person fifty grams of the poison and but the remedy is about five grams you see .... we have been eating apartheid for a long period .... using Bantu education for a long period. But with a short period it is not for us to vomit what has

been eaten so far. So it should be a process and a need for special people, special remedy, that will deal exactly with the disease of this attitude because it is a disease—we need to work on it.

Lucky contends that resistance is expected from the colonized and colonizer. Yet, how can we expect radical attitudinal change in a short time span? His metaphor speaks to the need for continuous engagement, including opportunities for dialogue among teachers, administrators, and others involved in the educational system. Such forums will provide spaces to engage critical educational issues that are currently rare across racial groups.

Lucky also calls for patience for teachers' negative attitudes toward curriculum change. He argues that teachers cannot be expected to be bulimic, vomiting all of apartheid's indoctrination, and that the history behind negative attitudes and practices needs to be addressed first. He suggests that a rethinking of the curriculum process has to take place at the grassroots level and calls for special "remedies." This is a provocative call, to be taken with serious consideration, if educational intervention in social reconstruction is to be successful. The teachers unanimously agree that patience is needed, but are troubled by the urgency to address issues now. They are acutely aware that time is not on the side of those who continue to be oppressed and marginalized within the post-apartheid state.

The teachers acknowledge that inadequate teacher training and buy-in to the reform process can be detrimental to the success of C2005. Despite their ambivalences it is clear that they are committed to ensuring the success of C2005. In Sabs' words, "As teachers we've got both a political and a moral duty to ensure—in fact more than that, even a professional duty to ensure—that C2005 succeeds because this is something coming about with changes in the education system, changes which are going to be useful, especially to us formerly oppressed people." The hope that he articulates for C2005 and the oppressed in South Africa echoes the optimism that the government has for its political power to equalize educational experiences. However, such optimism does not come with naïve pollyannaism and blind loyalty to the democratic governmental structure.

The teachers are critical of the government's role or lack thereof in placing structures that will ensure the success of C2005, particularly in formerly disenfranchised Black schools. They insist that their commitment as professionals cannot ensure success. They reference their marginalized settings not as total roadblocks but as persistent obstacles to the process of change for their students, the community, and themselves. They want to see the government play a more involved role, rather than simply mandating a curriculum and providing sparse training. Layla states that OBE cannot be successful in their schools compared to the formerly White schools because those schools "have smaller classes, more resources .... If we had those kinds of facilities, those smaller classes, we could also do these things." The reference to facilities and other resources is a signal to structural and financial privileges that former White schools enjoyed from the apartheid government and continue to enjoy, thereby enabling themselves to be better prepared and organized to implement the new curriculum. Teachers argue that C2005 favors those schools and widens, rather than eliminates, the privilege gap in the post-apartheid era. They question the integrity of the government in mandating such a curriculum without providing the support needed by marginalized school environments.

The teachers display enigmatic struggles of demonstrating support for a government that everyone wants to believe has the power to change so that the previously oppressed have hope for a better life. At the same time they do not want to become passive recipients of a system that in practice and at the grassroots level is not working for the learners and communities it intends to uplift. The complexity and entanglement of these issues are not lost on the teachers. As their narratives and vignettes reveal, there are no simple answers and solutions. The teachers argue that self-critique and reflection as well as appropriate accountability and responsibility from the various players within the educational environment are urgently needed. The five teachers are not afraid to critique their own complicities and are also prepared to enact their responsibility to educational change.

Un/settling C2005's Ideological Promises

The teachers' marginalized educational environments have become the "ethno-scapes" (Appadurai, 1991) from which they theorize a transformative national educational agenda and raise questions about the interconnectedness of ideology, instruction, and curriculum. Building on Appadurai's neologism, I indicate the "dilemmas of perspective and representation" through the narratives of Black educators. Their words unveil the teachers' complexities, convictions, and ambivalences to the (im)possibilities of teaching and learning as an empowering vehicle for social change in South Africa.

The teachers are skeptical about the possibilities of C2005 as "transformative" for themselves and their students. While they utilize the "transformative" rhetoric of C2005, they are ambivalent about its ideological translation in the lives of their educational communities. Their narratives raise the same query posed by Abdi (2002) on whether political change in South Africa will translate into a different country educationally, socially, and economically. While Abdi acknowledges that this may be unattainable in such a short time span, he states that "even the changing of the constitution, the flag, and national anthem, as symbolically useful as they are, are not still projects that effect concrete changes in peoples' lives" (pp. 108–109).

The teacher narratives suggest that the end of political apartheid has not birthed the end of educational, economic, or racial apartheid and inequity in South Africa's educational environments. What does this indicate for the counterhegemonic promise of C2005? One could conjecture that, if apartheid era discriminations continue to take place, the fissures in the already vulnerable curriculum are likely to rupture into dissent and resistance, not unlike what took place during apartheid. Sab's hope for the role of education in healing apartheid wounds and its promise in C2005 could ultimately remain a symbolic utterance for the masses. Thus, C2005's legacy may become an archival document, simply a "peculiar(ly) hypothetical 'performative' utterance," reputed for its inability to "perform the acts it names" (Pechey, 1994, p. 156). More fatally, in the current historical and political moment, the legacy of apartheid remains fairly intact in townships and urban schools, creating in South Africa's second democratic decade a national liberation with local oppression.

Notes

1. I use the term "race" not as an essentialized concept but as a means to illustrate the apartheid ideology and practice that are based on the racial categorizations of White, African, Coloured, and Indian to name and differentiate the citizens of South Africa.

2. The term "Black" has its roots in the Black Consciousness Movement (BCM) of the 1960s in South Africa. It was an inclusive term to refer to Africans, Coloreds, and Indians who were marginalized and struggled under the apartheid regime. The apartheid government appropriated the term in the late 1970s to refer to Africans only. However, the term Black remains an inclusive and collective term for the oppressed and those aligned with the liberation movement.

3. See Hlatshwayo (2000) and Nkabinde (1997) to explore the forms and organization of indigenous education prior to colonization, and of the impact of Western/colonial education on the continuation and survival of indigenous education in South Africa.

4. The word "Bantu" in the Nguni group of languages means people. However, the South African apartheid government usurped and officially used it to refer to the indigenous South African (Nkabinde, 1997). See Hlatshwayo (2000), Kallaway (1986), and Nkabinde (1997) for analyses of the Bantu Education's apartheid and labor ideology.

5. During the Soweto student insurrection in 1976, more than 1,000 Black students were

killed (Kunnie, 2000). The students were protesting against the Bantu education system and the government policy of mandating Afrikaans as a second medium of instruction in Black schools, in addition to English.

6. Ongoing evaluations of C2005 have resulted in the current document referenced as Revised National Curriculum Statement (RNCS) (Department of Education of South Africa, 2001). Central to RNCS is a call for an education for social justice and citizenship that was developed from the vision and values of the constitution and C2005.

References

Abdi, A. (2002). *Culture, education, and development in South Africa: Historical and contemporary perspectives*. Westport, CT: Bergin & Garvey.

Alexander, N. (1990). *Education and the struggle for national liberation in South Africa: Essays and speeches*. Braamfontein: Skotaville, Educational Division.

Appadurai, A. (1991). Global ethnoscapes: Notes and queries for a transnational anthropology. In R. G. Fox (Ed.), *Recapturing anthropology: Working in the present* (pp. 191-210). Santa Fe, NM: School of American Research Press.

Bassey, M. O. (1999). *Western education and political domination in Africa: A study in critical and dialogical pedagogy*. Westport, CT: Bergin & Garvey.

Christie, P., & Gaganakis, M. (1989). Farm schools in South Africa: The face of rural apartheid. *Comparative Education Review, 33*(1), 77-92.

Department of Education of South Africa. (2001). *Revised national curriculum statement grades R-9 (schools)*. Pretoria: Department of Education.

Erickson, F. (1986). Qualitative methods in research on teaching. In M. C. Wittrock (Ed.), *Handbook of research on teaching* (pp. 119-161). New York: Macmillan.

Hlatshwayo, S. A. (2000). *Education and independence: Education in South Africa, 1658-1988*. Westport, CT: Greenwood.

Jansen, J. D. (1990). Curriculum in a post-apartheid dispensation. In N. Nkomo (Ed.), *Pedagogy of domination: Toward a democratic education in South Africa* (pp. 325-339) Trenton, NJ: Africa World Press.

Kallaway, P. (Ed.). (1986). *Apartheid and education: The education of black South Africans*. Johannesburg: Raven.

Kamler, B. (2001). *Relocating the personal: A critical writing pedagogy*. Albany: State University of New York Press.

Kunnie, J. (2000). *Is apartheid really dead?: Pan-Africanist working-class cultural critical perspectives*. Boulder, CO: Westview.

Lather, P. (1992). Postmodernism and the human sciences. In P. Kvale (Ed.), *Psychology and postmodernism* (pp. 88-109). Newbury Park, CA: Sage.

Maylam, P. (2001). *South Africa's racial past: The history and historiography of racism, segregation, and apartheid*. Hampshire, UK: Ashgate.

Mbeki, T. (2002). *Remarks of President Mbeki on the occasion of the state banquet in honour of President Ciampi of Italy, 15 March 2002*. Retrieved November 13, 2008 from http://www.anc.org.za/ancdocs/anctoday/2002/at11.htm

McLaren, P. (Ed.). (2003). *Life in schools: An introduction to critical pedagogy in the foundations of education*. Boston, MA: Pearson.

Mohamed, Y. (1990). The power of consciousness: Black politics 1967-77. In R. Cohen, Y.

Muthien, & A. Zegeye (Eds.), *Repression and resistance: Insider accounts of apartheid. African discourse series, 2* (pp. 250-271). London: Hans Zell.

Motala, E., & Pampallis, J. (Eds.). (2002). *The state, education and equity in post-apartheid South Africa: The impact of state policies.* Aldershot, Hampshire, UK: Ashgate.

Mzamane, M. V. (1990). Towards a pedagogy of liberation: Education for a national culture in South Africa. In M. Nkomo (Ed.), *Pedagogy of domination: Toward a democratic education in South Africa* (pp. 365-382). Trenton, NJ: Africa World Press.

Nkabinde, Z. P. (1997). *An analysis of educational challenges in the new South Africa.* New York: University Press of America.

Pechey, G. (1994). Post-apartheid narratives. In F. Barker, P. Hulme, & M. Iverson (Eds.), *Colonial discourse, postcolonial theory* (pp. 151-171). New York: St. Martin's Press.

Ramphele, M. A. (1999). *Across boundaries: The journey of a South African woman leader.* New York: Feminist Press.

Satyo, S. (1999). Eleven official languages: One plus one equals two. In K. K. Prah (Ed.), *Knowledge in black and white: The impact of apartheid on the production and reproduction of knowledge* (pp. 149-158). Cape Town: Centre for Advanced Studies of African Society.

Simon, R. (1987). Empowerment as a pedagogy of possibility. *Language Arts, 64*(4), 370-381.

Smith, L. T. (1999). *Decolonizing methodologies: Research and indigenous people.* London: Zed.

Subreenduth, S. (2003a). Black teachers (re)negotiation and (re)construction of their pedagogical practice within South Africa's post-apartheid curriculum. Unpublished dissertation, Ohio State University.

Subreenduth, S. (2003b). Using a needle to kill an elephant: The politics of race and education in post-apartheid South Africa. *Inquiry: Critical Thinking Across the Disciplines, 12*(2), 65-74.

Subreenduth, S. (2006). "Why, why are we not allowed even ...?": A de/colonizing narrative of complicity and resistance in post/apartheid South Africa. *International Journal of Qualitative Studies in Education, 19*(5), 617-638.

Wilson, F., & Ramphele, M. A. (1989). *Uprooting poverty: The South African challenge.* New York: W. W. Norton.

PART THREE

CULTURAL STUDIES

CHAPTER 9

The Future in the Present: The Status of Sport and Intellectual Labor in C.L.R. James' *Beyond a Boundary* and His Other Works

CAMERON MCCARTHY

> We live in a world in the throes of a vast reorganization of itself.
> — James, 1980, p. 135

> The Cricket field was a stage on which selected individuals played representative roles which were charged with social significance.
> — James, 1963/1983, p. 72

As a consequence of the new driving logics of globalization and the information age articulated most profoundly in the workings of flexible capitalism, all late-modern institutions and forms of association are coming under the banner of new identities. The dynamics associated with globalization (the rapid and constant dispersal of cultural and economic capital across national boundaries, the intensification and rapidity of movement and migration of people across borders, the amplification of electronic mediation, and the work of the imagination of the people) reveal themselves in what Zygmunt Bauman (2000) and Richard Sennett (1998) describe as a general lightness of being or liquidity of social relations and social arrangements of late-modernity. These developments are critical to the way in which sport and intellectual labor are being transformed in our time. Although, as I will show via the example of cricket, C.L.R. James's postcolonial theorizing is overtaken by such events, his writings provide an important nexus. James effectively brought together in his *Beyond a Boundary* (1963/1983) the twin concerns of intellectual endeavor and sport, the everyday ritual of exertion and exercise of the body with the ivory tower and canonical practice of abstract thought. He did so in a seamless manner that is exemplary and instructive for the contemporary observer reflecting on these two spuriously, but often, rigidly separated domains.

The examination of the relationship of sport to the ordeal of intellectual labor and the fortunes of modern oppressed people has not been systematically pursued in contemporary scholarship, even in cultural studies. Indeed, there is a tendency to separate intellectual practice from labor entirely (Cantor & Schomberg, 2003). This is the ideology that often guides how the academic understands his/her project. A professional distance is established separating the academic from the backbreaking occupation of the lower orders. Sport is pushed to the side as a practice associated with spectacular leisure, surplus, and waste. Intellectuals, even the public intellectuals of our times, are content to occupy the *nom de guerre* of the pedant as opposed to the moudain.[1]

C.L.R. James drew his line in the sand against the pedant. Reading sport as an extension of popular culture and drawing on the reservoir of cultural forms, he recognized a crisis of meaning in contemporary life, a crisis of theodicy that flashed across all cultural work in modern times (James, 1993). James understood it as the central problem of social integration of modern subjects into modern life. In the historical specificity of the center/periphery relationship of England and the British West Indies, this crisis of meaning took on a particular articulation and poignancy, as Caribbean societies were at a point of transformation to self-government and independence from the turn of the twentieth century to the 1960s. James suggested that the tensions of transforming plantation society were articulated in cricket more profoundly than any other Caribbean popular arts. They were articulated within the field of cultural production, as reflected in the relations between and among the institutions of cultural production (schools and cricket clubs), the social position of cultural producers (cricketers), their cultural brokers (club and national selectors), and the markets of symbolic belief (mass audiences in the Caribbean, India, Australia, and England, defined by class, race, locality, region, and nation). He maintained that cricket as a popular art rooted in the Caribbean masses constituted a great window on modern social realities.

James was a man of the world and his scholarship was fashioned from autodidactic training, relentless reading, and a persistent interest in the social and political significance of the quotidian encounters of human actors registered in popular culture. He was the quintessential *moudain* (Bourdieu, 1984), puttering about in the world, tinkering with thought experiments and political action. In his grammar schooling at Queens Royal College in Trinidad, sport was integral to education as part of the fulfillment and rounding out of the cultivated social subject, a colonial version of the cosmopolitan and liberal amateur that was the educational project and desired social outcome of Oxbridge schooling. The British grammar school in the colonies, as Edward Said (2000) points out, was a place of moral incorporation of colonial subjects into empire, a place of letters and preparation for the gentleman orientation to the world of constant cultivation. Cricket, soccer, tennis, and swimming were never simply school games, but points or doorways of conjuncture linking the colony to empire in the preparation and molding of particular types of intellectual mentalities, subjectivities, and initiation into the Enlightenment sensibility of the modern citizen.

But it was precisely on this terrain of cultural reproduction that resistance to colonialism was launched by organic intellectuals whom James identified in his work. Overdetermined along lines of metropole and periphery, sport took on a particular conjunctural significance. Integrated into the organization of the British public school in the colonies, sport was fused to letters in his postcolonial imagination. Reading Thackeray's *Vanity Fair* (1847/1962) and cricket books, writing on "The Novel as an Institution of Reform" and the prowess of Australia's Donald Bradman, W. G. Grace of England, Ranjitsinhji of India, or Learie Constantine of Trinidad, were interrelated activities (James, 1963, p. 27). In these practices, James demonstrated an acute attention to detail, character, form, technique, and the general vicissitudes and casuistry of human life as part of the elaboration of world forming context, affiliation, and feeling. He was keen to relate "structured, meaningful cultural activities to a given time and place," and "the importance of the handful of individuals who achieve mastery" in their connection to the articulation of needs, aspiration, desires, and interpretations of mass audiences (Smith, 2006, p. 47). An example of this is his assessment of the English all-rounder Frank Wooley: "[Wooley] gave to thousands of his countrymen a conception of the beautiful which artists struggle to capture in paint on canvas.... They recognized in him something beyond the average scorer of runs, some elegance of line and harmony of movement" (James, 1938, p. 17).

In *Beyond a Boundary*, James (1963/1983) offered a contextual and relational examination of sport, an early form of cultural studies methodology in which he deployed demystifying techniques of interpretive theory and contextual analysis. He explored the power relations that informed the social inequality that existed and still exists in the Caribbean. Above all, interested in the postcolonial struggle, he situated sport organically in the evolving social relations of class and race in the Caribbean and in the social integration of modern subjects into modern life. He addressed the problem of theodicy and meaning of sport as a partisan and cosmopolitan set of practices of global significance in which the fate of the working class seemed centrally at stake. Sport provided the basis for James to explore the emergence of the subaltern intellectual types emerging out of the colonial context and to track, map, and check empire as he did throughout his life. The inaugurating site and focus of his analysis, the cricket ground and pitch in Tunapuna, Trinidad, was a source of intellectual alchemy, a kind of working intervention in an inchoate form, a visible laboratory of the world in microcosm.

Sport as Context and Discourse: The Cultural Work of Cricket

I seek to make sense of James' *Beyond a Boundary* as a meditation on the labor of sport, understood as cultural work, and its relation to intellectual labor as a form of meaning production linked especially, in the time that James was writing, to the fortunes of the downtrodden peoples of the Caribbean. I am not interested in sport understood and reduced to game playing, the statistical records and annals of, say, cricket, baseball, basketball, and so on, but with sport as a productive and deployed practice and discourse within an evolving colonial and neocolonial political and moral system. It is in sport that James found models and prototypes of the organic intellectual and the embodiment of the broader struggle for independence in the Caribbean. He also explored the articulation of sport to social stratification and the tissues and sinews of the cultures, values, prejudices, needs, desires, and capacities of the social actors in the emergent postcolonial context. James claimed cricketers were in the intellectual vanguard who were more keenly articulating the aspirations of the Caribbean masses, the struggle for independence, and collective consciousness than the arts of writing, painting, and general scholarly production.

The great value of *Beyond a Boundary*, then, is its presentation of imperialist relationship as a complex tissue of articulations between metropole and colony and its reworking of the center/periphery thesis. Sport was integral to this story as James saw it as organically connected to the weaving, the warp, and the woof of the social fabric of societies that were caught in a grand sweep of change.

Why did sport matter to British public schooling in the Caribbean? Why did sport matter to the emergent middle classes? It mattered as an encoded instrumental and expressive organizing principle of competition. It rearticulated the idea of jousting from aristocratic society to the emphasis on achievement and credentialing of emergent professional middle classes. This is captured, for instance, in grammar school songs throughout the region, such as Combermere in Barbados and its "Lives are in the making here / Mighty undertaking here / We are arming for the fight / Pressing on with all our might," or Queens Royal College of Trinidad with its motto: "Certant Omnes Sed Non Omnibus Palma" (All strive but the prize is not for all), or Lodge School of Barbados and its unofficial school song, "We are fighting back." The pattern variable of achievement displaced ascription in the articulation of bourgeois interest and ethic. But this was never a clean break. In the Caribbean, the struggle was long delayed and belatedly enjoined.

The principle of sporting competition was central to the organization of knowledge in the grammar school. It was aligned with and encoded into a meritocratic ideology that rested on individual ability and effort, and explained the enormous socioeconomic gaps that existed between and among the classes by implied or direct references to differences in capacity, competence, and effort as opposed to birthright and ascription. To attend the West Indian grammar school (a colonial bequeath and facsimile of the British public school), you had to, and you still have to, test in. The "proof of the pudding" (James, 1963, p. 217) was in legitimation processes to be demonstrated by the Caribbean working classes. Indeed, it was not uncommon for working-class families of my generation to have a child in the public grammar school and one or several others in the comprehensive, more vocational schools. The children were dressed differently for the different types of schools in accordance with their different social status. The children of the working-class family going to the grammar school wore uniforms that were neat and tidy, while their counterparts, sometimes in the same family, who attended the more vocational school were less well-dressed, less neat, less tidy. Parents would rationalize the difference in treatment by referring to the differences in the ability of their children and, in so doing, rationalize the system of unequal educational provision in the islands. The grammar school examination that James passed was proof that the working-class or lower middle-class child had opportunity to seize if he or she had the ability or competence.

James counterposed movement against stasis in the portrayal of the early modern Caribbean people. He showed the dwellers of the islands moving within a constricted field of options within the region, to the metropole, and back again to the periphery, seeking to improve their educational or economic options in "the great struggle for happiness." These societies were also moving and changing between the early 1900s and 1960s, as reflected in the efforts of a new black and brown political leadership, rising on the crest of working-class protests and demands for change, and their push for West Indian self-government. Indeed, in 1932 when James went to England on the invitation of Learie Constantine, the famous Trinidad and West Indies all rounder and the first black cricketing star, he was on board a ship that took cooks, maids, and transportation workers to England. In writing about cricket, James used it as a barometer to check the pulse of society as a whole.

In cricket, the nationalist character of the emerging peoples of the British West Indies was being asserted as ebullient, contradictory, and determined. Each cricketer discussed by James represented a type of everyman, a figure of cricket and a social character defined by and defining the political culture evolving in the Caribbean. It is to be noted that the movement of Caribbean bodies, ideas, and so forth within the Black diaspora is not well documented in the social science literature, Gilroy's *The Black Atlantic* (1993) aside. But even Gilroy decenters the Caribbean in the story of the movement of Black bodies and ideas in the triangular nexus of England, the United States, and the Caribbean. A better recording of this movement is to be found in postcolonial literature. In Mittleholzer's *Corentyne Thunder* (1970), Geoffrey experiences the voyage out in his exile to England and the voyage in, in his return to Guyana as disorientation and instability. African American activists and artists like Michelle Gibbs and Howard Fuller worked in Grenada during its Revolution of 1979-1983. And Langston Hughes operated between Cuba, Haiti, and New York in an earlier period. In part, this chapter contributes to the location of the Caribbean within the Black diaspora as a site of its own orchestrations and energies.

To properly examine C.L.R. James' *Beyond a Boundary* and its implications for sports, we must begin to put the novel in context and read it in relation to his entire oeuvre and his central project of foregrounding the intellectual's relationship to the working class and identifying particular types of intellectual consciousness as they are articulated to movement and change. I draw on the work of White (1973), particularly his concept of emplotment, to better understand and assess the intellectual types that appear in James' books, such as *Beyond a Boundary* (1963), *The Black Jacobins* (1938/2001), *Mariners, Renegades and Castaways* (1978), and *American Civilization* (1993). White (1973) defines emplotment as the form of explanation in which "the 'meaning' of a [his]story" is derived from the "kind of story [romantic, comic, tragic, satiric] that has been told" by a chronicler (p. 7). The historian classifies and orders past structures and processes to explain what they mean. In this sense, the historian both records and makes history. It also means that the historical text is not so much a social science document, but as a poetic act and process and therefore subject to textual analysis.

James' mode of organization of the story of the intellectual-mass relationship is largely romantic-epic or heroic in the sense that human actors are shown to overcome the contradictions of world experience and almost impossible forms of material constraint. But there are elements of tragedy and irony in the intellectual's relationship to the masses, for example, in James' story of Toussaint L'Ouverture and the Haitian Revolution. I call attention to the significance of emplotment in James' work because of what I see as his investment in the ennoblement of the working class and his tendency to connect the working-class subjectivity to grand narratives and movement in history. In this sense, his work is connected to the philosophy of consciousness tradition and anticipates the Marxist humanism illustrated in Thompson's *The Making of the English Working Class* (1964), Williams' *The Long Revolution* (1961), and Hall's "Cultural Identity and Cinematic Representation" (1996). Marx and Hegel (1973) are very important to him. Intellectual work is registered neither in the professional pedant operating in the ivory tower nor in the dumb and mute forces of economic production working themselves out in the dialectic of structure versus superstructure, but in the expressive orders and mobilized capacities of working-class subjectivities pushing back on the circumstances that constrain them.

Circumstances are not simply given, but are produced in human struggle and work. I believe James' emplotment of intellectual types in *The Black Jacobins*, *Mariners, Renegades and Castaways*, and *American Civilization*, books that offer an epical and heroic sense of subaltern struggle against impossible odds, derived from James' intellectual apprehension of the thorough integration of sport into the formal grammar school experience and the cultural work it is asked to perform. The organization of the grammar school into the competitive houses referenced in the Harry Potter books of J. K. Rowling is an illustration of the structural integration of sporting as a tool for the organization of knowledge and pedagogy. Sport was part of the traditional liberal arts notion of the healthy body, mind, and disposition. The mind or brain in cognitive psychology, "faculty method," and curriculum theory during the late nineteenth century and early twentieth century was understood as muscle-like which needed to be exercised through competitive actions and tasks (Kliebard, 1995). The body was not to be neglected since it had its own needs for expenditure, optimization, and aesthetic motion that, when fully deployed, allowed the individual to achieve intense states of elemental purity, collective association, affiliation, and feeling. The body was the handiwork of god and empire, a vessel in and through which the moral compass of honesty and fair play helped to make school children into colonial elite adults. Sport played a major role in the nexus of health, hygiene, and modernization under imperialist trusteeship. If the body could be linked to the mind in an imperialist project of domination, the body and its deployment in sport also could be associated with counter-hegemony.

It is through the articulation of culture, education, and sport in the colonial context that James saw the West Indian cricketers as intellectual actors organically linked to the masses and as representatives of the craving for change and decolonization in the Caribbean. He identified three types of intellectuals. First, there was the *organic intellectual* as embodied in trailblazing Afro-Caribbean cricketers like Clyde Walcott, Everton Weeks, and Frank Worrell (the famous "3 W's"), and Learie Constantine. Later Vivian Richards embodied forms of leadership that echoed the great organic leaders of revolutionary struggle such as Toussaint L'Ouverture, leader of the Haitian Revolution, discussed in *Black Jacobins* (James, 1938/2001), or Captain Arthur Cipriani, the white creole leader of the Trinidad labor movement discussed in *Case for West Indies Self Government* (James, 1933). The organic intellectual type is represented in the fictional world (which James saw as a social extension of reality) as echoed in the workers below the deck of Herman Melville's Pequod of *Moby Dick* (1851/1967), discussed in *Mariners, Renegades and Castaways* (James, 1978). Arrayed together, their sense of collectivity is expressed as physical and sensuous forces acting back upon the material world.

The second type of intellectual was the product of the over-rationalization of modern society. He was an organization man full of resentment who directed change towards the maintenance of authoritarianism. This was the *resentment intellectual* in the characters of comic strips, crime detective novels, motion pictures, and radio soap operas that James (1993) identified in *American Civilization*. They were present in cricket, the planter-mercantile elite that controlled the West Indies Cricket Board, and the colonial legislatures that held the fate of the black and brown cricketers in their hands. They were present in the Marlebourne Cricket Club and the British colonial administrators for whom a black captain of a cricket team was, as late as 1960, still a matter to be deferred.

The third intellectual type was the *relational or contextual intellectual* who, like James himself, moved within and beyond cricket and across different terrain like England, the United States, Africa, and Mexico. This type changed context and operated relationally. This type of intellectual was found in cricketers like Learie Constantine who took a particular brand of politics to England by attempting to achieve direct intervention in the colony and the metropole. In 1943, Constantine was refused service in a British hotel because of his color. He took the owners of the hotel to court and won his case. Later, he wrote *Colour Bar* (Constantine, 1954), with his friend C.L.R. James, which dealt with racial prejudice in Britain.

Intellectual Exemplars

Organic Intellectual

The organic or subaltern intellectual can be found in James' portrayal of historical figures like Toussaint L'Ouverture in *The Black Jacobins* (James, 1938/2001), or in the polyglot, racially diverse crew of the Pequod in Herman Melville's *Moby Dick* (1851/1967). These intellectual types emerge directly from the masses and seem inextricably bound to their fate. They rise and fall as they express a sense of community and operate within the transformation of the fetters of society that constrain a group's will to power and desire for the good life. For this model, Toussaint L'Ouverture is the preeminent example. Challenging any easy or presumed a priori relationship between the charismatic leader and the people, James critiques this model as retaining elements of vanguardism or "Messiahanism" (Singham, 1968). In Toussaint, James shows the complexity of the organic intellectual and the tensions between the will and expectations of the masses and revolutionary intellectual leadership. Toussaint's revolutionary struggle was launched in Haiti in part as a consequence of his revisionary application of the French texts of Voltaire, Rousseau, and Robespierre, and the watchwords of the French Revolution, "Liberté, Egalité, Fraternité." But L'Ouverture established a new constitution for San Domingo and himself as ruler for life. L'Ouverture eventually grew distant from the people, was lured onto a French ship for negotiations with Napoleon's brother, LeClerc, and was captured and shipped to France where he was imprisoned at Fort de Joux in the Jura Mountains where he died in 1802.

In *Beyond a Boundary*, James (1963/1983) identifies star cricketers such as Learie Constantine, George Headley, Gary Sobers, Frank Worrell, and Rohan Khanai both as sportsmen of the highest caliber and as intellectual leaders of the grandest political idea of the West Indian nation. He argues that cricket represents the first distinctive cultural institution to be elaborated indigenously in the region. By excelling at the English game, the sportsmen destroyed antediluvian supremacist beliefs that, for example, greeted the West Indies team on their first tour to England in 1896 when the black players (only 5 out of a team of 15) were portrayed in some British papers as naked coons who lacked the cultural sophistication for the game. (Here, the coon stereotype, associated with white peasantry of the U.S. South before it was attached to Black people [Roediger, 1991], slid across the Atlantic to England.) The white elite in the Caribbean saw the game as an extension of their cultural heritage. The rise out of the colonial paradigm in cricket parallels the rise out of the nineteenth-century novel genre and the birthing of West Indian literature. C.L.R. James is linked to both the decolonization of sport and the emergence of a decolonizing literature that focuses attention on the agroproletarian realities of the Caribbean rather than the foibles of the English Royal Court or the self-satisfied middle class of Jane Austen's *Emma* (1998). Even as he was contracted to write a cricket column for the *Guardian* newspaper in Lancashire, England in 1932, James was putting the finishing touches on *The Case for West Indies Self Government* (1933) and *Minty Alley* (1933/1993), the first Caribbean novel published in England. After its publication and during the second rising of the nationalist paradigm in cricket, there was a formidable rise of West Indian writers, such as George Lamming (*In the Castle of My Skin* [1953/1997] and *Water with Berries* [1971]), V. S. Naipaul (*Mimic Men* [1969], *A House for Mr. Biswas* [1961], and *Miguel Street* [1959/1971]), Wilson Harris (*Palace of the Peacock* [1960], *Companions of the Night and Day* [1975], and *Carnival* [1985]), Edward Mittleholzer (*A Morning at the Office* [1964] and *Corentyne Thunder* [1970]), and Roger Mais (*The Hills Were Joyful Together* [1978]), who were engaged in the reinvention of the British nineteenth-century novel. Interestingly, there are few direct allusions to this literary ferment in *Beyond a Boundary*.

It is clear that the fields of cultural production are co-articulated. Cricket was endogenously rooted in the masses as a site of opportunity for young, working-class, West Indian men. Working-class men had few other choices in a highly stratified colonial social formation. Going into a trade or to the sea (both Frank Worrell's and Gary Sobers' fathers were seamen) or joining the secondary labor market in England or the United States were more likely occupational opportunities than professionalization through higher education, since access to this avenue of social uplift was impeded by the colonial model of white supremacy and the brutal color and class stratification in the islands. After emancipation, the British colonial government signed a Faustian pact with the West Indian planter-mercantile class that undermined educational access and committed many black working-class youth to the secondary labor market.

Cricket occupied a powerful imaginary universe in which epic struggles would be played out. In the emergent West Indian literature, writers such as Lamming sought to express the philosophical disposition and historical currents that drove the masses. The protagonist "G" in the *Castle of My Skin*

(Lamming, 1953/1987) goes to New York as a stevedore, joins Marcus Garvey's United Negro Improvement Association movement, and returns to launch a struggle for labor unions in Barbados. Labor unions were the incubator for political protest and political party formation that articulated the interests of black working and emergent middle classes. Cricket therefore was participating in a wider political culture, tapping the energies of the Caribbean black and brown masses yearning for unrestricted access to the public sphere. Yet this access was limited. The sponsorship approaches to education for the masses cut a thin social swath, carving out a talented tenth for eventual tertiary education. An even smaller elite segment at the top of the structure would be educated in the citadels of Oxford and Cambridge.

What is remarkable about the story of West Indian cricket as seen through James is that, the West Indies—a scattered set of tiny islands divided from each other by geography, history, and psyche, and by lines drawn as far back as the Navigation Acts of 1651 that regulated trade within a hermetically sealed dyadic relationship between the metropole and each individual colony, rendering them a squabbling pecking order—would produce a material sense of a pan-Caribbean nation in cricket and reach world supremacy in that sport from 1962 to 1970 and from the mid-1970s to 1994, a few years after James died and *American Civilization* (James, 1993) was published posthumously.

This was achieved on incredibly slender and unstable resources for the economic commitment of the planter-mercantile elite and West Indian colonial governments was paltry. Cricket declined as an invested interest of white West Indian elites as the sport became dominated by the black working class. Consequently the world superstar cricketers from the West Indies such as Gary Sobers were paid less than the most inferior cricketers on the Australian and English teams. The idea of productive and constructionist nationalism and its dynamic fuel for West Indian cricket, therefore, rested on the psychic force and the grounded anticolonial mentalities of the players themselves. The sense of pan-Caribbean nation did not and does not exist with vitality anywhere else in West Indian institutions of culture, politics, or economics. Indeed, the colonial bequeath of subnationalism has produced the most vigorous pecking order in the islands. In contemporary times, with the impact of globalization on sports, West Indian cricket has suffered something of diremption or breaking up of the national paradigm.

The context of anticolonial struggle that West Indian cricket and cricketers articulated during the period assessed by James is a broad context of struggle in which what Homi Bhabha (in James, 1993) describes as the "magic arts of interpretation" are in play in the African diaspora and throughout the third world. In the decolonizing period of West Indian cricket, other powerful anticolonial movements were feeding into the Caribbean imaginary. The civil rights movement worked as a material and symbolic generator of subjugated knowledge and resistance. So were the struggles for independence in Africa and Asia. The emergence of socialism within the region that began with Guyana in the early 1950s and Cuba at the end of that decade was a significant backdrop. It was a period marked by dense popular works, such as "James Brown Live at the Apollo, October 1962," "Miles Davis Live at the Plugged Nickel," Ornette Coleman's launch of free jazz and harmolodics in *The Shape of Jazz to Come* (1959), Max Roach and Abbey Lincoln's *We Insist! Freedom Now Suite* (1960), LeRoi Jones/Amiri Baraka's *The Blues People* (1963) and *Dutchman and the Slave* (1964), and Dennis Scott's *Echo in the Bone* (1969). It was the period of burn baby burn, black exploitation films, rising independence movements in Ghana and Tanzania in Africa, and Jamaica, Trinidad, and Barbados in the Caribbean. These developments fed back into the Caribbean scene (Beckles, 1998; Manley, 1988). They fed into Afro-Indian alliance for the West Indian cricket nation that broke free but also pasted over the contradictions of subnationalisms visceral in the Caribbean.

Resentment Intellectual

The context of the organic intellectual leading struggle for change has to be qualified. Nationalism in the Caribbean, sporting nationalism, operated on a slender material base and in a hostile theater of local and imperialist white supremacy. It meant cricket in the Caribbean would have to turn its back on its colonial past as a white-dominated sport. The sport broke free from the white elite stranglehold at the price of chronic underfunding. A further issue that helps to delimit the field of production of the cricket intellectual is the resentment factors built into modern life in the Caribbean and elsewhere. The resentment is driven by a worldview produced from the great struggle for theodicy in the churning industrial momentum of capitalism. Modern life produces alienation and the problem of social integration of subjects into modern institutions.

Counterposed to the figure of the organic intellectual is the authoritarian or resentment type intellectual. The latter, as Paulo Freire (1970) warns in the *Pedagogy of the Oppressed*, are the vanguardists who lead by commands, edicts, and pronouncements without consultation with the will of the popular, and who cut themselves off from the humanizing processes associated with the masses. In the most extreme form, they are what Friedrich Nietzsche (1996) in

Genealogy of Morals calls the resentment type. The resentment intellectuals define their identity through the negation of the other. They exist in real or imaginary exile from society's working poor, and are driven by a dangerously narrow-minded program of retributive morality. We live in the ascendancy of this type of intellectual in Washington, D.C. But the most vivid embodiment of the totalitarian intellectual is the white professional middle-class suburban resident who rails against the government and against paying taxes and welfare programs for the poor, and who is hopelessly addicted to the idea of security systems and prison expansion. James points to the resentment intellectual type in the paranoid detective Sam Spade, played by Humphrey Bogart in the 1941 film version of *The Maltese Falcon*, and in Captain Ahab in Herman Melville's *Moby Dick* (1851/1967). In the Caribbean, the figure is articulated in the persistence of imperialist imperatives that serve to check anticolonial initiatives. The U.S. naval bases in Trinidad and Barbados are supreme examples of this. Contracted by the British colonial authorities and the United States in the 1940s without the input of Caribbean people, the bases operated as states within states with U.S. naval personnel possessing de facto authority to interdict locals while being immune from the local legal system. The bases parallel the emergence of West Indian cricket and reinforce the stifling conditions of the colonial paradigm and local white supremacy mythology. The dual imperialist project is marked by a racialization that is structurally integrated into the social order and manifests in the organization of cricket.

James called attention to the operation of race in the organization of cricket in Trinidad into tier one, tier two, and tier three clubs. At the zenith of the color/class system was the all-white Queens Park and Shamrock clubs. At the nadir were the all-black Stingo (the club of "The plebeians: the butcher, the tailor, the candle stick maker, the casual laborer, with a sprinkling of the unemployed," as James [1963/1983, p. 56] called them, of "no social status whatsoever") and Shannon, a club that served as a staging ground for black talent and aspiration. In the middle was the Maple Club for light skin or brown people. Similar markings divided the Caribbean educational provision into the hierarchy of A, B, and C schools (Williams, 1994). The elite resentment gaze on popular culture was articulated as well in the legal and juridical attack on popular expression in carnival, calypso, and the hostile lines of demarcation drawn in schooling against Caribbean cultural form, history, and letters. Right up until the late 1980s and into the 1990s, Caribbean school youth read the letters of Europe and the United States while being ignorant of the writings of James, Lamming, and Naipaul, alumni of the most illustrious schools of the region. The nationalist rising in cricket occurred within a cultural field of hostility to indigenous cultural form and white domination of the structure and determinations of the sport.

Contextual Intellectual

The third type of intellectual presented in *Beyond a Boundary* seems to work past the impacted localism and nationalism of the first two types. This figure is a cosmopolitan and anticipates the future of the Caribbean that is linked to the rest of the world. Along this framework, West Indian cricketers were integrated into a complex web of relations that exceeded the Caribbean, which involved travel to England, India, Australia, Pakistan, Africa, and within the Caribbean. As James (1963/1983) puts it,

> Time would pass, old empires would fall and new ones take their place, the relations of countries and the relations of classes had to change, before I discovered that it is not quality of goods and utility which matter, but movement; not where you are or what you have, but where you have come from, where you are going and the rate at which you are getting there. (pp. 116-117)

Cricketing life played out at the highest level involved movement and migration as part of the labor process. The contextual intellectual can be linked to literature and to James' work. This third figure, the relational or contextual intellectual, is what Henry Louis Gates (1988) describes as a revisionary actor, committed to rewriting the master narratives of domination. The figure is, in part, foregrounded in James himself, autobiographically disclosed in *Beyond a Boundary*, his most theoretically and methodologically integrated manuscript.

The struggle is to link the personal to the popular, the agonistic private to the turbulent public, the high to the low. To do this, the contextual intellectuals must work across the roadblocks and separations that capitalism and imperialism have fabricated to divide and conquer the masses and subaltern groups embattled in the project of change. They are versed in the magic arts of interpretation, and their special prerogative is a deconstructive assault on the taken-for-granted and naturalized terrain of the West. The tools of the master will be used against his own house, a position that Audre Lorde (1982) advances in *Zami: A New Spelling of My Name*. In Derek Walcott's play *Ti-Jean and His Brothers* (1999), the peasant woodcutter Ti-Jean brings down the planter-devil by building alliances with the rejected animals of the forests. He organizes across and beyond his class location and species. Together they burn down the plantations and humiliate the planter class. Without alliance across difference, the planter can continue to exploit the peasants and treat them as beasts of burden.

In *Beyond a Boundary*, James struggles with the class and color divides that reveal themselves in the British public school educational system and in the legacies of cricket operating in Trinidadian society in the early part of the twentieth century. It is precisely these divides that inform the production of the postcolonial intellect. Within the very heart of French and English literature, James would launch a revisionary strike for the case of West Indian equality and self-government. He would graft claims for political autonomy to the quest for a West Indian cultural autonomy founded in the popular arts of the masses and in the critical interpretation of the contradictory themes and nuances within Western cultural forms. Moreover, James insists that the contextual intellectuals must be ceaselessly vigilant about the excesses and pitfalls of nationalism and must be willing to engage in self-criticism. They must be open to suggestion, open to the voices of the masses, and open to the historical variability and nuance of the struggle of the masses for a better life.

West Indian cricketers operated within the national paradigm and within the international framework of the British Commonwealth, propagating and proclaiming the game and its values around the world. For example, Trinidadian Learie Constantine (1902-1971) established himself as the first "superstar" of Caribbean cricket on tour in England with the West Indies in 1928. Employed as a professional by the Nelson club in the Lancashire League, he drew huge crowds from 1929 to 1937, and through his insistence and demands he was one of the highest paid cricketers in the world at the time. This ran against the grain of the experience of his colleagues who were poorly paid. According to James, Constantine would probably have stayed in Trinidad if, at the beginning of his career, he could have found a decent job or realized his desires to be a solicitor there. During the Second World War, Constantine worked for the British government in the Ministry of Labor ministering to West Indian workers as they struggled to find employment and decent working conditions in the British labor market. He later moved to London, where he worked as a highly successful broadcaster and qualified as a barrister at the age of 52. He returned to Trinidad in the 1950s. But after serving as chair of Eric Williams' People's National Movement and as a minister in Williams' first two administrations, Constantine resigned due to a falling out with Williams. Constantine would leave the country, representing Trinidad as High Commissioner to London. He was elevated to the House of Lords with the title Baron Constantine of Nelson and Maraval, expressing a dual identity as Trinidadian and Black Briton.

It could be argued, drawing on James, that Constantine was by philosophical disposition a Black nationalist and pan-Africanist who paradoxically was embraced by white Briton because of his prowess as one of the greatest cricketers of his time. He was an example of the reach of sportsmen across provincial distinctions and locations. Constantine was therefore at the shifting site of the time/space compression and distanciation that defined the contextual intellectual life of the West Indian cricketer. He dwelled in the two worlds of home and exile. In life and cricket, he was a cultural and political actor, a cricketer and a writing intellectual who sought to confront hegemonic white supremacy even as he entertained mainly white spectators around the world.

Another illustration of the complex role and location of West Indian cricketers during the period of nationalist rising identified by James is Frank Worrell. Born in Barbados, he took up citizenship in Jamaica in his youth after his parents migrated to New York. He would eventually become a member of the Jamaican Senate. Underscoring their appreciation for the high level of cricket and sportsmanship that Worrell's West Indies team evinced in a 1960–1961 test tour, thousands of Australians poured out onto the streets in Melbourne to say goodbye to his team. Worrell was the first nonwhite West Indian to captain the West Indies cricket team for an entire test series. He was so internationally revered for his leadership qualities that, when he died of leukemia in 1967 at the age of 42, a funeral service was held for him at Westminster Abbey in England (*Barbados Nation Newspaper*, 2007). He was the first ever sportsman to be accorded such a tribute.

The significance of the Constantine and Worrell examples and the knighting of West Indian cricketers like Gary Sobers speak to the contradictory facts of the cultural practice of cricket and the multivariate function of cricketers in the center/periphery arrangements. Within James' tripartite framework, cricketers fell in more than one organizing discourse. They were organic intellectuals committed to modeling a kind of pan-West Indian nationalism as well as subnationalists working to hold the banner up for their individual islands in interisland and intercolonial cricket. They also were contextual intellectuals working as cosmopolitans though always operating within the delimiting frame of the British Commonwealth, even as the sun had set on the dream and grandeur of the British Empire.

Conclusion

James' analysis of cricket as a social extension of an emergent West Indies transitioning out of colonialism is a study in a long durée. Slender economic resources, small size, high density of population, the enormous shadow of

United States, the very active and powerful presence of its media, and a less resonant but persisting British imperialism are political, economic, and cultural relationships that set structural terms against which contemporary Caribbean societies must navigate. In *Beyond a Boundary*, James attempts to understand these dynamics by carefully studying the cricket social context and cricket players who, operating within the field of cultural production and the sport's labor process, formed an intellectual cadre that articulated a new nationalist imaginary. The national imaginary proved to be an expansive, pan-Caribbeanist, and Afro-Indian alliance against white supremacy and British imperialism. The emergence of an organic intellectual type committed to anticolonial struggle, as James points out, always operated in an adversarial context, a context informed by resentment logics that were both system based and cultivated by intellectual types, such as the supremacist imperialist defenders Trollope, Carlyle, and Froude, members of the colonial bureaucracy, and local white elites who drew lines of distinction between black and white people.

In colonial societies where white elites emulated Europe, indigenous cultural forms, including carnival, calypso, letters, theater, painting, and sport, suffered a hostile gestation. Impoverished and neglected, the cultural arts suffered vicious local hostility. Cricket first emerged as the cultural capital of the white West Indian elite and later as a reluctantly transferred beneficence or patrimony of the black and brown lower orders and from which, given the overdetermined nature of uneven development in the islands, one could fashion a future if he were lucky to make it to the West Indies cricket team. It was upon this tiny fracture in the firmament of British colonialism and white domination that I would argue a full inter-island nexus of aspirations for change became focused. Cricket became a social extension of the reality of people who were denied too long a secure space in the public sphere. Cricket was what "they knew, who only cricket knew" (James, 1963/1983, p. xix). It became, according to historian Hilary Beckles (2003), a mass sport in the Caribbean before the masses had the right to vote, before free secondary schooling for the working people, before socialized health care, and so forth. Through its black and brown players, cricket also was a site of theodicy linked to nationalism and anticolonialism. Cricketers concentrated their extraordinarily keen antisupremacist and anticolonial energies at a time when other indigenizing cultural institutions were not as secure. Players who sought to assert an antisupremacist achievement on the field were precursors of, or operated in tandem with, the rise of indigenous struggle for self-governance and change and the blossoming of indigenous black and brown political leadership in the islands.

The significance of James' analysis in *Beyond a Boundary* is linked to a rising of the nationalist paradigm. Although James was an internationalist and his discussion of the relational or contextual intellectual anticipates and maps a role for the intellectual working across different fields and national boundaries, the limits of *Beyond a Boundary* are the limits of the neo-Marxist paradigm that is, in part, central to James' underlying framework and method of interpretation of cricket and society. His framework, in its operationalization in cultural studies scholarship, has held fast to the nation as the unit of analysis for understanding and intervening in modern human relations. This can be seen in a broader context as an aspect of the limits of modern social science that defines its key operating term "society" as a projection and facsimile of the nation, understood as coterminous with bounded, geographically drawn territory. Within this framework and the intellectual work of cricketers such as Gary Sobers, Frank Worrell, Rohan Khanai, Learie Constantine, and Vivian Richards, the Caribbean was the special case of the not-yet-nation, the nation waiting to be born from the ruins of subnationalisms that colonialism and the Navigational Acts of 1651 had gestated.

However, as cricket in the Caribbean entered the new millennium, formidable currents associated with the movement of cultural and economic capital, the intensification of electronic mediation, the amplification and intensification of the circulation of images—in short, globalization articulated within the vectors of advanced capital—threw out new circumstances onto the terrain of sports, especially cricket. Cricket could not separate itself from a larger dynamic in which the contradictory but real gains of the nationalist paradigm (black and brown leadership in the political structure as well as the nationalization or partial nationalization of key economic sectors, such as the dairy industry, transportation, water, electricity, the health care system, and schooling from primary to tertiary education, were examples of an expanded public sphere under the nationalist paradigm) came under considerable strain (Beckles, 1998). Neoliberal values of the universalization of the enterprise ethic began to take hold in the cultural forms of the islands. Carnival, cricket, the economic forms, the social welfare systems, all began to be turned inside out, deepening the vein of privatization and debilitating the Fabian socialist and Keynesian social welfare pact that had been established between the masses and their political leadership in the middle part of the twentieth century. Even traditional sections of the economy dominated by the planter-mercantile elite, such as the plantation, were being turned inside out for touring, tourism, and the tourist dollar.[2]

With respect to cricket, James' investment and ambivalent relationship to the precapitalist values of the sport and the public school code it ideologically reproduced and buttressed are in the current historical moment shown to be a little old-fashioned. The public school code of shared responsibility, discipline, artistic and aesthetic values and craft, models of thoughtfulness, associative investments, and cultural resistance, has been thrown into disarray in the twenty-first century. The kind of analysis that becomes articulated in James' depiction of organic intellectual types (read isomorphically back into class and race position) now seems to be overtaken by events.

The enticements and blandishments associated with new capital inflows starting in West Indies and world cricket in the late 1970s when Australian entrepreneur Kerry Packer, who set up an almost irreverent brand of cricket (one-day cricket) that, like sports in the United States, placed an emphasis on same-day clarification of winners and losers, would transform the fundamental features of the game that James extolled. Packer's one-day World Series contests were a sign of things to come. His new entrepreneurial codes changed the terms of cricket from the collection code of its feudalist framework to an integrated code in which cricketing structures became more penetrated by commodity values and less tied to the mechanical solidarity and the rituals of collective affiliation. The smashing of the public school code by the one-day cricket paradigm was reflected profoundly and paradoxically in the "look" of the game. The more formal all-white attired model of the game, five-day test cricket, still persisted, but it had to coexist with the more flashy instant result version. Competitors now wear an array of flag-colored uniforms of red and green, blue and red, ultra marine and gold or maroon or whatever. The color schemes seem to mix a light nationalism with fashion and spectacle, and suggest the new lightness of being of cricket. With the advent of one-day cricket, the cricketer has become a performer, a new century medieval troubadour, a professional rooted to region but only in part. His eye is cast upon possibilities of making a professional life unmoored from the responsibilities of nation or the school tie. He has become an entertainer, flashing on the surface of life. Shallow is the new deep for the cricketer. The recently retired Trinidadian superstar Brian Lara was offered £3 million by a batting manufacturer to simply "continue playing cricket" (Beckles, 1998, p. 5). This was more money than the world's greatest cricketer, Gary Sobers, was able to make in his entire cricketing life.

What these developments foreground is the fact that West Indian cricket, managed by the West Indian Cricket Board of Control, exists on incredibly slender resources and lacks the financial backing of the new national governments and the white-dominated merchant class. These are the new terms of twenty-first century cricket and society in the West Indies in which the modern cricketer and the social relations of the production of cricket have been transformed by the commodification of the sport—less as an organic intellectual and more an entertainer. Indeed, Brian Lara asked in his retirement speech that he be remembered for entertaining spectators and giving everyone a good time.

What James would make of this is impossible to say. There seems to be a need, however, to develop a new paradigm of analysis of cricket that addresses the features of globalization as they have impacted the sport and society in the Caribbean. A process that is emptying out the contents and values associated with the game. A process in which self-promotion over one's team, where betting, gambling, and fixing of the sport are not the terms that scandalized the C.L.R. James of *Beyond a Boundary*. In a time of neoliberalization and globalization, cricket is constituted by new symbolic and material developments. Cricket now dwells and cohabits with online gaming, entertainment, intensified electronic mediation, and hypermarketization in an age when the cricketer has become less a citizen and more a vessel for the maximization of consumption. The connections between sport and globalization have intensified in the Caribbean and throughout the world in the new millennium. Indeed, West Indies cricket is caught in powerful forces that it does not control. The forces and operations of neoliberalism or the universalization of the enterprise ethic now command sport. Sport carries forward and serves as the quintessential vehicle of the Horatio Alger myth as a form of disembedding from collectivity. This is a perverse and distorted luminescence, the false clarity of the self-sufficient, individual athlete acting with full interiority upon the world around him. I believe that increasingly the made-for-television, made-for-prime-time quality of media coverage has lifted sporting activities into an other-worldly arena of the spectacle. In this framework, the nation declines as an institutional or organizing principle of major importance.

Notes

1. Bourdieu (1984) conceptualizes the "pedant" and the "moudain" as two different types of intellectual subject. The first one (the pedant) is the doctrinaire academic whose understandings of social life are generated almost exclusively from book knowledge. The moudain by contrast derives his or her knowledge from the world and worldly encounters, and thrives on experience.

2. The hierarchical structure of domination associated with the plantation became

transcoded in the new era as the nostalgia for the way we used to be—a colored museum of black style, music, dance, and food as in "De Plantation: Roots and Rhythms"—a standing variety show for tourists visiting Barbados, which serves up a potpourri of down memory lane acts that are free of the noise of social class hierarchy and white supremacy that might be unpalatable to North American or British tourists. The health care systems in the Caribbean constitute another site that has come under neoliberal logics. What emerged from postwar, anticolonial struggle as a comprehensive, national public health care system with clinics all over the island became, with pressures of NAFTA, the World Bank, and IMF, a denationalized system that accommodated to privatization. This process bifurcated the health care system into public and private. Some of the best personnel, doctors, and nurses moved out into the brave new world of privatized medicine. The public systems of health care are in a state of disinvestment and decline. Middle-class people in the islands can now join Americans in participating in a privatized health care system, choosing one health care plan or another such as Blue Cross Blue Shield.

References

Austen, J. (1819/1998). *Emma*. London: Penguin.
Barbados Nation Newspaper. (2007, March 11). Brief service in Sir Frank's memory. *Barbados Nation Newspaper*, 1.
Bauman, Z. (2000). *Liquid modernity*. Cambridge: Polity.
Beckles, G. (1998). *The development of West Indies cricket: Vol. 2—The age of globalization*. Kingston, Jamaica: University of West Indies Press.
Beckles, G. (2003). *A nation imagined*. Kingston, Jamaica: Ian Randle.
Bourdieu, P. (1984). *Distinction: A social critique of the judgment of taste*. Cambridge, MA: Harvard University Press.
Cantor, N., & Schomberg, S. (2003, March/April). Poised between two worlds: The university as monastery and market place. *Educause*, 38(2), 12–21.
Constantine, L. (1954). *Colour bar*. London: S. Paul.
Freire, P. (1970). *Pedagogy of the oppressed*. New York: Seabury.
Gates, H. L. (1988). *The signifying monkey*. New York: Oxford University Press.
Gilroy, P. (1993). *The black Atlantic*. Cambridge, MA: Harvard University Press.
Hall, S. (1996). Cultural identity and cinematic representation. In H. A. Baker, Jr., M. Diawara, & R. Lindeborg (Eds.), *Black British cultural studies: A reader* (pp. 210–222). Chicago, IL: University of Chicago Press.
Harris, W. (1960). *The palace of the peacock*. London: Faber.
Harris, W. (1975). *Companions of the day and night*. London: Faber.
Harris, W. (1985). *Carnival*. London: Faber.
James, C.L.R. (1933). *Case for West Indies self government*. London: Hogarth.
James, C.L.R. (1933/1993). *Minty alley*. Oxford: Blackwell.
James, C.L.R. (1938/2001). *The black Jacobins: Toussaint L'Ouverture and the San Domingo revolution*. London: Penguin.
James, C.L.R. (1963/1983). *Beyond a boundary*. New York: Pantheon.
James, C.L.R. (1978). *Mariners, renegades and castaways: The story of Herman Melville and the world we live in*. Detroit: Bewick/Ed.
James, C.L.R. (1980). The West Indian middle classes. In *Spheres of existence: Selected writings* (pp.

131-140). London: Allison & Busby.

James, C.L.R. (1992). The revolutionary answer to the negro problem. In A. Grimshaw (Ed.), *The C.L.R. James reader* (pp. 182-189). Oxford: Blackwell.

James, C.L.R. (1993). *American civilization*. Oxford: Blackwell.

Jones, L. (1963). *Blues people: Negro music in white America*. New York: Morrow Quill.

Jones, L. (1964). *Dutchman and the slave*. New York: Harper and Row.

Kliebard, H. (1995). *The struggle for the American curriculum*. New York: Routledge.

Lamming, G. (1953/1987). *In the castle of my skin*. New York: Schocken.

Lamming, G. (1971). *Water with berries*. London: Penguin.

Lorde, A. (1982). *Zami: A new spelling of my name*. Trumansberg, NY: Crossing.

Mais, R. (1978). *The hills were joyful together*. London: Penguin.

Manley, M. (1988). *A history of West Indies cricket*. London: André Deutsch.

Marx, K., & Engels, F. (1973). *The communist manifesto*. London: Penguin.

Melville, H. (1851/1967). *Moby dick or the white whale*. New York: Bantam.

Mittleholzer, E. (1964). *A morning at the office*. London: Penguin.

Mittleholzer, E. (1970). *Corentyne thunder*. London: Heinneman.

Naipaul, V. S. (1961). *A house for Mr. Biswas*. New York: Knopf.

Naipaul, V. S. (1969). *The mimic men*. London: Penguin.

Naipaul, V. S. (1971). *Miguel street*. London: Penguin.

Nietzsche, F. (1996). *The genealogy of morals*. Oxford, UK: Oxford University Press.

Said, E. (2000). *Out of place: A memoir*. New York: Knopf.

Scott, D. (1969). *Echo in the bone*. Unpublished play, University of the West Indies.

Sennett, R. (1998). *The corrosion of character*. New York: Norton.

Singham, A. (1968). *The hero and the crowd*. New Haven, CT: Yale University Press.

Smith, A. (2006). "A conception of the beautiful": C.L.R. James' *Glasgow Herald* cricket articles. *International Journal of the History of Sport, 23*(1), 46-66.

Thackeray, W. M. (1847/1962). *Vanity fair*. London: Penguin.

Thompson, E. P. (1964). *The making of the English working class*. New York: Pantheon.

Walcott, D. (1999). *Ti-Jean and his brothers*. New York: Samuel French.

White, H. (1973). *Metahistory: The historical imagination in nineteenth-century Europe*. Baltimore, MD: Johns Hopkins University Press.

Williams, E. (1994). *Education in the British West Indies*. New York: A & B Distributors.

Williams, R. (1961). *The long revolution*. London: Chatto and Windus.

CHAPTER 10

Multicultural and Creole Contemporaries: Postcolonial Artists and Postcolonial Cities

RINALDO WALCOTT

> A city must remain open to knowing that it does not yet know what it will be.
> — Derrida, 1998, p. 17

> [T]he city increasingly mediates circuits of political engagement and cultural reproduction at a post-national scale of analysis. It is important politically because the city becomes the disruptive force in the reproduction of cultural and political form, the mediating field through which newness comes into the world after the cosmopolitan loses its populist gloss.
> — Keith, 2005, p. 188

September 11, 2001; March 11, 2004; and July 7, 2005, mark significant moments for cities at the beginning of the twenty-first century. The events that made the cities of New York, Madrid, and London leak into each other in ways that would not have been evident before is buttressed by a narrative of fear and terror that has come to dominate numerous city spaces in our new colonial present (Gregory, 2004). More than any human geography, the city has become the dominant site in the Western imagination with its accompanying narratives of threat and fear in the Age of Global Terrorism and virus-fueled pandemics of all kinds, such as HIV/AIDS, SARS, avian flu, and Ebola. The intimacies of city life have always carried a narrative of fear and threat and thus a constant lurking danger or violence. The city also has been a place of possibility, experimentation, and pleasure of anonymity, coupled with the promise of something "to come." The triumph of the Age of Global Terrorism and viral pandemic hysteria is that discourses of the city as a site of danger have become dominant in our times. That danger has become the prevailing metaphor and trope of the city requires that we pay careful attention to how this moment has come to be and how it organizes contemporary forms of human life since most of human life happens in cities.

We must think of the narratives of the city as central to the interventions that Left or progressive scholars working in the Humanities, Social Sciences, and spaces in-between can make to what we might call, hijacking a phrase from David Scott (1999), the new "problem-space" of the city. Scott describes the problem-space as "conceptual-ideological ensembles, discursive formations, or language games that are generative of objects, and therefore questions" (p. 8). To think of the city as a new "problem-space" is to make sense of the city as a space and place that "must remain open to knowing that it does not yet know what it will be," as Jacques Derrida (1998) puts it. I turn to Scott and Derrida in accounting the city because I intend to suggest that the city is the site where critique as a continued strategy for living a life becomes possible.

This chapter concerns itself with thinking of the city and multiculturalism as sites for the productions of "new forms of human life" (Wynter, 1995, p. 13) or a human to come. It makes sense of the ways in which artists and theorists whom I term postcolonial have reimagined and reproduced the city as a space of desire and as "a democracy to come" (Derrida, 2005). In the chapter, I focus on the works of Dionne Brand and Stuart Hall. In the case of Brand, I am interested in metropolitan artists in postcolonial spaces who produce art meant to do something. The perspective that art is meant to do something does not deaestheticize art; rather it suggests that the aesthetics of art are political scripts and narratives of a kind. My attention is to moments or fragments of artistic insight that allow us to glimpse into the "to come" of the city that might act as counternarratives to the ongoing utterances of life's complex intimacies. Artists offer us evidence of the past and present with a sensibility of a future-possible—a process.

I begin the chapter with the recent traumas of Western metropolitan cityscapes because it has become difficult to think of the city without thinking about 9/11 and its after-effects. Since that moment, the city has come to be marked as a new site of a coming tragedy, a tragedy that appears to be more imaginable than any time before. The hole left in the ground where the World Trade Center stood seems to stand in for the new contestations of city life and living. At this moment, reading Michel de Certeau's (1984) "Walking in the City" might give one an eerie experience and sensation. The essay's aerial view from the 110th floor of the World Trade Center offers a vantage point from which the ruins of the twin towers bookmark the old and a contested coming anew of New York city landmarks. de Certeau's essay seeks to map the city as a space analogous to the act of speech and thus walking in the city comes to mark a kind of speech act. The enunciative aspects of walking in the city in our new speech moment bring fear, threat, and suspicion of other walkers. The other walkers, many of whom are migrants to metropolitan city-spaces, are inscribed with the mark of threat and danger as well as hyperrealized with the mark of terrorist and/or polluted viral carrier. The poetics of an intimate and possibly political resonance of city life is characterized by the viciousness of modernity's most powerful invention: the city. As Derrida (2005) teaches us in "(No) More Rogue States":

> However much one may try to contain the effects of September 11, there are many clear indications that if there was a trauma on that day, the United States and throughout the world, it consisted not, as is too often believed of trauma in general, in an effect, in a wound produced by what had effectively already happened, what had just actually happened, and risked being repeated one more time, but in the undeniable fear or apprehension of a threat that is worse and still to come. (p. 104)

It is the still to come that sits at the foundation of the ongoing narratives of threat and fear that continue to shape our common world. One of the central apprehensions of the worst still to come is the place of the postcolonial migrant within the metropolitan city. The fear and threat have been proclaimed as an end to multiculturalism. But I argue that the task for scholars is that we need to struggle with the idea of multiculturalism, for Stuart Hall (2000) tells us "we have no better terms to think the situation with" (p. 209). I also suggest that we need to up the ante in the struggles around the idea of multiculturalism and offer something more, something that is simultaneously empirical, imaginary, and to come. The something I offer is creole-ness.

Cities and the End of Multiculturalism

In an episode of the television show *Will and Grace*, Grace hires an identifiable (or at least we are to believe so from the name and look of the person and other references) Middle Eastern woman to work in her design firm. Grace hires her not because she is the most qualified but because Grace wants to right a wrong.[1] The character of the Middle Eastern woman is played over the top so that her Middle Eastern name is extremely long, there is an assumption of gender victimization, and a dislocated sense of place and racial discrimination are offered as central markers of the woman's experience. These assumptions produce the desire in Grace to right a wrong through the act of hiring her. The woman turns out to be a horrible employee, even worse than Karen (which for those familiar with the show will know to be quite significant). But Grace's intent to right a wrong does not allow her to fire the new employee. After losing Grace's best client because of the employee's incompetence and finding out that the woman is Jewish, Grace finally acts. Grace proclaims to the woman how pleased she is to learn that she is Jewish because Grace is Jewish, too. After the two women bond very briefly, Grace fires her, stating that she cannot discriminate against her own and that she will see her now former employee at prayers. Such is the resolution to Grace's dilemma of hiring the wrong person and regaining her client. I found the episode a curious statement on contemporary fears and threats as well as the proclaimed demise of multiculturalism.[2]

Grace's desire to right a wrong by making an offer of employment is understood by her as an act that her Western metropolitan privilege can make available. Western liberalism as the savior of victimized others, especially by their own kind, becomes the underlying theme. However, her claim that she cannot discriminate against her own makes use of a shared but differentiated Jewish-ness to undermine the altruism of her act. The act is ultimately embedded in a multiculturalism that makes us all the same. Such enactment of the politics of difference is not the kind of ethnopolitics that I am hinting at. The comedic moves in *Will and Grace* function to undo and render the political impact of identifying a wrong that can be righted but is obscured by our commonalities. This should not be surprising since the show's entire run was about a sexless gay man who becomes so normalized on heterosexual terms that we can tolerate him since he is just like one of "us" only with a few gay quirks.[3] An assumed uncomplicatedness of belonging, identity, and even nation becomes the grounds of regulation, containment, and refusal. But when one sits outside of these grounds, there can be no doubt that identity comes to the fore again.

There is much more that can be said about the *Will and Grace* episode, but I am more interested in how we got there in the first instance, and how the demise of multiculturalism can make any kind of sense in this historical moment. I am interested in the heuristic claim of demise because it is a claim that, if made unintelligible, might allow for a moving away from the narratives of threat, fear, and danger that have become dominant in our postcolonial times. The numerous discourses of multiculturalism might be understood as an inadequate but necessary compromise of postcolonial and post-civil rights eruptions and their moderate success to provide new forms of human life in the West. In the historical-present, or our new colonial present, those who have been historically colonized experience both hyperimperialism and the older vulgar colonial practices that target largely but not exclusively those whom the threat, fear, and danger narratives are meant to confine, control, and contain.

In this regard the cities of the metropolitan West are not just multicultural, that is cities constituted of racial, ethnic, and cultural differences, but are also postcolonial in the sense that they are a break with the regime of earlier moments of colonial arrangements in condition and in figuration. Both former colonizer and colonized now occupy the same geopolitical space. The multicultural, for me, is one index of the postcolonial condition of anticolonial and neocolonial utterances and desires, of a global postcolonial to come. It is only in fact through the arrivals and departures of the colonial venture, both old and new, that a global postcolonial to come is possible. Thus the assault on the nascent appearance of a postcolonial to come as encapsulated in the claim of a demise of multiculturalism in the post-9/11 world is much more in line with older versions of colonial and imperialist orders than with the newer versions of the global financiering of the world, a neocolonial condition called the New World Order, the Age of Global Terrorism, or Globalization. Such names obscure the ongoing workings of colonial practices in which we conceptually apprehend overlapping colonial conditions of old and new.

As Stuart Hall (2003) points out concerning the forced migrations caused by various upheavals,

> Migration is the joker in the globalization pack.... In the new globalization everything moves with a new fluidity: capital, investment, goods, messages, images.... Only labor—people—are supposed to stay still.... Nevertheless, against the grain of the system, the second half of the 20th century and the first years of the 21st have seen an unprecedented explosion of the largely unplanned movement of peoples. (p. 195)

The unplanned movements of people have arrived by and large in metropolitan places and reconfigured those spaces as something other than their conventional history when new arrivals bring with them and make immediately present other histories that had been subjugated and/or discredited. Multiculturalism is, then, both the containment of such histories and their excess. It is not too much to claim that the desire to see a disappearance of multiculturalism as a desire for a postcolonial to come is shrouded in a need to reaffirm and replicate older and newer forms of colonial and imperialist mechanisms of authority and military biopower. Much of the new colonial and imperialist authority and energy are expended on limiting migration and its impacts. To engage Hall's assessments again:

> Migration constitutes a disruptive cultural force within globalization. Unlike earlier phases, where the problems of religious, social, and cultural difference were held at a safe distance from the metropolitan homelands, contemporary migration intrudes directly into, disturbs, challenges, and subverts, metropolitan cultural space. It projects the vexed issue of pluralism and difference into the settled monocultural spaces of the Western metropolis. It has produced an epistemic rupture, generating the thematics of a new problematic—that of the postcolonial moment. (p. 196)

One of the central emergent narratives of the new marking of the city is the proclamation of the death of multiculturalism. But a truism is in order: cities are by their very nature multicultural. So what kind of multiculturalism is over or being referenced to in claims of its death? The kind that is being named as dead, and rightly so, is state multiculturalism. What I am suggesting is that it is our responsibility to keep alive and relevant the idea of multiculturalism. The idea of multiculturalism is central to how we might live the intimacies of postcolonial cities and their migratory conditions and politics. The idea of multiculturalism helps us to make sense of how postcolonial cities come to be and how the state has responded to the historical positioning of the phenomena of living colonial, postcolonial, and metropolitan crimes simultaneously. The idea of multiculturalism is one that both conceptually and pragmatically grapples with the fact that the culture, ethnicity, and race are meaningful categories to many people and have become the basis upon which they organize themselves into voluntary and forced collectivities. The idea of multiculturalism acknowledges the fluid and influx nature of claims based on racial, ethnic, cultural, and other differences as never static but always in a process of unfolding tensions and possibilities.

Since the end of the Second World War, metropolitan places in the West have been pedagogically preparing for the threat and fear that have come to characterize our present. The riots of Nottinghill and Nottingham in the 1950s; the civil rights movement; the women's movement; the antiwar and antinuclear movements; the post-civil rights fires of the Black cities of the United States and thus the production of the burnt-out ghetto inner-city; the gay and lesbian movement; the race riots of the 1970s and 1980s in Britain;

the Reagan/Bush years of heightened security characterized by racialized helicopter surveillance of Black and Latino communities; heightened immigration border controls; and the production of the fear of refugees have been contained by the discomforting politics of state multiculturalism that sought to curb struggles for a democracy to come. Out of these movements and politics has come the political context from which the multicultural idea and thus the state multicultural compromise sprang. The state multicultural compromise might be characterized by the state attempts to fix identity markers as the basis of its multicultural policies. Such fixing could not allow for fluidity and the constant changes that occur in a multiculture; thus in moments of crisis the multicultural compromise fails to hold as a pack that is capable of resolving difficult questions and concerns. The compromise has been called into question by many as identity politics, and has produced a scholarly impasse of essentialism and antiessentialism that jettisons the ethicopolitical and the ethnopolitical in favor of unmasking shoddy political claims based upon struggles over state power. Now is the time to think of state power again and to think of it in the context of the ethicopolitical and ethnopolitical, both ethics and ethnicity/identity. We need to be vigilant not only about how state power positions us in political terms, but also how new paradigms of ethnicity are being positioned within and across states. The machinery of citizenship, ethnicity, and nation has resurfaced (if they ever did go away) in ways that we must urgently re-engage.

The most recent manifestations of the overlapping history are the murder of Theo Van Gogh in Amsterdam; the bombing in London, England; the riots in France's banlieues; and the continued intra-Black and other forms of minoritized violence in North American cities. The tremors of the continuing postcolonial and post–civil rights crises tell much about the unfolding of overlapping colonialisms ushered in by the neoliberal global reordering within the terms of mobility of finance capital and a decentered global production line. The above outbreaks, to use language from the viral pandemic, are only symptoms of a much larger malaise. Let me take as an example the claims being made concerning the bombing in London.

The shock or the worse to come, to return to Derrida, of the London bombing centers on the allegation that the bombers were British-born Muslims. The assumption is that they should have been counted on to be loyal to the nation. The shock is that they were not loyal to the state, that they had reoriented themselves to what has been termed a fundamentalist perspective of the world, and that their "new" homeland (for it is always new for such bodies) was at odds with "their" ways of knowing and being. The condition of being at odds, which if we follow Fanon (1967) is the condition of the colonized, was meant to be apprehended by various incarnations of state and corporate multiculturalism, a multiculturalism meant to salve the wound of colonial and postcolonial displacement and dislocation and persistent racisms in the West. Bringing some identifiable members of marked racial and ethnic groups into the field of consumption and/or as representable models of capitalist success was and is meant to demonstrate that entering the circles of the elite nation always remains possible. The youth, both symbolically and literally, are supposed to demonstrate that one does not have to leave anything of their "cultural selves" behind to enter the realm of the elites. The shock is that state multiculturalism was supposed to produce forms of being that made use of anthropologized and objectified culture and cultural practice as the basis from which second- and third-generation youth born of British colonial adventures would come to be contained in Britain. That the anthropologized cultural objectification of the other's culture failed to contain, but might have succeeded in other ways, in this case to produce a radical, if perverted, sense of resistance, is the moment of crisis in the announcement of the failure of multiculturalism. In that sense, state multiculturalism has failed and so it should. But the idea of multiculturalism is one that we must nonetheless continue to work with (Hall, 2000).

The failure is in the state's inability to quell the conditions of diasporicity, migrant subjectivities, and racisms of all kinds. The migrant subjectivities that continue to be the form and condition through which second and third generations of postcolonial subjects live their lives in the metropolitan space is of crucial necessity for us to consider. If the allegations of the London bombing are correct, what we are faced with is the stunning defeat of state multiculturalism as we witness it being unmasked within the conditions of our new colonial present. The colonial present is coterminus with a new imperialism that seeks to control the movement of peoples and to reconstitute identity, nation, and ethnicity as conditions for a politics of suppression of the creole conditions of metropolitan human life. The actual story in the much-vaunted announcements of the demise of multiculturalism across Europe and North America is grounded neither in empirical evidence nor in the imagination. The attack is really launched at the idea of multiculturalism and the creole present it can bequeath us. Thus, we might think of the bombing of London as one of the difficult moments of creolization since we can never just think of creolization as a happy story, even though it is also a story of possibility.

The claim of the demise of multiculturalism then only functions in regard to state multiculturalism and the policies that flow from such regulation.

There are many kinds of multiculturalism, but the evidence of a lived and everyday multiculture does not disappear in the face of metropolitan elites decrying and claiming the demise of state multicultural polices. Instead the everyday and banal multiculturalism that we live in intimate urban spaces functions as the back drop for a move toward a more creole experience.

Creole Cities: A Postcolonial to Come

The last scenes of Isaac Julien's 1991 film *Young Soul Rebels* offer a glimpse of a community to come as the white, the black, the male, the female, the gay, the heterosexual come together dancing to African American music having formed a new and more hopeful affiliation within the context of racism and nationalism of the 1970s. The moment of affiliation in the film comes from a recognition of differences and a political solidarity based on a poetics of relation within and across national and psychic boundaries. Julien captures the changing relations of race, nation, gender, and sexuality as the substance of what Hall (1996) terms as "new ethnicities." The moment of new ethnicities that Julien cinematically represents is what I call everyday or popular multiculturalism. It is a multiculturalism that occurs from below, driven by the intimacies of urban life. It is also a multiculturalism on its way to creolization. Creolization is the result of multiple differences and their intimate encounters producing "mutual mutations" (Glissant, 1997) as the point toward further and more opacity in terms of cultural formations, expressions, and articulations. It is only possible in a multiculture. The film utters the imagined and material context of multicultural London at that time. The images of a differently racialized and ethnicized London in the post-July 7, 2005, moment utters yet another one. They are the creole children of the racism and nationalism that Julien's film calls into question. They are the creoles of London, now misrecognized as fundamentalists of all sorts.

The development of creole society, as Kamau Brathwaite (1971) calls it, is a society "caught up in some kind of colonial arrangement with a metropolitan European power" (p. xv). Brathwaite writes about the Anglo-Caribbean and in particular Jamaica when he offers that definition. He suggests that creole society is a complex situation where external metropolitan forces pressure the colonial polity to make constant internal adjustments between master and slave, elite and laborer, and so on "in a culturally heterogeneous relationship" (p. xvi). I contend that much of Brathwaite's terms for the conditions of creole society manifest themselves in the metropolitan space, especially in conditions concerning cohabitation and uneven acts of power. Thus Brathwaite's definition requires a bit of fine-tuning when relocated elsewhere. Before I offer that fine-tuning, let me be clear that creolization takes place in the context of unequal and brutal power arrangements alongside forms of severe cultural dominance. As Hall (2003) points out, creolization could not take place without extensive transculturation. It arises out of the brutal context and unequal power relations through which differing cultures come into contact and engagement with each other. In the period of transatlantic slavery and its aftermath, the early state of the plantation society and the state of our times have been the arbiter of uneven power and its brutalizing qualities. The importance of creolization as a term to think with is its location between brutality and something different, something more possible, if I can use such a phrase, the fusing and mixing of cultures forced to cohabit together that render something else possible (Hall, 2003, p. 193). Humanists and social scientists must think of new possibilities and enter empirical and imaginary evidences into the public sphere and the public debate of our new realities.

The longue durée of multicultural metropolitan spaces have been in the midst of a creole process for some time now. Most city spaces are creole places even if we don't think of them in those terms. In *Times Square Red, Times Square Blue*, Samuel Delany (2001) plots one moment of creole sensibility in New York City prior to its Disney-fication. He articulates a sexual community whose existence is both marginalized and demolished by the remaking of Times Square as a middle-class playground. What is powerful about his observations and analyses is that he understands what is missing: the comingling of people across race, class, and culture through sexual desire and practice. In one of Delany's central claims about the city, he writes:

> I propose that in a democratic city it is imperative that we speak to strangers, live next to them, and learn how to relate to them on many levels, including the sexual. City venues must be designed to allow these multiple interactions to occur easily, with a minimum of danger, comfortably, and conveniently. This is what politics—the way of living in the polis, the city—is about. (p. 193)

The politics of city living has been chronicled by a number of artists from the former colonies and of the disposed in the West and by their descendents. I am interested in artists who have constituted a migratory subjectivity in relationship to transatlantic slavery and colonial history because I believe that such artists bring a unique position to articulating the city. In the Canadian context, no contemporary artist has consistently grappled with the city and its multivalent contours like the poet, novelist, and essayist Dionne Brand.

Brand has been writing about the city as a material and imagined place since 1983 with her *Winter Epigrams and Epigrams to Ernesto Cardenal in Defense of Claudia*. Over that time the city has changed and evolved from a cold and frigid place to one in which alienation, celebration, pain, shame, and pleasure live up close to each other. Brand's poetry, fiction, and essays chronicle a history of the evolving cityscape of Toronto since the 1970s. For instance, a relatively recent essay in *Brick Magazine* reflects on the joys and pleasures of women's boxing at a local Toronto gym where she attended to witness a friend's debut in the sport, a sport that has become a lesbian underground practice in many major cities (Brand, 2005a). She chronicles the economies of city living with a language evocative of the tight spaces we negotiate. Her conception of the city is different from where I began with *Will and Grace* in that Brand's city is not one where elites right wrongs, but rather where the ingredients of creole-ness are realized in what Glissant (1997, p. 138) terms as the "unimaginable turbulence of Relation." The multiculturalism of Brand's city embeds the violent intimacies of everyday life, state practices, and the hopefulness of living together in moments of mutual recognition that are the signs that provide movements and thus possibility for something else to come into being. In "Thirsty," Brand (2002, p. 7) writes:

> History doesn't enter here, life, if you call it that
> on this small street is inconsequential,
> Julia, worked at testing cultures and the stingy
> task, in every way irredeemable, of saving money
>
> Then Allan came, his mother, left, came ill
> squeezing a sewing machine into a hallway
> and then the baby. Already you can see how
> joylessness took a hold pretending to be joy

The poem "Thirsty" comes out of the tragedy of a police shooting a black man in the early 1980s. Brand does not vindicate; she offers a reading of the city in which entanglements of pain and beauty might signal one response to the traumas of the place. She writes of Toronto as a "city that had never happened before." But if we bring Brand's uttering into conversation with Derrida, we have generations of cities since all cities suffer the condition of having not happened before. "Thirsty" is a poem very local in its articulations, a kind of eulogy to Toronto, but much wider in its impact and call to an ethics of living together in a community of which we might demand an ethicopolitical in accord with a Derridean hospitality to the stranger.

In "Land to Light On," Brand (1997) is more pensive about the city. The poem might be read at first as a disappointment in and refusal of the nation-state as a place of ethical belonging. She gives up on land to light on declaring, "I don't want no fucking country, here, there or all the way back." She moves to the hyper-immigrant local of Toronto to call nation and world into question and to demand an ethical accounting of the pain of movement. Thus "Land to Light On" is dedicated to making sense of how movement facilitates a particular kind of politics.

In Brand's essays and short stories, the same kind of attention is paid to the city as the locus from which to view and engage a larger politics concerned with the international ethicopolitical and ethnopolitical. Anyone familiar with Toronto as a space and place would not be surprised why one of Canada's best living poets would find such inspiration in Toronto. In *What We All Long For*, Brand (2005b) writes Toronto like it has never been written before, and maps places, spaces, and people like a cartographer's poetics denuded of its science. The novel monumentalizes Toronto through the ordinary and the every day. Brand works with a notion that the city has never happened before and thus her narration is in keeping with the to come aspect that I have been delineating. Her novel is in fact a counterpoint to the neoconservative desire to have multiculturalism disappear as though these conditions are only possible in state announcement and legislation. In fact *What We All Long For* ushers in the creole city.

The characters in the novel are a group of 20-some young people of color who resemble the kinds of folks accused in the London bombing. They either have migrated to the city at a very young age or were born of first-generation migrant parents for whom their children's cultural difference is both shared and confusing. But this is not a novel about generational conflict. It is about migrant subjectivity even when there is no place to return as is the case for the second generation and after. It is a novel about how cultural difference is lived as a moment as something else to come. Brand neither celebrates nor denounces multiculturalism; she writes its possibilities and outcomes. One of its outcomes is a creole sensibility or condition with the vicious pleasures that such entails.

Let me focus on one strand of the novel. The novel concerns itself with various reasons why migration happens. It also allows me to advance the idea of how violence is a central aspect of seriously accounting for our multicultural present and its process toward a creole-ness to come. A key strand in the novel concerns the character Quy, who is the brother of Tuyen, a young aspiring artist. Quy is lost by his family when they flee Vietnam in the 1970s. Quy does

Multicultural and Creole Contemporaries 173

not hold onto his mother's hand strong enough, and she loses him as the refugees run to the boats. Quy makes his way to Thailand where he becomes part of the underworld and eventually makes his way to Toronto. Quy's mother is inconsolable by her loss, and his sister Tuyen wishes for Quy's return so that she might be given the space for self-expression in a family with strict demands for the youngest girl child. Tuyen is neither Vietnamese nor Canadian; she is her very local self, more captured by the poetics of the urban than by any national geography or imaginary.

For much of Quy's life, he is state-less, calling to mind certain aspects of Agamben's insights on the place of law and no law.[4] Quy is the kind of refugee who sits in a wasteland contained by law but for which no law can speak on his behalf. The place of law without law has recently been hyper-actuated in legislation like Homeland Security and the Security Certificate in Canada, but refugee claimants find themselves at such junctures more so now. Quy's existence from the tragic evening in Vietnam has been to exist below the radar of state organized human life.

Through a series of events, Tuyen discovers Quy's existence in the city. She approaches him and arranges for him to meet the family. While waiting outside the family home, Quy is apparently murdered for his car.[5] Quy's death at the hands of a stranger, but one familiar to his sister, is a moment in the novel where the politics of a creole to come announces its most brutal aspects. In the novel Brand is not romantic about the city; she writes its violence and joys, its pain and laughter, its sorrow and fruit. The city is not a locus of resolution; it functions as the place where resolution might be possible. The intimacy of living close and living together can act as the conduit to a different kind of conversation. I suggest that our task as scholars is to make that conversation happen better than it has been happening.

The tragic circumstances of Quy's apparent death act as one of the conditions through which the multicultural space and place of Toronto is not romanticized. The textures of Brand's narration of Toronto's cityscape recoil with his death, and simultaneously propel the cityscape forward as new knowledges, new ways of being, and new relations are found in the aftermath. There is no single aspect of Brand's novel that makes it utter the deep textures of Toronto's creole sensibility and form. Its textures, both thick and thin, pervade the work and, in its most hopeful ethnographic sense, give the reader a sense of what pervades the landscape and the possibilities to come. In this sense creolization is a process toward what Sylvia Wynter (1995, p. 13) calls "new forms of human life." How might scholars think of these new forms of life to come? The elements of the novel that move us toward the tragedy of the violence that Quy encounters allow us to apprehend how those who know each other in the aftermath will be forced to plot new ways of being in the world they intimately inhabit—a move toward a creole reality. The new modes of being can only be but accessed as new modes of human life in the aftermath of the violent reconfiguration of knowing and living a life together.

Conclusion: New Forms of Human Life

The urgencies of our new colonial moment have found scholars searching for rehabilitating and resuscitating concepts of all kinds to think these new conditions. No other concept has made a firmer return than cosmopolitanism.[6] Let us take Kwame Anthony Appiah as our example. In *Cosmopolitanism: Ethics in a World of Strangers*, Appiah (2006) asks, under what rubric to proceed in this moment. He answers: "not globalization" and "not multiculturalism." In my view, Appiah creates a false separation multiculturalism and cosmopolitanism. Each idea inflects the other and thus it is not possible to have one without the other. What Appiah fails to do, but which he does better in *The Ethics of Identity* (Appiah, 2005) yet does not go far enough, is to think about the state. The idea of multiculturalism, as entangled in state and corporate discourses, pollutes it no more than cosmopolitanism's colonial history.

So, why not multiculturalism? I think it is the overall frames from which Appiah's inability to challenge state power explicitly precedes that he reduces the idea of multiculturalism down to state and corporate multiculturalism. He finds in the history of cosmopolitanism more to work with, but does not recognize the state and corporatist reduction of the latter to the language of global citizen. What is significant, for me, about Appiah's arguments in *Cosmopolitanism* is that his examples approach what I have been calling creolization. However, his fear of ethnicity does not allow him to go there. By his fear of ethnicity, I mean to signal that, in every instance in Appiah's text where ethnicity rears its head as a meaningful attachment, his practice is to argue that it is a faulty idea. I argue, however, that the move is not to undermine such passionate attachments, but rather to point out how the attachments are in a long process of movement and possibility elsewhere. To approach the situation from the place I am suggesting, one cannot fear ethnicity as a problem but one must embrace it as a meaningful and yet not fully possible marker of self and collectivity. When we think of these ideas in the context of the city, we recognize what Michael Keith (2005) points out: "the city increasingly mediates circuits of political engagement and cultural reproduction at a post-national scale of analysis. It is important politically because the city becomes the disruptive force in the reproduction of cultural and political form, the mediating field through which newness comes into the world after the cosmopolitan loses its populist gloss" (p. 188). Thus in cities (and elsewhere), ethnicity and its claims are both a crutch and a lever toward something other and something more in conscious and not so conscious ways.

I am suggesting that the ethnopolitical is important because we must confront the ways in which the new colonialism and imperialism continue to make identity a locus of control, containment, and regulation. The recent pass of a knee-jerk identity politics critique has now reached its conclusion, meaning that we can no longer make the claim that identity does not matter and that it is far more the problem than the resolution of problems. Previous critiques of identity politics too easily dismiss appeals to identity in an effort to mobilize a politics that might move beyond self-recognition into one that might activate a practice of care for those whom we did not share anything in common with. The critiques of identity politics that many of us quickly fell victim to shifted the politics of the dispossessed. But in the post-9/11 world, identity has reemerged as a function of the state to mark, contain, surveil, and incarcerate in a fashion that requires a reengagement with identity claims.

In the postidentity politics moment, the only stable category that those of us on the Left had was class. It was a curious moment, for clearly we did not do the work to make the interventionist politics of various identity groups garner real traction. Such is particularly evident when class, which is heavily racialized in the spaces I have been discussing, is reproduced in our studies as a kind of empty category in which the "real problem" of identity, race, is not essential to understanding it. In much of Left humanities and social sciences, class has become a signifier of a transcendent identity category: it is an identity without an identity, and race and culture only enter to sully it. The ethnopolitical is not an appeal to essentialize identity, but rather to highlight the ways in which identity, especially ethnicity, matter in our colonial present. As Diana Fuss (1989) states back in the heady days of the essentialist/constructionist argument, "To insist that essentialism is always and everywhere reactionary is, for the constructionists, to buy into essentialism in the very act of making the charge; it is to act as if essentialism has an essence" (p. 21). I am not making a case for ethnopoliticality as the only ground of a renewed collective politics, but I am arguing for the language of ethnicity as a central element for how we approach a collective politics of the possible and thus a postcolonial to come, out of our present multicultural and submerged creole present.

Finally, it would have been noticed that much of the conceptual scaffolding of my argument has been built through artists and intellectuals who have a relation of some sort to a region we call the Caribbean. I would not want for such attention to be interpreted as chauvinism, but I do want to place on the conceptual agenda a piece of potentially difficult knowledge. The archipelago of poverty, as Wynter (1992) calls it, is a place that has produced an interesting and arresting relation to modernity, both within and against it. Most Caribbean people are people who must make themselves native to a place they are not from. Caribbean people also occupy a place that drove the engines of the modern industrial world, and play a significant role in migratory practices to the former and now new again colonial powers. The unique place of the Caribbean as extension of Europe, Africa, and Asia; as amputation and extension; as overseas department; as import and export; as slave, free, indentured, and in-between; as backyard of the United States, makes it a place where the cosmopolitical takes route in all the messiness that ethnicity brings with it. I suggest that it is the utter uniqueness of the place and the ways in which it struggles to live both the ongoing moments of creolization and a democracy to come in the backyard of new empire and our new colonial present that it has much to offer us as the people of that place continue to "quarrel with history" (Glissant, 1989).

Notes

1. See Spivak (2004, 2005) for a discussion on human rights and metropolitan understandings of how they might participate in the righting of wrongs.

2. For those interested in what Will and Jack were doing in this particular episode, they were having a *Brokeback Mountain* moment at a gay cowboy bar in the city.

3. While the chapter makes reference to a number of queer artists and queer texts, it is not interested in queer-ness as a privileged identity. In fact it argues that queer identity claims are only one among others in the present multiculture arrangements of human life. What is often important about queer-ness when it is asserted is that it operates at a number of in-between and bridging positions which work to make more visible the limits of other identity claims.

4. I draw on Agamben (2005) to point to how "states of exception" position people in precarious relation to the state. In his rendering of how the law works in such situation, the law is simultaneously upheld and under erasure. Such a position produces a kind of "no man's land" or sets up those caught in the gaps of law with no recourse to law.

5. It is not entirely clear that Quy dies; what is clear is that great violence has occurred. Violence is a constitutive element of the process of creolization, which must be dealt with if creole-ness is to be acknowledged as constitutive of a difference process after the encounter.

6. Paul Gilroy (2005) in *Postcolonial Melancholia* favors the term conviviality rather than cosmopolitanism. Gilroy's term is important in part because it recognizes the element of living together. Nonetheless it is faulty because it does not allow for thinking of new modes of being in the context of living together as an emergent site of new possibilities.

References

Agamben, G. (2005). *State of exception* (K. Attell, trans.). Chicago, IL: University of Chicago Press.
Appiah, K. A. (2005). *The ethics of identity*. Princeton, NJ: Princeton University Press.
Appiah, K. A. (2006). *Cosmopolitanism: Ethics in a world of strangers*. New York: W. W. Norton.
Brand, D. (1997). *Land to light on*. Toronto, ON: McClelland and Stewart.
Brand, D. (2002). *Thirsty*. Toronto, ON: McClelland and Stewart.
Brand, D. (2005a). Manos de piedras. *Brick Magazine 76* (winter).
Brand, D. (2005b). *What we all long for*. Toronto, ON: Vintage Canada.
Brathwaite, K. (1971). *The development of creole society in Jamaica, 1770–1820*. Oxford, UK: Clarendon.
de Certeau, M. (1984). *The practice of everyday life*. Berkeley: University of California Press.
Delany, S. (2001). *Times Square red, Times Square blue*. New York: New York University Press.
Derrida, J. (1998). Generations of a city: Memory, prophecy, responsibilities (R. Comay, trans.). In J. Knechtel (Ed.), *Open city: Alphabet city no. 6* (pp. 12–27). Concord, ON: House of Anansi Press.
Derrida, J. (2005). *Rogues: Two essays on reason*. Stanford, CA: Stanford University Press.
Fanon, F. (1967). *Black skin, white masks*. New York: Grove.
Fuss, D. (1989). *Essentially speaking: Feminism, nature and difference*. New York: Routledge.
Gilroy, P. (2005). *Postcolonial melancholia*. New York: Columbia University Press.
Glissant, É. (1989). History, histories, and stories. *Caribbean discourse: Selected essays* (J. M. Dash, trans.) (pp. 61–97). Charlottesville: University of Virginia Press.
Glissant, É. (1997). *Poetics of relation* (B. Wing, trans.). Ann Arbor: University of Michigan Press.
Gregory, D. (2004). *The colonial present*. Oxford, UK: Blackwell.
Hall, S. (1996). New ethnicities. In D. Morley & K. Chen (Eds.), *Stuart Hall: Critical dialogues in cultural studies* (pp. 441–449). London: Routledge.
Hall, S. (2000). Conclusion: The multi-cultural question. In B. Hesse (Ed.), *Un/settled multiculturalisms: Diasporas, entanglements, transruptions* (pp. 209–241). London: Zed.
Hall, S. (2003). Creolization, diaspora, and hybridity in the context of globalization. In O. Enwezor, C. Basualdo, U. M. Bauer, S. Ghez, S. Maharaj, M. Nash, & O. Zaya (Eds.), *Créolité and creolization: Documenta 11 platform 3*. Ostfildern, Germany: Hatje Cantz.
Keith, M. (2005). *After the cosmopolitan?: Multicultural cities and the future of racism*. London: Routledge.
Scott, D. (1999). *Refashioning futures: Criticism after postcoloniality*. Princeton, NJ: Princeton University Press.
Spivak, G. (2004). Righting wrongs. *South Atlantic Quarterly 103*(2/3), 523–581.
Spivak, G. (2005). Use and abuse of human rights. *boundary 2, 32*(1), 131–189.
Wynter, S. (1992). Rethinking "aesthetics": Notes towards a deciphering practice. In M. B. Cham (Ed.), *Ex-Iles: Essays on Caribbean cinema*. Trenton, NJ: Africa World.
Wynter, S. (1995). 1492: A new world view. In V. Hyatt & R. Nettleford (Eds.), *Race, discourse, and the origin of the Americas: A new world view*. Washington, DC: Smithsonian Institution Press.

CHAPTER 11

Border Crossing with M.I.A. and Transnational Girlhood Studies

LISA WEEMS

Rolling Stone magazine named *Kala*, the sophomore production of Sri Lankan British hip-hop artist M.I.A., its 2007 Album of the Year. Like much of the "progressive" press that review M.I.A.'s work, *Rolling Stone* points to the political imagery and rhetoric in her music. The reviewers write, "*Kala* explores worldwide war zones, talking about 'Third World democracy' and 'putting people on the map that [have] never seen a map'" (Christgau, Fricke, Hoard, & Sheffield, 2007, p. 7). They refer to *Kala* (Arulpragasum, 2007) as an "international block party" marked by "a Day Glo sensibility" but with "the political rage of Public Enemy," and conclude that M.I.A. "remains a criminal-minded art freak with a true rock & roller's love of flash and sensation and irresponsible shit-talking" (ibid.). M.I.A. is constructed as an "intelligent Sri Lankan party girl" (Widner, 2007) and the poster child of Third World democracy.

What meaning can we make of the current commercial success of M.I.A. as a cultural worker in transnational popular media?[1] What kind of cultural work (e.g., political analysis and sociocultural pedagogy) is at play in the performance art of M.I.A.? What is the significance of this work for postcolonial theorizing, global studies of youth culture, and a burgeoning field of transnational girlhood studies?

I investigate the performance art of M.I.A. to examine questions of gendered postcolonial resistance and agency within the cultural and political contexts of globalization. I draw upon research on transnational cultural productions that foreground cultural hybridity in racial and national boundary crossing, and extend them to attend to issues of gender and sexual politics among young women in diaspora (Chow & Ang, 1993). Following M. Jacqui

Alexander's (2005) writing on "pedagogies of crossing," I examine the interplay of "gendered and sexualized power that is simultaneously raced and classed yet not practiced within hermitically sealed or epistemically partial borders of the nation-state" (p. 4). I analyze the performance art of M.I.A. to explore three forms of border crossing (cultural hybridity, local and global forms of ethnic violence, and sexual politics) in relation to dominant narratives of gender, race, and nation in cultural theory and practice. Finally, I discuss how her pedagogy of crossing provides a useful starting place to articulate a transnational feminist framework for theorizing postcolonial girlhood and the field of transnational girlhood studies.

Global Youth, Girlhood Studies, and a Hybrid Framework for Understanding M.I.A. and Transnational Popular Culture

My examination of the performance art of M.I.A. both sutures and expands two separate but related projects: (1) to provide a rich description of the cultural and political dimensions of the position of a refugee rebel girl; and (2) to argue for a transnational approach to the study of girlhoods. The first aim is necessary because there is relatively little research regarding the experiences and symbolic representations of the positions of Sri Lankan girls in either domestic or diasporic contexts (Mathieu, 2006). My analysis expands the literature in youth studies to understand how globalization affects different groups of girls differently. My second aim invites a fundamental shift in the way "girlhood" is theorized. I argue that gender studies has been dominated by the voices, theoretical orientations, and sites of analysis that center on White, middle class, Western/Northern, heterosexual women at the exclusion of nondominant or subaltern perspectives. Transnational feminism also suggests that our object of analysis needs to attend to the ways in which knowledge and its production are linked to global capitalism and imperialism. Thus, I am arguing for a shift in the field of girlhood studies to consider the ways in which global capitalist and imperialist dynamics operate within the material practices and representations of "girlhood" or "the girl child." In other words, "girlhood" becomes a site that consolidates assumptions and practices regarding difference, colonial power, and economic relations between and among gendered subjects in transnational contexts. What is at stake in this cultural politics is the extent to which youth (girls and boys) can create, inhabit, and transgress the discursive positions to which they are subject.

The art of M.I.A. represents a new generation of postcolonial cultural productions that reflects the fluid ethnoscapes (Appadurai, 1996) made possible by transnational migration of cultural, informatic, ideological, technological, and financial forms of currency and recognition. Appadurai (1996) writes, "the imagination has become an organized field of social practices ... a form of work ... and a form of negotiation between sites of agency and globally defined fields of possibility" (p. 31). Scholars in global youth studies have pointed to the ways in which popular culture provides real and imagined networks of affiliation and border crossing in terms of race and nationality (Dimitriadis & McCarthy, 2001; Dolby & Rizvi, 2008). They also have noted the central role of music in crossing ethnic and aesthetic borders and its potential to create political change. What has not been addressed, however, is the role of gender and sexuality among girls in the production, distribution, circulation, and reception of such hybrid cultural productions. For example, issues related to gender appear in only 7 of the approximately 50 articles included in oft-cited texts in global youth studies (McCarthy, Hudak, Miklaucic, & Saukko, 1999; Maira & Soep, 2004; Muggleton & Weinzierl, 2003). Of those 7, only 5 articles focus on girls as gendered subjects located within cultural, racial, and national politics. Thus, the question raised by Angela McRobbie (2000) remains pertinent: is it that girls are not active in subcultural activities, or could it be that the conceptual apparatus of global youth studies marginalizes the activities in which girls are producers of cultural hybridity? Extending McRobbie's query, I wonder if and what types of gendered postcolonial agency might be rendered visible by making explicit a theoretical framework of transnational feminist practice.

Similarly, the field of girlhood studies tends to be populated with constructions of gender and sexuality among Western/Northern and White young women (Brumberg, 1997; Kearney, 2006: Lamb & Brown, 2007) and the institutionalized spaces they inhabit (Aapola, Gonick, & Harris, 2005; Bettis & Adams, 2005; Mitchell & Reid-Walsh, 2005). Although there are a few exceptions (Brown, 2008; Jiwani, Steenbergen, & Mitchell, 2006), the trend is to credit the "emergence" of girlhood studies with the sociocultural phenomenon of "girl power" or "riot grrl" movement in the United States in the 1980s. While studies may include girls of color within and outside of the United States, the discursive production of "girlhood studies" articulates that the subject of this field remains a White, middle class, heterosexual female living in the United States, Canada, UK, or Australia.[2]

An effect of these theoretical and empirical blindspots is that the lived experiences, cultural productions, political interventions, and theoretical contributions of "Third World girls" remain somewhere between invisible and underexplored. I use the term Third World girls similar to Mohanty's articulation of "Third World women" and Anzaldúa's "Women of Color" to mark a political solidarity. For Mohanty and Anzaldúa, these terms are not intended to suggest a prediscursive essentialist lived experience, but rather an ideological solidarity. Central to my argument is that M.I.A.'s cultural productions are insightful in terms of theorizing gendered postcolonial agency, and that an analysis of her work moves the logics of both global youth studies and girlhood studies beyond their limits.

The conceptual lens of border crossing is paramount in that the postcolonial critic is mindful of the ways in which subjectivity is constituted by sociocultural, political, economic, and geographic hybridity, multiplicity, and migration (Anzaldúa, 1999). The emphasis on fluidity is also attentive to the ways in which power/knowledge plays a role in constructing the possibilities and limits of ways of thinking and being (Foucault, 1980). In *Pedagogies of Crossing*, Alexander (2005) offers a conceptual framework for theorizing the impact of the material and psychic dimensions of imperialist, racialized, national, class-based, and sexual domination. She argues, "hegemony works as spectacle, but more importantly as a set of practices that come to assume meaning in people's everyday lives" (p. 5). The source material for her analysis ranges from the institutionalization of same-sex discrimination in the Bahamas to White gay tourism and from the "feminist-led" divisive politics at New School's "diversity" initiative to the "blackening of U.S. welfare policy." Emergent in her analysis is a framework that calls for critique of imperialist heteropatriarchy and for new alliances of transnational solidarity through "sacred possession" of our complicity and humility yet power to invoke change. What is important about Alexander's framework is the call for vigilance to the ways in which our subject positions demand complicity into practices of assimilation and domination. As she states, "Our hands are not clean" (p. 264). Yet through pedagogies of the sacred, including the creation of alternative, transgressive, and not-yet articulated histories, we can engage in the necessary work of "healing" ourselves, our communities, and the global landscape.

M.I.A's biography characterizes the kind of border crossing that postcolonial scholars have written in terms of inhabiting multiple, hybrid cultural positions. Her music and art signify the type of Alexander's pedagogy of crossing that seeks justice through acts of "re-membering" subaltern history and representation (Rhee, 2006). M.I.A. speaks out against imperialism, and recognizes the economic and psychic "costs" associated with colonial and sexual domination in everyday life.

M.I.A. the "Refugee Rebel": Border Crossing the War Zones of Global and Ethnic Violence

M.I.A. invokes global border crossing in "Buckey Done Gun," a song in her first album *Arular* (Arulpragasum, 2004). She starts with "London / Quiet Down, I need to make a sound / New York / Quiet Down, I need to make a sound / Kingston / Quiet Down, I need to make a sound / Brazil / Quiet Down, I need to make a sound." The lyrics, combined with video imagery of Tamil youth throwing grenades, signals the everyday landscape of war-torn geographies. M.I.A. not only names several intercontinental locations to define a global network, but uses this imaginary network of affiliation to call for solidarity among its members to "fight back" and work together for "third world democracy." London, New York, Kingston, Brazil all become "sites of agency and globally defined fields of possibility" (Appadurai, 1996, p. 31) for youth affected by and speaking about violence.

Born in the late 1970s, M.I.A./Maya represents one of the 700,000 members of the Tamil diaspora displaced by the past 30 years of civil war within and across the borders of India and Sri Lanka. In Sri Lanka, Tamils consist nearly 18 percent of the general population and are often characterized as a "militant" ethnic group even though only a small subset of Tamils identifies with the Liberation Tigers of Tamil Elam (LTTE) (Jayasena, 2007). M.I.A. was born in Hounslow, London, but moved back to Sri Lanka with her family within her first year of childhood. Around the age of 10, M.I.A., her siblings, and mother fled war-torn Sri Lanka to London. Her father, cited in her biographies as a member of the LTTE with a code name of Arular, left the family to fight for a separate geopolitical state (Tamil Eelam) on the northeastern periphery of Sri Lanka. Although the ethnic conflict in Sri Lanka predates her childhood, the 1980s witnessed violent ruptures due to the injunction of Sinhalese-only language and cultural policies. Thus, when M.I.A. sings, "I was missing in action / can you please come get me," it is unclear whether she is languishing for her father, a reconnection with Sri Lanka or other nation-state.

Her messages are complex and conflicting: does she advocate for violence ("Muscle in the gun slip"), or articulate the violent realities of being poor, brown, and illegal ("Police I try to avoid them / They catch me hustling they say deport them")? Her "true" stance on the role of violence is ambivalent given her desires for sovereignty ("I'll fight you just to get peace") and "Third World democracy" for "independent foreigners" in the "world town." Although questions surrounding her support of violence and LTTE have become major points of contention within the Desi blogosphere, the U.S. and British media seem to buy into this rendering of M.I.A.[3] The representation of M.I.A. as a supporter of LTTE terrorism (whether accurate or not) has been reported as the source for her denial of entry into the United States in 2006.[4] M.I.A. used this refusal of entry as an opportunity to explore a more global sound and political message in her second album *Kala* in two ways. First, she set up musical production in Ghana, Angola, Trinidad, Sri Lanka, and Australia, purposefully incorporating indigenous aesthetics into her music through sounds, local musicians, and dancers. Second, M.I.A. constructed lyrics that highlight local political themes and social conditions. M.I.A. is thus engaging in "cultural appropriation," as some critics have raised, and shining a spotlight on issues of violence, war, and cultural survival. In a 2007 interview, she notes the unintended political benefits of being denied entry:

> Me not being able to get into the country actually forced me to go to Africa and India, which actually works out worse for whoever wants me to shut up, because the worst thing you can do is make Africa look cool, or like make India look cool.... They just made it a step closer for a bridge to get built between modern developing countries and modern Third World and America, which is what needs to happen.[5]

Her songs specifically address the everyday "underbelly" of global capitalism that involves relations of power with differential effects for those who are "buying the shit" and those making or selling it. In "Hussel" M.I.A. writes, "We do it cheap hide our money in a heap / Send it home and make 'em study." In "Sunshowers" she writes, "He got Colgate on his teeth / and Reebok classics on his feet / At a factory he does Nike / And then he helps the family." These passages illustrate the influence of branding and transnational corporate consumption. They also highlight how global capitalism asymmetrically affects those who are producing commodities for cheap wages and those consuming such goods associated with U.S. cultural capital. In addition, M.I.A. analyzes the impact of the global economy on issues related to domination and violence. In "Sunshowers" she writes, "Semi-9 and snipered him / On that wall they posted him / They cornered him / And then just murdered him / He told them he didn't know them / He wasn't there, they didn't know him / They showed him a picture then; / Ain't that you with the Muslims?" M.I.A. calls attention to the racialized and Orientalizing profiling and violence that haunt brown bodies across geopolitical boundaries, especially after 9/11. Violence within nation-states does not just occur as a result of ethnic conflict; one of the features of the New World Order is that domination and violence can operate as state-sanctioned ritual or routine that requires little evidence to wield its deadly force.

Her songs directly and indirectly connect global capitalism with imperialist violence. Throughout "Paper Planes," sounds of a cash register are interspersed with gunshots, which were considered "controversial" enough that they were edited out of her live performance on the David Letterman Show in 2007 (Widner, 2007). M.I.A. describes the everyday life of hustling, whether drugs or visas, reminding us of the easy slippage between the war on terror, the war on drugs, and the war on poverty. The song also samples the Clash song "Straight to Hell" that describes the situation of Amerasian immigrants in a post-Vietnam, postindustrial context of "homelessness" and "hopelessness." In other words, living on the borders is a dangerous "game."

What intrigues me most is her incisive analysis of *how* persons trapped within the intimate dynamics of domination participate in the cultural and economic systems that render them subordinated ("Every dollar just keeps me down more"). M.I.A. is keenly aware that part of the everyday struggle in the underbelly of globalization and cultural imperialism is dealing with our complicity in maintaining the status quo. In "20 Dollar" she writes, "Do you know that cost of a.k.s / Up in Africa / 20 dollars aint shit to you / But that's how much they are / So they gonna use the shit just to get far." Countless examples of people living at or below the poverty line, from undocumented nannies working for elected officials in the United States to Iraqi police whose target is determined by the highest bidder, have little "choice" in the means or path to financial stability. In the global economy, the gap between those whose ethical dilemma is whether or not to fly to Jamaica for spring break and whether or not to give up a child for transnational adoption is growing at rates unseen in the previous century.

The increasing gap between rich and poor has been a function of and exploited by economic and racial dynamics within and across nation-states and sociocultural boundaries (Appadurai, 1996). Jacqui Alexander (2005) and Lisa Lowe (2006) argue that global capitalism also has been a function of and exacerbated by dimensions of gender and sexualization in arenas such as labor, violence, and intimacy. While issues of child prostitution, sexual violence, and low wages for women's labor are not unique to the twenty-first century, new technologies such as mass and digital medias make possible new formulations of imperialist sexual exploitation. As Ann Stoler (2006) suggests, scholars interested in the effects of empire should examine how "matters of the intimate are critical sites for the consolidation of colonial power" (p. 4).

Border Crossing and Sexual Politics: A Transnational Feminist Approach to Girlhood Studies

The third type of border crossing I wish to discuss is how M.I.A. is positioned by and positions herself within discourses of sexual politics. I elaborate on the contexts within which she is positioned as a female Tamil refugee rebel, and then discuss how she articulates a position of resistance and agency in the song "10 dollar" by mobilizing the discourses of global capitalism, patriarchy, and "porno-tropics" (McClintock, 1995) that frame the strategies of resistance available to Third World girls.[6] A closer examination of "10 dollar" is particularly useful for articulating a transnational feminist approach to girlhood studies in multiple ways. First, it foregrounds M.I.A. as an example of a postcolonial young female who is an agent of culture and knowledge production. The subject of the song, the Chinna girl, is portrayed as an active sexual agent who works within and against the dynamics of intimacy within inequitable geopolitical and socioeconomic relations. My analysis thus pushes for a move away from constructions of girlhood dictated by social and economic conditions of the global North and its academies.[7]

Discourses of sexual politics in Western feminism often center on issues of equal pay, reproductive rights, body image, and self-esteem. While these issues may resonate with some women across the globe, feminists of color and postcolonial feminists note that assumptions about the universalism of women's oppression mostly reflect a Western, white, middle-class, heterosexual bias (Hernandez & Rehman, 2002). Mohanty (2003) locates this tension less with individual women involved in "Western feminism," admittedly a generalized universalizing construct, and more with the tendency in sociocultural and political theory to make generalizations to legitimize political claims toward socioeconomic progress. Working within and against the construct of "strategic essentialism" (Spivak, 1990), Mohanty (2003) suggests that "it is possible and desirable to articulate a politics of 'Third World feminist struggles'" that pay vigilant attention to the ways in which "imagined communities are historically and geographically concrete" with "boundaries that are necessarily fluid" (p. 47). The dual emphasis on the materiality and constructedness of the constitution of "Third World feminist struggles" should be underscored. Such politics allows us to investigate how issues of power and domination are culturally and locally specific, yet connected to macroeconomic, social, and political dimensions of sexual politics and globalization.

Transnational, feminist, postcolonial, and queer scholars contend that global imperialism creates a fetishization of "brown" and "native" bodies that simultaneously invokes fear and a need for colonial rule, yet fuels a sexual fascination that transpires into sexual tourism (Puar, 2005). Third World bodies become the site of exotic fantasy. Colonizers ranging from British Anglo heterosexual men to U.S. white gay men and lesbians imagine a mutual attraction and seek engagement through physical, psychological, and/or spiritual forms of intimacy (Povinelli, 2006). This imagined "reciprocal arrangement," however, typically involves financial transaction underpinned by an asymmetrical economy of money, status, or position. Yet as McClintock (1995) argues, studies of colonial power must include a discussion of desires, pleasures, and agency that "question[s] the binary verities of dominance and resistance" (p. 141). The postcolonial subject navigates existing "circuits of knowledge production" as much as she creates new relations, dynamics, and affective responses to the complex interplay of what Stoler (2006) refers to as the "tense and tender ties" of colonial intimacy. In line with such scholarship, I investigate the lyrics of "10 dollar" to illustrate "how habits of the heart and comportment have been recruited to the service of colonial governance but [are] never wholly subsumed by it" (Stoler, 2006, p. 4).

The song "10 dollar" tells the story of a modern day "third world Lolita." The main character is a "young Chinna girl" from a small town. Like Lolita, this Chinna girl is not a "village virgin" but rather a "platinum digger" with "her sights on a bigger world" (Arulpragrasum, 2004).[8] The story goes that she went to the shop and didn't have "enough" (presumably money), but she "clocked him looking right at her / So she sucked on a lollipop." The song continues, "Chinna girl grew up to be a big girl" who still wanted this "bigger world," and she saw her ticket when she caught "a Yorkshire banker, a geezer / staring right at her / so she sucked on a lollipop." This "dial-a-bride from Sri Lanka" saw that this Yorkshire banker, this old time geezer could help her get (out) with things, like money, a plane ticket, and even a visa.

According to the song, the bride "paid him with her knees up." But M.I.A. seems hopeful and writes, "Years later, started to ease up / Got her own way, shouted out, 'see ya.'" The song ends with several iterations of the chorus, "What can I get for 10 dollar? / Anything you want." It is unclear who the "speaking I" is in the chorus (Butler, 1993). Is it the "young Chinna girl" asking the shopkeeper or the Yorkshire banker the price of what she wanted? And what was it that she wanted? Is it a calling card, a visa, a plane ticket? Or is the "speaking I" the shopkeeper or the banker asking, as they would a prostitute, what they could get for a small bill? The latter interpretation would make sense, but the previous verse says that the bride "paid" the banker (presumed husband). In the act of paying the banker, does this not imply some agency through economic exchange? Although dominant discourses on sex work construct the worker as a "victim," several activists and scholars maintain that sex work can be consensual (and perhaps desirable) even in the context of imperialist heteropatriarchy.[9] This tension raises questions about complicity in theorizing agency and resistance related to "critical sites for the consolidation of colonial power" (Stoler, 2006, p. 4). What is the price of freedom for young women in the global economy given the "tense and tender ties" of intimacy?

According to the United States Citizenship and Immigration Services (USCIS), there are between 4,000 and 6,000 *documented* cases of international marriages brokered through legal means (Scholes & Phataraloaha, 1999, p. 3). This figure does not account for the number of girls and women who are illegally "smuggled" into the United States, Great Britain, and Germany to serve as domestic or sex workers through externally mediated financial transactions. It also does not take into account the informal and formal arrangements made by individuals, families, community networks, and inter/national organizations to facilitate the im/migration of persons for reasons ranging from traditional matchmaking to relocation to improve one's quality of life.

How we interpret this data, of course, depends on the discursive frameworks of the reader. Should we gather, from this data, that "third world young women" are being exploited at alarming rates through international sex traffic? As Bhattacharyya (2005) and Davidson (2005) argue, much of the national and international laws on international marriage assumes that men are dangerous and that the potential brides either are or will become victims of sexual abuse.

Perhaps this view is taken by George W. Bush when he signed into legislation the Trafficking Victims Protection Act that puts more government restrictions on the types of international marriages or kinship arrangements permissible by law and managed by USCIS. But could we alternatively interpret from this data that there is something else happening that explains why so many young women, particularly from Eastern Europe, Eastern and South Asia are willing/able to participate in the "risky business" of international marriages? How and who would determine what kinds of intimate relationships are a product of choice or coercion?

While I do not diminish the suffering that may accompany life in either the sex trade or the "mail bride" industry, I want to highlight the ways in which both Western feminist and U.S. political discourses position women who participate in such work as "victims" who need to be "rescued." For example, Agustín (2007) is critical of the "rescue industry" noting that discursive practices associated with the antitrafficking movement employ the very "disempowering" imperialist and capitalist agendas it supposedly "protects" against. As M.I.A. points out in her music, immigrants, refugees, and persons of the Third World can and do resist through economic, political, and cultural discursive practices. Whether it is selling drugs, a.k.'s, or participating in armed combat, such as suicide bombing, those at the "underbelly" of systemic domination fight back and "give 'im a run at his own game" (Arulpragasum, 2004). But what is the "game" that M.I.A. references in "10 dollar"?

Although there are no spaces free of global capitalism, patriarchy, and racialized violence, it is important to take into consideration the particular contexts of power/resistance framing the story and actions of the dial-a-bride from Sri Lanka. First, we need to remember that Sri Lanka is a former colony of Britain that gained its independence in 1948. However, like many former colonies, economic and political life continues to be beholden to the West, and retains external and internal antagonisms as a result of neocolonialism, high rates of poverty, and effects of natural disasters. Since the deregulation of international trade agreements in the latter half of the twentieth century, many Western-owned corporations set up manufacturing plants to take advantage of cheap labor. Thus, it is no coincidence that the Sri Lankan bride sets her sights on a "Yorkshire banker" not only because he is a wealthy man, but also because he symbolically represents the colonizer of which she wants revenge.

Second, "10 dollar" foregrounds one of the strategies made possible by patriarchy, sexual manipulation, of which all characters are complicit. Both the shopkeeper and the Yorkshire banker are enticed by a seemingly innocent girl whom they see as an opportunity to get what they want. The girl, who turns out to be not so innocent, capitalizes on their fetish as a passport to a particular commodified freedom. Whether it is the commodity of food or a visa, it is the girl who comes out of the exchanges with some things. I should underscore that, while the girl uses (and loses, some may argue) something in the exchanges, she successfully leverages objects that will tangibly translate into material survival and geographic mobility. Moreover, she is aware of the importance of these commodities in the long-term trajectory of her life.

Finally, how should we read the sexual and racialized politics of "10 dollar"? The name of the song and the intertextual references may be clues to interpret some of the dynamics. The line "What can I get for 10 dollar?" is a direct reference to a scene in the Stanley Kubrick film *Full Metal Jacket*, where two U.S. soldiers solicit a Vietnamese prostitute by asking the same question, "What can I get for 10 dollars?" To which she replies, "Anything you want." Since the film *Full Metal Jacket* is a scathing critique of the psychosocial effects of imperialist wars, the song can be located in anti-imperialist and antiwar discourses. These discourses resonate across M.I.A.'s music, not just making explicit references to historical injustices against third world countries but also in the current context of U.S. economic and military imperialism worldwide. In the "bonus" song of the first album, M.I.A. sings, "You can watch the t.v. / You can watch the media / President Bush doing takeova." She adds, from the "Prime Minister to your employer / ego-lovers need more power." Going through a list of nation-states, she asks, "Who the fuck's your president?"

Fighting back in the "new world order," according to M.I.A., is about "guerrilla warfare." Flipping the 1960s rhetoric in the U.S. attempts to win the "hearts and minds" of the Vietnamese, M.I.A. shows that what it takes for subaltern resistance is not just to put "guns up" but to play out warfare through the cultural scripts available to Third World women, such as "you suck, you blow" which shows up repeatedly in her songs. Her claim that she is a soldier, "a nice, nice fighter," can be read as the lollipop sucking Lolita or the female Tamil Tiger "Bird of Freedom" who might have a grenade stuffed inside her dress or basket.[10] She contests the U.S. and European imperialist discourses that construct Third World girls as props to legitimize the "assistance" "liberation" of (primarily male) military troops in order to "free" them from the assumed limits of "primitive" societies and as the presumed innocent victims and survivors of "terrorist attacks."[11] Yet, the fact that girls living in war zones, such as the Freedom Birds, comprise 42 percent of the active armed military (Mathieu, 2006) reminds us that the discourses of girlhood are not a mere product of local cultural scripts or transnational political and economic campaigns, but a hybrid space of contested terrain. Explanations of how and why girls participate in arenas of conflict are as varied and intricate as the roots and effects of sex, race, and war. What seems clear, however, is that desires for "freedom" require attachments of intimacy to ideas, practices, and objects that stretch beyond the limits of logic. Asked if she would give up her life to be a suicide bomber, one female Tamil soldier confessed to an Al-Jazeera reporter, "Yes, if the leader permits me, yes I would" (Grey, 2007).

While the connection between the female suicide bomber and the dial-a-bride may not be obvious in the context of Western-based girlhood studies, M.I.A.'s biographical position and symbolic representations make explicit the "tense and tender ties" of colonial intimacy. Singing from the position of a Sri Lankan/British refugee rebel girl, M.I.A.'s project demonstrates how global capitalism and imperialism shape the possibilities and limitations of particular forms of agency for girls/young women in transnational contexts. Whether it is the Bird of Freedom or the modern day Lolita, both figures employ the duplicitous images of their embodied "innocence" to fight back and fight for "liberation" for themselves and/or their communities.

Conclusion

M.I.A's cultural work pushes the limits of the logic of multiple fields of scholarship, global youth studies, and girlhood studies more specifically. By taking up the position of the Chinna girl, M.I.A. suggests that Third World girls are neither "free" nor "innocent" in mapping their destinies in transnational contexts that privilege heteropatriarchy, imperialism, and global capitalism.[12] Yet M.I.A., like the Chinna girl, exercises agency in navigating the local and global environments in which she is positioned.

Jacqui Alexander's notion of pedagogies of crossing is instructive in providing a framework to understand how Third World girls are actively involved in making meaning of their lived experiences. Employing a framework of border crossing suggests that Third World girls are engaged in making strategic decisions at "the crossroads, the space of convergence and endless possibility; the place where we put down and discard the unnecessary in order to pick up that which is necessary" (Alexander, 2005, p. 8). For the Chinna girl, this may imply sexual brokerage with the Yorkshire banker. For M.I.A., it may mean gaining success as a celebrity Third World girl within U.S. media outlets. For the female postcolonial critic, it may suggest working within and against academic subdivisions to suture a theoretically hybrid framework such as a transnational feminist approach to studies of girlhoods. The "costs" are certainly not the same across various contexts, but the point is to put these points of border crossing into conversation regarding the psychosocial effects of heteropatriarchy, global capitalism, and imperialism.

I end with Chandra Mohanty's vision for the field of women's studies and the need for comparative feminist studies. For Mohanty (2003), a comparative feminist model:

> is based on the premise that the local and the global are not defined in terms of physical geography or territory but exist simultaneously and constitute each other.... Differences and commonalities thus exist in relation and tension with each other in all contexts. What is emphasized are relations of mutuality, co-responsibility and common interests, anchoring the idea of feminist solidarity.... the focus is not just on the intersections of race, class, gender, nation, and sexuality in different communities of women but on mutuality and co-implication, which suggests the interweaving of the histories of these communities. (p. 242)

Following Mohanty, I suggest that the study of girlhoods must take into account how sociocultural productions of "the Western/modern girl" coexist alongside images of the exoticized "Third World" or "primitive" Other girl who is demonized for practices that represent the "dirty, pretty things" of the underbelly of globalization (i.e., hustling, prostitution, and military combat) (Giardina, 2008). As M.I.A. suggests, freedom fighting must take place on multiple fronts: the battleground, the workplace, the bedroom, and even the classroom.

The postcolonial challenge in education has many faces, issues, and debates. In this chapter, I point to some of the literature within postcolonial, transnational, and global youth studies as useful frameworks for understanding the contemporary scene of globalization and education. Working through the gap within each of these literatures, my analysis of the performance art of M.I.A. seeks to articulate a transnational feminist approach to the study of girlhoods. M.I.A., a Sri Lankan/British "refugee rebel girl" who produces popular yet anti-imperialist music, shows how "subaltern" young women not only personally navigate through the dynamics of global capitalism, imperialism, and sexual politics, but also epitomize the kind of pedagogy of crossing that is attainable and necessary to the larger project of shifting the real and imaginary spaces of "sacred possession."

Notes

1. Drawing on cultural studies (Spivak, 1999), I use the term *postcolonial* to link with cultural "work" (academic, aesthetic, activist, etc.) that references the historical, sociocultural, and psychological conditions, dynamics, and politics of European and U.S. imperialism in Africa, the Americas, and Asia/Pacific. The term *transnational* signals the "ethnoscapes" (Appadurai, 1996) created by economic, informational, technological, cultural, political, and ideological flows across, within, and between nation-states. The term *global* is an artifact of modernist discourse in anthropology that serves as a signifier of orientalism (Said, 1978) equating United States/United Kingdom with "home" and non-United States/United Kingdom with "travel." Like the term international, global is often deployed unproblematically within and outside academic discussions of contemporary political, economic, and social practices without attention to its link to imperialist discourses of "development." Grewal and Kaplan (2000, p. 1) coined the term "transnational feminist practices" as a theory and method to "break down the disciplinary divides between American studies and Area studies, women's studies and ethnic studies, as well as between studies of high and low culture."

2. See Weems (in press) for an analysis of the field of girlhood studies as a contested terrain in terms of racial and national dimensions of gender, sexuality, and the definitions of "girlhood."

3. See Sepia Mutiny (http://www.sepiamutiny.com/sepia/archives/001043.html) and Desi

Blogs (http://desiblogs.blogspot.com/2004/07/maya-arulpragasum-next-big-thing.html) for a sampling of the debates about M.I.A.'s political beliefs among South Asians across the globe.

4. The actual reason why M.I.A. was denied entry to the United States is unknown. However, this did not stop formal news stories and informal blogging on the matter. Retrieved November 1, 2008, from http://www.asiansinmedia.org/news/article.php/music/1321

5. Retrieved November 1, 2008, from http://sundaytimes.lk/070826/Interntional/i517.html

6. See Weems (under review) for a discussion on how transnational media outlets participate in the production and circulation of M.I.A. as a "Tamil hottie."

7. Thanks to Aliya Rahman for helping me crystallize this point.

8. Chinna is the Tamil word for a female villager. The term "village virgin" is an effect of modernist and imperialist discourses on gender and geography that is taken for granted yet rarely theorized in postcolonial studies. It references the practice of locating and procuring an innocent or sexually pure female from a village who will maintain the mandates of "tradition" despite a transnational sexual contract.

9. For example, the Sex Workers' Rights Advocacy Network (SWAN) is a group of international sex workers who educate themselves and others about the complex economic, political, and health dimensions of sex work in Europe and Asia. Retrieved November 1, 2008, from http://swannet.org/en/node/955

10. It is claimed by the LTTE that a Bird of Freedom was responsible for the 1991 assassination of Rajiv Gandhi, the former prime minister of India. Retrieved November 1, 2008, from http://english.aljazeera.net/NR/exeres/41D90602-2717-4E42-B47B-180816031476.htm

11. Bush, G. W. (2007, January 23). State of the union address.

12. For an exploration of the virgin/whore dichotomy and its particular effects on Third World and postcolonial women, see Gloria Anzaldúa's (1999) discussion of the intertwined figures of *la virgen* and *la malinche*.

References

Aapola, S., Gonick, M., & Harris, A. (2005). *Young femininity: Girlhood, power and social change.* New York: Palgrave Macmillan.

Agustin, L. M. (2007). *Sex at the margins: Migration, labour markets and the rescue industry.* London: Zed.

Alexander, M. J. (2005). *Pedagogies of crossing: Meditations on feminism, sexual politics, memory, and the sacred.* Durham, NC: Duke University Press.

Anzaldúa, G. (1999). *Borderlands = la frontera* (2nd ed.). San Francisco, CA: Aunt Lute.

Appadurai, A. (1996). *Modernity at large: Cultural dimensions of globalization.* Minneapolis: University of Minnesota Press.

Arulpragasum, M. (2004). *Arular* [CD]. Santa Monica, CA: Interscope.

Arulpragasum, M. (2007). *Kala* [CD]. Santa Monica, CA: Interscope.

Bettis, P., & Adams, N. G. (2005). *Geographies of girlhood: Identities in-between.* Mahwah, NJ: Lawrence Erlbaum Associates.

Bhattacharyya, G. (2005). *Traffick: The illicit movement of people and things.* London: Pluto.

Brown, R. N. (2008). *Black girlhood celebration: Toward a hip-hop feminist pedagogy.* New York: Peter Lang.

Brumberg, J. J. (1997). *The body project: An intimate history of American girls.* New York: Random

House.
Butler, J. (1993). *Bodies that matter: On the discursive limits of "sex"*. New York: Routledge.
Chow, R., & Ang, I. (1993). *Writing diaspora*. Bloomington: Indiana University Press.
Christgau, R., Fricke, D., Hoard, C., & Sheffield, R. (2007, December 27). The top 50 albums of 2007. *Rolling Stone*, p. 7. Retrieved December 30, 2007, from http://www.rollingstone.com/news/story/17601851/the_top_50_albums_of_2007
Davidson, J. O. (2005). *Children in the global sex trade*. Cambridge: Polity.
Dimitriadis, G., & McCarthy, C. (2001). *Reading and teaching the postcolonial: From Baldwin to Basquiat and beyond*. New York: Teachers College Press.
Dolby, N., & Rizvi, F. (Eds.). (2008). *Youth moves: Identities and education in global perspective*. New York: Routledge.
Foucault, M. (1980). *The history of sexuality*. New York: Vintage.
Giardina, M. (2008). Consuming difference: Stylish hybridity, diasporic identity, and the politics of youth culture. In N. Dolby & F. Rizvi (Eds.), *Youth moves: Identities and education in global perspective* (pp. 69-84). New York: Routledge.
Grewal, I., & Kaplan, C. (2000). Postcolonial studies and transnational feminist practices. Retrieved November 13, 2008, from http://social.chass.ncsu.edu/jouvert/v5i1/grewal.htm
Grey, K. (2007). We are freedom fighters. *LankaNewspapers.com*. Retrieved March 10, 2008, from http://www.lankanewspapers.com/news/2007/7/17613_space.html
Hernandez, D., & Rehman, B. (Eds.). (2002). *Colonize this!: Young women of color on today's feminism*. New York: Seal.
Jayasena, N. (2007). Where have all the Tamils gone?: Ethnicity and the body in the films of Prasanna Vithange. Unpublished manuscript.
Jiwani, Y., Steenbergen, C., & Mitchell, C. (2006). *Girlhood: Redefining the limits*. Montreal and New York: Black Rose.
Kearney, M. C. (2006). *Girls make media*. New York: Routledge.
Kubrick, S. (Producer/Director and Writer), & Hasford, G. (Writer). (1987). *Full metal jacket* [Motion picture]. California, United States: Warner Brothers Pictures.
Lamb, S., & Brown, L. M. (2007). *Packaging girlhood: Rescuing our daughters from marketers' schemes*. New York: St. Martin's Griffin.
Lowe, L. (2006). The intimacy of four continents. In A. L. Stoler (Ed.), *Haunted by empire: Geographies of intimacy in North American history* (pp. 191-212). Durham, NC: Duke University Press.
Maira, S., & Soep, E. (2004). *Youthscapes: The popular, the national, the global*. Philadelphia: University of Pennsylvania Press.
Mathieu, A. (2006). *Reaching the girls in South Asia: Differentiated needs and responses in emergencies*. Formal report of the United Nations Girls Education Initiative (UNGEI). Kathmandu, Nepal: United Nations Children's Fund (UNICEF).
McCarthy, C., Hudak, G., Miklaucic, S., & Saukko, P. (Eds.). (1999). *Sound identities: Popular music and the cultural politics of education*. New York: Peter Lang.
McClintock, A. (1995). *Imperial leather*. New York: Routledge.
McRobbie, A. (2000). *Feminism and youth culture* (2nd ed.). New York: Routledge.
Mitchell, C., & Reid-Walsh, J. (2005). *Seven going on seventeen: Tween studies in the culture of girlhood*. New York: Peter Lang.
Mohanty, C. T. (2003). *Feminism without borders: Decolonizing theory, practicing solidarity*. Durham, NC: Duke University Press.

Muggleton, D., & Weinzierl, R. (Eds.). (2003). *The post-subcultures reader*. Oxford and New York: Berg.

Povinelli, E. A. (2006). *The empire of love: Toward a theory of intimacy, genealogy, and carnality*. Durham, NC: Duke University Press.

Puar, J. K. (2005). Queer times, queer assemblages. *Social Text, 23*(3-4), 121-139.

Rhee, J. (2006). Re/membering (to) shifting alignments: Korean women's transnational narratives in US higher education. *International Journal of Qualitative Studies in Education, 19*(5), 595-615.

Said, E. (1978). *Orientalism*. New York: Pantheon.

Scholes, R., & Phataraloaha, A. (1999, February). Appendix A: The mail order bride industry and its impact on U.S. immigration. *International matchmaking agencies: A report to Congress*. United States Citizenship and Immigration Services, Washington, D.C.

Spivak, G. C. (1990). *The postcolonial critic: Interviews, strategies, dialogues*. New York: Routledge.

Spivak, G. C. (1999). *A critique of postcolonial reason: Toward a history of the vanishing present*. Cambridge, MA: Harvard University Press.

Stoler, A. L. (2006). Intimidations of empire: Predicaments of the tactile and unseen. In A. L. Stoler (Ed.), *Haunted by empire: Geographies of intimacy in North American history* (pp. 1-22). Durham, NC: Duke University Press.

Weems, L. (in press). Not M.I.A.: Postcolonial girls' agency and the need for transnational girlhood studies. *Girlhood Studies*.

Weems, L. (under review). From "Freedom Bird" to "Tamil hottie": The transnational politics of sexuality in media representations of M.I.A. *Feminist Media Studies*.

Widner, J. (2007). M.I.A., LCD, ACL. *Dallas Observer*. Retrieved December 7, 2007, from http://www.dallasobserver.com/2007-09-20/music/m-i-a-lcd-acl/

CHAPTER 12

Postcolonial Studies as Re-education: Learning from J. M. Coetzee's *Disgrace*

APARNA MISHRA TARC

> "Perhaps that is what I must learn to accept. To start at ground level. With nothing. Not with nothing but. With nothing. No cards, no weapons, no property, no rights, no dignity."
> "Like a dog."
> "Yes, like a dog."
>
> — Coetzee, 2000, p. 205

In the ruins of the failed colonial apartheid state is a glimmer of learning. Uttered by Lucy, the daughter of the main protagonist David Lurie in J. M. Coetzee's highly acclaimed novel *Disgrace* (2000), the words contain a painful lesson for those marred by colonial pasts. In bearing and being witness to the state of disgrace characterizing post-apartheid South Africa, Lucy learns how to be differently human. The demand to respond to the suffering of others, she suggests, defying both the white Afrikaner patriarchs and the black African anti-colonialist revolutionaries that rule her worlds, is one of remembrance and redress articulated in and as forms of learning. What Lucy seeks by submitting to her place in South Africa's traumatic colonial past is the possibility of a shared, negotiated community and future with others afflicted by South Africa's brutal history of mass violence.

Postcolonial studies are slow to come to education, in part, because postcolonial studies threaten to undo education, to unravel the passionately held-onto thought and knowledge of the modern Western-educated student and scholar. Postcolonial studies have long been associated with literary or "post"-

informed theories, and have been sidelined by critical theorists and positivists alike for their supposed non-material, non-empirical significance. In this chapter I demonstrate how postcolonial studies can and do affect the social in schools, in aesthetic and artistic movements, and in the political arena. The potential effect of postcolonial studies on political and social life, I argue, using the exemplary case of J. M. Coetzee's *Disgrace*, is pedagogical (Dimitriadis & McCarthy, 2001). My reading of this novel follows the re-education of David Lurie as he begins, reluctantly, to situate his subject formation and dehumanizing treatment of women and blacks in South Africa's disgrace-full colonial history. While re-education is a process that both colonized and colonizer must undergo in the aftermath of long and systematic mass violence, my analysis focuses on the re-education of the South African colonizer through the "difficult" learning of the seemingly ordinary, banal figure of David Lurie (Britzman, 1998, 2003, 2006). I also focus on the role that the female figures play in the novel's narration of disgrace and in my analysis of Lurie's process of re-education. I demonstrate how the ethico-aesthetic pedagogy of the novel moves the main character and, with him, the reader to think and act differently in the world with all sentient beings. Re-education as postcolonial studies can be a means of social movement towards repairing existing dysfunctional colonial institutions and broken human relations. Pedagogical interventions, as engaged by political figures, artists, and activists, provide the grounds for life-sustaining and less violent social and political movements of change and justice.

As Paulo Freire (1982) points out, if colonizing education has the means to create a particular kind of capitalist subject, an ethically responsive education has the means to intervene in this wide-reaching capitalist formation. After all, Gayatri Spivak (1992) insists, the British empire utilized the less coercive agent of English literacy and not brute violence to rearrange the desires and dreams of its colonial subjects: "Literature buys your assent in an almost clandestine way and therefore is an excellent instrument for a slow transformation of the mind. For good and ill" (p. 279). We might look to an ethically responsive postcolonial literacy and literature to intervene in the global practice of a market-driven, instrumentalized version of English education towards the creation of a socially responsive global imaginary. A significant challenge for postcolonial education scholars, then, is to attend to the difficult task of engaging with suppressed histories of mass violence. This past violence can be linked to contemporary civil and ethnic conflicts reasserting themselves throughout the globe in state, civil, and sporadic conflict in relation to global forces reorganizing transnational human relations and hierarchies (Appadurai, 2006). In the wake of increased global flows, forces, and movement, debates over how to decolonize former colonized states from imperialist forms of governance seem all but in memory.

Without attending to the colonial past of injustice structuring our deeply divided worlds, the current era risks reanimating imperialist desires for global dominance while simultaneously summoning half-abandoned calls for retribution in anti-colonial states and societies. A new and volatile history, centered on non-responsive, unaccountable capital, inserts nations and their citizens through structural adjustment plans and market-driven Western education into a rapidly polarizing, global economy (Hall in MacCabe, 2008). Disregarding the colonial histories leading to the present social and economic inequities between the West and others, warns Fazal Rizvi (2007), promotes an ahistorical acceptance of the new global order and market-created social imaginary. While this order and imaginary presents itself as the promise of the future for a powerful few, it suppresses the dreams of emancipation from violence and poverty longed for by the majority of the world's inhabitants. Fortified by their past and present collusion with imperialist and corporate power, elite classes, whether they are of the "democratically elected," ruling, revolutionary, or military classes (Appadurai, 2006), take the restructuring opportunity that globalization affords to construct nations in their own image and interests.

Arjun Appadurai (2006) attributes the recent worldwide upsurge of violence against immigrants and refugees to the pressures of forced global migration stemming from civil conflict in ex-colonial nations. The influx of foreigners from warring states compels some nations to rebuild themselves according to self-preserving narratives of birthright, entitlement, and purity. The official narratives serve to secure from foreigners a claim to resources and nominal standards of living. Formerly colonized nation-states are not giving way to new formations of transnational solidarity, and the elites within these states are working diligently to preserve a hyper-nationalist brand of itself, a brand that is grounded in racial intolerance and guarded by the twin high-security gates of ethnic purity and superiority. The enforced establishment of identity giving way to renewed nationalist uprisings plunges fragile, emerging democracies into chaos and bloodshed.

Caught in the middle of volatile returns to new nationalisms are ethnic and religious minorities. The minority populations are forced en masse from their homelands and, in the process of global redistribution, become socially and politically unrecognizable in their new countries. Ethnic minorities are without citizenship and without recourse to the rule of law afforded by the infrastructures of a civil society and stable governance (Agamben, 2005). In addition, minorities are being socially reassembled according to the commodity value of their bodies, knowledge, and labor (Appadurai, 2006). The number of migrant workers, largely from lower socio-economic sectors of third world and post-Soviet era nations, who are recruited for domestic service work, organ donation, and sex trades, attests to the growing feminization, reclassification, and commodification of women, the poor, and the racialized (Sassen, 2002). Consequently it is neither sustainable nor safe only to reclaim minority status and history as the way to social justice. Postcolonial education scholarship has the responsibility to intervene in what may well be an ominous and more vicious return to misogyny, othering, and abjection occurring within minority groups in the ex-colonies and ex-colonial nations. The "new" violence and hatred, set starkly against the global scramble for capital and commodities, are orchestrated by dominant elites and enacted by the marginalized upon other marginalized people (Appadurai, 2006).

In light of ethnic conflicts worldwide, the stakes are high for postcolonial scholars and activists to resituate forces of globalization in histories of oppression and failed liberation movements (Rizvi, 2007). The anti-colonial imaginary of "beyond colonization" needs to reorient itself towards, what Stuart Hall terms as, "the beyond of the global economy" (Hall in MacCabe, 2008, p. 18). As nations find themselves dependent on corporate benefactors, the terms "colonizer" and "colonized" by which anti-colonizing movements once operated no longer exist. Local elites have moved to secure their place and claim to dwindling resources in former anti-colonial states and ghettoized communities where homegrown militia of mostly young, disenfranchised men wage brutal warfare over women, children, minorities, and each other. For the inhabitants of ghettoized communities and urban slums in "emerging nations," there is no end to war, violence, and despair.

The challenge for educators in classrooms and grassroots social movements is to bring to the forefront the dysfunctional modes of human relating that have given way to the present geopolitical and social formations. With other scholars working in the area of historical remembrance, I see a large part of this project as supporting formerly traumatized populations in pedagogical practices that address, heal, and bridge socio-economic divisions within and between minority and dominant groups (Pinar, in press; Simon, Rosenberg, & Eppert, 2000; Simon, 2005). The task requires scholars and activists to perform what Appadurai (2006) characterizes as "the hardest of analytical exercises" (p. 46): to conduct interdisciplinary examinations of the viscerally experienced and materially lived histories of colonization and genocide leading to this globalizing moment. The imperative is "hard" in terms of educational research because "conventional emphasis on racism's material and discursive history tends to ignore this phenomenon's impalpable forms" (Lane, 1998, p. 4). Educational research traditionally fixates on the observed and measurable even though much of our learning and socialization occur below the surface of what can be seen and known (Britzman, 2006). Literary and artistic depictions of mass violence can teach us how to engage with the "anxieties, fears and seductions" manifesting inside of our individual, social, and political (un)consciousness (Appadurai, 2006).

Judith Butler (2004) writes, "If we are interested in arresting cycles of violence to produce less violent outcomes, it is no doubt important to ask what, politically, might be made of grief besides a cry for war" (p. vii). Although framed as a political imperative, the demand Butler makes is profoundly pedagogical. Arresting cycles of violence in the production of less violent outcomes can come about only through the less violent act of learning, by our being pedagogically moved to change the way we have learned to relate to others and to reorient our socialization away from brutal regimes of thinking and being (Lévinas, 1969). For the difficult learning, I turn to sustained literary engagements with practices of historical remembrance. Based on lessons from Coetzee's *Disgrace* of what it means to represent, bear, face, and learn from violence and one's place in a violent human history, I suggest that what might be politically and pedagogically inserted between the cry of sorrow and the cry for arms is postcolonial studies as re-education, a potentially reparative, justice-oriented, and socially altering curriculum.

Learning from *Disgrace*

Jacques Derrida (1986) cites South African apartheid as an exemplary case of European colonization. Apartheid, Derrida writes, is the most heinous and disgraceful of social experiments, inscribing in the body while instituting in civil structures the ultimate form of apartness made legitimate by an extreme form of state-sanctioned racial segregation. Remembering apartheid is to learn how to be differently human from the personal and public histories archiving the modern, social-scientific experiment of race.

J. M. Coetzee's *Disgrace* takes on the risky remembering. The novel seeks to pedagogically immerse readers in the violent affects of ambivalence that structure the racist colonial scene. The resurfacing of affect in the narrative articulating human and historical conflict serves to restage, in literary form, the imagined perverse desires and sadistic impulses driving European colonial projects (Pinar, 1993). As with an analysis, the novel functions by entering into the bodies of its characters to expunge unspeakable narratives of suffering, failed repression, and dangerous memories. Unlike, or perhaps in response to, the religious overtones of the African National Congress' (ANC) Truth and Reconciliation Commission (TRC), the novel wrestles with the difficult question of what it means to forgive the unforgivable. The novel suggests that our present means of learning from the past are inadequate. *Disgrace* imagines how we might recover and remake dehumanized bodies and human relations from our formative education in violent, sexist, and racist educational institutions. Through its ethico-aesthetic pedagogy, it invites us to consider how we might rebuild a relatively balanced psychosocial state of lived community from one seemingly beyond repair.

The novel is educationally and politically significant for a number of reasons. First, *Disgrace* has reached a critical mass of readers in South Africa and beyond; its worldwide appeal is worth considering from an educational and political standpoint. Second, it offers readers an engagement with the other's violence that resists further violating through the intrusion of objectifying and sensationalizing apparatus like mass media. Third, its ethico-aesthetic and formal operations pedagogically move us to take in and take into historical account the disturbing scenes of human violence. As learners, teachers, and scholars, we have much to learn from Coetzee's painstakingly attentive and disciplined textual practice and teachings. Many of the main characters in Coetzee's novels are failed teachers who manage, despite their limitations, to move us to think otherwise by asking us to engage with the ethical, moral, and social conflicts leading to their undoing. There is a significant role for literature in our political movements toward justice if we can learn to teach, think, and act differently by learning from a novel's pedagogical lessons.

Disgrace is set in the aftermath of South African apartheid. The narrative revolves around an aging, white, English professor struggling to find meaning for himself in his own and the nation's newly fallen state. No longer heady with power in terms of youth, sexual virility, and whiteness, David Lurie is a typically overlooked and seemingly benign kind of colonial figure: an aging, indifferent, and deeply disappointed one. A former university English teacher who is attached to humanist knowledge and aware of racial injustice, he is, at the same time, unmoved to shake the privilege of Afrikaner whiteness and the accompanying perverse male desire from his body (Pinar, 1993). Bound to his version of a humanist education, which contains an eclectic curriculum of selected triumphant and tragic European works, he moves in the world with ease and without thought to (ab)using women and words to construct a palatable narrative for his actions and ontological views. Lurie internalizes a tautological narrative that helps him justify his self-serving, bordering on cruel, sexual and epistemic treatment of others. When he is found guilty of abusing his academic power with a female student, he retreats to his daughter's farm rather than take responsibility, utterly disgraced and without moorings. Barely clinging to the racist and educational ideals of South Africa's past, he is confronted by his daughter Lucy's personal will to accept the starkly changed relations of power between blacks and whites in the aftermath of apartheid. When Lucy is violently gang raped, set on fire, and locked in a room by her black neighbors, her father is rendered impotent and helpless to do anything to stop the attack on himself and his daughter. Lurie's weak capacity for response is further disabled by the prospect of Lucy's pregnancy with her rapist's child. He is left shaken by Lucy's determination to recover from the trauma of rape while trying to learn how to live and raise her child with her attackers on their terms.

The novel implies that populations affected by mass violence need to re-enter history as fully re-formed subjects, subjects who can participate in their nation's future despite and in spite of the social, economic, and racial divisions wrought by an unrelenting past and exacerbated by a rapidly restructuring present. The novel's unstated call for re-education as a radical subject and social reformation is directed at those affected by mass violence across generations, whether they are ex-colonialists struggling to come to terms with a legacy of brutality or the ex-colonized attempting to form a co-habitable society with their oppressors and enemies. Re-education, as I conceptualize in the chapter, is not in the order of "reformation of character ... counseling ... recantation, self criticism or public apology" (Coetzee, 2000, p. 66). Rather re-education is a way of responding to and showing concern for the lives of others. Re-education redevelops within us our human capacity for responding to and feeling for others by virtue of being born from and dependent on (m)others (Klein, 1937/1984; Lévinas, 1969).

Lurie seems unmoved to respond to the suffering inflicted by him or others, deeming "re-education" as "compromising" himself to others rather than a means by which he might learn to be affected by the lives of others (Coetzee, 2000, p. 66). In contrast, his daughter Lucy seems to intuitively subject herself to re-education as providing a way for blacks and whites to move forward in South Africa. Lucy's re-education begins by engaging with the lives of others through encounters that seem to redevelop the originary capacity to feel for others. Lucy's example of ethical redress is just this: a way to literally bear the suffering of others by taking that suffering upon herself or, as she puts it, to "pay the price" for the wrongs suffered by blacks in the hands of her white (fore)father(s). Mark Sanders (2002) suggests that the novel parallels Lucy's gesture by bearing the disgrace of apartheid that many white South Africans still refuse to admit:

> The work enters into the wager of elaborating, in its own way, upon disgrace. *Disgrace* not only takes it upon itself to narrate the fall from grace of Professor David Lurie of Cape Technical University, but, through its syntax, performs disgrace, what it is to be in disgrace, and, perhaps, what it takes to end disgrace. (p. 363)

The novel takes the aesthetic risk of reanimating the affects of disgrace circulating through the lives of its characters. *Disgrace* places the reader in a face-to-face encounter with the other's suffering as and in the form of relearning. I conceive re-education, a process rejected by David Lurie in the novel, as a sustained and committed engagement to repairing our seemingly irreparable, damaged, and damning relationships with others. Part of this learning involves what Ngugi wa Thiong'o (1986) calls "decolonizing the mind" through a curriculum of reparation that learns from and responds to histories of mass violence and dehumanization.

Franz Fanon's (1967) pedagogical project, often read only for its material or revolutionary significance, is of existential historical remembrance, grief, and mourning. Fanon comes to terms with an internalized self-violence that is brought about by a racist education, an education binding him to a dehumanizing version of black existence that he refuses and is helpless to accept. Not only do we need to decolonize our nations and ourselves, but we also need to learn how to decolonize our dysfunctional relations with others in order to learn how to live with and "among" them. Fanon attempts to work out the persisting effects of colonialism and racism to repair the blight of (self) loathing afflicting him so that he might enter into Western history as a newly formed and ready subject to wage "hand-to-hand bodily struggle" with the psychosocial, epistemic, and material effects of persecution (Derrida, 2005, p. 99). Without attention to the trauma that wounds of colonialism and racism leave in the minds and bodies of their subjects, Fanon insists that there is little way for racialized peoples to restore their humanity to its original full state.

The double bind of racism, as Homi Bhabha (1994) articulates, is mutual misrecognition in which colonizer, native informant, and colonized are perpetually bound together by splitting ambivalence and paranoid suspicion. In the novel, Coetzee figures the double bind in the mirror of the narrative where white and black South African characters and the reader are forced to "view" the distortions they have created of self and other through the narrative's asymmetrical and distorted lens. The reader is made to trust neither the image of blacks, women, and white South Africans, nor the "potentially resurfacing" images of self and other that she has learned to internalize through her formative education (Britzman, 2006). Through the formal and aesthetic operations Coetzee uses to structure the text, the dynamics of misrecognition plaguing the characters in the novel penetrates the reader. The reader finds herself making identifications with and defending against the distorted and disturbing images of self and other. The dynamics of misrecognition structuring *Disgrace* and taken in while reading make for the reader a disturbing and unsettling literary and/or learning experience (Britzman, 2006; Mishra Tarc, 2007).

To engage in postcolonial studies as the critical practice of historical remembrance is to examine and intervene in dysfunctional human relations that perpetuate mass violence. Postcolonial studies as re-education asks us to willingly learn from our formative education in colonizing and racist schools of thought to become open to becoming otherwise. Roger Simon (2005) conceives of historical remembrance as a form of pedagogy that

> Intentionally ... affirms or transforms established practices of historical memory through person-to-person encounters or the staging of engagement with text or image. As a pedagogical form, remembrance incorporates a set of evaluations that structure what memories should inform our social imaginations as well as a detailed set of operations for presenting and engaging historical representations intended to provoke and solidify particular affect. (p. 17)

The educator's responsibility is to listen carefully to the text of remembrance and to support students' or community members' engagement with the material accordingly. The formal and aesthetic operations of the text become a "teacher" from which we are given the opportunity to learn. Learning to read elusive affective material responsively is an ethical imperative taken on by educators and students engaging with the other's life narratives. The attentive hearing of the other's suffering is what I conceive as a "literacy of the other," an interpretive practice that redevelops the capacity to "feel for" the appeal to language and others that human suffering makes (Mishra Tarc, 2007).

Re-education as "Difficult" Learning

The point of learning from *Disgrace* is not to determine the veracity of the events taking place in the novel. We should not place this fictional accounting of history on the same level as historical testimony or witnessing. Literary testimony performs a different pedagogical function compared to the public hearing of the ANC's TRC. The TRC transcripts describe the commission as "letting the victims speak, to grant them a hearing, to hear them, in their own languages" (in Sanders, 2002, p. 3). The novel *Disgrace* functions instead as a response to the narratives of witness emerging out of the TRC. It seems to highlight the limits of commissioning forgiveness in officially directed memorials, apologies, and practices of historical remembrance. In response to the immense pressures to forgive that the TRC seems to place on victims of apartheid, the novel inserts itself in the aporias of forgiveness, in the cloistered psychical space of confused conflict where meaning breaks down and where one has neither the capacity nor the resources to forgive or be forgiving. Forgiveness is instead, as Derrida (2001) writes, an open question and a potential reopening wound that render the conditions for unconditional forgiveness (im)possible. The public hearing of historical remembrance performs an important function because it can potentially force those who have perpetuated unspeakable acts to answer to those who have suffered from them, to determine "the truth about abuses in apartheid South Africa" (Sanders, 1999, p. 3). However, the public hearings also risk failing to deliver the truth if those who commit violent acts refuse to acknowledge or admit to them. The abusers' refusal of the victims' truth has the troubling effect of further violating the victims.

Through the depiction of David Lurie's academic hearing in *Disgrace*, the novel argues indirectly that the TRC failed the victims of apartheid by not reaching the perpetuators of violence. As Hannah Arendt (1963/1994) comments in the trial of Nazi war criminal Adolf Eichmann, perpetrators have a diminished capacity for meaningful response due to the dehumanizing nature of their crimes. If there is no remorse on the part of the perpetrators, there is nothing to forgive on the part of the victims. Even if there is remorse, the victim may be unable and/or unwilling to forgive. More problematic, Derrida (2001) points out, is the condition in which the living are not in the position to offer forgiveness to the dead, leaving the living infinitely responsible for attending to the suffering of apartheid's victims.

The aporias of forgiveness that plague the TRC are mimed in the novel's staging of the academic hearing held by Lurie's peers. The inquiry seeks to examine the professor's alleged sexual misconduct with Melanie Issacs, an underage, female, "coloured" student. Lurie's easy admission of guilt of sexual misconduct with a student troubles senior professor Dr. Farodia Rasool. After Lurie's admission, Rasool struggles with how the committee can "make" the professor take responsibility for his actions:

We are going around in circles, Mr. Chair. Yes, he says he is guilty; but when we try to get specificity, all of a sudden it is not abuse of a young woman he is confessing to, just an impulse he could not resist, with no mention of the pain he has caused, no mention of the long history of exploitation of which this is a part. That is why I say it is futile to go on debating with Professor Lurie. (Coetzee, 2000, p. 53)

Lurie's lack of understanding of and denial of responsibility for his actions echo the testimonies given by prominent and ordinary white Afrikaners to the TRC. Such a position is exemplified by former Prime Minister P. W. Botha, who did not attend the "circus-like proceeding" and refused to admit to any wrongdoing (Krog, 1998). Similarly Lurie resents being put on display for his colleagues. He also refuses to fashion his admission according to, what he sees as, Rasool's presumptive finding of guilt and standards of moral behavior. To his female colleague's outrage, Lurie nonchalantly attributes his actions to an uncontrollable sexual impulse, which he claims belies mere explanation. The unaccountable rationale for his actions seems to contain a concerted effort to deny any wrongdoing. The truth of the matter leaves the committee without a reason and way to proceed. On the basis of his passive hostility and admission of guilt, Lurie's peers released the professor from his academic duties.

The spectacle of David Lurie's hearing gives us insight into the limits of public hearings for securing recognition of wrongs or justice for victims of mass violence (Arendt, 1963/1994). The findings of the proceedings depend much on the participants' anticipated wish to produce their form of moral justice or desired effect. In Lurie's case, things go terribly awry. The hearing seems to give him an opportunity to mount a defense for his questionable actions. Resting his case on an inexplicable and uncontrollable desire for younger women of color, a desire he seems to attribute to a sexual suggestion brought about by their mere existence, Lurie gives "reasons" for his perverse, uncontrollable masculine sexual desires and, by association, those driving the colonial scene. Dr. Rasool's likening of Lurie's alleged rape of his student to the historical and contemporary sexual crimes perpetuated by white men on women of color fails to register with his diminished capacity to feel for the humanity of women of color. Lurie's persistent failure to recognize and respond to women's humanity, the novel implies, is the source of his disgrace. His disaffected and unremorseful public admission of guilt serves to justify Lurie's and his countrymen's sexual crimes against women of color, much to his female colleague's surprise and dismay. The public inquiry into his alleged sexual misconduct leaves all those concerned without recourse to its desired end of seeking out truth, justice, learning, repentance, and forgiveness.

Despite Lurie's defense against any suggestion that he needs to reconsider his worldview and take responsibility for his actions, the events that unfold after the trial imply otherwise. Re-education as difficult learning from the wrongs of the past is the only catalyst that moves him to situate his demeaning attitude and treatment towards women of color in South Africa's colonial past. Lurie's position on the objectified status of women, his daughter suggests, is a direct result of his misogynist and racist South African education, conditioning him to dehumanize women of color into objects of sexual desire and punishment. Lucy points out this schooling to him when he struggles with how he might support her after she, too, is sexually attacked by a gang of men: "Maybe, for men, hating the woman makes sex more exciting. You are a man, you ought to know. When you have sex with someone strange—when you trap her, hold her down, get her under you, put all your weight on her—isn't it a bit like killing?" (Coetzee, 2000, p. 158). At first affronted by being put in a misogynist position, Lurie is struck silent and taken aback. The pointed accusation of "you ought to know" transports him haphazardly from the scene of Lucy's rape, to his childhood, to his own treatment of women, and to wondering "if he has it in him" to develop the capacity needed to respond to the tyranny of white Afrikaner patriarchal history by trying feel that history from the position of the other, the violated bodies of countless, faceless women (Coetzee, 2000, p. 160). The primal Electra-like conflict between father and daughter has a pedagogical effect on Lurie: finally he seems able to learn.

Historical remembrance demands something beyond public inquiries, something resembling what Deborah Britzman (2006) calls "difficult" learning, a passing through the other's unbearable experience to gain a sense of and feeling for the other's truth. Our present ways of representing and engaging with traumatic history are limited by our incapacity to convey the inconceivable dimension of history, the depth of human perversity and violence that leaves lives and communities torn apart. The version of truth that public hearings permit is prone to, at best, assimilating the suffering of others into one's own frame of reference and, at worst, disavowing or making spectacle of the victim's testimony (Arendt, 1963/1994). Instead of an end to the victim's suffering, we might see truth and reconciliation commissions as a beginning to face violence and as a way to open us up to the possibility that we might be able to learn from the lives of others.

The questions that *Disgrace* poses to national practices of historical memory exercise what Roger Simon (2005) describes as the public's democratic right to call into question both the social imagination previously secured by particular remembrances and the social interests and ethical visions supporting such an imagination. Such a process does not mean mindlessly accepting all contesting counter memories, but means learning to hear what is being asserted within them and seriously consider the claim they make on our understanding of the present. (p. 17)

Rather than accept the official version of traumatic history as compiled and archived by the ANC or Afrikaners, the novel dares to suggest that official versions of remembrance seem to foreclose trauma's violent and lasting effects. It moves to affectively and imaginatively reanimate human suffering in literary language rather than renarrate the trauma of others by rewriting the other's experience into an "acceptable" form as dictated by the official record. The affective content of this suffering has an unsettling effect, not only on readers but also on the characters struggling to make sense of how they can recognize and relate to each other in the wake of mass violence. Shoshana Felman and Dori Laub (1992) write that literary testimony appeals to the reader to witness and respond to historical trauma in the act of writing/reading the other's account of suffering. If the appeal is to have any pedagogical impact, literary testimony must be able to transfer a sense of the other's trauma to the reader. Only then can our practices of reading and writing acknowledge the human lives they claim to address.

Testifying to historical trauma takes the risk of failing to remember the past and failing to heal past injuries. Despite the risks, as Jean Francois Lyotard (1990) indicates, one attempts to inscribe the unrepresented of the past into historical record. The novel *Disgrace* wrestles with the difficult task of writing into historical record the experience of trauma and loss from inside of the wounded body out. To preserve the remainder, the traumatic affects of violence trapped in historical memory, is to summon up the courage to imagine and restage in writing the effects of unthinkable violence riveting through the minds and actions of human actors. The novel writes against dominant forms of representation that function to save the memory, to describe, explain, and recount extreme violence, since empirical forms fail to respond to the persisting and trans-generationally transmitted effects of mass torture, maiming, and killing. Through its formal and aesthetic operations, the novel forces Lurie and the reader *to feel* the utter senselessness and terror of human violence when the narrative, suddenly and without prior warning, thrusts Lurie into the scene of his daughter's brutal rape. The traumatic effects of apartheid's reign explode in this scene. Afterwards Lurie and the reader are left to reckon with the sources, material effects, and manifestations of apartheid's dehumanizing regime and to confront what he has become: as apartheid's native son.

It takes a violent sexual attack on his daughter and a physical attack on himself for Lurie to be moved from his former position of righteous indignance to one that confronts his place in the apartheid past. Only when the narrative turns the country's violence and racist ontology upon him, when he and his daughter become victims of the after-effects of violence and racism, is Lurie able to gain a sense of what it means to be held captive and without mercy at the hands of unloving others. Something more than knowing has to occur, something inwardly and materially life-altering has to be passed through, the novel seems to insist, for learning to begin. But more than this: if we are to arrest existing cycles of violence, we must reckon with the sorrow and rage that victims of atrocity are forced to manage but never really move past. *Disgrace* reckons with the rage and sorrow of victims of atrocity in order to pedagogically respond to the injury festering within the individual and collective bodies of post-apartheid South Africa.

The child Lucy is carrying as the result of the violent rape also moves Lurie to change and make something other of himself. As Lucy takes the rape of her body to produce a life, the novel implies that a more loving human relation might be produced from the experience of mass violence. The mixed-race child conceived by violence and marked by history, metaphorically and tragically, holds the novel's only tangible sense of hope for the future, an inarticulate and impossible hope but hope nonetheless:

> And now, lo and behold, *the child*! Already he is calling it *the child* when it is no more than a worm in his daughter's womb. What kind of child can seed like that give life to, seed driven into the woman not in love but in hatred, mixed chaotically, meant to soil her, to mark her, like a dog's urine.
>
> A father without the sense to have a son: is this how it is all going to end, is this how his line is going to run out, like water dribbling into the earth? Who would have thought of it! A day like any other day, clear skies, a mild sun, yet suddenly everything is changed, utterly changed!
>
> Standing against the wall outside the kitchen, hiding his face in his hands, he heaves and heaves and finally cries. (Coetzee, 2000, p. 199)

By confronting the violence propagated "by his line," Lurie is finally able to feel for and bear the considerable weight of his place in history. While critical response to this passage has been predictably hostile, I think we must work hard to resist a closed reading of the scene and its aftermath as "realistically" depicting a white woman's brutal rape at the hands of murderous black men.[1] Instead the confrontation between blacks and whites attempts to exact a sense of and feeling for justice for past wrongdoing committed to and experienced by black South Africans.

The scene of Lucy's rape allegorically articulates to Afrikaners a feeling of what justice might entail for black South Africans. Justice, the novel suggests, cannot be served until white South Africans like Lurie pass through the relentless effects of their dehumanizing social experiment and are subjected to imagining and feeling what it might be like to live an existence bereft of mercy at the hands of others. The scene's force of violence attempts to articulate the depth and perversity of apartheid violence, and not of black men, that Lurie must be made to bear to be moved finally to learning. The rape scene further works against the force of its allegory, against its suggestion that whites must now be subjected to a vengeance-driven retributive violence to atone for their roles or complicity in an apartheid past, although there is an implication that some form of redress towards black society is necessary. Rather, the scene appeals to Afrikaners to imagine and feel for the tremendous violence that apartheid leaves on the bodies of black South Africans by returning them to the scenes of their crimes to face the evil that resides in their history. The scene also appeals to blacks to return to that history to examine apartheid's psychical and material effects residing inside their bodies and communities in order to resist repeating and working out the violence on vulnerable and innocent others. The novel's pedagogy reorients reconciliation towards re-educating how to recognize the depths of humanity that still stirs in the dehumanized and the dehumanizer, a reconciliation that must take place with the other in concerted acts of self and mutual repair.

"Things to Learn": Towards a Reparative Curriculum

Reparative learning can come in the form of a literary intervention that challenges the Afrikaans and colonized readers to consider what the future holds for all South Africans if they are to continue to live out the life-killing effects of apartheid. The pedagogical intervention is faintly hopeful, leaving us with the image of Lurie's sorrow and tenderness for his grandchild yet to be. The child will be born into a society still possessed by apartheid's horrific memory, with no warning of the ruined world that awaits her, and conceived in bloodshed. *Faintly* hopeful because the birth of the mixed-race child signals but does not guarantee the death of David's line, "running out like water dribbling into the earth," and by association the death of his kind of privileged inhumanity and cruel indifference. For the child's sake, *for all of our sake*, we can only hope (Morrison in McGeveran, 2008).

Pinar (2008) characterizes the curricular imperatives of a work such as Coetzee's as reparative because the novel is open rather than closed to the complicated and dialogical conversation that needs to accompany difficult learning: "Neither empathy nor accusation supports the understanding of suffering or moves us to redress it; the interest in, the openness to, the other presumed by conversation can" (p. 26). Without a reparative curriculum, a curriculum that attempts to use autobiographical, artistic, and aesthetic resources to learn *from* as well as about past violence, the colonizer, the colonized, and the faceless masses in-between are doomed to live a partial and fractured existence.

An encounter with *Disgrace* can immerse readers into the affective trauma of mass violence. Because affect is unthematizable, the novel resists one's impulse to assimilate the other's incomparable suffering into our own. The novel invites us, instead, to feel our way through the violent conflicts of competing histories and bodies as experienced by differently situated characters. The novel is reparative because it can potentially move the reader to think diferently and become different, thereby demonstrating that our fragile sociality can be altered by a fictional encounter with traumatic history.

Our engagement with *Disgrace* can develop in us the capacity to hear what literary testimony does not say in words but by feeling (Britzman, 1998). "*There may be things to learn,*" Lurie finally admits at the end of the novel (Coetzee, 2000, p. 218, italics added). We sense that these things may have nothing and everything to do with learning how to be a grandfather to a mixed-race child who is conceived in racial hatred and sexual brutality and will be born into a country still traumatized by extreme violence. His belated admission and appeal to learning sets the conditions for reparation, conditions that can only emerge after Lurie passes through and faces up to the unforgivable violence white South Africans committed to others.

A curriculum of reparation lends itself to postcolonial studies in education. Engaging pedagogically with works that archive the affective material of colonial history, students and communities are given the chance to enter into the difficult practice of learning, however removed and secondary, from unspeakable events. Literary works of historical witness give students and community members opportunities to practice responses to and concern for the "symbolic" and "real" lives of those affected by mass violence. Novels such as Coetzee's serve as public pedagogies inviting the willing to engage with the contesting memories and narratives organizing traumatic history. It is understandable that those most pained by Coetzee's *Disgrace* are South Africans, black, coloured, and white, many of whom are still caught in apartheid's grip. It is probably too soon and too late for South Africans to appreciate the prophetic depth of Coetzee's art. As I read of the "new" violence perpetrated by blacks against immigrants and foreigners in South Africa (Bearak & Dugger, 2008), I am reminded of David Lurie's words of consolation to Lucy and all sentient beings left scarred by the immense reach of human violence: "'It was history speaking through them,' he offers at last. 'A history of wrong. Think of it that way, if it helps. It may have seemed personal, but it wasn't. It came down from the ancestors'" (Coetzee, 2000, p. 156). Without a re-education that orients us towards working through histories of genocide, apartheid, and imperialism, human beings are bound to dehumanizing and violent impulses and condemned to repeat them. We are living in a time of great violence against those with the least power and recourse to justice in our human community. As indicated by the violence against mostly African and South Asian ethnic minorities in South Africa today, the violence rippling across the globe is no longer between black and white, colonizer and colonized but, as Appadurai (2006) suggests, waged between friends, neighbors, and even kin. The novel holds a lesson for those who think that learning about or analyzing histories of oppression is enough. As *Disgrace* demonstrates with its risky yet insightful teaching, we have everything to lose by not facing up to and engaging with the remnants of violence that remain trapped in our historical (un)consciousness and we are unable to break free.

To learn from the past, we must be open to participating in a complicated conversation facilitated by an openness to listen and respond to the suffering of others and by a willingness to rethink how it is that we are subject to history as well as our personal lives and experiences. Postcolonial studies as a reparative curriculum offers us a chance to remake our former worlds and estranged human relations by changing how it is we think of justice as a painful and internally motivated relearning how to be differently human. Justice as re-education requires starting over again at ground level, as Lucy suggests in the epigraph opening this chapter: possessing "nothing. Not with nothing but. With nothing" (Coetzee, 2000, p. 205). We must give up everything to become the trusting and loyal creatures we once were. From *others* we are afforded the gift of existence, a chance to learn to live beyond the worlds we make and live.

Note

1. Peter MacDdonald's (2002) remarkably balanced article entitled "Disgrace Effects" discusses the hostile responses to the novel by many South African journalists, writers, and academics. For example, MacDdonald points to the African National Congress' submission to the South African Human Rights Commission (SAHRC) describing the novel as "'report[ing]' on the still pervasive idea of the black as a 'faithless, immoral, uneducated, incapacitated primitive child,' a version of white racism they traced back to J. B. M. Hertzog, the father of 'so-called pure Afrikaner nationalism'" (SAHRC, 2000b). The ANC's argument centered on Lucy's rape or, more accurately, on Lucy and her father David's subsequent conversation about the meaning of the brutal violation" (MacDdonald 2002, p. 123). The ANC's interpretation of the novel and its author as racist is understandable given the dynamics of self-other misrecognition that Coetzee depicts in the novel. I view the charge of racism as a gut-reaction to the aesthetic effect of misrecognition that the novel mirrors and emits in the relationships between characters and between narrative and reader. I also argue that reducing the author's fictional restaging of racist acts and attitudes to the author's presumed and/or actual beliefs fail to do justice to both Coetzee, the artist and human being, and to the potentially reparative "complicated conversation" about race that Coetzee attempts in the novel (Pinar, in press).

References

Agamben, G. (2005). *The state of exception* (K. Attell, trans.). Chicago, IL: University of Chicago Press.

Appadurai, A. (2006). *Fear of small numbers: An essay on the geography of anger*. Durham, NC: Duke University Press.

Arendt, H. (1963/1994). *Eichmann in Jerusalem: A report on the banality of evil*. New York: Penguin.

Bearak, B., & Dugger, C. (2008, May 18). South Africans take out rage on immigrants. *New York Times*. Retrieved June 3, 2008, from http://www.nytimes.com/2008/05/20/world/africa/20safrica.html?hp

Bhabha, H. K. (1994). *The location of culture*. New York: Routledge.

Britzman, D. P. (1998). *Lost subjects, contested objects. Towards a psychoanalytic inquiry of learning*. Albany: State University of New York Press.

Britzman, D. P. (2003). *After-education: Anna Freud, Melanie Klein, and psychoanalytic histories of learning*. Albany: State University of New York Press.

Britzman, D. P. (2006). On being a slow reader: Psychoanalytic reading problems in Ishiguro's *Never let me go. Changing English, 13*(3), 307–318.

Butler, J. (2004). *Precarious life: The powers of mourning and violence*. London: Verso.

Coetzee, J. M. (2000). *Disgrace*. London: Vintage.

Derrida, J. (1986). Racism's last word. In H. L. Gates, Jr. (Ed.), *"Race," writing and difference* (pp. 329–358). Chicago, IL: University of Chicago Press.

Derrida, J. (2001). *On cosmopolitanism and forgiveness* (M. Dooley & M. Hughes, trans.). London: Routledge.

Derrida, J. (2005). *Sovereignties in question: The poetics of Paul Celan* (T. Dutoit & O. Pasanen, eds.). New York: Fordham University Press.

Dimitriadis, G., & McCarthy, C. (2001). *Reading and teaching the postcolonial: From Baldwin to

Basquiat and beyond. New York: Teachers College Press.
Fanon, F. (1967). *Black skins, white masks.* New York: Grove.
Felman, S., & Laub, D. (1992). *Testimony: Crises of witnessing in literature, psychoanalysis, and history.* New York: Routledge.
Freire, P. (1982). *Pedagogy of the oppressed.* New York: Continuum.
Klein, M. (1937/1984). *Love, guilt, and reparation, and other works, 1921-1945* (Vol. 1). New York: Free.
Krog, A. (1998). *Country of my skull.* Johannesburg: Random House.
Lane, C. (1998). *The psychoanalysis of race.* New York: Columbia University Press.
Lévinas, E. (1969). *Totality and infinity: An essay on exteriority* (A. Lingis, trans.). Pittsburgh, PA: Duquesne University Press.
Lyotard, J. F. (1990). *Heidegger and "the Jews"* (A. Michel & M. S. Roberts, trans.). Minneapolis: University of Minnesota Press.
MacCabe, C. (2008). An interview with Stuart Hall, December 2007. *Critical Quarterly, 50*(1-2), 12-42.
McDonald, P. (2002). Disgrace effects. *Interventions, 4*(3), 321-330.
McGeveran, T. (2008, January 28). Toni Morrison's letter to Barack Obama. *New York Observer.* Retrieved October 27, 2008, from http://www.observer.com/2008/toni-morrisons-letter-barack-obama
Mishra Tarc, A. (2007). Literacy of the other: Making relations to language. Unpublished doctoral thesis, York University, Canada.
Ngugi, W. T. (1986). *Decolonizing the mind.* London: James Currey.
Pinar, W. (1993). Notes on curriculum as racial text. In C. McCarthy & W. Crichlow (Eds.), *Race and representation in education* (pp. 60-70). New York: Routledge.
Pinar, W. (2008). *On the agony and ecstasy of the particular: Identity politics, autobiography, cosmopolitanism,* unpublished conference paper. Retrieved October 25, 2008, from http://csics.educ.ubc.ca/Projects/CSSE.pdf
Pinar, W. (in press). *The worldiness of a cosmopolitan education: Passionate lives in public service.* New York: Routledge.
Rizvi, F. (2007). Postcolonialism and globalization in education. *Critical Methodologies, 7*(3), 256-263.
Sanders, M. (1999). Reading lessons. *Diacritics, 29*(3), 3-20.
Sanders, M. (2002). Disgrace. *Interventions, 4*(3), 363-373.
Sassen, S. (2002). Global cities and survival circuits. In B. Ehrenreich & A. R. Hochschild (Eds.), *Global woman: Nannies, maids, and sex workers in the new economy* (pp. 254-274). New York: Metropolitan.
Simon, R. I. (2005). *The touch of the past: Remembrance, learning, and ethics.* New York: Palgrave Macmillan.
Simon, R. I., Rosenberg, S., & Eppert, C. (Eds.). (2000). *Between hope & despair: Pedagogy and the remembrance of historical trauma.* Lanham, MD: Rowman & Littlefield.
SAHRC. (2000a). Faultlines: An inquiry into racism in the media. Retrieved May 3, 2009, from http://www.gov.za/reports/2000/racism.pdf
SAHRC. (2000b). Inquiry into racism in the media. *Hearings transcripts, XIV 3/3:* 121-42.
Spivak, G. (1992). The burden of English studies. In R. S. Rajan (Ed.), *The lie of the land: English literary studies in India* (pp. 275-299). London: Oxford University Press.

PART FOUR

Gender and Sexuality

CHAPTER 13

Decolonizing the Flesh:
The Body, Pedagogy, and Inequality

ANTONIA DARDER

> The Body is our medium for having a world.
> — Merleau-Ponty, 2002

> [T]he body is also directly involved in a political field; power relations have an immediate hold upon it; they invest it, mark it, train it, torture it, force it to carry out tasks, to perform ceremonies, to emit signs.
> — Foucault, 1995

> I know with my entire body, with feelings, with passion and also with reason. It is my entire body that socially knows. I cannot, in the name of exactness and rigor, negate my body, my emotions and my feelings.
> — Freire, 1995

Our bodies constitute primacy in our material relationships with the world. Without considering the materiality of the body, all notions of teaching and learning are reduced to mere abstractions. This represents a misguided attempt to situate the mind as an independent agent, absent of individual and collective emotions, sensations, yearnings, fears, and joys. Nevertheless, it is the body that provides the medium for our existence as subjects of history and politically empowered agents of change. But, as Peter McLaren (1998) reminds us, "bodies are also the primary means by which capitalism does its job" (p. xiii). We are molded and shaped by the structures, policies, and practices of domination and exclusion that violently insert our bodies into the alienating morass of an intensified global division of labor.

In *Pedagogy and the Politics of the Body*, Sherry Shapiro (1999), as other feminist theorists before her, contends that "any approach committed to human liberation must seriously address the body as a site for both oppression and liberation" (p. 18). Yet, seldom is the significance of the body made central to discussions of emancipatory pedagogy. Educational efforts to reinvent the social and material conditions in classrooms are often devoid of close consideration to the significance of the flesh in mediating conditions of teaching and learning, that is, unless the discussion turns to "classroom management," a convenient euphemism for the covert and overt regulation and control of students' corporeality.

Meanwhile, the classroom exists as an arena where abstract knowledge and its construction are objectified, along with the students expected to acquiesce to its alienating function, limiting rationality, and technocratic instrumentalism. Hence, the production of knowledge is neither engaged nor presented as a historical and collective process, occurring in the flesh and its sensual capacities for experiencing and responding to the world. Instead, as Christopher Beckey (2000) argues in *Wicked Bodies*, "the flesh, the material aspect of the body, is seen as a hindrance which must be overcome, negated, and transcended" (p. 71), as if it were not involved in the act of knowing at all.

We as teachers know that teaching and learning can invoke a multitude of sensations and responses, including excitement, pain, joy, anger, pride, and frustration. Paulo Freire (1998) refers to these human responses when he considers the process of studying: "Studying is a demanding occupation, in the process of which we will encounter pain, pleasure, victory, defeat, doubt and happiness" (p. 78), all physical sensations of the body.

Students as Integral Human Beings

The notion of students as embodied and integral human beings has received limited attention in discussions of classroom praxis in the United States (Darder, 2002). Missing even in multicultural discussions of pedagogy is a more complex understanding of humanity and the significance of the body to intellectual formation. Such discussions have been left to educators whose tendency has been to overemphasize the role of subjectivity or fall into an overpsychologizing of the self. No matter how well meaning, this view often fails to address the material conditions and issues of power and privilege at work in the lives of historically disenfranchised students.

The reticence in education to engage issues of the body also has been tied to scholarly tendencies to ignore material analysis of societal structures and the political apparatus of public schooling that shapes classroom life. The historical absence of the body has been so because "bringing the body into critical discussion is ... [considered] potentially disruptive and subversive" (Levy, 2000, p. 82) to the social order of schooling. Grounded in such a worldview, many educators assume that teaching and learning are solely cognitive acts. As such, teachers do not concern themselves with the physical nature of their students, unless one is deemed as "inappropriate," at which time administrators or psychologists are summoned to evaluate and hopefully "fix the problem."

To support students in becoming *full subjects of history*, Freire urges teachers to grapple with the fact that students construct knowledge through the multitude of collective interactions of the body with the world. Amanda Sinclair (1999) reminds us that

> the immediate impact of a person's body on another is profound. A great deal happens before a person opens their mouth. Emotions are aroused, judgments are made. Comfort or discomfort levels are established well in advance of verbal communication. We unconsciously or consciously register and make judgments about stature and voice. Bodies elicit feelings of excitement and admiration, attraction and desire, envy and distaste. (p. 3)

The material conditions and histories of students are made visible by their bodies. Their histories of survival are witnessed in their skin, teeth, hair, gestures, speech, and even the movement of their arms and legs. If "bodies are maps of power and identity" (Haraway, 1990, p. 2), then teachers must work to engage students' physical realities more substantively, in an effort to forge an emancipatory practice of education. It is not enough to rely on abstract learning processes, where only the analysis of words and texts are privileged in the construction of knowledge. Such educational process of estrangement functions to alienate students from the world around them, from themselves, and from each other.

Thus, teachers and students must labor in the flesh: teaching and learning must be anchored in a material understanding of our human existence, as a starting place for classroom praxis and our struggle to reinvent the world. Freire (1993) posits this as vital to critical pedagogy, in that

> We learn things about the world by acting and changing the world around us. It is [in] this process of change, of transforming the world from which we emerged, [where] creation of the cultural and historical world takes place. This transformation of the world [is] done by us while it makes and remakes us. (p. 108)

However, there is nothing automatic or "natural" about social change. Nor is it a process that can solely rely on calculating logic or cold rationality, given the manner in which the body's sentient forces overwhelmingly shape human experiences and responses to social structures. Struggles in the name of social justice must, then, hold steadfast the fullness of our human existence if we are to craft truly emancipatory ways of teaching and learning.

Schooling and the Flesh

In our efforts to understand the process of schooling, teaching and learning have to be acknowledged as human labor that take place within our bodies and incorporate, consciously or unconsciously, the totality of our being. The corporeal phenomenon is always at work as we strive to make sense of the material conditions and social relations of power that shape our particular histories. In *Teaching to Transgress*, bell hooks (1994, in Kazan, 2005, p. 379) describes an awareness of her body within the traditional classroom:

> I have always been acutely aware of the presence of my body in those settings that, in fact, invite us to invest so deeply in a mind/body split so that, in a sense, you're almost always at odds with the existing structure, whether you are a black woman student or professor. But if you want to remain, you've got, in a sense, to remember yourself—because to remember yourself is to see yourself always as a body in a system that has not become accustomed to your presence or to your physicality.

Through such awareness of presence, teachers can begin to build a practice of education where students are not being asked to confront themselves and each other as strangers, but rather as fully embodied human beings from the moment they enter the classroom. A critical praxis of the body must seek to contend in the flesh with the embodied histories of the disenfranchised, as well as the social and material forces that shape the conditions in which we teach and learn.

Freire (1993) speaks to the undeniable centrality of the body in the act of knowing:

> The importance of the body is indisputable; the body moves, acts, rememorizes, the struggle for its liberation; the body in sum, desires, points out, announces, protests, curves itself, rises, designs and remakes the world ... and its importance has to do with a certain sensualism ... contained by the body, even in connection with cognitive ability .... [I]t is absurd to separate the rigorous acts of knowing the world from the [body's] passionate ability to know. (p. 87)

This sensualism, with its revolutionary potential to nurture self-determination and the empowerment of students as individuals and social beings, is systematically stripped away from the educational process of public schooling. Most teachers "already well-versed in maintaining a grey world of unsexy knowing ... are well placed to take up the challenge" (McWilliams, 2000, p. 29) of policing expressions of passion, excitement, and physicality within the classroom, particularly when working with youth.

Conservative ideologies of social control, historically linked to Puritanical views of the body as evil, sensual pleasure as sinful, and passions as corrupting to the sanctity of the spirit, continue to be reflected in the narrow, rule-based pedagogical policies and practices of schooling today. The sensuality of the body is discouraged in schools through the prominent practice of immobilizing students' bodies within hard chairs and desks that contain and restrict their contact with one another and the environment around them. Viviane Laroy (2002) contends that

> The body is not usually granted a lot of space in our educational system; it is nothing more than what allows us to remain seated for hours and to move from one classroom to another and to meet the requirements ... 90% of the time spent in schools is typically in a state of immobility. Learning is reduced to an airborne exchange of knowledge between different minds: the knowledge in the teacher's mind is transmitted to the learners, defined as minds able to receive new knowledge or not. (p. 1)

Laroy argues that this tradition of fettered bodies is anchored in three classical paradigms, Socrates, Christianity, and Pavlov's dog. In the classical tradition, the sensual body is quickly subordinated to the mind and intellect is privileged over the senses (Seidel, 1964). In Christianity, the separation between the body and the soul constitutes an essential pedagogical concern in preserving purity of thought. In the Pavlovian model, the body is transformed into an instrumentalized object to be manipulated and controlled through external stimulus in the process of learning.

Such views of teaching and learning ultimately lead to pedagogical practices that do emotional and psychological violence through their erasure of the body and the annihilation of the flesh in the traditional rubric of classroom life. Accordingly, inequalities are reproduced in class through racialized, gendered, and homophobic perceptions and distortions of male and female bodies, embodied within the pedagogy of even the most well-intentioned teachers. Consequently, students from communities where the body with its senses and spontaneities is given greater primacy in the act of knowing and being are often coerced into sacrificing their knowledge of the body's sensuality, creativity, and vitality, in favor of an atomized, analytical, and instrumental logic of being. In light of such tendency, we as teachers need "to reflect on what bodies we give 'permission' to in our classrooms and the extent to which we let those bodies speak" (Kazan, 2005, p. 394) or move freely. Reflections may prove, for example, significant to explaining the overwhelming tendency of teachers and school officials to label African American and Chicano boys as hyperactive or attention deficit when they find it difficult to comply with common expectations of immobility.

Similarly, Susie O'Brien (2000) argues that "the corporeal, physical and sexual realms are unwelcome intrusions" (p. 46) into the everyday world of the classroom. The systematic disembodiment of students in the process of learning begins early in their academic formation. Despite child development theories asserting that human beings are sexual beings even before birth, sexuality as an ever-present phenomenon is repressed and denied within the four walls of the classroom. This is the case at puberty when adolescent bodies are sensitive to heightened and confusing sensations. Seldom do teachers, many of whom are not comfortable with their own sexuality, critically engage questions of sexuality beyond the often repeated cliché of "raging hormones" to connote teenage sexuality. Meanwhile, students are not only pedagogically abandoned, but also left at the mercy of media and corporate pirates that prey upon the bodily sensations, emotions, and stirrings of youth (Rushkoff, 2001). Henry Giroux (1998) argues that

> In the slick world of advertising, teenage bodies are sought after for the exchange value they generate in marketing an adolescent sexuality that offers a marginal exoticism and ample pleasures for the largely male consumer. Commodification reifies and fixates the complexity of youth and the range of possible identities they might assume while simultaneously exploiting them as fodder for the logic of the market. (p. 41)

Frightened by their own corporeal ambivalence and the physicality of students' bodies, education policymakers institute practices that coerce teachers into silence, limiting any discussion about one of the most significant aspects of humanity. The message is clear: everyone, especially youth, is expected to check their sexuality (along with other aspects of their lived histories) at the door prior to entering school. Despite the difficulties and hardships that such silence portends for many students, such as isolation and increasing rates of suicide among gay youth, schools act as moral leaders, much like churches, policing and repressing the body's participation.

The minimalism of U.S. schools in the area of human sexuality can be contrasted with other parts of the world where straightforward facts about the "birds and bees" are considered a pedagogical imperative. In Sweden, for example, compulsory sex education has been in place since 1956, given their recognition of sex as a natural human act and the frank acknowledgment that most people become sexually active before they are 20 years old. Students learn at an early age about sexuality, reinforcing a more open and positive view of sex and the body. Curriculum begins at age 6 with anatomy and from age 12 on, topics are more geared toward developing tools for taking responsibility for their sexual lives. The outcome is that Sweden's rate of teen pregnancy and sexually transmitted diseases is among the lowest in the world (Grose, 2007).

The issue of teen pregnancy also illustrates how school practices and policies associated to the body are inextricably tied to gendered ideologies of power and control. Sinclair (1999) reminds us that schools, like most institutions, are only able to "assimilate women's bodies so long as they conform to a neutral or desexualized form." Young teen mothers violate the norm by "drawing attention to their femaleness, their sexuality, and difference from the male norm" (p. 5). Hence, teen pregnancy is addressed by "excommunicating" and exiling young expectant mothers from the school campus while young fathers are left virtually untouched by the same system.

Missing, even in the university, is the willingness to contend with the sexuality of students in their process of academic formation despite the fact that "intense desires are played out in the university classroom" (O'Brien, 2000, p. 49). In keeping with the mind/body split, educators ignore the manner in which learning is both visceral and sensual. Consequently, the severing of the body's desires and sensations from the construction of knowledge interferes with students' capacity for self-knowledge. Such practices also thwart our knowledge of "the other," rendering us alienated and estranged to any human suffering that exists outside of the particular and limited scope of our identities, whether linked to gender, ethnicity, sexuality, skin color, ability, or spirituality. Spender (1995) argues that the absence of pedagogical engagement with the body inhibits the development of empathy and respect for those deemed as "the other." Thus it should be no surprise to learn that many traditional curricular policies and practices, which reinforce abstract, fragmented, and decontextualized theories of teaching and learning, seldom function in the interest of oppressed populations. Instead, students are objectified, alienated, and domesticated into passive roles. Schools discourage us from thinking about ourselves as bodies (Kazan, 2005). This not only interferes with student achievement, but also sabotages social agency and the evolution of consciousness. This is visible when emotional and physical needs of students are ignored in an overriding effort to obtain their obedience and conformity.

In spite of major institutional efforts to control the body's desires, pleasures, and mobility in the classroom, students seldom surrender their bodies completely or acquiesce readily to authoritarian practices, providing the impetus for resistance (Shapiro, 1999). Many students engage in the construction of their cultural forms of resistance that may or may not always function in their best interest. Paul Willis (1977/1981) exposes this phenomenon in his ethnography of working-class kids in England. Then as it is today, expressions of youth resistance are enacted through counterculture alterations of the body, including clothing, hairstyle, posturing, manner of walking, way of speaking, piercing, and tattooing. They represent not only acts of resistance but also alternative ways of experiencing and knowing the world that are generally perceived by school officials as both transgressive and disruptive to the social order. Such views of students are exacerbated by what Giroux (1998) contends is a "new form of representational politics [that] has emerged in media culture fueled by degrading visual depictions of youth as criminal, sexually decadent, drug crazed, and illiterate. In short, youth are viewed as a growing threat to the public order" (p. 29).

Teachers, whose bodies are similarly restricted, alienated, and domesticated by their workplace, are under enormous pressure to follow strict policies and procedures for classroom conduct, while expected to dispense prepackaged curriculum, instead of employing more creative and critical approaches that are grounded in the actual needs of students. Given the impact of disembodied practices, teachers experience an uphill battle in meeting standardized mandates that extricate students' bodies from the equation of their learning. Nowhere is this more apparent than in low-income schools across the nation where teaching-to-the-test fronts as the "rigorous" and "scientific" curriculum of choice, even in many colleges and universities.

Along with teaching-to-the-test, there exists what Katherine Hayles (1999) terms as *incorporated knowledge*, notions of gender, sexuality, and "race" that are "deeply sedimented into the body and ... highly resistant to change" (p. 205). It constitutes knowledge that is generally beyond the reach of conscious view, given its habitual and ritualized nature. Its outcomes include repressive educational policies and practices that marginalize the knowledge and languages of oppressed populations, infantilize adult students, criminalize youth of color, and render suspicious any ideas or uses of the body that are perceived as existing outside of narrow mainstream views of normalcy. Incorporated knowledge associated with classroom management reproduces a variety of authoritarian classroom practices through teachers' efforts to maintain physical control of students. Even when teachers struggle within the classroom to implement more liberating strategies, they are often forced to become masters of deception, saying what the principal or district office wishes to hear, while doing behind closed doors what they believe is in concert with a democratic vision of education. Having to shoulder the hidden physical burden of such duplicity can drive some of the most effective teachers out of their chosen vocation, irrespective of their political commitment. Their experience of alienation and stress often becomes intolerable. Those who begin to feel defeated may in frustration begin to adopt more authoritarian approaches to manipulate and coerce "cooperation," while justifying the means in the name of helping students succeed academically.

What cannot be overlooked is the manner in which authoritarian practices are designed not only to "blindfold students and lead them to a domesticated future" (Freire, 1970, p. 79), but also to alienate and estrange teachers from their labor. Concerned with the need to restore greater freedom, joy, and creativity in the classroom, Freire (1998) urges teachers to reject their domesticating role and work to challenge the authoritarianism of standard policies and practices of pedagogy, curriculum, and school administration, which require an open process of dialogue, for "in classrooms, with the doors closed, it is difficult to have the world unveiled" (p. 9).

A critical praxis of the body is salient to rethinking university education, where there seems to be little pedagogical tolerance for the emotional needs of adult learners. "Somewhere in the intellectual history of the West there developed the wrongheaded idea that mind and heart are antagonists, that scholarship must be divested of emotion, that spiritual journeys must avoid intellectual concerns" (Lifton, 1990, p. 29). Such tradition sets an expectation, for example, that professors and students compartmentalize themselves within the classroom without any serious concern for the manner in which the essence of university education is tied to major moments of life transitions. Students are asked to make major intellectual commitments and material investments related to the direction of their uncertain futures. They also are expected to engage their studies and research as objective, impartial observers, even when the object of their study is intimately linked to conditions of human suffering.

Moreover, Freire (1993) argues that the traditional academic expectations of the university reinforce pedagogical myths. These include that feelings corrupt research and its findings; intuition should be feared; emotion and passion must be negated; and science and technology rule. These myths "end in convincing many that, the more neutral we are in our actions, the more objective and efficient we will be [in our knowing]" (p. 106). Hence, students are slowly but certainly socialized to labor as uncritical, descriptive, "neutral" scholars who are dispassionate and disembodied in their intellectual constructions of the world. The outcome is scholarship conceived through a deeply estranged way of knowing where values are restricted to scientific definitions and knowledge is divorced from human emotions and connections. Seldom does such an approach to knowledge guide or encourage students to grapple with moral questions that challenge the social and material relations of inequality that function to sustain human suffering in the first place.

Critical Principles for a Pedagogy of the Body

As our consciousness becomes more abstracted, we become more detached from our bodies. One could say that a hidden function of public schooling is to initiate and incorporate poor, working class, and students of color into social and material conditions of labor that normalize their alienation and detachment from the body. Such function is absolutely necessary for social control and the extraction of surplus labor, given that the body is the medium through which we wage political struggle and through which we transform our historical conditions as individuals and social beings (Eagleton, 2003). Hence, the perception of students as integral human beings is paramount to both questions of ethics and the development of critical consciousness. All aspects of our humanity, with their pedagogical needs, are present and active at all times; that is to say, all aspects of our humanity are integral to the process of teaching and learning. To perceive students in terms of only the mind or only one way of knowing can translate into an objectifying and debilitating experience for students, despite the intellectual and cultural strengths they bring to their education.

Students must therefore be acknowledged, respected, and treated as entering the classroom as whole persons. The degree to which this is possible is linked to the skill of teachers to be fully present, to negotiate the process of learning *with* their students, and to establish meaningful interactions in the classroom community. Such a horizontal view of student-teacher relationships goes hand in hand with obliterating the myth that an impersonal and emotionally distant approach to engaging students is professionally and pedagogically correct. It also counters beliefs among elitist mentors who brutalize their students through humiliation and cultivation of self-doubt, insisting that it engenders rigorous scholarship. What we often find is a reproduction of pedagogical brutality in their mentees who, having survived the hazing of privilege, now feel special and entitled. They defend dehumanizing pedagogical relations of power as they become the new gatekeepers of the discipline. Nowhere is this condition more devastating to watch than in students from oppressed communities who, "earning" entry into the elite group, embrace their position as a sign of "empowerment."

At issue is the reproduction of veiled class distinctions that educators enact in the classroom and in the "real world." Ira Shor and Paulo Freire (1986) insist that

> What we do in the classroom is not an isolated moment separate from the "real world." It is entirely connected to the real world and it is the real world which places both powers and limits on any critical course. Because the world is in the classroom, whatever transformation we provoke has a conditioning effect outside our small space. But the outside has a conditioning effect on the space also, interfering with our ability to build a critical culture separate from the dominant mass culture. (p. 26)

Nathan Snaza and Timothy Lensmire (2006) likewise argue that "we must cease to think of our lives separate from the operations of capital.... School *and* society is a false dichotomy: school *is* society" (p. 15, italics in original text).

Accordingly, critical principles that support a pedagogy of the body oblige educators to be cognizant of the larger social, political, and economic conditions that shape their lives and the lives of their students. In brief, the following provides a summary of important pedagogical considerations related to decolonizing the body within the context of teaching and learning:

- Teachers must engage the emotional and physical responses and experiences of students in the process of teaching and learning. Their responses and experiences are recognized as meaningful indicators of strengths and limitations that students face in the process of their intellectual formation and social consciousness.
- Knowledge must be understood as a historical and collective process emanating from the body's relationship to the world. The body is primary in the construction of knowledge and development of moral thought or, as Connell (1987) reminds us, "in the reality of practice, the body is never

outside history" (p. 87).
- The mind and its cognitive capacities have to be understood as only one medium for the construction of knowledge. Hence, students are seen as integral human beings whose minds, bodies, hearts, and spirits are implicated in the process of teaching and learning. Our practices must reach into the students' innermost emotional and psychic centers if we are committed to a pedagogy of emancipation.
- The knowledge derived from the body's interactions with the world constitutes a significant dimension of a critical educational praxis. Classroom and community relationships, materials, and activities must reflect this knowledge through cultural integrity with the communities in which students reside.
- Teaching and learning must be understood as a process of human labor that is tied to the material conditions and social relations of power that shape classroom life. Hence, the question of power and the uses of authority must be interrogated consistently.
- Knowledge construction has to be seen as a collective, historical phenomenon that takes place continuously within and outside of school. To privilege school knowledge and ignore the knowledge and power of lived experiences limits students' social agency and diminishes important opportunities for active participation in their process of learning.
- Teachers must create meaningful interactions and activities in classrooms and communities that support students to grapple honestly with the tensions of differences in worldview, whether related to class, race, gender, sexuality, ability, or culture, and their consequences within contexts of inequalities.
- The knowledge that teachers have of their own bodies, including their sexuality, is an important aspect in their ability to effectively interact with and competently educate diverse student populations.
- Acts of resistance connected to the body can signal meaningful alternative ways of knowing and relating to the world. Opportunities must be created for students to reflect, affirm, and challenge the meaning of acts of resistance in their lives.
- Opportunities must be created in classrooms and communities that permit students to control aesthetic and physical conditions, including the definition and execution of knowledge construction, aesthetics, politics, fashion, voice, and participation.

The above principles for a critical praxis of the body are linked to decolonizing the body from educational and social constraints that repress the development of voice, disrupt democratic participation, and thwart the self-determination of disenfranchised populations. Educators must work together with students, parents, colleagues, and the community to challenge the conditions of their labor in schools that render them passive and domesticate their dreams.

Forging an Emancipatory Vision: Love, Ethics, and the Body

Forging an emancipatory vision of schooling calls us back home to our bodies in a world where all aspects of our daily life, such as birth, death, marriage, family, school, work, leisure, parenthood, spirituality, and even entertainment, are monitored and controlled (Lefebvre, 1971). The historical colonization of our bodies has left many of us numb, alienated, fragmented, defenseless, and at the mercy of capital. The consequence, as Richard Brosio (1994) reminds us, is a deep sense of personal and collective dissatisfaction generated by a marketplace that cannot satisfy the human needs of the body, needs that can only be met through relationships that break the alienation and isolation so prevalent in our lives today. Through integrating principles that sustain a critical praxis of the flesh, teachers can begin to create a space in which emotional intimacy can thrive, nourishing academic development and human connection among students. Terry Eagleton (2003) urges us to recognize that the origin of emancipatory possibility and human solidarity resides squarely in the body. For it is through the collective interactions of integral bodies in the classroom that the possibility of moral thought can be awakened. This constitutes a very important aspect of pedagogy since, as Eagleton suggests, it is moral thought that places our bodies back into history and creates a place for us to grapple with the impact of structural inequalities, social and economic injustice, and the curtailing of human rights.

Moreover, it is the absence of a truly democratic moral language and practice of the body that stifles our capacity for social struggle today. Many educators across the country bemoan, justifiably so, the conditions created by high-stakes testing and other accountability measures that negatively impact their labor. However, despite their frustration, educators have struggled for the past eight years to communicate a clear and coherent emancipatory moral message to challenge the shallow economistic moralism of the Bush administration's educational panacea, No Child Left Behind (Karp, 2003). Some would argue that the lack of a coherent political project is a direct result of teachers' alienated complicity with the status quo and the contradictions inherent in their lack of politics within a highly charged political arena. Rather than exercising a language of economic efficiency and neoliberal accountability, life in schools and society requires the development of a moral political language that can safeguard the dignity and integrity of all human differences that are intrinsic to a pluralistic nation. Genuine democracy requires the body's interaction with the social and material world in ways that nurture meaningful and transformative participation. It must exist as a practice in which human beings can interact individually and collectively as empowered subjects of their lives.

Freire emphasizes the significance of love and the importance of ethics in education. He embraces love as an emancipatory and revolutionary principle, compelling us to become part of a new decolonizing culture that nurtures human connection, intimacy, trust, and honesty from the body out into the world. In the same vein, Shapiro (1999) writes, "With love we affirm and are affirmed. In the sociopolitical struggle against death from hunger, disease, exploitation, war, destruction of the earth, and against hopelessness, there is a great and growing need for our capacity to become 'body-full' with love" (p. 99). For Eagleton (2003), love means to comprehend the moral and the material as inseparably linked. It constitutes an essential ingredient of a just society and the political principle that must motivate struggles for social justice and human rights. It is grounded in the mutuality and interdependence of human existence. Also inherent is the understanding that we as educators are never at liberty to be violent, cruel, brutal, or authoritarian in the name of being pedagogically rigorous or scientific, actions that belie an ethos of democracy or enlightenment.

Freire (1993, 1995, 1998) contends that ethics is a significant point of departure for our private and public lives. It constitutes a political and moral question. Without morality, our politics and pedagogy can result in an instrument of oppression. Eagleton (2003), however, reminds us that morality cannot be confused with moralism. Morality in a critical pedagogical context entails exploring deeply the quality of our sensations, ideas, and practices, a process that teachers and students cannot accomplish by abstracting life from our social surroundings, from our cultures, or from our histories of survival. It requires educators to bring together in their teaching the moral and political as well as the particular and universal, acknowledging that nothing can survive in isolation. Through collective struggles to decolonize our bodies, consciousness is born. Through collective actions with students, colleagues, and communities, we can work together for the shifting of consciousness and for the transformation of material conditions. They require our participation in the actual settings in which we live and work. To not act in the immediacy of our workplace or lived environment can place us in danger of living out an abstracted or "false consciousness," one that can cause us to lose touch with the grief or empathy for others that human oppression stirs in the human soul.

Muriel Rukeyser (1996) writes, "a true consciousness is the confession to ourselves of our feelings; a false consciousness disowns them" (p. 49). Ultimately it is this disowning that leads to the corruption of the mind and the body. It is the outcome of an overabundance of contrived representations and images in schools, society, and the media that repeatedly tell poor, working class, and racialized populations that our lives are worthless, beckoning us to abandon ourselves daily in the name of capital. At a time when our civil liberties are being undermined, great moral courage is required to voice our dissent against policies and practices that betray the oppressed, rendering them disposable and expendable. To counter debilitating conditions in classrooms and society, we need a revolutionary pedagogy committed to the unfettering of the body by embracing the liberation of humanity as sensual, thinking, knowing, and feeling subjects of history. It entails rewriting the body into our understanding of pedagogy by calling forth the establishment of new social, political, and economic conditions that can reap new possibilities for public schooling. For classroom conditions that begin with the primacy of the body carry radical possibilities for reconnecting students deeply to their development as fully integral human beings. Most importantly, since the body is the material foundation of our yearning for human liberation, it is only in our bodies that we can ultimately enact a revolutionary love, a love grounded in shared human kinship, political self-determination, and economic justice.

References

Beckey, C. (2000). Wicked bodies: Toward a critical pedagogy of corporeal differences for performance. In C. O'Farrell, D. Meadmore, E. McWilliam, & C. Symes (Eds.), *Taught bodies* (pp. 57–80). New York: Peter Lang.
Brosio, R. (1994). *A radical democratic critique of capitalist education.* New York: Peter Lang.
Connell, R. (1987). *Gender and power.* Cambridge: Polity.
Darder, A. (2002). *Reinventing Paulo Freire: A pedagogy of love.* Boulder, CO: Westview.
Eagleton, T. (2003). *After theory.* New York: Basic Books.
Foucault, M. (1995). *Discipline and punish.* New York: Vintage.
Freire, P. (1970). *Pedagogy of the oppressed.* New York: Seabury.
Freire, P. (1993). *Pedagogy of the city.* New York: Continuum.
Freire, P. (1995). *Pedagogy of hope.* New York: Continuum.
Freire, P. (1998). *Teachers as cultural workers.* Boulder, CO: Westview.

Giroux, H. (1998). Teenage sexuality, body politics and the pedagogy of display. In J. Epstein (Ed.), *Youth culture: Identity in a postmodern world* (pp. 24-55). Malden, MA: Wiley-Blackwell.

Grose, T. K. (2007, March 26). Straight facts about the birds and bees. *U.S. News and World Report.* Retrieved September 20, 2008, from http://www.usnews.com/usnews/news/articles/070318/26sex.htm

Haraway, D. (1990). A manifesto for cyborgs. In L. Nicholson (Ed.), *Feminism/postmodernism* (pp.190-233). New York: Routledge.

Hayles, K. (1999). *How we become posthuman: Virtual bodies in cybernetics, literature, and informatics.* Chicago, IL: University of Chicago Press.

hooks, b. (1994). *Teaching to transgress.* New York: Routledge.

Karp, S. (2003, Spring). Equity claims don't pass the test. *Rethinking Schools Online.* Retrieved September 20, 2008, from http://www.rethinkingschools.org/special_reports/bushplan/ESEA173.shtml

Kazan, T. (2005). Dancing bodies in the classroom: Moving toward an embodied pedagogy. *Pedagogy, 5*(3), 379-408.

Laroy, V. (2002). The body in a pedagogy of being. *Humanizing Language Teaching, 4*(6). Retrieved September 20, 2008, from http://www.hltmag.co.uk/nov02/mart.htm

Lefebvre, H. (1971). *Everyday life in the modern world.* London: Penguin.

Levy, B. (2000). Pedagogy: Incomplete, unrequited. In C. O'Farrell, D. Meadmore, E. McWilliam, & C. Symes (Eds.), *Taught bodies* (pp. 81-90). New York: Peter Lang.

Lifton, R. (1990). The genocidal mentality. *Tikkun, 5*(3), 29-32, 97-98.

McLaren, P. (1998). Foreword. In S. Shapiro, *Pedagogy and the politics of the body: A critical praxis* (pp. ix-xviii). New York: Garland.

McWilliams, E. (2000). Stuck in the missionary position. In C. O'Farrell, D. Meadmore, E. McWilliam, & C. Symes (Eds.), *Taught bodies* (pp. 27-37). New York: Peter Lang.

Merleau-Ponty, M. (2002). *The phenomenology of perception.* New York: Routledge.

O'Brien, S. (2000). The lecherous professor. In C. O'Farrell, D. Meadmore, E. McWilliam, & C. Symes (Eds.), *Taught bodies* (pp. 39-55). New York: Peter Lang.

Rukeyser, M. (1996). *The life of poetry.* Ashfield, MA: Paris.

Rushkoff, D. (2001). *The merchants of cool: A report on the creators and marketers of popular culture for teenagers.* Retrieved September 20, 2008, from http://www.pbs.org/wgbh/pages/frontline/shows/cool/

Seidel, G. (1964). *Martin Heidegger and the pre-Socratics.* Lincoln: University of Nebraska Press.

Shapiro, S. (1999). *Pedagogy and the politics of the body: A critical praxis.* New York: Garland.

Shor, I., & Freire, P. (1986). *A pedagogy for liberation: Dialogues for transforming education.* South Hadley, MA: Bergin and Garvey.

Sinclair, A. (1999). *Body and pedagogy.* Retrieved September 20, 2008, from http://www.mbs.edu/index.cfm?objectid=951E3441-123F-A0D8-42535588B213E90B

Snaza, N., & Lensmire, T. (2006). Abandon voice?: Pedagogy, the body and late capitalism. *InterActions: UCLA Journal of Education and Information Studies, 2*(2). Retrieved September 20, 2008, from http://repositories.cdlib.org/gseis/interactions/vol2/iss2/art3

Spender, D. (1995). *Nattering on the net: Women, power and cyberspace.* Melbourne: Spinifex.

Willis, P. (1977/1981). *Learning to labour: How working class kids get working class jobs.* New York: Columbia University Press.

CHAPTER 14

Postcolonial Subjects, Black Feminism, and the Intersectionality of Race and Gender in Higher Education

HEIDI SAFIA MIRZA

In order to tackle the issue of race and gender inequality in higher education, it is imperative to understand the nature of power relations and how racialized, classed, and gendered boundaries are produced and lived through black/postcolonial female subjectivity.[1] In this chapter, I ask the still necessary and fundamental questions that underpin black feminist struggles to find a voice in higher education. How do racial and gender distinctions structure the experiences of black and ethnicized women in places of higher learning? This question points to the issue of black and ethnicized female subjectivity and the way "difference" is organized through social relations in political and economic structures, policies, and practices. In the context of endemic race and gender inequality, why is there a persistent expression of educational desire and optimism among black and ethnicized women? To answer these questions, I take an insider black feminist view of how gender and race difference is lived out in the contingent historical specificity of universities. My aim is to clarify our understanding of the ways in which structures of power reproduce social divisions in the lives of black and ethnicized women. I examine the processes of social inequality and systematic institutionalized discriminatory practices in the context of raced and gendered human agency that frames black female struggles for life chances and educational opportunities.

Black Feminism and "Embodied Intersectionality"

A black feminist framework seeks to reconfigure multidimensional marginality using an intersectional analysis where race, class, gender, and other social divisions are theorized as lived realities. Intersectionality, a term coined by Kimberley Crenshaw (1989, 1991), rearticulates concerns about black female marginality in mainstream theorizing voiced in the scholarship of African American feminists, such as Angela Davis, Audrey Lorde, and Patricia Hill Collins.[2] Intersectionality provides a complex ontology of "really useful knowledge" that reveals the everyday lives of black and ethnicized women who are simultaneously positioned in multiple structures of dominance and power as gendered, raced, classed, colonized, and sexualized "others." It signals a move away from the inadequate additive models of double or triple jeopardy and the seemingly meaningless listing of never-ending hierarchies of multiple social positions and identities (Butler, 1990). Black and ethnicized women, of different ages, with various caring responsibilities, coming from particular cultures, religions, nation-states, with or without citizenship/human rights, live in the dominant modalities of race, class, and gender (Brah, 1996; Skeggs, 1997). A black feminist epistemology is contextual and contingent and examines the differentiated and variable organizing logics and beliefs that structure women's lives in various historical times and geographic places (McKittrick, 2006; Yuval-Davis, 2006).

The notion of "embodied intersectionality" seeks to make sense of black or "othered" women's symbolic and narrative struggles to define the materiality of their educational experiences (Ahmed, 2000). Simmonds (1997) writes of such embodied experience: "The world I inhabit as an academic is a white world ... in this white world I am a fresh water fish that swims in sea water. I feel the weight of the water on my body" (p. 227). Hers is a powerful statement about the costs of marginality for black women and their profound experiences when moving between "worlds" of difference. As black feminists, we need to ask questions about what shapes these worlds and how we are implicated in racist and sexist discourses through our inclusion, exclusion, choice, and participation.

Postcolonial Bodies:
"Being and Becoming" Gendered and Raced Subjects

Experience, as revealed by black and ethnicized female oral histories, autobiographies, diaries, and photographs, reveals the ways in which regulatory discursive power and privilege are "performed" or exercised in the everyday material worlds of the socially constructed "black woman." I draw on such personalized "embodied" narratives to demonstrate the processes of "being and becoming" gendered and raced subjects of academic and educational discourses (Gunaratnam, 2003; Mirza, 2009).

There is a hidden genealogy of black women's presence in higher education in England. Cornelia Sorabji, who was Indian, went to Somerville Hall in Oxford University in 1889.[3] She was the first woman to study law in a British university (Burton, 1998; Visram, 2002). What must it have been like for the first woman of color in an elite white male university in Britain? Sorabji was by no means a feminist or a radical; in fact, she supported British rule and was against Gandhi's independence movement for India. Always wearing a sari, she received special treatment and privileges at Somerville. She was given a fire to dress in the morning, was chaperoned to lectures, and was introduced into influential literary and political circles. Although she was never allowed to practice as a solicitor in Britain, she demanded and received special dispensation to sit her law exams as a woman in college. She wrote that the male students were kind, giving up a book if the librarian said that she wanted it. However, such treatment exasperated her, and she said of her tutor, "I wish he would treat me like a man and not make gallant speeches about my intellect and quickness of perception" (Visram, 2002, p. 95). Sorabji returned to India and championed the property rights of the Purdahnashin (veiled women confined to the private domain by religious practice), but lived her final years in England in an asylum where she died in 1954 (Vadgama, 2004). Such sad revelation makes me wonder about the "weight" of living a nonwhite existence in a consuming white world.

For postcolonial women of color, it is impossible to escape the body and its reconstructions as we negotiate our embodied social situations. Casey (1993) describes how black women's innocent expectations and eager quest for knowledge can take them on an unexpected journey "to another place" where they are transformed by the consuming, monolithic power of whiteness: "young black women set off into the white world carrying expectations of mythic proportions ... their odysseys, they believe will transform their lives ... but separated from their cultural communities these young women's passages turn out to be isolated individual journeys ... 'into the heart of whiteness'" (p. 132). Being a curiosity, a special case, "one in a million," can be an emotional and professional burden to black women in the academy. To be an exotic token, an institutional symbol, a mentor and confidant, and a natural expert of all things to do with race, is something that many black women recount in their academic careers (Essed, 2000; hooks, 1994; Mirza, 1995; Razack, 1998; Williams, 1991; Wright, Thompson, & Channer, 2007). But we need to be careful in how we situate these "tales of women with dark skin" for, as Bhattacharyya (1998) argues, such heroic "new" stories by themselves do not counter invisibility and negative stereotypes deeply embedded in our thinking.

In a similar narrative of marginality and neglect, the story of Indian women suffragettes reveals our collective amnesia about black women's presence in higher education. I stumbled upon a small crumpled photograph of the Indian suffragettes at the 1911 Women's Coronation Procession.[4] The photo was tucked away in a dark display cabinet of the "World City Gallery" at the Museum of London. The procession was a rally organized by the suffragettes to highlight their struggle during the coronation celebrations of George V. There were 60,000 women, 1,000 banners, and a column of marchers that snaked for seven miles. Under a banner with an elephant emblem were Indian women suffragettes. I did not know that there were Indian suffragettes since Indian women remain largely outside of British suffragette historiography (Visram, 2002). I learned that one of the most active Indian suffragettes was Sophia Duleep Singh, whose sisters Bamba and Catherine (daughters of the Maharaja of Punjab), went to Somerville with Cornelia Sorabji in 1890.

I was excited by the revelation of Indian women as activists, scholars, and writers. Women like me marched in demonstrations at a time when we were not even supposed to have an existence! Excavating such erasure of black women's genealogy in British academia exposes a "countermemory" that tells a different "truth." Spivak (1988) calls such negation of black women from discourse a form of "epistemic violence." I had thought that the struggle for space in higher education was a "white woman's history," as indeed I thought that the suffragette movement was a white woman's movement. But I have been learning that history is about what gets chosen to be revealed by whom and when.[5] Mohanty (1993) writes against a hastily derived notion of "universal sisterhood" that assumes a commonality of gender experience across race and national lines: "I have tried to demonstrate that this (feminist) scholarship inadvertently produces Western women as the only legitimate subjects of struggle, while Third World women are heard as fragmented, inarticulate voices in (and from) the dark" (p. 42).

For me, the question in the instance of revelation is, as Mohanty suggests, not just acknowledging their "difference," but rather the more difficult question of the *kind of difference that is acknowledged and engaged*. The kind of difference that I found should not have surprised me. The Indian women at the procession were described by a governor of an Indian province in terms of their "oriental" appearance: "Particularly striking and picturesque ... in beautiful dress ... the most significant feature of the whole procession, as they demonstrated the 'women's' question was without race, or creed, or boundary" (Visram, 2002, p. 164). In contrast to the staunch, serious, and defeminized white middle-class suffragettes, these "strange and exotic creatures" were described as nonthreatening in their ability to bring about change through their harmonious multicultural "otherness." A spectacle to be gazed upon, it was as if these Indian women were "known better than they know themselves" (Mirza, 1997a, p. 20). Simmonds (1997) discusses how racial knowledge is constructed about the other and the experience of being a "curiosity": "Adorned and unadorned I cannot escape the fantasies of the western imagination .... [T]his desire for colonized bodies as spectacle ... is essentially an extension of the 'desiring machine' of capital" (p. 232).

By telling the stories of Cornelia Sorabji and Indian suffragettes, I am not advocating the narratives of "black women were there too" as some sort of a triumph, that numbers and presence is all. This would be to invoke a benign multiculturalism that suggests that diversity in and of itself, that is, mere presence of black women, signals the attainment of equality. I tell the stories of these lost and invisible pioneers because as Mohanty (1993) explains,

> The challenge of race resides in a fundamental reconceptualization of our categories of analysis so that differences can be historically specified and understood as part of larger political processes and systems .... [D]ifference seen as benign variation (diversity), for instance, rather than as conflict, struggle or threat of disruption, bypasses power as well as history to suggest a harmonious, empty pluralism. (p. 42)

For black women, like Carby (1997), existence is not just about physical space; it is also about the power to occupy a historical space: "The black woman's critique of history has not only involved us coming to terms with absences: we have also been outraged by the ways in which it has made us visible, when it has chosen to see us ... we cannot hope to constitute ourselves in all our ill conceived presences that invade herstory from history, but we do wish to bear witness to our own herstories" (p. 45).

Race and "The Politics of Containment" in Higher Education

> Whereas racial segregation was designed to keep blacks as a group or class outside centers of power, surveillance now aims to control black individuals inside centers of power when they enter the white spaces of the public and private spheres. (Collins, 1998, p. 20)

Black women are increasingly visible in public spaces as professionals in previously homogenous raced/gendered places, such as universities, the judiciary, and the media. Collins (1998) suggests that the shift in the positioning of race, gender, and class through changing power relations and privatization has led to reconfigured patterns of institutionalized racism. In what she calls the "new politics of containment," surveillance strategies become important when middle-class black women enter institutional spaces of whiteness in the devalued public sphere from which they were hitherto barred. She argues that black women are watched in desegregated work environments to ensure they remain "unraced" and assimilated (p. 39). Being seen as assimilated is as important as standing out since it can invoke feelings of need, rejection, and anxiety within the "white other" (Ahmed, 2004). To be unassimilated or "stand out" invites a type of surveillance that appears benign but can be deeply distressing for black women.

Surveillance means being accountable and having more attention than others heaped upon you. A black female professor related when she was first appointed with fanfare and excitement. She was a "special case," one in "a million," a black female trophy. She was in the university news (front page and the Web), and was invited to high profile functions and events. Although it was not her job, in the first week she has to publicly present a detailed plan for delivering equal opportunities and race equality for the next five years to the senior managers and executives of the university. By the third month, she had been required to write five reports on her targets, attainments, and strategies, and found herself accountable to three different line managers since it could not be decided to whom she should report (to the executive administration, the academic area, or the faculty). Their "kind and supportive" attention was all consuming, but she received no real support for her academic research and teaching. Finally she became ill. No other professor had received such exhausting and intense level of scrutiny or expectation over a short period of time.

There is an irony to the heightened visibility of the "invisible" in the polite and genteel corridors of higher education. A national survey of ethnic minorities in higher education found that black women were more likely than any other group to report being the victim of sexual harassment and discrimination at work (Carter, Fenton, & Modood, 1999). This raises questions about the safety of black women in public spaces. The high profile case of Anita Hill, an African American attorney, against African American Supreme Court Justice Clarence Thomas demonstrates how sexual harassment can be racialized within institutional contexts. Hill lost her case because, some argue, of how the "black woman" is constructed and given meaning in the public discourse on "race" (Morrison, 1993). Hill did not fit the stereotypes of "the black woman": she was neither an overachiever nor a welfare mother. Since she could not be easily understood in the public mind, she did not receive sympathy. She was labeled as a "traitor to the race" because of her public denouncement of a senior black male colleague. As Collins (1998) points out, the "black woman" is predetermined by an already written script: "surveillance seems designed to produce particular effects—black women remain visible yet silenced; their bodies become written by other texts, yet they remain powerless to speak for themselves" (p. 38).

Black women's journeys into higher education, as Casey (1993) writes, are journeys into the "heart of whiteness" where a homogenous identity, "the black woman," is created by "a white gaze which perceives her as a mute visible object" (p. 111). Being a "mute visible object" is something that consumes our very being and, as hooks (1994) argues, black women need healing strategies and healing words to deal with the anguish that sexist oppression creates in daily life. She suggests black women need to theorize from a "place of pain ... which enables us to remember and recover ourselves" (p. 74). hooks explains that such a location is experienced and shared by those who are "aware" of the personal and collective struggle engendered by various forms of domination, such as homophobia, class exploitation, racism, sexism, and imperialism. She suggests courageously exposing the "wounds" of struggle that will teach and guide us to new theoretical journeys that challenge and renew inclusive feminist practices.

Such a "place of pain" manifests in many ways. Recently I attended an equal opportunities workshop where we were asked to identify experiences of institutional racism. A young Iranian woman, a graduate student, recounted how her husband, a qualified medical doctor, experienced racial discrimination when he tried to get a placement in the National Health Service. A white male member of the workshop, an established academic said to her, "Don't worry, love, it wouldn't happen to you as you are so attractive." In that moment, black women were reduced to no more than their embodied "otherness" as mute visible objects. His comment was made possible by the unspoken power of his authorative gaze. Williams (1991), an African American law professor, talks of the collective trauma such everyday incursions into selfhood engenders:

> There are moments in my life when I feel as though part of me is missing. There are days when I feel so invisible that I can't remember the day of the week it is, when I feel so manipulated that I can't remember my own name, when I feel so lost and angry that I can't speak a civil word to the people who love me best. These are times I catch sight of my reflection in store windows and I am surprised to see the whole person looking back ... I have to close my eyes at such times and remember myself, draw an internal pattern that is smooth and whole. (in hooks, 1994, p. 74)

The Excluding Power of Whiteness in Higher Education

We have established a small but important community of women scholars of color in Britain. I belong to a generation of postcolonial women who have struggled together in the world of academe since the 1970s, and many of us are now professors! There is also a new generation of hopeful young women of color challenging the traditions of the academy, but even then we are so few in number! Data on higher education staff shows that there are 15 black and 80 Asian women professors in the UK, out of a total of 14,305 professors.[6] Maybe I was deluded by our newfound status and assumed that a few black feminists having a place in the academy means we are no longer considered an endangered species! Higher education in Britain still remains a "hideously white"[7] place that is rarely open to critical gaze (Back, 2004). It is not a place one expects to find many "black bodies." Being a body "out of place" in white institutions has emotional and psychological costs to the bearer of that difference (Puwar, 2001).

There are costs to "just being there" in higher education. Black and minority ethnic students are more likely to leave university before completing their course. As Connor, Tyers, Modood, and Hillage (2004) argue, the most influential reasons are the unmet expectations about higher education. While financial and family difficulties and institutional factors such as poor teaching and wrong subject choice also feature, ethnic minority people report "the feeling of isolation or hostility in academic culture" (p. 60). These are worrying findings as they signal the fact that many black students do not feel they belong. Reay, David, and Ball (2005) shed light on the process of exclusion felt by young, working class, and ethnic minority people seeking to enter higher education. They suggest that young people can engage in a process of self-exclusion when making university choices. Drawing on Bourdieu, they write that processes of exclusion work through having "a sense of one's place which leads one to exclude oneself from places from which one is excluded" (p. 91). As one student in their study says about going to an elite university, "What's a person like me doing in a place like that?" According to the researchers, "Choosing to go to university ... for the working classes is about being different people in different places, about who they might be but also what they must give up" (p. 161).

Processes of exclusion in higher education are difficult to unpack as they are underscored by the complex dynamics of class, gender, and race. Experiences are complex and relational and are located at the intersection of structure, culture, and agency (Brah, 1996). For some, the university can be a positive experience. As Housee (2004) demonstrates, South Asian young women can find spaces in the university to express assertive and independent personas that enable them to freely express their religious identity. In opposition to the stereotype of Asian women as victims and recipients of patriarchal culture, they were "fighting back ... and were not going to accept racism, sexism or any other -ism" (p. 69).

While spaces of opposition can and do open up, Back (2004) suggests that there are two antagonistic forces at play in higher education. One moves unconsciously and haphazardly toward what Hall (2000) calls "multicultural drift," and the other remains the "sheer weight of whiteness" (Back, 2004). In some institutions the "sheer weight of whiteness" is overt and almost impenetrable. Research examining the University of Cambridge shows how elite culture is self-reinforcing. It was seen by others as a white, male, "tough and macho" culture that was "secretive, intimidating and insular." It was assumed by people at Cambridge that those in privileged positions were there because of their ability and merit. However, research indicates that over 70 percent of readers and professors had a degree from Cambridge, a third of the academics had no experience from any other university, and the majority had been there for over 20 years (Schneider-Ross, 2001).

Puwar (2004) draws on Bourdieu and Foucault to explain how cultures of exclusion operate within contested social spaces such as universities:

> Social spaces are not blank and open for any body to occupy. Over time, through processes of historical sedimentation, certain types of bodies are designated as being the "natural" occupants of specific spaces.... Some bodies have the right to belong in certain locations, while others are marked out as trespassers who are in accordance with how both spaces and bodies are imagined, politically, historically and conceptually circumscribed as being "out of place." (p. 51)

Puwar suggests that black bodies out of place are "space invaders." There are several ways in which black bodies are constructed when they do not represent the "racial somatic norm" within white institutions (Puwar, 2001, 2004). First, there is "disorientation": a double-take as you enter a room as if you are not supposed to be there. You are noticed and it is uncomfortable, like walking into a pub in a town where you don't live. There is confusion as you are not the "natural expected occupant of that position." I know this well: in many meetings, even though I am a professor, I have been mistaken as the coffee lady. Even students do a double-take when they see me as the social theory lecturer. Second, there is "infantalisation": you are not only pigeon-holed into being "just a race expert" but also seen as less capable of being in authority. This can mean black staff are assumed to be more junior than you are, and there is constant doubt about your skills that can affect career progression. Third, there is the "burden of invisibility" or hypersurveillance: you are viewed suspiciously and any mistakes are picked up and seen as a sign of misplaced authority. You have to work harder for recognition outside of the confines of stereotypical expectations, and can suffer disciplinary measures and disappointment if you do not meet expectations in your work performance.

Sometimes I am shocked by the deeply racist comments I hear in everyday life in the higher echelons of our "civilized" universities. Recently I was on a search committee for the appointment of a chair in a prestigious university. I was sent an e-mail by a senior white male academic about the applications. He described several in terms of their research and then one from a "not very incredible Indian." Why was "the Indian" racialized but not the others? What difference did it make that he was Indian? What was I being "told" in this message? Was it "all Indians want to come to England and will try anything"? Or that "Indian qualifications are not very good and, anyway, an Indian can never be as good as a white (British) academic"? Why did the white male academic who sent the e-mail not think about what he was saying to me, a woman of Indo-Caribbean heritage? Was it because even though I am one of them (an Indian), I am now one of us (an honorary white who can speak their language)? Why did he say it at all? Maybe because he could. Fanon's (1952/1986) parallel analysis can help us understand the personal costs of the racialized phenomena of "a not very credible Indian":

> "We have a Senegalese teacher. He is quite bright.... Our doctor is colored. He is very gentle." It was always the Negro teacher, the Negro doctor.... I knew, for instance that if the physician made a mistake it would be the end of him and all those who came after him. What could one expect after all, from a Negro physician? As long as everything went well he was praised to the skies. But look out, no nonsense under any conditions... I tell you I was walled in; no exception was made for my fine manners, or my knowledge of literature, or my understanding of quantum theory. (p. 117)

Marginality, Resistance, and Transforming the Academy

From the diaries of Cornelia Sorabji (Visram, 2002) and the eloquent lectures of Patricia Williams (1997), we can begin to open up and understand the complex multidimensional world that black women inhabit on the margins of white institutions. We need to understand black women's agency and subjectivity in relation to their space on the margins. Marginality, as hooks (1991) argues, can be a radical location in which black women can situate themselves in relation to the dominant group through "other ways of knowing." hooks recounts her own story of leaving home, going to the university, and becoming an academic: "When I left that concrete space on the margins, I kept alive in my heart ways of knowing reality.... (I was) sustained by remembrance of the past, which includes recollections of broken tongues that decolonize our minds, our very beings" (p. 150). She argues that we should reclaim the word "margin" from its traditional use as a marker of exclusion and mobilize it as an act of positive appropriation for black women:

> Marginality is a central location for the production of a counterhegemonic discourse—it is found in the words, habits and the way one lives.... It is a site one clings to even when moving to the centre ... it nourishes our capacity to resist.... It is an inclusive space where we recover ourselves, where we move in solidarity to erase the category colonizer/colonized. (pp. 149-150)

Black and ethnicized women occupy a "third space" (Mirza & Reay, 2000) or a "hidden counter public" sphere (Fraser, 1994) where members of subordinated social groups invent and circulate counterdiscourses that in turn permit them to formulate oppositional interpretations of their identities, interests, and needs. In our research on African Caribbean women educators in black community schools (also called supplementary or Saturday schools), Diane Reay and I found black women working alongside the dominant educational discourse. In their space on the margin, with their quiet and subversive acts of care and "other ways of knowing," they operate within, between, under, and alongside mainstream educational and labor market structures. By doing so, they subvert, rename, and reclaim opportunities for their children through the transformative pedagogy of "raising the race," a radical pedagogy that ironically appears conservative on the surface with its focus on inclusion and dialogue with the mainstream (Mirza, 1997b, p. 274).

Black and ethnicized women appear to seek social transformation through educational change. The African Caribbean women teachers in black supplementary schools, like those working and studying in universities and schools, struggle for educational inclusion in order to transform opportunities for themselves and their children. In covert and quiet ways, unlike street riots that signal masculine social change, the women work to keep alive the black communities' collective desire for self-knowledge and their belief in the power of schooling to militate against racial barriers (Fordham, 1996). As Casey (1993) writes, education acquires a different meaning in the context of racist oppression: "In a racist society ... to become educated is to contradict the whole system of racist signification ... to succeed in studying white knowledge is to undo the system itself ... to refute its reproduction of black inferiority materially and symbolically" (p. 123).

For African Caribbean women, educational institutions are not just mechanisms through which individuals are unconsciously subjected to the dominant ideological system but rather, as Freire (2004) argues, education is the terrain on which they acquire consciousness of their position and struggle. Just as black women educators have developed a strategic rationalization of their situation and opportunities, so too have black women in higher education developed a sense of their space on the margin through self-actualization and self-definition.

Conclusion

I began by asking the question, How do racial and gender distinctions structure the experiences of black and ethnicized women in places of higher learning? The chapter addresses the issue of black ethnicized female subjectivity by exploring the way race and gender is systematically organized through social relations in places of higher learning. Cornelia Sorabji and the Indian women suffragettes in the late nineteenth century are symbolic of the erasure of an ethnicized black feminist/womanist presence in mainstream (white) educational establishments. An analysis of their "embodied" subjectivity illuminates the invisible ways in which their raced and gendered intersectional "differences" are lived out in the contingent historical specificity of academic and educational discourses. They are "mute visible objects" excluded through processes of containment or surveillance, and located on the margins of structures that conceal the technologies and power of monolithic whiteness.

The second question, Why is there a persistent expression of educational desire and optimism among black and ethnicized women? is addressed through an understanding of the ways in which women of color continually resist and rename the regulatory effects of the discourses of educational inequity and subjugation in higher education. Ultimately, black and ethnicized women challenge systematic and institutionalized discriminatory practices through their collective agency and educational desire for personal transformation through educational opportunities.

The power of intersectional analysis reveals how educational institutions must be seen, not just as mechanisms through which individuals are unconsciously subjected to dominant ideological systems of race, class, and gender, but rather as sites of struggle. My aim in the chapter has been to explore the multiple and complex ways that structures of power reproduce racialized and gendered social divisions in the everyday lives of black and ethnicized women in higher education. A black feminist epistemology is a powerful tool that opens up ways of seeing multiple structures of dominance and power in spaces of learning and teaching. The chapter shows the need to be vigilant of the quiet, invisible, organizing logics of race, class, and gender that ultimately structure the "real" embodied experiences across time and space for postcolonial black and ethnicized women.

Notes

1. Black is used to mean women of visible difference (Bhavnani, Mirza, & Meetoo, 2005). This includes women of color, such as those of African and Asian origin unless otherwise specified (Brah, 1996; Mirza, 1997a).

2. See Patel (n.d.) for a summary of Crenshaw's intersectionality presentation at the 2001 World Conference Against Racism. For additional discussions on intersectionality, see Brah and Phoenix (2004), McCall (2005), Phoenix and Pattynama (2006), Prins (2006), and Symington (2004).

3. For an image of Cornelia Sorabji, see the National Portrait Gallery Web site at http://www.npg.org.uk/live/search/person.asp?LinkID=mp61443. See also (Mirza, 2009).

4. For an image of Indian women suffragettes, see the Museum of London Web site at http://www.museumoflondon.org.uk/MOLsite/piclib/pages/bigpicture.asp?id=1032. See also (Mirza, 2009).

5. I was a member of the Mayor's Commission for African and Asian Heritage (MACCH) from 2003 to 2005. During this time, we took evidence as to the "forgotten" contribution of minority communities to the historical wealth of Great Britain and the institutional and organizational shortcomings in recognizing and displaying this contribution (Greater London Authority, 2005).

6. The 2006/7 HESA staff return data estimate that there are 15 black female professors and 80 Asian female professors in the UK. There are 14,305 professors in Britain: 2,595 are white women, 14,305 are white men, 55 are black men, and 545 Asian men. There are 55 women and 225 men categorized as "other" that includes mixed race. I thank the HESA information service for permission to reproduce these figures. Please see HESA (www.hesa.ac.uk) for definitions of ethnic categories.

7. The BBC was called "hideously white" by Greg Dyke, the BBC director general in 2001, for being 98 percent white. With less than 1.3 percent black and minority ethnic staff in higher education in UK (Carter et al., 1999; THES, 2004), higher education can be called hideously white as well.

References

Ahmed, S. (2000). *Strange encounters: Embodied others in post-coloniality*. London: Taylor and Francis.

Ahmed, S. (2004). *The cultural politics of emotion*. Edinburgh: University of Edinburgh Press.

Back, L. (2004). Ivory towers?: The academy and racism. In I. Law, D. Phillips, & L. Turney (Eds.), *Institutional racism in higher education* (pp. 1–6). Stoke on Trent: Trentham.

Bhattacharyya, G. (1998). *Tales of dark skinned women: Race, gender, and global culture.* London: University College London Press.

Bhavnani, R., Mirza, H. S., & Meetoo, V. (2005). *Tackling the roots of racism: Lessons for success.* Bristol: Policy.

Brah, A. (1996). *Cartographies of diaspora: Contesting identities.* London: Routledge.

Brah, A., & Phoenix, A. (2004). Ain't I a woman?: Revisiting intersectionality. *Journal of International Women's Studies, 5*(3), 75–86.

Burton, A. (1998). *At the heart of empire: Indians and the colonial encounter in late Victorian Britain.* Berkeley: University of California Press.

Butler, J. (1990) *Gender trouble: Feminism and the subversion of identity.* New York: Routledge.

Carby, H. (1997). White women listen!: Black feminism and the boundaries of sisterhood. In H. S. Mirza (Ed.), *Black British feminism* (pp. 45–53). London: Routledge.

Carter, J., Fenton, S., & Modood, T. (1999). *Ethnicity and employment in HE.* London: Policy Studies Institute.

Casey, K. (1993). *I answer with my life: Life histories of women teachers working for social change.* New York: Routledge.

Collins, P. H. (1998). *Fighting words: Black women and the search for justice.* Minneapolis: University of Minnesota Press.

Connor, H., Tyers, C., Modood, T., & Hillage, J. (2004). *Why the difference?: A closer look at higher education minority ethnic students and graduates* (DfES Research Report No. 552). London: HMSO.

Crenshaw, K. (1989). Demarginalizing the intersection of race and sex: A black feminist critique of antidiscrimination doctrine, feminist theory and antiracist politics. *University of Chicago Legal Forum,* 138–167.

Crenshaw, K. (1991). Mapping the margins: Intersectionality, identity politics, and violence against women of color. *Stanford Law Review, 43*(6), 1241–1299.

Essed, P. (2000). Dilemmas in leadership: Women of colour in the academy. *Ethnic and Racial Studies, 23*(5), 888–904.

Fanon, F. (1952/1986). *Black skin, white masks.* London: Pluto.

Fordham, S. (1996). *Blacked out: Dilemmas of race identity and success at Capital High.* Chicago, IL: University of Chicago Press.

Fraser, N. (1994). Rethinking the public sphere: A continuation to the critique of actually existing democracy. In H. A. Giroux & P. McLaren (Eds.), *Between borders: Pedagogy and the politics of cultural studies* (pp. 74–98). New York: Routledge.

Freire, P. (2004). *Pedagogy of indignation.* Boulder, CO: Paradigm.

Greater London Authority. (2005). *Delivering a shared heritage: The mayor's commission on African and Asian heritage.* London: GLA.

Gunaratnam, Y. (2003). *Researching "race" and ethnicity: Methods, knowledge, power.* London: Sage.

Hall, S. (2000). Conclusion: The multicultural question. In B. Hesse (Ed.), *Un/settled multiculturalisms: Diasporas, entanglements, transruptions* (pp. 209–241). London: Zed.

hooks, b. (1991). *Yearning: Race, gender and cultural politics.* London: Turnaround.

hooks, b. (1994). *Teaching to transgress: Education as the practice of freedom.* New York: Routledge.

Housee, S. (2004). Unveiling South Asian female identities post-September 11: Asian female students' sense of identity and experiences of higher education. In I. Law, D. Phillips, & L.

Turney (Eds.), *Institutional racism in higher education* (pp. 59-70). Stoke on Trent: Trentham.
McCall, L. (2005). The complexity of intersectionality. *Signs, 30*(31), 1771-1802.
McKittrick, K. (2006). *Demonic grounds: Black women and the cartography of struggle.* Minneapolis: University of Minnesota Press.
Mirza, H. S. (1995). Black women in higher education: Defining a space/finding a place. In L. Morley & V. Walsh (Eds.), *Feminist academics: Creative agents for change* (pp. 142-152). London: Taylor and Francis.
Mirza, H. S. (1997a). Introduction: Mapping a genealogy of Black British feminism. In H. S. Mirza (Ed.), *Black British feminism* (pp. 1-30). London: Routledge.
Mirza, H. S. (1997b). Black women in education: A collective movement for social change. In H. S. Mirza (Ed.), *Black British feminism* (pp. 268-277). London: Routledge.
Mirza, H. S. (2009). *Race, gender and educational desire: Why black women succeed and fail.* London: Routledge.
Mirza, H. S., & Reay, D. (2000). Redefining citizenship: Black women educators and "the third space." In M. Arnot & J. Dillabough (Eds.), *Challenging democracy: International perspectives on gender, education, and citizenship* (pp. 58-72). London: RoutledgeFalmer.
Mohanty, C. T. (1993). On race and voice: Challenges for liberal education in the 1990s. In B. Thompson & S. Tyagi (Eds.), *Beyond a dream deferred: Multicultural education and the politics of excellence* (pp. 41-65). Minneapolis: University of Minnesota Press.
Morrison, T. (Ed.). (1993). *Race-ing justice, en-gendering power: Essays on Anita Hill, Clarence Thomas and the social construction of reality.* London: Chatto and Windus.
Patel, P. (n.d.). Notes on gender and racial discrimination. Retrieved February 24, 2008, from http://www.eurowrc.org/13.institutions/5.un/un-en/12.un_en.htm
Phoenix, A., & Pattynama, P. (2006). Editorial: Special issue on intersectionality. *European Journal of Women's Studies, 13*(3), 188-192.
Prins, B. (2006). Narrative accounts of origins: A blind spot in the intersectional approach? *European Journal of Women's Studies, 13*(3), 277-290.
Puwar, N. (2001). The racialized somatic norm and the senior civil service. *Sociology, 35*(3), 351-370.
Puwar, N. (2004). Fish in or out of water: A theoretical framework for race and the space of academia. In I. Law, D. Phillips, & L. Turney (Eds.), *Institutional racism in higher education* (pp. 49-58). Stoke on Trent: Trentham.
Razack, S. (1998). *Looking white people in the eye: Gender, race and culture in courtrooms and classrooms.* Toronto: University of Toronto Press.
Reay, D., David, M., & Ball, S. (2005). *Degrees of choice: Social class, race and gender in higher education.* Stoke on Trent: Trentham.
Schneider-Ross Consultants. (2001). *Equality in the university: Setting the new agenda: A report on equality audit for Cambridge University.* Andover: Schneider-Ross.
Skeggs, B. (1997). *Formations of class and gender: Becoming respectable.* London: Sage.
Simmonds, F. N. (1997). My body myself: How does a black woman do sociology? In H. S. Mirza (Ed.), *Black British feminism* (pp. 226-239). London: Routledge.
Spivak, G. (1988). Can the subaltern speak? In C. Nelson & L. Grossberg (Eds.), *Marxism and the interpretation of culture* (pp. 271-314). London: Macmillan.
Symington, A. (2004). Intersectionality: A tool for gender and economic justice. *Women's Rights and Economic Change #9.* Retrieved February 24, 2008, from www.awid.org
Times Higher Education Supplement. (2004, October 22). Distinct lack of ebony in ivory towers.

Times, 18–19.

Vadgama, K. (2004, March 27). *Cornelia Sorabji*. Lecture presented at the Politics and Pioneers of South Asian History seminar in Museum of London, UK.

Visram, R. (2002). *Asians in Britain: 400 years of history*. London: Pluto.

Williams, P. J. (1991). *The alchemy of race and rights: The diary of a law professor*. Cambridge, MA: Harvard University Press.

Williams, P. J. (1997). *Seeing a color-blind future: The paradox of race*. New York: Noonday.

Wright, C., Thompson, S., & Channer, Y. (2007). Out of place: Black women academics in British universities. *Women's History Review, 16*(2), 145–162.

Yuval-Davis, N. (2006). Intersectionality and feminist politics. *European Journal of Women's Studies, 13*(3), 193–209.

CHAPTER 15

Dis/locating Oriental Citizen-Subject Makings: A Postcolonial Reading of Korean/Asian American Women's Narratives

JEONG-EUN RHEE

Drawing on Edward Said (1979/1995), historians, literary critics, ethnic studies scholars, and critical educators argue that orientalism has been integral in making U.S. national identity (Chow, 1993; Tchen, 1999). Said's concept examines British, French, and U.S. imperialist discourses on the Middle East, and his thesis provides a postcolonial theoretical ground to analyze how Asian people and cultures have been represented as antithetical and inferior to those of Europeanized America (Kang, 1995; Subedi, 2008). This is reflected most significantly in the history of U.S. immigration and nationalization laws, beginning with the Chinese Exclusion Act of 1882, the first law to ban immigration to the United States on the basis of nationality, thereby introducing a new legal category of "aliens ineligible for citizenship."[1] As such, the construction of the racialized "oriental" as fundamentally foreign to the U.S. nation-state has been more than discursive; it has historically materialized in U.S. laws (Coloma, 2006; Lowe, 1996).

Orientalism encompasses an imperialist desire of the occident. As Said (1979/1995) states, "It *is*, rather than expresses, a certain *will* or *intention* to understand, in some cases to control, manipulate, even to incorporate, what is a manifestly different (or alternative and novel) world" (p. 12, italics in original). In its expansionist mission through the continuous pursuit of Manifest Destiny in the Pacific, the United States occupied and governed Hawai'i, the Philippines, Guam, and the American Samoa since the 1890s, although the Philippines and Guam gained formal independence in 1946 and limited self-governance in 1949, respectively (Coloma, 2006). Through the Cold War Containment doctrine manifested in Korean and Vietnam Wars, the U.S. will was to contain Koreans, Cambodians, Hmongs, Laotians, and Vietnamese (Miyoshi, 1996). The construction of Asians as both yellow peril and model minority in U.S. domestic cultural discourses reflects this imperialist desire to know, define, control, manipulate, and incorporate the other. Through contradictory encompassing and distancing, different national and ethnic gendered Asians have been placed "within" the U.S. nation-state and marked as "foreign" and "outside" of the national polity (Lowe, 1996).

"Asian American" is an enigmatic term that includes people from vastly diverse ethnic, linguistic, national, religious, cultural, and immigration backgrounds and histories whose only common experience is that of having been labeled and treated as "orientals" in a supposedly "occidental" nation (Yanagisako, 1995). This political term was forged to develop panethnic solidarities across different Asian American communities and with other racialized groups of African Americans, Native Americans, and Latino/as in the 1960s and 1970s (Coloma, 2006; Lowe, 1996). Grounded in the U.S. geography yet excluded from the dominant U.S. historical narration, the politics of Asian Americans consequently has sought to reclaim their rootedness in making the U.S. nation-state. It is critical to underscore that the (partial) inclusion and integration "won" through these struggles for Asians as Americans opened spaces to imagine Asian America.

What is equally important is to examine what has been made unsayable by the political fiction of Asian American inclusion in the U.S. nation-state. If Asian American narratives are subsumed only as domestic racial and ethnic minority experiences that are encompassed by the U.S. nation-building project, what will be unthinkable and unsayable in terms of their diasporic realities engendered by U.S. imperialism (McClintock, Mufti, & Shohat, 1997)? This chapter therefore looks into the Asian American citizen-making project of the U.S. empire-nation-state by interrogating the conceptual demarcation between the national and the international (e.g., Asian American, immigrant, and foreign Asian) and by bringing together individual, cultural, and historical narratives that reveal the transnational contours of citizen-making.

The chapter examines the narratives of four Korean/Asian American subjects drawn from my larger study on U.S. higher education (Rhee, 2002). As I analyze the changing nature of U.S. citizenship for these women, I also explore the alternative understandings that emerge when their narratives are read through the history of U.S. domination of Korea (Kim & Choi, 1998). My purpose is not to develop a redemptive criticism in which minority subjects, particularly Korean/Asian American subjects, become included or assimilated successfully as part of a pluralist United States. By interrogating the fissures and gaps that interrupt the allegedly U.S. multicultural national identity, I illustrate instead the postcolonial dilemmas of Korean/Asian Americans to discuss the possibilities and limitations of the U.S. citizen-making project.

Participants and Citizenship

The chapter narrates the stories of four women: Anna, April, Sammy, and Sarah.[2] Legally, all of them are U.S. citizens. At the time of the interview, April and Sarah were graduate students, Anna was a full-time housewife of a Korean (international) male student, and Sammy was a university faculty member. April and Sarah were born in Korea in the 1970s, were adopted by white parents, and were brought to the United States when they were very young. So, they are naturalized U.S. citizens. In the 1960s Anna and Sammy were born into Korean international student families in the United States, grew up mostly in Korea, and then came back to the United States—Anna for her husband's graduate schooling and Sammy for her education. So, they are U.S. citizens by birth.

Korean Emigration:
An Imperialist Lineage of Korean American Citizen-Making

To contextualize their narratives, this section includes a brief historical account of Korean emigration to the United States. Positioning Korean emigration—not immigration—as a necessary historical context is to develop a transnational cartography of how U.S. imperialism in Korea has created a continuity between the destruction of social relations in Korea and the migration of Koreans to the United States (John, 1996). It also points out how U.S. imperialist culture prepares emigrants for the domestic racialization process of U.S. citizen-making.

Penetrating Missionaries, Emitting Emigrants: 1882–1945

The official relationship between Korea and the United States began with the Korean-American Treaty of 1882, 16 years after the first arrival of U.S. merchants in the Korean peninsula (Kim, 1997). By 1900, a small number of Korean students, diplomats, and merchants (fewer than 50) made their way to the United States (Abelmann & Lie, 1995). From 1903 to 1905, a total of 7,226 Koreans were then recruited by U.S. Protestant missionaries to work in the plantations of Hawaii and to replace the mostly Japanese workforce that initiated strikes for better pay and labor conditions (Kim, 1997).[3] In 1908 the United States and Japan established the Taft-Katsura Treaty in which the United States supported the colonization of Korea by Japan (1909–1945) in return for Japan's promise not to invade the Philippines. During the Japanese occupation of Korea, U.S. missionaries took a major role in establishing the country's K-16 school system, without much prohibitive regulations from the colonial government (Suh, 1984). The educational, religious, and social influences of U.S. missionaries contributed to a pro-American attitude among the colonized Korean population, which consequently increased their power to promote the transnational emigration of Koreans to the United States (Bark, 1984).

Post-1945: The U.S. Military Occupation

After the Second World War, when Korea gained independence from Japan, the relationship between Korea and the United States became increasingly intense, complex, and unequal. Elaine Kim and Chungmoo Choi (1998) argue that "Korean modern history is a palimpsest of multiple layers of Japanese colonialism and neo-imperial domination, especially by U.S. hegemony, which superimposed its systems on political and social infrastructures of Japanese colonial rules" (p. 2). In 1945, Korea was split in half: the United States took control of the southern part of the peninsula, and the Soviet Union claimed the northern part (Kim, 2003).[4] The national division proceeded the U.S. military occupation of South Korea from 1945 to 1948 (Kim, 1991). The overall attitude of the U.S. Army Military Government in Korea (USAMGIK) is revealed in the following statement of U.S. Commanding General Hodge:

> I'm enough of an imperialist to want to preserve the standards of living we've achieved in the U.S. and I firmly believe that we have benefited the nations into which we have extended our influence. All nations with a high standard of living have been imperialist. Our imperialism hasn't been a bad imperialism. (Cumings, 1981, p. 248)

Under the USAMGIK, the imperialist discourses of civilizing mission, Western-style development, and capitalistic democracy imbued the social and cultural realms of the U.S.-controlled nation-building project in Korea (Cho, 1998, 2000).

The Korean War from 1950 to 1953 claimed more than four million lives, left Korea still divided into two (allegedly enemy) nations, and separated countless families without any promise for unification. After the Korean War, more than one million U.S. military personnel continue to be stationed in South Korea (Abelmann & Lie, 1995, p. 57). For the past 50 years, the political, military, economic, and cultural domination of the United States over South Korea has increasingly solidified (Cumings, 1981; Miyoshi, 1996). Under the continuing domination of the United States, Choi (1998) points out that Korea's "postcolonial" status has not really taken place; Korea's "postcoloniality" has been "deferred."[5]

Three Modes of Emigrations: You Are Here So We Will Be There

The social impact of the U.S. military on Korean life can be seen in the approximately 28,000 Korean women who married U.S. G.I.s between 1950 and 1972 and became the largest group of Koreans to emigrate to the United States (Abelmann & Lie, 1995, p. 58). Close to 100,000 Korean women came to the United States as brides of U.S. soldiers in the last half of the twentieth century (Yuh, 1999, p. xxiii). Yuh (1999) argues that the U.S. presence in Korea not only created the physical context (military bases and camptowns) where Koreans and Americans met, it also helped to create the social and cultural contexts (militarized prostitution, local civilian employment on bases, and the lure of the United States) that made marriage to U.S. soldiers appealing to Korean women.[6]

> Their marriages are a consequence of a half century of American military domination over Korea, a domination that includes the sexual subordination of Korean women, the glaring contrast between Korean poverty and American wealth, between Korean backwardness and American modernity, and the resulting lure that America has held for many Koreans.... Marriages between Korean women and American soldiers may be personal choices at the individual level, but at least for the women, these choices are profoundly shaped by the context of Korean subordination to American domination. Korea is inscribed as the feminine other while the United States takes on the role of the masculine superior. This is reflected in the male dominated, masculine, and strong U.S. military occupying a weak Korea in need of protection. This gendered context of neo-imperialism is a major factor in the skewed gender profile of intermarriages between Koreans and Americans. (Yuh, 1999, p. 2)

As a result of marriage-based immigration, the sex ratio of Koreans in the United States was significantly disproportionate over a long period. Statistics from the Immigration and Naturalization Services indicate that women represented 81 percent of the total number of Koreans in the United States in 1965, 67 percent in 1970, 58 percent in 1975, and 55 percent by 1990 (Abelmann & Lie, 1995, pp. 58, 202). While the four participants of this project do not reflect this mode of emigration, it must be noted that cultural discourses on Korean emigrant women invoke these gendered and sexualized dimensions of U.S. imperialism.

Another large group of Korean emigrants to the United States was "war orphans," who were categorized as such due to interracial union, the loss of parents, wartime dislocations, or poverty. The Korean government established an agency called *Yangyeonhwe* in 1954 to help Amerasian children to be adopted in their fathers' country. This policy was driven by the combined factors of strong prejudice against racial mixing, the stigma attached to Korean women's association with foreign men, the patriarchal belief that children belong to their paternal lineage, and the lack of social and economic resources to provide appropriate care for children. However, even after Korea has achieved economic prosperity, intercountry adoption has continued because of Korea's patriarchal Confucian culture and social structure in which unmarried mothers and children born out of wedlock are stigmatized and nonrelated adoptions are avoided (Chun, 1989). Consequently, it was assumed that most children adopted after the postwar period were born to unwed mothers. It is estimated that over 45,000 Korean children were adopted into U.S. families between 1962 and 1983 (Abelmann & Lie, 1995), the same period when Sarah's and April's adoptions took place.

The final large group of post–Korean War migrants consisted of mostly male students who came from the upper echelon of Korean society. It is not certain how many stayed in the United States, but it is not difficult to speculate that their experiences were qualitatively different from military brides and adoptee children. Whether they have stayed in the United States or returned to Korea, their U.S. tastes, styles, and credentials, along with their socioeconomic elite positions, confer high status and authority in Korea's public and private spheres. This group is central in the analysis of how the United States secured a place in the dreams and plans of a sizable number of Koreans (Bark, 1984). Both Anna's and Sammy's U.S. citizenships were the result of their parents' emigration to the United States as international students and as members of the Korean privileged elite.

Predicaments of the South Korean Nation-Building Project

What has made the above historical reality particularly insidious is that discourses in South Korea have constructed the United States as the benevolent "Big Brother" who saved Korea from Japanese imperialism and communism, at least until the 1980 Kwangju uprising, a brutal massacre of civilians in which the United States was implicated (Lee, 1988; Lee, 1995). The pro-American discourse that frames U.S. involvement in Korea as heroic and generous has been fed through strict "thought control policies" by the United States as well as Korean elites and military authoritarian regimes supported by the U.S. government. As a result, critics of the United States have been punished, and alternative or resistant dialogues have been labeled as antinational or communist (Kim, 1991). In addition, because official dominant discourses both in Korea and the United States deny the paradigm of U.S. imperialism, the colonized-colonizer relationship between these two countries is more ambiguous and ambivalent. The citizen-making project under Korean elite and military regimes is therefore seriously implicated in and complicit to U.S. imperialism.[7]

The Oriental Body and U.S. Imperialist Citizenship

The brief historical account above serves as the analytical point of "departure" to examine the four women's narratives in my study. This section explores how Korean emigrants have been incorporated as Korean American citizen-subjects and what they have sought in this process. I interrogate how categories of gender, race, and ethnicity are not simply domestic issues, but are intertwined, ruptured, and resisted in relation to the power dynamics of the U.S. empire-building in Korea (Kaplan, 1993). To highlight each woman's particularity and their collectivity, I relay their narratives separately and make occasional juxtapositions with the other stories to delineate convergences among them.

Sarah: (White) American in an Oriental Body, So Am I Definitely American?

Sarah's narrative of conflicting fragmented selves opens a visceral space to examine how every individual is always already constituted by ideological discourses and how U.S. orientalism affects Asian American subject formation. Sarah, who was adopted when she was seven months old, grew up in an "average" white suburban, middle-class family as the only child of color. Even though she checks the box "Asian American" for her race, she does not identify with the term "Korean." As Sarah points out, "The magazine for Korean Americans, they have this whole issue on Korean adoptee and adoptee experiences, they had this cartoon and one of the 10 cartoons was, you know that you're an adoptee if you're … One of the things was you forget you're Korean until you see yourself in the mirror." She continues, "I have this, this really strange contradiction between how I think, and how I see myself, and how I appear to the outside world." Whenever her racially marked (Asian) body invokes the question of "Where are you from?" from (white) people, she remembers that, especially when she was younger, she used to say "Korea-but-I-was-adopted" to distance herself from Korea as much as to assert that "I'm more like you than I seem to be. Don't trust [the] exterior."

Since she has lived in the gap between being born in Korea and being culturally white, she also feels split between her racially embodied self and her sense of belonging in white culture. Sarah says,

> The hardest part I have about my identity is the contradictions because although I was raised in white middle class America and have just absorbed that mentality, not of choice but that's where my world view comes from. At the same time I know the experience of discrimination and prejudice and ethnic sexism. So it's kind of like I'm straddling two worlds.

Her discrepant experiences continue as she tries to make sense of being an American. On the one hand, being an American is like skin to Sarah, so embedded in who she is and thus inseparable. The embodied experience of living her entire life in the United States, speaking only English, growing up in a "typical" white middle-class family, and living with white cultural values and norms allows her to comfortably acknowledge and claim her American self. On the other hand, as Stuart Hall (1997) argues, the bodily representation has its own genealogy and marking. That is, how our bodies are read is not an individual but a historically collective act. Sara's racial difference, marked as foreign, never an embodiment of the U.S. empire-nation-state, creates a contradiction in the legitimacy and authenticity of her U.S. identification. Sarah indicates,

> Even though I'm a person of color, even though I'm a woman, I know that I'm not the most, I'm not like the representative in American in terms of the mythical order of white male and everything, I don't know.... am I definitely American? Well, it's like, I think it's funny, like you internalize what American means, and at the same time I assume I am an American and when I think American I think of white people.

While her sense of being American is assumed and normalized with her proper cultural performance and her membership in white U.S. culture where she was raised, her Asian body engenders incongruence and incompatibility with her identification: "when I think American I think of white people."

Sarah's conflicted relationship with her white cultural identity and her racially embodied self signifies the continuous reign of race regime in the allegedly multicultural U.S. empire, which insists on the homology of culture, race, and nationality. Within this regime, the politics of cultural assimilation mocks the unassimilable body. Sara indicates that, if she has not been cursed and/or blessed to deal with the disparity of how she thinks, how she sees herself, and how she appears to the outside world, she might have forgotten her Korean self a long time ago. Perhaps this disparity and incoherence that reminds both Sarah and the United States of what they want to suppress is a symptomatic clue of how the projects of U.S. nation-building and empire-building are historically conterminous and mutually defining through the paradigm of orientalism.

April: Asian American Only, Never American

April has negotiated this discrepant experience of being born in Korea and being adopted and raised to become American by identifying as an Asian American, but not as an American or Korean. Growing up in a racially mixed, working class, immigrant family in California, she sees herself at the intersection of multiple ethnic, cultural, and racial flows, if her class and sexual identities can be placed aside for a moment. April reveals that

> Like my mom is from Holland so there's a very deep European kind of influence in my life. I'm Korean—not that I know that much Korean but relating to people because I'm Asian. Do you know Karate? Do you know this and that? Oh you look so good in red. I can't believe you don't know how to use chopsticks. I know how to use chopsticks. All these things. And then like living in California you need to know Spanish. There are four different influences that never really mix. They're very divided, very specific also, and then also living in America.

April has maneuvered to situate herself amidst polyglot, multicultural, and multinational communities, due to her lack of mainstream connection. Knowing the power of positive and negative connotations that any identity brings to the subject, she would never just say, "I'm American." She indicates that "it would not be something I would ever say." Instead, she calls herself Asian American: "Because it's that, it's ambiguous and unspecific enough for me to contend with like being Asian because I look Asian. Like I've got Asian descent in me but yet my socialization, my education, and all that kind of stuff stems from being American." The term Asian American becomes an intriguing battle site where her agency is exerted through political dis/identification and works within and against the race regime of the U.S. nation-state that rejects and differentiates Asian immigrant/American subjects from "native, authentic and real" Americans. Her refusal to claim American ironically coincides with the U.S. refusal of Asians. Through these double rejections, the name Asian American is claimed.

April says, "Korean, I don't say that because I don't feel I have the groundedness in Korean culture to be able to say I'm Korean, even though I'm interested in it." Her statement bears more of a self-perceived disqualification than denunciation. April's line of reasoning was echoed by Sarah when she says,

> Because I feel like for me to claim a Korean identity I feel like I'd be an imposter. Like I'd be an imposter. That I would—to be ignorant about Korean culture, to not speak the language. To not know the history. To not know the cultural norms. To not know the ways in which people are supposed to interact.... It's just not—I feel like to say not having all that knowledge and then to say I'm Korean I feel like I would be an imposter or I would be unjustified in claiming that identity.

The logic highlights the postcolonial history of a nation-building project that erects the trinity of people/race, culture/language, and nationality to help solidify the imagined community of a geographic territory (Gupta & Ferguson, 1997). However, no nation is based on one essential culture and language shared by one intact ethnic group (Cho, 1998). Instead, the project of nation-building constructs fictive racial/cultural subjects and disciplines its citizens and noncitizens to idealize, totalize, and erase different segments of histories, relationships, and experiences (Kang, 1995; Kim & Choi, 1998). For April and Sarah, although they can claim an American identity, their hypervisible "oriental" bodies that signal the history of U.S. imperialism in Korea (and other Asian countries) preclude them from actualizing their American subjectivity. Constrained by the operations of U.S. nation and empire building that refutes hybridity, dislocation, and loss, what Sarah and April have been deprived of is the legitimate historicity and explanatory power of their complex transnational and postcolonial experiences as Korean adoptee women in the United States, which can emerge through "de/colonizing moves" (Rhee & Subreenduth, 2006).

Anna: Legally American by Birth but Always Korean

Anna's narrative depicts similar predicaments of a Korean/Asian American subject position within the orientalist discourses in the United States. Yet her explicitly transnational narrative disrupts the secure border of U.S. citizenship. For Anna, her travel "back" to the United States was implicated in the fact that she was born in the United States to a Korean international student family: she is legally American by birth. She says,

> Ever since I was young, people around me told me that (I should go back to America) since I was born and lived there for my first five years. You know I also had this admiration about America as a kid as well. So I simply accepted that someday I should go back. People in Korea even say that they would love to purchase U.S. citizenship if they can. So I thought it was my luck, blessing that I was born there. What a fortune.[8]

If the United States was not idealized and desired in the Korean society, she might not have persevered to maintain her U.S. citizenship. Since Korea does not allow dual citizenships for people who are older than 18 years old, Anna gave up her Korean citizenship and stayed in Korea with a visa after her high school graduation. Although this situation caused financial and personal inconveniences, she kept her American citizenship to travel back to the United States.

Juxtaposing Sarah's and April's current relationship with Korea with Anna's return to the United States offers a way to think about how these women are differently yet concomitantly involved with global power relations. In sharp contrast to Anna's acceptance of her U.S. citizenship as good fate, Sarah states,

> So part of me feels like even things like—I don't really understand how the Korean culture works because even things like domestic violence, rape, HIV which are all women's issues. How are Korean communities addressing those? I'm not sure. But I don't see the literature out on that. Or I don't see—I guess—hm. I guess I'm trying to think. I know—I don't want to sound like all Koreans have internalized this idea of sexism and femininity and there's no such a thing as a Korean feminist or a Korean-American feminist. I guess from a western perspective which is where I'm rooted in, it seems as if Korean culture and women in Korean culture are oppressed in a way that turns me off.

Even as Sarah admits that her construction of Korean culture derives mainly from media representations, stereotypes, and the internalization of othering practices in the United States, the impact of orientalist discourse on her "western" subject position looms large. "Korea" turns her off: "resorting to Orientalism to prove how un-Oriental she is" (Ma, 1998, p. 14). Sarah's Korean self is delegated as an incidental mark from which she wants to distance herself, while Anna has taken care of her U.S. citizen-self that in turn has enabled her to claim America. After all, both acts of Anna's embrace and Sarah's distancing reveal how self-other relations are constructed locally and globally in everyday identity narratives and practices.

While Anna's idealization of the United States as a better place has led her to come back to her birth country, she disclaims any U.S. cultural identity. For Anna, being Korean is as natural as breathing and does not need to be examined. Therefore, the way she narrates her Korean self begins with the negation of being American. While she has always felt that she is different from Koreans in Korea due to her U.S. citizenship and entitlement, she sees herself not as a Korean American or as an immigrant, but as a Korean. Even after raising her own family in the United States for the past eight years, Anna remains Korean, albeit an American citizen: "*I think I am just Korean because I was raised there. My way of thinking is Korean. I think I am Korean. Probably my daughter isn't since she is growing up here. I think I am Korean. Although legally American, my mind is Korean.*" Her sense of being Korean is affirmed through the racialized difference she perceives between herself and white Americans. She says, "First, we are different from American people, we look different." In this process, her citizenship is separated from her racialized cultural self. On the one hand, she is exercising flexible citizenship to accumulate economic and symbolic capital (Ong, 1999). On the other hand, her position is an additive evidence of the successful regulation and exclusion of Asian citizen-subjects in the impossible politics of assimilation in U.S. multicultural discourse (Yanagisako, 1995). Anna says,

> I don't know. It's hard to explain and name me. The way I feel about me is that I am neither Korean American nor immigrant. I am a person from Korea living in the U.S. In my understanding, what it means to be Korean American is that your appearance is Korean but your mentality is American. Then I ask myself whether my mindset is closer to U.S. culture or to Korean. I think I am still closer to Korean cultural side, so I am not Korean immigrant or American.

While her citizenship is included in the U.S. juridical contours, Anna insists that her body, culture, mindset, and mentality do not fit in the U.S. cultural citizenship. Hers is an incoherent narrative testifying that citizenship does not change the sociocultural conditions of Asian American abjection, saturated by orientalist history and epistemological structure that continue to delegitimize Asian American subjectivity.

Sammy: Impure Korean Performing American

Born to Korean international students in the United States and raised in Korea, Sammy shares a gendered binational narrative, which articulates how her choice refracts and reflects the multifaceted unequal power relations of social structures and discourses. Her narrative highlights different modalities of performing citizenship. Although she grew up mostly in Korea, she attended an American high school for a year and a half when her mother came to the United States as a visiting scholar. Then she attended college in Korea and came back to the United States for her graduate degrees. Sammy aspires to maintain her bilingual and bicultural competency that, she acknowledges, requires tremendous effort and commitment. She repeatedly emphasizes the importance of her English fluency in expanding her sociocultural connections and constituting her flexible self.[9] Putting aside the perplexing questions of "Does performing a certain behavior produce an identity?" or "Does the process of identification produce a particular form of performance?" her narrative reveals that her learned motivations, desire, and choices became integral in her cultural, national, and structural negotiations.

For Sammy, a bicultural mode of living becomes a strategy of impurity that enables her to refuse the sexually subordinate position of Korean women to Korean men. During her undergraduate years in a highly prestigious Korean university, Sammy had mostly male classmates. With her nonfeminine performance of aggressive and direct communication and swearing, she was treated as one of the guys and was frequently invited to male locker and drinking talks that sometimes included accounts of female sexual harassments and rapes. However, says Sammy, "It was too much information in terms of getting to know men's culture, masculine culture." Her five university years as an insider/outsider of Korean masculine world was enough to turn her into an enraged woman who could no longer trust Korean men. Her interactions with Korean male students in graduate schools in the United States substantiated, rather than undermined, her knowledge of Korean male culture. Her resistance to Korean women's position as sexually exploitable has guided her search for alternative spaces in U.S. society.

> My antagonism, resistance toward Korean men and Korean culture made me feel comfortable to associate with these identities of Korean American woman, Asian American woman. Because I didn't feel at ease and I didn't want to associate with Korean men and culture, and as I put this distance, I began to think I am American, I am an Asian American woman.

Performing an impure Korean woman through her intimate and sexual partnership with a white American man, she gains heretical power to resist the relentless governance of Korean patriarchal culture over her sexuality.[10] She emphasizes her impurity, fluidity, and mobility that cannot be contained by Korean national discourse. Ironically the heretical power demotes her to a position of a promiscuous woman whose sexuality needs to be disciplined and controlled by Korean men. She often finds herself becoming stiff and nervous in groups of Korean men in the United States. She sometimes tries passing as someone not Korean. Her uneasiness reinforces her hybrid Asian American acts as a distancing strategy from the constricting Korean cultural regime.

Sammy, at the same time, suspects that she might desire security in the United States through her association with a white man.

> Maybe a sort of security, American society is in fact a white society, isn't it? I'm not sure but I think, indirectly, I am gaining power, I don't often think I am a minority. For example, when my boyfriend throws a party, sometimes I am the only Asian there. I am very comfortable in the setting without being conscious of my race. Then suddenly it hits me "Oh, I was the only Asian there. You know I just totally forgot about it." I don't know how to interpret that. But, in American society where white represents a dominant culture, I may have unconscious desire in some extents to be with a white guy who has power.

She points out that analyzing her romantic relationship with her partner in structural and social terms can be convoluted when different markers are taken into account. She is more argumentative and dominating; she is five years older; she is a professor, he is a college student; she makes more money; and her parents disapprove of their interracial relationship. She would rather focus on the fact that her relationship is based on romantic feelings between individuals and that she feels more free and empowered. Paradoxically she indulges in the pleasure of being physically smaller and feminine compared to her well-built, white partner as she scoffs at short, scrawny Korean men who demand thin female bodies to secure their masculinity. Sammy states indifferently, "[Korean men] will say to me, here comes a big fat maid." However problematic her pleasure can be, that pleasure sustains Sammy to maneuver the complex and paradoxical layers of sexualized, nationalized, racialized, gendered, and postcolonial cultural relations. This reflects how the contradictory and incoherent forces of inclusion and exclusion, cooptation and resistance as well as location and dislocation generated by the projects of Korean and U.S. citizen-making play in "her" Korean/Asian American subject formation.

Recurring and Embodied Memories of Korean/Asian Americans at the Imperial Center

The material legacy of the repressed history of U.S. imperialism in Asia is borne out in the "return" of Asian immigrants to the imperial center. In this sense, these Asian Americans are determined by the history of U.S. involvement in Asia *and* the historical racialization of Asians in the United States.... Once here, the demand that Asian immigrants identify as U.S. national subjects simultaneously produce alienations and disidentifications out of which critical subjectivities emerge. These immigrants retain precisely the memories of imperialism that the U.S. nation seeks to forget. (Lowe, 1996, pp. 16-17)

Once the transnational and postcolonial history of Korean/Asian Americans is taken into account, we realize that the four women came to the United States for survival as adopted children, for academic, economic, and professional aspirations, and for gendered self-determination. Hoping for something "better," the adjective attached to the United States, was the common denominator that pushed them out of Korea. For these women, remembering "Koreans/Asians as Americans" forces the forgetting of the history of U.S. imperialism over Korea. When they are required to accede to "a political fiction of equal rights in the name of U.S. citizenry, generated through the denial of history, a denial that reproduces the omission of history as the ontology of the (U.S.) nation" (Lowe, 1996, p. 27), the gaps and disparities generated by their incoherent and unstable narratives as Korean/Asian American subjects disrupt the prevailing narrative of U.S. citizenship. While their narratives bare the traces of U.S. amnesia that represses the history of U.S. imperialism in Korea in exchange for their (dis)location as Americans, they also refute "the pluralist integration of Koreans/Asians as Americans" (Kang, 1995, p. 158). In fact, a postcolonial reading of the tensions and contradictions that the women have been working through reveals how putatively domestic cultural configurations of citizenship are never contained within the borders of the U.S. nation-state, but are always already the symptoms and determinants of U.S. imperialist relations outside of the nation-state. As long as U.S. orientalism defines Asia as antithetically foreign to its national identity as a way to justify the military, economic, political, and cultural practices of U.S. imperialism and exceptionalism, these struggles will spill over the politics of citizenship in the United States. Imperialism is not only about negotiating international relations, but also about consolidating domestic cultures (Kaplan, 1993, p. 14).

As Gupta and Ferguson (1997) write, "If one of the modes of operations of power is to attach identities to subjects, to tie subjects to their own identities through self-knowledge, then resistance serves to reshape subjects by untying or untidying that relationship" (p. 20). Reading the narratives through Gupta and Ferguson's formulation of resistance, they trouble the myth of national community in the homology of race, culture, and nation. By resisting

Korean patriarchy, Sammy renounces her memories of and attachments to Korea, and performs a new cultural/national subject position. By defying racism and orientalism in the United States, April disowns her legitimate space in the United States. By refusing to identify culturally with her legal U.S. citizenship, Anna unwittingly enacts a flexible form of citizenship. Sarah's insistence that she is not American because of her oriental body constitutes an embodied testimony against the myth that aliens can be transformed into Americans within the U.S. imperialist-national borders. The strategies, resistance, and transformation of these women may be reinscribing and deepening certain cultural discourses, such as Asian women fleeing from wretched conditions for a better life, the United States as white America, and the danger of contact between foreigner/colonizer and Korean/colonized women. Yet, by willingly dislocating themselves, their narratives fracture, interrupt, and intervene in those discourses as well.

The chapter displaces the fictional dichotomies between the national and the international, questions the Asian American citizen-making project of the U.S. empire-nation-state, and intervenes in the narrative of national development that omits the social realities of Korean/Asian American women. What Said (1993) writes is pertinent in understanding the significance of putting these women's narratives in print: "[N]ations themselves are narrations. The power to narrate, or to block other narratives from forming and emerging, is very important to culture and imperialism, and constitutes one of the main connections between them" (p. xiii). More importantly, my attempt to narrate the U.S. nation-state by (dis)locating Korean/Asian American citizen-subjects demands more narratives, dialogues, and interventions to engage the unthinkable and unsayable conditions of nations in order to undo the violence committed in the name of nationalism.

Notes

The author would like to thank Stephanie Daza and Binaya Subedi for their insightful feedback. The author is very grateful for the careful and critical reading, editing, and comments of Roland Sintos Coloma.

1. Even after the Naturalization Act of 1790 that made "free white persons" eligible for naturalization and an 1870 law that proclaimed the eligibility of persons of "African descent or nativity," the Chinese, Japanese, and Koreans were declared ineligible for U.S. citizenship in 1882 and 1924. The Immigration Act of 1917 prescribed an "Asiatic Barred Zone" that banned any immigrant laborers from India, Indochina, Afghanistan, Arabia, the East Indies, and other Asian countries to enter the United States. The Act was the "first" step in establishing a federal policy of restriction that favored national groups thought to be most "assimilable." The

Immigration Act of 1924 barred the immigration of all "aliens ineligible for citizenship," a shift from a denial of naturalization to a total ban on future Asian immigration. During this time period, Asians living and working in the United States were barred from U.S. citizenship, thereby making the demarcation unclear between Asian Americans and Asian aliens ineligible for citizenship (Kang, 1995, pp. 142-149).

2. The chapter presents findings from a larger project in which seven women participated. The study was conducted primarily using in-depth interviews with an average total interview time of about six hours for each person (Rhee, 2002). The names used are pseudonyms.

3. Within the intertwined historical contexts of severe famines in Korea and cost-cutting measures in Hawaiian plantations, Christian missionaries played an important role in promoting early Korean migration to the United States by constructing the United States as "the land flowing with milk and honey" (Kim, 1997, p. 3) as well as a place of modernity (Abelmann & Lie, 1995). The majority of the first migrant laborers to Hawaii came from the Youngdong Church of Reverend Jones in Inchon (Kim, 1997).

4. The Yongsan Garrison in Seoul, once the headquarters of the Japanese Imperial Army, became the headquarters for the U.S. military (Yuh, 1999, p. 20).

5. Hereafter Korea refers to South Korea, unless noted otherwise.

6. It is important to analyze how this form of marriage could be read as Korean women's defiance against Korean patriarchy.

7. The predicaments of postcolonial and/or neocolonial conditions are complicated by the emerging political struggles and anti-Americanism in Korea in the 1980s. Due to the Kwangju massacre, Koreans began to question Korea's historical, political, and economic relationships with the United States (Kim, 1998; Lee, 1988). As Korea became economically more prosperous and politically stable from the late 1980s to mid-1990s, the number of Koreans who emigrated to the United States decreased. In 1992 fewer than 20,000 South Koreans emigrated to the United States, the lowest number since 1972 (Abelmann & Lie, 1995, p. 77), while the number of Korean international students to the United States drastically increased. This is the time period when both Anna and Sammy came back to the United States.

8. When the interview data was translated from Korean to English, I italicized the text.

9. What Franz Fanon (1967) argues regarding the mastery of the master's language goes along with Sammy's emphasis on English fluency to gain cultural power.

10. See Kim and Choi (1998) and Rhee (2002) for more discussions of how Korean nationalist discourse has authenticated cultural identity through the regulation of Korean women's sexuality, particularly in response to foreign powers.

References

Abelmann, N., & Lie, J. (1995). *Blue dreams: Korean Americans and the Los Angeles riots*. Cambridge, MA: Harvard University Press.

Bark, D. S. (1984). The American educated elite in Korean society. In Y. Koo & D. S. Suh (Eds.), *Korea and the United States: A century of cooperation* (pp. 263-280). Honolulu: University of Hawaii Press.

Cho, H. (1998). Constructing and deconstructing "Koreaness." In D. C. Gladney (Ed.), *Making majorities: Constituting the nation in Japan, Korea, China, Malaysia, Fiji, Turkey, and the United States* (pp. 73-94). Stanford, CA: Stanford University Press.

Cho, H. (2000). "You are entrapped in an imaginary well": The formation of subjectivity within compressed development—a feminist critique of modernity and Korean culture. *Inter-Asia Cultural Studies*, 1(1), 49-69.

Choi, C. (1998). Nationalism and construction of gender in Korea. In E. H. Kim & C. Choi (Eds.), *Dangerous women: Gender and Korean nationalism* (pp. 9-32). New York: Routledge.

Chow, R. (1993). *Writing diaspora: Tactics of intervention in contemporary cultural studies*. Bloomington: Indiana University Press.

Chun, B. H. (1989). Adoption and Korea. *Child Welfare*, 68(2), 255-260.

Coloma, R. S. (2006). Disorienting race and education: Changing paradigms on the schooling of Asian Americans and Pacific Islanders. *Race Ethnicity and Education*, 9(1), 1-15.

Cumings, B. (1981). *The origins of the Korean war*. Princeton, NJ: Princeton University Press.

Fanon, F. (1967). *Black skin white masks*. New York: Grove.

Gupta, A., & Ferguson, J. (1997). Culture, power, place: Ethnography at the end of an era. In A. Gupta & J. Ferguson (Eds.), *Culture, power, place: Explorations in critical anthropology* (pp. 1-32). Durham, NC: Duke University Press.

Hall, S. (Ed.). (1997). *Representations: Cultural representations and signifying practices*. Thousand Oaks, CA: Sage.

John, M. (1996). *Discrepant dislocation: Feminism, theory, and postcolonial histories*. Berkeley, CA: University of California Press.

Kang, L. H. Y. (1995). *Compositional subjects: Enfiguring Asian/American women*. Unpublished doctoral dissertation, University of California-Santa Cruz.

Kaplan, A. (1993). "Left alone with America": The absence of empire in the study of American culture. In A. Kaplan & D. E. Pease (Eds.), *Cultures of United States imperialism* (pp. 3-21). Durham, NC: Duke University Press.

Kim, B. (2003). Paramilitary politics under the USAMGIK and the establishment of the Republic of Korea. *Korea Journal*, 43(2), 289-322.

Kim, C. (1991). *Changes in Korean elementary and secondary education in United States-occupied Korea, 1945-1948: A revisionist analysis of the effects on policy of progressive education*. Unpublished doctoral dissertation, Georgia State University.

Kim, E. H., & Choi, C. (Eds.). (1998). *Dangerous women: Gender and Korean nationalism*. New York: Routledge.

Kim, J. H. (1997). *Bridge-makers and cross-bearers: Korean American women and the church*. Atlanta, GA: Scholars Press.

Kondo, D. K. (1996). The narrative production of "home," community, and political identity in Asian American theater. In S. Lavie & T. Swedenburg (Eds.), *Displacement, diaspora, and geographies of identity* (pp. 97-118). Durham, NC: Duke University Press.

Lee, M. (1988). Anti-Americanism and South Korea's changing perception of America. In C. Moon, M. Lee, & R. McLaurin (Eds.), *Alliance under tension*. Boulder, CO: Westview.

Lee, S. H. (1995). Generation gap in Koreans' perceptions of the United States: A case of Korean broadcast journalists. In E. H. Shin & Y. Kim (Eds.), *Korea and the world: Strategies for globalization* (pp. 141-150). Columbia Center for Asian Studies at the University of South Carolina.

Lowe, L. (1996). *Immigrant acts*. Durham, NC: Duke University Press.

Ma, S. (1998). *Immigrant subjectivities in Asian American and Asian diaspora literatures*. Albany: State University of New York Press.

McClintock, A., Mufti, A. R., & Shohat, E. (Eds.). (1997). *Dangerous liaisons: Gender, nation and postcolonial perspectives*. Minneapolis: University of Minnesota Press.

Miyoshi, M. (1996). A borderless world: From colonialism to transnationalism and the decline of the nation-state. In R. Wilson & W. Dissanayake (Eds.), *Global/local: Cultural production and the transnational imaginary* (pp. 78-106). Durham, NC: Duke University Press.

Ong, A. (1999). *Flexible citizenship: The cultural logic of transnationality.* Durham, NC: Duke University Press.

Rhee, J. (2002). *Globalization, education, and identity: A critical auto/ethnography of traveling Korean (descendent) women in U.S. higher education.* Unpublished doctoral dissertation, Ohio State University.

Rhee, J., & Subreenduth, S. (2006). De/colonizing education: Examining transnational localities. *International Journal of Qualitative Studies in Education,* 19(5), Special issue.

Said, E. W. (1979/1995). *Orientalism.* New York: Vintage.

Said, E. W. (1993). *Culture and imperialism.* New York: Alfred A. Knopf.

Subedi, B. (2008). Contesting racialization: Asian immigrant teachers' critiques and claims of teacher authenticity. *Race Ethnicity and Education,* 11(1), 57-70.

Suh, D. K. (1984). American missionaries and a hundred years of Korean protestanism. In Y. Koo & D. S. Suh (Eds.), *Korea and the United States: A century of cooperation* (pp. 319-349). Honolulu: University of Hawaii Press.

Tchen, J. K. W. (1999). *New York before Chinatown: Orientalism and the shaping of American culture, 1776-1882.* Baltimore, MD: Johns Hopkins University Press.

Yanagisako, S. (1995). Transforming orientalism: Gender, nationality, and class in Asian American studies. In S. Yanagisako & C. Delaney (Eds.), *Naturalizing power* (pp. 275-298). New York: Routledge.

Yuh, J. (1999). *Immigrants on the front line: Korean military brides in America, 1950-1996.* Unpublished doctoral dissertation, University of Pennsylvania.

CHAPTER 16

Putting Queer to Work: Examining Empire and Education

ROLAND SINTOS COLOMA

> The aim of a theoretically-informed political practice must surely be to bring about or construct the articulation between social ... forces and those forms of politics and ideology which lead them in practice to intervene in history in a progressive way—an articulation which has to be constructed through practice precisely because it is not guaranteed by how those forces are constituted in the first place.
>
> — Hall, 1985, p. 95

The emergence of queer studies in academe and in the field of education has opened new doors for theoretical and empirical inquiries, enabling innovative conceptualizations and investigations of knowledge and culture, identity and difference, subjugation and resistance (Britzman, 1998; Kumashiro, 2002; Pinar, 1998; Tierney, 1997). As an analytical framework, it also has facilitated asking different questions and asking questions differently: What does queer theory and research reveal, critique, and enable? What if it is mobilized in ways that are different from the ways in which it is typically employed? What is a queer trespassing like, a dangerous yet useful move that gazes away from gay, lesbian, bisexual, and transgender (GLBT) subjects, and dallies with other realms of possibilities? What sorts of generative "positivities" (Lather, 2004) are produced when queer is no longer confined to a normalizing regime that constrains its powers to conventional objects of scrutiny? How do we construct and perform queer research that is "out beyond the censoring imaginary of the state and the information culture that consolidates the rule of its names"

(Berlant, 1997, pp. 172–173)? Asked another way, what happens when it functions as "an active intervention, a provocation: an interruption rather than a reproduction"? More specifically, "To what invention, what praxis, what revolution might we thereby come?" (Haver, 1997, p. 278).

This chapter engages queer theory by mobilizing it within, through and beyond the framework of sexuality and putting it to work in postcolonial and educational studies. It foregrounds the relevance of queer and sexuality as categories of analysis in research regarding imperialism and decolonization. Admittedly, there may be concerns raised about the combination of queer and postcolonial studies. Juxtaposing queer with postcolonialism may be perceived as a deterrent to the allegedly more central issues of class, race, and gender in investigations of empire, nation, power, and subjectivity. In response, I align myself with queers and feminists of color, like Angela Davis (1981), Audre Lorde (1984), Jacqui Alexander and Chandra Mohanty (1997), and Chela Sandoval (2000), who contend that the failure to utilize an intersectional viewpoint can lead to the damaging dislocation of identities, the exclusionary imagining and development of community, and the impossibility of progressive coalition building. Moreover, if the research is not about gay, lesbian, bisexual, and transgender individuals, communities, and concerns in the global South and in the diaspora, bringing a queer lens to postcolonialism may seem inappropriate. Indeed, my work is informed by scholars, such as Martin Manalansan (2003), Suparna Bhaskaran (2004), and Gayatri Gopinath (2005), who focus on GLBTs of color from historically colonized spaces. However, what profoundly interests me more is an intellectual and political "articulation," as conceptualized by Stuart Hall (1985), which sutures seemingly incongruent analytics, such as queer and postcolonial frameworks, in the project of decolonization. I strive to enact and extend what David Eng (2001) calls "queerness as a critical methodology" which "exceeds the question of sexuality" (pp. 216–217) by generating new critiques and praxis in the examination of empire and education.

My engagement with queer and postcolonial theories draws from my larger research on the history of Filipino/a schooling under U.S. rule in the early twentieth century (Coloma, 2004). After the United States took control of the Philippines at the end of the Spanish-American and Philippine-American Wars, the United States governed the country as a colony for over 40 years, and U.S. administrators and teachers introduced the common school system to Filipino/as. My initial formulations derived from the lens of postcolonial and ethnic studies that investigated the transnational oppression and resistance of peoples of color in the colony and the metropolis. As an intervention into postcolonial studies in general and as a reexamination of my previous findings in particular, this chapter emphasizes the usefulness of three queer approaches in postcolonial projects. First, by examining the theme of exclusion within the framework of sexuality, a queer approach can highlight the marginalization of "alter/natives" in scholarships and movements regarding empire and diaspora. Although my study did not focus on GLBTs in education and in U.S.-Philippine relations, the absence of GLBTs or queer perspectives in theoretical and empirical work marks a major limitation in most postcolonial research. Second, by examining the theme of normativity through sexuality, a queer approach can challenge the prevailing interpretive tropes used to depict imperialist encounters. Foregrounding same-sex relations, especially between and among U.S. and Filipino men in this case, does not necessarily intend to unveil homosexual acts or intimacies. Rather, it can shed light on the power of imperialist patriarchal masculinity, which aims to control both native men and women. Finally, by examining the theme of colonial subject position and agency beyond sexuality, a queer approach can explore a form of native power that renders useful and positive what has been utilized to inflict damage and pain. My research on a U.S.-trained Filipino educator reveals the ways in which a colonized individual mobilizes potentially destructive Western influences to enact counterhegemonic politics and performances.

Ultimately, I argue for the articulation of queer and postcolonial perspectives, especially since queer insights can offer pertinent perspectives on the themes of exclusion, normalization, and subject position and agency in studies of empire and education. I elaborate on queer approaches within, through, and beyond the framework of sexuality by reviewing the scholarly literature on postcolonial studies and then engaging my research data and findings. Since queer and postcolonial studies are relatively new in the field of education, a brief explanation follows to trace and mark, in broad strokes, their development in and significance to education.

A Genealogical Interlude:
Queer and Postcolonial Studies With/in Education

In the early 1990s, queer theory and research emerged to examine the constructions, performances, and meanings of sexuality and gender as well as the radical politics derived from centering same-sex relations and advocating for sexual difference (Butler, 1990; de Lauretis, 1991; Sedgwick, 1990). Undoubtedly, queer studies has built upon, complicated, and revised gay and lesbian studies. While gay and lesbian studies has focused generally on the realities and conditions of gay and lesbian individuals and communities, queer studies has not only included within its purview those of bisexuals, transgenders, and heterosexuals, but also questioned the very foundations of gay, lesbian, bisexual, transgender, and straight identities, groupings, and experiences (Hutchins & Ka'ahumanu, 1991; Thomas, 2000; Yoshino, 2000). In addition, it has drawn from and impacted other interdisciplinary fields, such as race/ethnic and women's studies as well as other analytical frameworks, such as deconstruction, Marxism, postmodernism, and psychoanalysis (Sullivan, 2003). However diverse its intellectual and political genealogy is, the central objects of inquiry in queer theory and research have remained the same: gay, lesbian, bisexual, and transgender subjects; the discourses and structures that construct and regulate them; and how GLBTs simultaneously shape and respond to these discourses and structures.

Queer studies has impacted and proliferated in various academic fields, including education. Queer projects in education have focused on the oppression and resistance of GLBT students and instructors in K-12 and higher education settings. They have investigated educational policies, programs, and practices that contribute to the marginalization of GLBTs, and have explored the struggles and strategies against homophobia and heterosexism (Lipkin, 1999; Macgillivray, 2003; Sears, 2005). This increasing body of research has addressed a wide range of issues, from personal identities and institutional cultures to educational foundations, curricula, and pedagogy (Talburt, 2000; Blackburn & Donelson, 2004). Many queer scholars and educators view their work as unapologetically oriented toward antioppression and social justice. Their intellectual and political contributions have helped to develop more inclusive spaces in K-12 schools and universities, in professional organizations such as the American Educational Research Association with the Queer Studies special interest group, and in academic publications such as the *Journal of Gay & Lesbian Issues in Education*.

About a decade earlier than queer studies, postcolonial theory and research emerged (Said, 1978). It has ushered in a radical way of analyzing the relationship between the West and the rest of the world by emphasizing the history and legacy of Western imperialism in Asia, Africa, and the Americas (Young, 2001). It has stressed the contemporary manifestations of empire through the ongoing occupation of indigenous territories and the neocolonial control of the global South through cultural, economic, educational, military, and political mechanisms (Beverley, 1999; Bhabha, 1994; Chakrabarty, 2000; Spivak, 1988). Intellectually and politically, it has drawn from national liberation and Marxist-based movements; it also has been inspired by and has impacted race/ethnic and women's studies, deconstruction, historical materialism, poststructuralism and psychoanalysis (Loomba, 2005). Like queer studies, postcolonial studies has derived its interpretive potency and social justice orientation from a wide range of frameworks in order to scrutinize the dynamics of Western domination and native resistance. Although postcolonial theory and research has predominantly focused on British colonialism, increasing attention is being paid to the expansion and operation of the United States as an empire (Kaplan & Pease, 1993; Trask, 1993).

Similar to its queer counterpart, postcolonial studies also has influenced the field of education. Postcolonial scholars in education have investigated the racial, national, and global developments and effects of school policies, programs, and practices both in the West and in its colonies. Offering new optics to view the intertwined local-global or, as Handel Wright and Karl Maton (2004) term, "glocal" contexts of education, they have raised new issues in the areas of comparative and international education, cultural studies, curriculum, higher education, multiculturalism, and teacher education (McCarthy, 1998; Ninnes & Mehta, 2004; Willinsky, 1998). The two notions of the United States as an empire and of the complicity of education in colonial governmentality are gaining ground in U.S. educational studies. An increasing number of scholars attend to the history and implications of U.S. colonial education, particularly in relation to indigenous peoples in the U.S. mainland and the inhabitants of former and current U.S. territories, such as Hawai'i, Puerto Rico, and the Philippines (Walsh, 1990; Benham & Heck, 1998; Reyhner & Eder, 2004; Coloma, 2005). Even a Postcolonial Studies special interest group was formed in the American Educational Research Association in 2004.

Admittedly, queer studies is a relatively new framework in education, and its combination with postcolonial studies is at a nascent state (Hawley, 2001). However, drawing primarily from queer of color theorists, I strive to develop queer possibilities in the project of decolonization in education and society at large. Roderick Ferguson (2004) defines "queer of color analysis" as the interrogation of the "normative and nonnormative articulations of social formations (political, economic, epistemological, and cultural)" (p. 149). Because social norms are connected to notions and practices of how things ought to be, they are powerful mechanisms to control individual and group thinking and behavior. Since norms are constructed and not innate, they become sites for struggles of definitions and performances. Queer of color analysis serves as a useful lens to investigate not only the themes of exclusion, normalization, subject position and agency, but also the subversive potentials of articulations and solidarities. Such an analysis can function to explore and expand the decolonizing borderlands of racial, gender, sexual, class, and geographical crisscrossing (Anzaldúa, 1987).

Within Sexuality: Examining the Exclusion of Alter/natives

Putting queer to work in empire and education entails the investigation of what has become "normal" and "not normal" in postcolonial and race/ethnic discourses, particularly in relation to queer sexualities. By examining colonized and racialized spaces within the framework of sexuality, a queer approach emphasizes the presence and impact of alter/natives within scholarly and political movements. By alter/natives, I mean gays, lesbians, bisexuals, and transgenders as well as deviant heterosexuals who defy conventional norms. A queer approach also mobilizes alternative readings to rethink and expand the constructions and meanings of sexualities in various cultures and communities. It is significant to draw attention to alter/natives since mainstream discourses and movements often mobilize queer sexualities to exclude and oppress individuals and groups who are not considered normal. The marginalization of queer sexualities and the privileging of heterosexuality can be traced, in part, to the complicity of education in K-12 and college settings. Almost all textbooks and classes perpetuate the notion of identity, family, and nation as heterosexual. What is worse is the elimination of queer references in the curriculum. For example, most discussions on the Harlem Renaissance sidestep or ignore the gay, lesbian, and bisexual identities of prominent figures, such as Alain Locke, Langston Hughes, Angelina Weld Grimké, and Alice Dunbar-Nelson (Schwarz, 2003). Queer existence is further obliterated when even the very limited discussions of sexuality in K-12 schools regarding topics such as abstinence and other sex-education programs remain premised on opposite-sex intimacies and relationships. As a result, compulsory heterosexuality and the heterosexual reproduction of progeny are deemed to be prerequisites for the continuation of family, community, and nation (Parker, Russo, Sommer, & Yaeger, 1991). References to nonconforming lives and experiences are usually suppressed or treated as a special case, construing non-heterosexuality as abnormal in mainstream curricula.

Gays, lesbians, bisexuals, and transgenders are further marginalized in mainstream postcolonial and race/ethnic discourses and movements (Mercer, 1996). For instance, major scholars in postcolonial studies, such as Edward Said and Frantz Fanon, either are silent about homosexuality or view it as a disease and exclusive to Western/white people. Certain leaders of postcolonial nations and race-based organizations, such as President Robert Mugabe of Zimbabwe and Eldridge Cleaver of the Black Panther Party, are outspoken about their denigration of queer sexualities, thereby buttressing homophobic attitudes within communities of color. The gay identity of Bayard Rustin, the chief architect of the 1963 March on Washington for Jobs and Freedom, is a source of conflict and tension within the U.S. civil rights movement, resulting in loss of public recognition for his pivotal role in the march (Kates & Singer, 2002). The explicit and implicit homophobia in scholarly discourses and political movements can lead to the continuous violence perpetrated upon GLBT individuals and groups, the dismissal of GLBT historical legacies and contemporary contributions, and the failure to forge meaningful coalitions based on combined vision and politics. What is often not tapped into is the power of coalitions, albeit contingent on issues, across and within racial and queer lines that can potentially counter divide-and-conquer strategies that are utilized to splinter communities, priorities, and actions.

More recently, queer and progressive heterosexual scholars and activists have attempted to disrupt the compulsory heterosexuality and c/overt homophobia in racialized communities (Eng & Hom, 1998; Leong, 1996). They not only stress the realities of GLBTs of color, but also make explicit the societal and analytical silences surrounding queer lives and sexualities. For example, the dominant historiography of Asian American studies centers on the lives of sojourner bachelor men in the late 1800s and early 1900s who toiled in the West Coast, Hawai'i, and Alaska, without any discussion of GLBTs (Takaki, 1989; Chan, 1991). Queer interventions contend that the absence of GLBTs in historical and literary texts does not signify the absence of queers. In fact, scholars, such as Melinda De Jesus (2002), argue for alternative or queer readings of canonical texts and empirical findings to productively complicate and reinterpret prevailing notions of sexualities. Others, such as Jennifer Ting (1995, 1998) and Nayan Shah (2001), posit the notions of "deviant heterosexuality" and "queer domesticity," respectively, to rethink the homosocial relations of, and the nonconjugal spaces inhabited by, Asian American men. The deviance and stigmatization of these men's relations and spaces is not necessarily due to these men's sexuality (regardless of heterosexual, bisexual, or homosexual orientation), but due to their disruption of conventional entitlements and performances of heterosexuality, such as opposite-sex marriage and the reproduction of progeny. Their deviance or queerness is a result of draconian U.S. immigration and antimiscegenation laws that prohibited the migration of Asian women and the intermarriage of Asian men and white women. Therefore, governmental control of family and national formations can produce queerness in individual subjectivities and communal spaces.

Queer theorizing is a powerful tool in discourses, movements, and research that embrace and celebrate difference, deviance, and defiance. Putting queer to work within the framework of sexuality contests the "normal" and "not normal" by reclaiming alter/native members of colonized and racialized groups and by offering alternative readings of social formations. Part of its significance is marking the absence of alter/native subjects in, and formulating alternative enactments of, theoretical, political, and empirical projects. Even though my study on Filipino/a schooling and U.S. imperialism in the early twentieth century did not unearth any records of GLBT educators and students, my findings by no means conclude that there were no queer Filipino/as or Americans during this time period. Since the archives are similar to mainstream narrations of history in that they both primarily focus on the lives and experiences of those who are considered dominant and normal, the recovery and inclusion of GLBTs and other alternatives in history is an important and necessary intervention.

Through Sexuality: Examining Heteronormative Analytics

A queer approach through sexuality extends the relevance of alternative theorizing by troubling the use of sexuality as a category of analysis. This second approach critiques formulations that mobilize sexuality yet do not acknowledge and challenge the heteronormative assumptions undergirding their projects. I use the term heteronormativity to denote the overt and covert privileging of heterosexuality and opposite-sex dynamics, regardless of sexual orientation and relations, as universal and given. A queer approach, instead, forwards same-sex analytics as a crucial intervention to investigate issues of identity and power and to disrupt heteronormative tropes, even in putatively critical and inclusive projects. I explore nationalist and feminist studies that are grounded in heteronormative assumptions and counter them with same-sex, especially male-to-male, empirical findings that illustrate the relations between the colonizer and the colonized. In this section, my investigation into the dynamics between and among Western and native men does not focus on confirming or denying whether these men engaged in homosexual acts and relations; moreover, the participation of Western and native women in empire and education merits a more detailed explanation that is beyond the scope of this chapter. Rather, I argue that putting queer to work through sexuality frames male-to-male interactions not in the absence of women, but within the ideology of imperialist patriarchal masculinity, which strives to control both native men and women.

In examinations of imperialism, nationalism, and decolonization, the categories of race and class prevail as the dominant interpretive perspectives (Wolfe, 1997; Young, 2001). They focus on the oppression and resistance of peoples of color that occupy the subjugated underclass in colonized and racialized communities. Feminist scholars question the monolithic representations of "the" colonized and critique the often male-centered and patriarchal bias in nationalist and postcolonial projects (Pérez, 1999). They posit the realities of women of color to underscore the heterogeneity and multiplicity of colonial experiences. In their use of sexuality, gender, race, class, nation, and empire as a combined interpretive lens, a number of feminists frame the dynamics between the colonizer and the colonized through the trope of rape (Paxton, 1999). The act and imagery of rape demonstrates the cultural, economic, military, and physical ravaging of dark natives by white imperialists. It illustrates how colonizers force their entry into a country and take advantage of native land, labor, resources, and bodies without native consent. The native woman in many historical, literary, and political accounts functions as the literal and figurative symbol of the colonized nation whose purity and honor have been tarnished by imperialist powers (Sharpe, 1993; Smith, 2005).

Feminists contend that the symbol of woman as nation often serves the patriarchal orientation of nationalist and anticolonial revolutionary movements (Caplan, Alarcón, & Moallem, 1999). They affirm that women are often the victims of rape and violence, but are concerned about the passive and marginal roles allotted to women in male chauvinist narrations of history. The depiction of women as pure and innocent, who are to be protected by men from other men, renders women without recourse to identity and agency. Simultaneously the ravaging of women through rape marshals native men into action to avenge both her individual and their patriarchal national honor, since she serves as the embodiment of the country. While feminists challenge male-centered and patriarchal narrations, the practice of putting queer to work interrogates the unmarked heteronormativity in postcolonial, nationalist, and feminist projects. A specific case in point: the trope of rape, which functions to illustrate the brutality of colonialism, is construed as an act between a man and a woman or, to put it in more base terms, an act in which a (Western white) man forcibly penetrates a (dark native) woman. Troubling the heteronormative assumptions of the trope of rape, a queer intervention complicates and extends feminist insights by contesting the narrow focus on opposite-sex encounters and addressing same-sex dynamics in empire and education.

While a heteronormative framework underpins the analytical tropes of sexuality and gender that interpret colonial entanglements, the empirical findings of my research study reveal the limitations of an opposite-sex framework and urge for the necessity of a same-sex perspective. Countering the prevalent figurative and literal depiction of imperialism as an act between a man and a woman, my research indicates that the interactions in the U.S.-controlled public schools in the Philippines were primarily between and among U.S. and Filipino men. My interest in highlighting the role of men is an effort neither to insist on the centrality of men as historical actors nor to reinforce male chauvinist narrations of history. Rather, complementary to feminist aims, my objective in putting queer to work through sexuality is to push the possibilities of scholarly and political work that can be undertaken under the combined rubric of postcolonial, feminist, and queer studies.

My archival research confirms the general findings in postcolonial studies in regard to the dominance of white men as the primary emissaries of colonial governance and education. Between 1901 and 1910, there were 723 to 928 U.S. educators in the Philippines. In the U.S.-controlled national office, all the directors and clerks were men; all the superintendents and deputy superintendents in charge of the school divisions were men; and at least two-thirds of the teaching staff were men (Bureau of Education [BE], 1910/1957, pp. 306-326). Due to the challenges of navigating a tropical country and the gendered prejudices of the times, U.S. colonial officials deemed the work of supervising and teaching Filipino/a natives a male domain. David Barrows, the Bureau of Education director, stated that

> The greater part of [the teacher's] time is spent in school visitations, sometimes on foot, sometimes by horse or vehicle, and frequently by *banca* or canoe on streams and *esteros* that connect the different hamlets of the municipality. This work, which must be followed throughout the stormy season, is frequently onerous and perilous, and can usually be successfully discharged only by men of strong constitution and more than usual courage and resolution. (BE, 1904/1954, p. 608)

Justifying the all-male administrative staff of the Bureau of Education, Barrows emphasized that "[t]his is the work which can obviously only be performed by a man, and for this reason the great majority of the teaching force is and must continue to be men" (BE, 1904/1954, p. 609).

What is missing in most postcolonial research is the enlistment of native men by Western powers in colonial governance and education. Since the dominant trope of sexuality and gender to investigate imperialism is premised on a heteronormative assumption, most postcolonial work explores the dynamics between Western male colonizers and native colonized females. Relegated to the margins is the role and participation of native men in collaborating with or resisting imperialist control. My archival research indicates that the dominance of men extended to the overwhelming appointment of Filipino male instructors and the enrollment of Filipino male students. In 1910, there were 8,275 Filipino/as employed by the Bureau of Education; male teachers consisted of 81.5 percent of the insular, 68.9 percent of the municipal and 70.3 percent of the apprentice staff. In addition, at least two-thirds of the native teacher candidates in the Philippine Normal School and the regional training institutes were men (BE, 1910/1957, pp. 320-321). In line with the demographic patterns of U.S. and Filipino/a educators, the Filipino/a students were mostly male, with schools having a boy-to-girl ratio of three-to-two. In 1910 with an enrollment of 451,938 students, boys consisted of 61 percent, 78 percent, and 83 percent of the total students at the primary, intermediate, and secondary levels, respectively (BE, 1910/1957, p. 310).

It is important to specify and foreground the identities of individuals and groups in studies of empire and education for multiple reasons. It stresses that terms such as colonizer and colonized, administrator, teacher, and student are not neutral but are already racialized, classed, gendered, and sexualized within the discourses of particular sociohistorical moments. To frame the interactions within the U.S.-controlled school system in the Philippines as predominantly between and among men is an interpretive endeavor not to marginalize the presence and contributions of women, but to underscore the techniques of imperialist patriarchal masculinity that privilege men and perpetuate their power. The U.S. school administrators, all of whom were men, were cognizant that their numbers were relatively few and needed local representatives. Conferring and extending U.S. imperialist male power, entitlement, and chauvinism in the colonial territories, they recruited and trained mostly male Filipino teachers to carry on the task of instructing native students in the public schools. The homosocial dynamics between U.S. and Filipino educators condoned the belief and practice that the work of school administration and pedagogy needed to be performed by men. By focusing on men and their interactions, putting queer to work through sexuality signals the heteronormative orientation that prevails in postcolonial and feminist studies, attends to empirical findings that counter and reinterpret prevailing tropes, and expands the identities of the actors involved to include homosocial dynamics.

Beyond Sexuality: Examining Subject Position and Agency

This final section explores the possibilities of mobilizing queer insights that go beyond the framework of sexuality and put them to work to address native agency and decolonization. It foregrounds one of queer theory's central tenets, as articulated by Eve Kosofsky Sedgwick (1997): how "selves and communities succeed in extracting sustenance from the objects of a culture—even of a culture whose avowed desire has often been not to sustain them" (p. 35). Queer theory and research scrutinizes how one gains nourishment from and utilizes that which is meant to inflict harm and pain. It recuperates and transforms something, like the term queer, which is intended to be damaging, in the service of self-determination and social justice. This approach takes what seems to be paradoxical and contradictory not as a source of paralysis, hypocrisy, or negativity, but as a powerful weapon for subversion and counter-hegemony. Such a move directs attention to colonial schooling, its manipulation of and influence on colonized natives, and the various ways in which the colonized use it for multiple purposes.

Discussions in postcolonial and race/ethnic studies concerning Western schooling primarily focus on its damaging impact on native individuals and national culture, economy and psyche. For instance, scholars of Philippine and Filipino/a American studies argue that the U.S. colonial education in the archipelago and abroad has been severely detrimental to Filipino/as, resulting in the continuation of the patron-client relations of Western control and native dependency. They contend that the U.S. curriculum served as a "miseducation" (Constantino, 1966) since it depicted the United States as a benevolent hero that rescued the country from Spanish theocracy and indigenous primitivism yet concealed its ulterior military, economic, and political motives in Asia, while demeaning and uprooting Filipino/a culture. They also point out how the advanced training and the professional brain drain of Filipino/as have primarily benefited the United States and not the Philippines (Choy, 2003). While I am in agreement with their emphasis on the deleterious effects of colonial education, I also want to highlight the ways in which the colonized mobilized the empire's tools for more revolutionary and decolonizing purposes.

Scholars and activists remain adamantly critical of those who seem to have gained from and collaborated with Western imperialist powers. Frantz Fanon (1967) indicts African native elites as bourgeois intermediaries and pawns who, during and after colonial rule, buttress and replicate imperialist hierarchy by serving the interests of Western structures and organizations and subjugating poor and working-class natives. Cherríe Moraga (1986) illustrates the ways in which women are depicted in Chicano nationalist renditions of history as either the revered and unblemished virgin, as embodied by La Virgen de Guadalupe, or the complicit sell-out who sleeps with the enemy, as represented by Malintzin Tenepal who was the translator and mistress of the Spanish conqueror of México, Hernan Cortez. Established in the scholarly discourses and political movements of colonized and racialized communities is a binary configuration of the native as either complicit or resistant to imperialism.

Putting queer to work to examine empire and education beyond the framework of sexuality can disrupt the limited options embedded in critical nationalist projects where the colonized can choose from only two polar positions of either the collaborating traitor or the resisting freedom fighter. Like other interpretive perspectives influenced by poststructuralism and deconstruction, queer theory and research seeks to destabilize compartmentalizing binaries and to discover multiple possibilities for subject positions and revolutionary acts. Building upon the previous section's focus on same-sex male dynamics, this queer approach facilitates the proliferation of questions regarding colonial power and resistance: What roles do native men take in the context of Western imperialism and education? Do the colonized only take the dominated role, without contracting, acquiescing to, or opposing colonialism? Do they become feminized or emasculated since they occupy the subjugated position? How do colonized natives assert their resistance to work within and against the structures and discourses of imperialism?

The queer approach of finding subversive and revolutionary sustenance from physical and psychological pain exceeds the complicit/resistant binary by foregrounding the ways in which the colonized appropriate and take advantage of the tools of empire. As an example of how native men navigate within and against empire and education, I offer the life and career of a Western-trained, Filipino (heterosexual) man named Camilo Osias (1887-1976) as a case study (Coloma, 2005). I put queer to work beyond sexuality by marshalling it to understand Osias' paradoxical yet decolonizing performance. Osias came of age during Filipino/a revolutions against Spanish and then U.S. colonizers (1896-1902) and during the United States's entrance into global imperialism, including the acquisition of the Philippines. His imperialist education took place in a Spanish grammar school and a U.S.-run high school in the Philippines, as well as in Western Illinois State Normal School and Teachers College at Columbia University in the United States (1905-1910). His U.S. schooling in the archipelago and abroad removed Osias first from his family and then from his native country. The U.S. curriculum was filled with ideas and representations that glorified the culture, heroes, history, and geography of the United States, yet was devoid of those from the Philippines. Upon his return to the islands, he became a member of the U.S. colonial system of schooling, one of the limited career paths available to educated natives that were sponsored by the government. He initially became a teacher, then a superintendent and curriculum specialist, and finally the highest-ranking Filipino administrator in the national Bureau of Education (1910-20s).

In becoming a revolutionary educator, Camilo Osias mastered the English language and the Western knowledge acquired from U.S. teachers and curriculum in the Philippines and abroad. Osias tempered the colonizing effects of U.S. education by sustaining his nationalist disposition through studies of Philippine heritage and maintenance of native languages and by being actively involved in anticolonial movements and struggles for national independence. Elected senator to the Philippine legislature in 1925, Osias became a Resident Commissioner to the United States in 1929. As a nonvoting member in the U.S. House of Representatives, he lobbied U.S. legislators and gave compelling speeches, first, to pass the Hare-Hawes-Cutting bill, known as the Philippine Independence bill and, then, successfully to override U.S. President Herbert Hoover's executive veto (Osias & Baradi, 1933). This bill preceded the Tyding-McDuffie Act of 1934, which established a commonwealth period and, after the Second World War, the Philippines became independent in 1946.

The decolonizing implications of Osias' agency were realized through the construction and performance of a hybrid subject position that juxtaposed Western and native influences and worked within and against the discourses and structures of U.S. imperialism and schooling. What is particularly queer in Osias' performance is how he deviantly disrupted the either/or binaries of colonizer and colonized and how he defiantly recycled and reworked the damaging tools of empire into subversive weapons for individual and national self-determination. His knowledge of U.S. history and ideals of liberty and equality, his command of the English language, and his prolonged interactions with people from the United States enabled him to have a strong understanding of Western imperialist views, codes, and rhetoric. By strategically occupying the positions of Western and native, he mobilized the knowledge and skills to work within and against empire. Osias' move is strategic in Gayatri Spivak's (1985) sense of "a strategic use of positivist essentialism in a scrupulously visible political interest" (p. 342). Osias enacted a queer and postcolonial agency that moved beyond the dichotomy of complicit or resistant to imperialism and, instead, led toward the process of decolonization.

While I do not portray Osias as a representative of all colonized natives, he serves as an example of how it was possible to utilize Western education yet remain committed to the decolonizing struggles of his native country. Elsewhere, I framed his revolutionary performance as an example of "disidentifying nationalism" that transcended the binary of conforming to the U.S. colonial agenda or invoking a separatist and precolonial nativism (Coloma, 2005). In interrogating contested spaces of empire and education where the dominant logic is challenged, I draw from José Esteban Muñoz (1999), whose study of performances by queers of color launch possibilities for counterhegemonic public knowledge, spaces, and actions. Like Muñoz, I attend to

> unveiling moments in which the majoritarian public sphere's publicity—its public discourse and reproduction of that discourse is challenged by performances of counter-publicity that defy its discriminatory ideology. Counterpublicity is disseminated through acts that are representational and political interventions in the service of subaltern counterpublics. (Muñoz, 1999, p. 147)

Raised in the tumultuous era of wars and uprisings and shaped by imperialist education in the Philippines and the United States, Osias worked within and against the tensions of dominant and subordinated cultures and moved beyond becoming a victim or accomplice of colonialism. The oppositional power of "disidentifying nationalism" (Coloma, 2005) as a queer and postcolonial agency generates a radical decolonizing awareness and praxis that marshals yet undermines the dominant culture "in the service of subaltern counterpublics." In putting queer to work beyond the framework of sexuality, revolutionary individuals and groups modify lessons learned from the top in order to advocate for and with those at the bottom.

Queer and Postcolonial: A Borderland for Decolonization

The borderland is a relevant site to analyze and draw attention to the nonnormative in various communities as projects of decolonization are enacted. It is a fitting location to juxtapose two seemingly incongruent fields—queer and postcolonial studies. Describing the borderland, Gloria Anzaldúa (1987) writes that it is a place for the "squint-eyed, the perverse, the queer, the troublesome, the mongrel, the mulatto, the half-breed, the half dead; in short, those who cross over, pass over, or go through the confines of the normal" (p. 25). In many ways, this chapter traverses an intellectual and political borderland as it puts queer approaches to work within, through, and beyond the framework of sexuality to examine empire and education. By offering innovative perspectives on issues of exclusion, normalization, same-sex dynamics, subject position, and agency in the context of imperialism, queer theory and research help to extend postcolonial, race/ethnic, feminist, and educational studies. Queer insights unpack the marginalization of alter/native subjects and alternative readings in scholarly discourses, research projects, and political movements. They question the privileging of heterosexuality, challenge the dominant tropes used to depict imperial entanglements, and put a spotlight on imperialist patriarchal masculinity. Finally, they disrupt the dichotomous binary of native collaborator and resister, and forward a hybrid subject position and agency that mobilize the tools of imperialism to advocate for marginalized and decolonizing politics.

My use of queer theory and research to examine empire and education is meant as a double intervention. The first move works within and through the framework of sexuality by recognizing the presence and contributions of gays, lesbians, bisexuals, and transgenders and simultaneously questioning the compulsory heterosexuality in communities of color, in the global South, in the diaspora, and in struggles for individual and collective self-determination. The centrality of GLBTs is not meant as a mere request for inclusion; it is a demand to foreground the heterogeneity, multiplicity, and hybridity of subject positions within colonized and racialized groups and to challenge the heteronormative constructions of individuals, communities, and nations. While the first move highlights GLBTs and questions heteronormativity, the second move puts queer theory to work beyond sexuality by engaging areas, such as postcolonial studies, that are not often considered within the purview of queer studies. It demonstrates that queer theory and research can substantially contribute to the examination of imperialism, subjugation, and resistance. It enacts the powerful possibilities of articulation, as conceptualized by Stuart Hall (1985), which juxtaposes different positions, constituencies, and ideologies for progressive and revolutionary projects. Through these separate yet intertwined interventions, I mobilize queer theory and research within postcolonial and educational studies in order to explore the discursive, empirical, and political potentials for revolutionary solidarities across borderlands.

References

Alexander, M. J., & Mohanty, C. T. (Eds.). (1997). *Feminist genealogies, colonial legacies, democratic futures*. New York: Routledge.

Anzaldúa, G. (1987). *Borderlands: The new mestiza = La frontera*. San Francisco, CA: Aunt Lute.

Benham, M., & Heck, R. (1998). *Culture and educational policy in Hawai'i: The silencing of native voices*. Mahwah, NJ: Lawrence Erlbaum.

Berlant, L. (1997). *The queen of America goes to Washington city: Essays on sex and citizenship*. Durham, NC: Duke University Press.

Beverley, J. (1999). *Subalternity and representation: Arguments in cultural theory*. Durham, NC: Duke University Press.

Bhabha, H. K. (1994). *The location of culture*. New York: Routledge.

Bhaskaran, S. (2004). *Made in India: Decolonizations, queer sexualities, trans/national projects*. New York: Palgrave Macmillan.

Blackburn, M. V., & Donelson, R. (Eds.). (2004). Sexual identities and schooling. *Theory Into Practice, 43*(2), 99-167.

Britzman, D. P. (1998). *Lost subjects, contested objects: Toward a psychoanalytic inquiry of learning*. Albany: State University of New York Press.

Bureau of Education (BE) (1904/1954). *Fourth annual report: Department of Public Instruction*. Manila, Philippines: Bureau of Printing.

Bureau of Education (BE) (1905/1954). *Fifth annual report: Department of Public Instruction*. Manila, Philippines: Bureau of Printing.

Bureau of Education (BE) (1906/1957). *Sixth annual report: Department of Public Instruction*. Manila, Philippines: Bureau of Printing.

Bureau of Education (BE) (1910/1957). *Tenth annual report: Department of Public Instruction*. Manila, Philippines: Bureau of Printing.

Butler, J. (1990). *Gender trouble: Feminism and the subversion of identity*. New York: Routledge.

Caplan, C., Alarcón, N., & Moallem, M. (Eds.). (1999). *Between woman and nation: Nationalisms, transnational feminisms, and the state*. Durham, NC: Duke University Press.

Chakrabarty, D. (2000). *Provincializing Europe: Postcolonial thought and historical difference*. Princeton, NJ: Princeton University Press.

Chan, S. (1991). *Asian Americans: An interpretive history*. Boston, MA: Twayne.

Choy, C. C. (2003). *Empire of care: Nursing and migration in Filipino American history*. Durham, NC: Duke University Press.

Coloma, R. S. (2004). Empire and education: Filipino schooling under United States rule, 1900-1910. Unpublished doctoral dissertation, Ohio State University.

Coloma, R. S. (2005). Disidentifying nationalism: Camilo Osias and Filipino education in the early 20th century. In E. T. Ewing (Ed.), *Revolution and pedagogy: Interdisciplinary and transnational perspectives on educational foundations* (pp. 19-37). New York: Palgrave Macmillan.

Constantino, R. (1966). *The Filipinos in the Philippines and other essays*. Quezon City, Philippines: Malaya.

Davis, A. Y. (1981). *Women, race & class*. New York: Random House.

De Jesus, M. L. (2002). Rereading history, rewriting desire, reclaiming queerness in Carlos Bulosan's *America is in the Heart* and Bienvenido Santos' *Scent of Apples*. *Journal of Asian American Studies, 5*(2), 91-111.

De Lauretis, T. (Ed.). (1991). Special issue on queer theory. *differences, 3*(2).

Eng, D. (2001). *Racial castration: Managing masculinity in Asian America*. Durham, NC: Duke University Press.

Eng, D., & Hom, A. (Eds.). (1998). *Q&A: Queer in Asian America*. Philadelphia, PA: Temple University Press.

Fanon, F. (1967). *Black skin, white masks*. New York: Grove.

Ferguson, R. (2004). *Aberrations in black: Toward a queer of color critique*. Minneapolis: University of Minnesota Press.

Gopinath, G. (2005). *Impossible desires: Queer diasporas and South Asian public cultures*. Durham, NC: Duke University Press.

Hall, S. (1985). Signification, representation, ideology: Althusser and the post-structuralist debates. *Critical Studies in Mass Communication, 2*(2), 91-114.

Haver, W. (1997). Queer research; or, how to practise invention to the brink of intelligibility. In

S. Golding (Ed.), *The eight technologies of otherness* (pp. 277-291). New York: Routledge.
Hawley, J. C. (Ed.). (2001). *Postcolonial, queer: Theoretical intersections*. Albany: State University of New York Press.
Hutchins, L., & Ka'ahumanu, L. (Eds.). (1991). *Bi any other name: Bisexual people speak out*. Boston, MA: Alyson.
Kaplan, A., & Pease, D. E. (Eds.). (1993). *Cultures of United States imperialism*. Durham, NC: Duke University Press.
Kates, N., & Singer, B. (Producers & Directors). (2002). *Brother outsider: The life of Bayard Rustin* [Film]. San Francisco: California Newsreel.
Kumashiro, K. K. (2002). *Troubling education: Queer activism and antioppressive pedagogy*. New York: RoutledgeFalmer.
Lather, P. A. (2004). Foucauldian "indiscipline" as a sort of application: Qu(e)er(y)ing research/policy/practice. In B. Baker & K. E. Heyning (Eds.), *Dangerous coagulations?: The uses of Foucault in the study of education* (pp. 279-304). New York: Peter Lang.
Leong, R. (Ed.). (1996). *Asian American sexualities: Dimensions of the gay and lesbian experience*. New York: Routledge.
Lipkin, A. (1999). *Understanding homosexuality, changing schools: A text for teachers, counselors, and administrators*. Boulder, CO: Westview.
Loomba, A. (Ed.). (2005). *Postcolonial studies and beyond*. Durham, NC: Duke University Press.
Lorde, A. (1984). *Sister outsider: Essays and speeches*. Freedom, CA: Crossing.
Macgillivray, I. K. (2003). *Sexual orientation and school policy: A practical guide for teachers, administrators, and community activists*. Lanham, MD: Rowman & Littlefield.
Manalansan, M. F. (2003). *Global divas: Filipino gay men in the diaspora*. Durham, NC: Duke University Press.
McCarthy, C. (1998). *The uses of culture: Education and the limits of ethnic affiliation*. New York: Routledge.
Mercer, K. (1996). Decolonisation and disappointment: Reading Fanon's sexual politics. In A. Read (Ed.), *The fact of blackness, Frantz Fanon and visual representation* (pp. 114-131). London, United Kingdom: Institute of Contemporary Arts.
Moraga, C. (1986). From a long line of vendidas: Chicanas and feminism. In T. de Lauretis (Ed.), *Feminist studies, critical studies* (pp. 173-190). Bloomington: Indiana University Press.
Muñoz, J. E. (1999). *Disidentifications: Queers of color and the performance of politics*. Minneapolis: University of Minnesota Press.
Ninnes, P., & Mehta, S. (Eds.). (2004). *Re-imagining comparative education: Postfoundational ideas and applications for critical times*. New York: RoutledgeFalmer.
Osias, C. (1971). *The story of a long career of varied tasks*. Quezon City, Philippines: Manlapaz.
Osias, C., & Baradi, M. (1933). *The Philippine charter of liberty*. Baltimore, MD: French-Bray.
Parker, A., Russo, M., Sommer, D., & Yaeger, P. (Eds.). (1991). *Nationalisms and sexualities*. New York: Routledge.
Paxton, N. L. (1999). *Writing under the Raj: Gender, race and rape in the British colonial imagination, 1830-1947*. New Brunswick, NJ: Rutgers University Press.
Pérez, E. (1999). *The decolonial imaginary: Writing Chicanas into history*. Bloomington: Indiana University Press.
Pinar, W. F. (Ed.). (1998). *Queer theory in education*. Mahwah, NJ: Lawrence Erlbaum.
Reyhner, J. A., & Eder, J. (2004). *American Indian education: A history*. Norman: University of Oklahoma Press.

Said, E. W. (1978). *Orientalism*. New York: Pantheon.
Sandoval, C. (2000). *Methodology of the oppressed*. Minneapolis: University of Minnesota Press.
Schwarz, A. B. C. (2003). *Gay voices of the Harlem Renaissance*. Bloomington: Indiana University Press.
Sears, J. T. (Ed.). (2005). *Gay, lesbian, and transgender issues in education: Programs, policies, and practices*. New York: Harrington Park.
Sedgwick, E. K. (1990). *Epistemology of the closet*. Berkeley: University of California Press.
Sedgwick, E. K. (1997). Paranoid reading and reparative reading; or, you're so paranoid, you probably think this introduction is about you. In E. K. Sedgwick (Ed.), *Novel gazing: Queer readings in fiction*. Durham, NC: Duke University Press.
Shah, N. (2001). *Contagious divides: Epidemics and race in San Francisco's Chinatown*. Berkeley: University of California Press.
Sharpe, J. (1993). *Allegories of empire: The figure of the woman in the colonial text*. Minneapolis: University of Minnesota Press.
Smith, A. (2005). *Conquest: Sexual violence and American Indian genocide*. Cambridge, MA: South End.
Spivak, G. C. (1985). Subaltern studies: Deconstructing historiography. In R. Guha (Ed.), *Subaltern studies IV: Writings on South Asian history and society*. New Delhi, India: Oxford University Press.
Spivak, G. C. (1988). *In other worlds: Essays in cultural politics*. New York: Routledge.
Sullivan, N. (2003). *A critical introduction to queer theory*. New York: New York University Press.
Takaki, R. T. (1989). *Strangers from a different shore: A history of Asian Americans*. Boston, MA: Little, Brown.
Talburt, S. (2000). *Subject to identity: Knowledge, sexuality, and academic practices in higher education*. Albany: State University of New York Press.
Thomas, C. (Ed.). (2000). *Straight with a twist: Queer theory and the subject of heterosexuality*. Urbana: University of Illinois Press.
Tierney, W. G. (1997). *Academic outlaws: Queer theory and cultural studies in the academy*. Thousand Oaks, CA: Sage.
Ting, J. P. (1995). Bachelor society: Deviant heterosexuality and Asian American historiography. In G. Y. Okihiro, M. Alquizola, D. Fujita Rony, & K. S. Wong (Eds.), *Privileging positions: The sites of Asian American studies* (pp. 271-280). Pullman: Washington State University.
Ting, J. P. (1998). The power of sexuality. *Journal of Asian American Studies, 1*(1), 65-82.
Trask, H. K. (1993). *From a native daughter: Colonialism and sovereignty in Hawai'i*. Monroe, ME: Common Courage.
Walsh, C. E. (1990). *Pedagogy and the struggle for voice, issues of language, power, and schooling for Puerto Ricans*. New York: Bergin & Garvey.
Willinsky, J. (1998). *Learning to divide the world: Education at empire's end*. Minneapolis: University of Minnesota Press.
Wolfe, P. (1997). History and imperialism: A century of theory, from Marx to postcolonialism. *American Historical Review, 102*(2), 388-402.
Wright, H. K., & Maton, K. (2004). Cultural studies and education: From Birmingham origin to glocal presence. *Review of Education, Pedagogy & Cultural Studies, 26*(2-3), 73-89.
Yoshino, K. (2000). The epistemic contract of bisexual erasure. *Stanford Law Review, 52*(2), 353-461.
Young, R. J. C. (2001). *Postcolonialism: An historical introduction*. Oxford, UK: Blackwell.

PART FIVE

METHODOLOGIES

CHAPTER 17

Postcolonial Technoscience, Toleration and Anti-imperialism, and Education and Psychology

BERNADETTE BAKER

In a special edition of *Social Studies of Science* dedicated to postcolonial technoscience, Warwick Anderson (2002) argues that "Too often the 'postcolonial' seems to imply yet another global theory, or simply a celebration of the end of colonialism. But it may also be viewed as a signpost pointing to contemporary phenomena in need of new modes of analysis and requiring new critiques. Some older styles of analysis in science studies—those that assume relatively closed communities and are predicated on the nation-state—do not seem adapted to explaining the coproduction of identities, technologies and cultural formations characteristic of an emerging global order" (p. 643). Shifting between suspending the term postcolonial in quotes and invoking it as a commonsense adjective, he takes up the difficulty of definition, on the one hand, appearing to prescribe what postcolonial technoscience studies would look like and on the other refusing to say definitely what it is: "At the most basic level, a postcolonial perspective would mean that metropole and postcolony are examined in the same 'analytic frame.' But we would go beyond a recommendation of analytic symmetry and inclusion, and seek to understand the ways in which technoscience is implicated in the postcolonial provincializing of 'universal' reason, the description of 'alternative modernities,' and the recognition of hybridities, borderlands and inbetween conditions" (ibid.).

Amidst a messiness that he was trying to both point to and not confine too rigidly, Anderson enumerates three bodies of literature: colonial critique, postcolonial theory, and historical anthropologies of modernity, arguing that they risk simplification but might be helpful for conceptual purposes. He notes that "For fifty years or so, beneath various deployments, the 'postcolonial' has proven a productively ambiguous intellectual site," and concludes that "It is futile to try to draw a definite boundary around postcolonial studies of science and technology: the enterprise is surely as heterogeneously populated as the terrain it describes. To list the canon of postcolonial science studies would be to miss the point. Like 'modernity,' it just keeps on mutating" (Anderson, 2002, p. 645). However, he outlines a preferred approach: "Even the most local of studies should imply a network, suggesting connections with other sites through the traffic of persons, practices, and objects. The recent emergence of richly textured, multi-sited studies of modern technoscience attests to the importance of both situating knowledge and tracing its passage from site to site" (ibid.). Postcolonial technoscience should, at the minimum, involve identification of either a carrier or a motion (traffic, passage) between sites.

In response, Itty Abraham (2006) argues that postcolonial technoscience as elaborated by Anderson is inadequate for explaining how science is never simply about science, but also about nation-building, and that focusing on contact zones of clashing knowledges is problematic, particularly if local knowledge is conceptualized as "alternative": "The proximity of modern nationalism and its ideological reliance on 'local knowledge' is too direct to ignore. Exploration of this possibility is crucial...the ideological work of alternative knowledge ends up reproducing and reinforcing the national scale over all others, since these are not debates over science, but always about something else" (p. 210). After positing that Anderson's analysis is primarily about political economy, Abraham moves to distinguish "postcolonial technoscience" as per Anderson, from "postcolonial science studies." Abraham's argument is then divided into two parts: in part one, efforts of scholars and political figures to recuperate an authentic Indian science inspired by what Abraham calls "Great-Tradition Hindu" are examined; part two concerns meetings or interviews conducted with laboratory scientists practicing science in contemporary India. In setting up the work that juxtaposition does, Abraham argues dubiously that Anderson positions postcolonial as an index and reference to the third world, as prime site of weakness and underdevelopment. In attributing this move to Anderson, he critiques the view that geopolitical entities are stable and speak for themselves. Without an awareness that they are not, "place becomes a metonym for a unique way of thinking tied to geocultural assumptions" (ibid.).

Like Anderson, the practice of science is linked in the analysis to the possibility for and phenomena of colonialism, the term power operates as a universal law governing all relationships, and similarly the term postcolonial slips into and out of contestation, quotation marks, and commonsensical adjectival status—for instance, "Science and technology is, in a material and cultural sense, central to postcolonial visions of third world states and anti-colonial movements." Abraham (2006) goes on to argue that universalist claims of science are not so pure: "Modernity, nation, and later, state all pass through and are interpellated in the institutions and cultures of modern western science. However, colonial and later postcolonial science was always a contradictory formation. Though science presents itself as universal knowledge, it is never able to do so unambiguously in a location distant from its putative origins in Western Europe. Science's conjoint history with colonial and imperial power implies a constant representation of its condition in order to pass as universal knowledge in the colony" (p. 211).

Abraham's paper highlights a complex synergy between domestic and transnational effects: "This domestication of science is a necessary step in the remaking of the Indian nation as an exclusionary political project, a project which in turn leads to a new scale of violence against the nation 'others'" (p. 213). The study of science in relation to India leads Abraham to question in one sense whether there is an essentializable India, to interrupt the reduction of "knowledge" to "place," to elevate an appeal to excess, surplus, incompletion, and instability. This means that: "Returning to Anderson's original formulation, it becomes clear that a postcolonial techno-science that focuses on 'contact zones' of clashing knowledges is dangerously incomplete unless firmly situated in political and institutional context." What should be sought is "an uneven and unsettled place where location no longer offers a one-dimensional and stable reference to knowledge," where "science as myth, as history, as political slogan, as social category, as technology, as military institution, as modern western knowledge, and, as instrument of change" suggests the surplus of meaning which inspires scholars and political figures alike to attempt to contain and employ it "as a source of geo-cultural certainty and stability" (pp. 213–214).

We have important circularities in play here: Anderson invokes terms such as political and difference as automatically understood in order to argue for the importance of liminality, hybridity, and inbetweenness, which then need to be reordered and clarified via examples that specify and particularize what such ambiguity would look like. Abraham, on the other hand, has to reduce Anderson's messiness to a single-statement proposition on political economy and delimit his own sources and study to nation-building primarily in relation to India in order to argue that it is reductive to think knowledge in terms of place. The analyses intersect in another way: the binaries that Anderson and Abraham seem to agree on as the most useful for persuading the reader are theory/practice and concrete/abstract. Anderson chides abstract theories and puts emphasis on the concrete, material, and richly textured, while Abraham elevates studies of the actual practice of science—with *practice* italicized—as the strategy for illustrating disagreement over what India was or is.

The circularity, from which Dipesh Chakrabarty (2000) tries to extricate historiography, could be brought into focus by examining how such distinctions came to be lodged as persuasive categories, how they attained their cache. How did the paradoxical elevation of practice and the concrete as moral high grounds in methodological claims come to be so honored even in arguments that appear oppositional, and even where such analyses assert the importance of challenging any claims to a universalized Western rationality?

I suggest that such wrangling over postcolonial technoscience versus postcolonial science studies is not better engaged or sidestepped simply by invoking an historical turn, nor are they weaknesses, nor do they need to be corrected, straightened, or relieved of their contradictions. They are symptomatic of broader and narrower issues that cannot be artfully or directly addressed by defining or not defining how to study technoscience and/or nation-building. The debate seems fundamentally to be limited and made possible by at least one particular principle of production, that is, the comparative act, a belief that comparing two or more entities tell us something rather than nothing. In short, one of the interesting problems driving science studies debates over postcolonial studies is not a universalized Western rationality per se but that the way of illustrating the problem with belief in such a rationality is mediated by conventions in other sciences, that is, largely in the social sciences that have held in their academic institutionalization in multiple locations such a troubled relation with the versions of the rational accepted in biophysics and medicine.

By focusing on biophysical laboratory science and medicine, science studies debates have eschewed the opportunity to attend to how the formation and politics of the social sciences, in which postcolonial technoscience analyses are so frequently housed, have staged the noticing of sameness/difference, the drawing of distinction between things, how this housing and staging within social science might inspire the difficulties of articulation, inciting the patterns of saying and unsaying that characterize appeals to liminality, surplus, and excess, the struggle with entification and essentialization, with contradiction around declaring binaries as problematic and relying on select ones anyway. Anderson's and Abraham's analyses seem to operate implicitly within a so-called metaphysics of presence that apparently speaks for itself in regard to how that which is perceived becomes perceivable, treating as a given the operation of social sciences and problematizing instead Western biophysics, medicine, and rationality through narrative forms that remain beneath the radar and naturalized as authorial voice.

The construction of questions about postcolonial science studies and postcolonial technoscience, the categories in the questions and their circularity and logocentrism, need to come under interrogation, then, from a different direction that takes cognizance of how the formation of social sciences have participated in the very possibility for such debates, the "voices" in which they can be written, and the analytical strategies, such as comparative thinking that are embedded in them. In particular, I am interested in how a so-called modern episteme, formalizing across the second half of the nineteenth century most tellingly in "Europe" and the "New World," projected and transformed the act of comparison as a principle of knowledge-production, simultaneously elevated and aligned it with perception (Crary, 2001), and pinned perception with increasing regularity to (belief in a) mind and its new organic home in the body, the brain (Richardson, 2001).

I have argued elsewhere that the *act of comparison*, the *elevation of the terms practice and practical, colonial and/or imperialist processes*, and *perception attributed to mind* comprise an important coagulation of discourses that inscribe particular value systems and worldviews into educational and psychological discourse as normative at the turn of the twentieth century (Baker, 2007). I want to unpack, with the potency of the quadratic equation assumed as background (which interpenetrates Anderson's and Abraham's analyses), the question of the human, child-mind, and the possibilities and limits for anti-imperialist discourse. I do so not via inspecting the colonies for what they can reveal or expose about the self of a center and not by assuming diffusion from a center to a periphery, nor by claiming I can step outside of such equation or the proclivities of the social sciences at large. More modestly, I want to explore from within the complicated trajectories and their (un)knowable limits the vexed formation of such sciences and their leaky objects, amid anti-imperialist critiques that were mounted from protests in the United States—while giving talks to teachers. Hence, William James, education, and psychology.

James, Anti-Imperialism, and the Principles of Toleration

James (1842–1910), a professor at Harvard University for several decades, is well-recognized for writing across what appears today as a range of disciplines, including theology, physiology, psychology, philosophy, education, psychoanalytics, medicine, and psychical science. Less recognized is his vociferous participation in the Anti-Imperialism League, founded in 1898 to protest the U.S. invasion of Cuba and the Philippines and which Andrew Carnegie, Mark Twain, and 50,000 other Americans joined in its first few years. James reputedly stated in regard to what Tavares (2009) calls "the forgotten war": "God damn the US for its vile conduct in the Philippine Isles!"[1] Virtually neglected in James' enormous oeuvre is his 1899 volume *Talks to Teachers on Psychology: and to Students on Some of Life's Ideals* in which he writes in the Preface the opening plea to live and let live in regard to the Philippine invasion and discusses throughout the United States he would like to see instead.

> The facts and worths of life need many cognizers to take them in. There is no point of view absolutely public and universal. Private and uncommunicable perceptions always remain over, and the worst of it is that those who look for them from the outside never know *where*. The practical consequence of such a philosophy is the well-known democratic respect for the sacredness of individuality, ... is, at any rate, an outward tolerance of whatever is not itself intolerant. These phrases are so familiar that they sound now rather dead in our ears. Once they had a passionate inner meaning. Such a passionate inner meaning they may easily acquire again if the pretension of our nation to inflict its own inner ideals and institutions *vi et armis* upon Orientals [sic] should meet with a resistance as obdurate as so far it has been gallant and spirited. Religiously and philosophically, our ancient national doctrine of live and let live may prove to have a far deeper meaning than our people now seem to imagine it to possess. (James, 1899/1915, p. vi)

Talks was based on a series of lectures that James delivered to schoolteachers from 1892 onward. It urged an inscription of humanity as practice-oriented and contained critiques of the Philippine invasion. It drew on his very popular two-volume *Principles of Psychology* for content, simplifying it as he noted for his intended audience. It was spectacularly successful when published with several additional essays, reprinted 23 times until 1929, adopted in undergraduate programs around the country, and becoming the most popular teacher education text in the early decades of the twentieth century. However, it remains almost completely unknown and unstudied in the field of education today.

James popularized the term pragmatism, argued that humans have been designed for practical affairs, and lectured that human biology was directed toward functionality and adaptation. Attention to such contours of "Being" is important for unpacking how the limits and possibilities of anti-imperialist discourse and of liberal toleration, linked as these are in James, could take shape in onto-epistemological hierarchies, in the effort to systematize perception and to absorb the "shock of difference." His writings lay at the confluence of several rivers deeply involved in shaping a valley between subject, environment, and perception, including debates over "German" philosophical idealism and laboratory psychology, "French" clinical psychoanalysis, "British" and "Swedish" Protestantisms, and the emergence of "American" pragmatism. In the Jamesian oeuvre, it is not his participation in the Anti-Imperialism League that is the most informative site for unpacking the complexity and complicity of such formations with the possibilities and limits of critical discourse. I suggest that a richer site lies in the minutiae of the developmental theory and its associationist psychology in what it meant to be a human and a child.[2]

The aim in taking his lectures seriously as something more than just a précis of his *Principles of Psychology*, which is the trend among Jamesian commentators, is not to suggest checklist implications for policy, nor to elevate or pillory James. It is rather to further elaborate postcolonial technoscience insights in the realm of social sciences such as education and psychology as an ethics of how disciplinary divisions of knowledge instantiate certain values at their point of inception, and to thus interrogate "the way systems of knowledge protect and isolate their primary categories from external accountability" (Carrette, 2007, p. viii). Some primary categories of education and psychology such as human, child mind, practice, and perception were formed in the nexus between domestic and transnational circulations of discourse, which set the boundaries of Being, mechanics of operation, and foci of importance, embedding processes that might today be recognized as colonizing and/or imperialist as integral to psychological and educational theories.[3]

Reinscribing the Human: Theory of Development and Associationist Psychology

The sequence, human–mind–consciousness–rational-thought-that-is-procedural, inherited at a minimum from Descartes, constituted a broader parameter of the lectures. *Talks'* version of associationist psychology is more indebted, however, to the proto-typical forms found in Locke's *Essay on Human Understanding*, an attribution that James makes across his writings. Associationist theories argued generally that sensation of things was the primary route to knowledge-production, that sensing something through the (now) five portals led to the formation of simple ideas that then become grouped into complex ones.[4] The associationist theories of the late 1800s were radically modified by the advent of Darwin's evolutionary theory, its appropriation into various forms of Social Darwinism (e.g., Spencer and Galton), and the difficulties that early psychologists had reconciling Protestant theologies with mammalian ontologies. The theory of association James described was interpenetrated by such concerns, operating in terms of its "internal" logic via appeals to *sensation, consciousness, focus/margin,* and *substitution-inhibition.* In *Talks,* James argues that "an associational constitution" is natural, that is, inborn: "we" arrive in a condition ready to associate new with old. Noticing something is indebted to what has already been noticed. For James, a biologic conception of man is unavoidable and what its acceptance permits is elaborated, namely that "We cannot escape our destiny, which is practical; and even our most theoretic faculties contribute to its working out" (James, 1899/1915, pp. 25-26). The (normal) infant under such a theory of associationism that is now sensational *and* biologic is portrayed as "a behaving organism," not as a Lockean gentleman-in-waiting. The child is comported out of a narrative of historical evolution and a concern for excess, complexity, machinery, and biology.

> Man, we now have reason to believe, has been evolved from *infra-human ancestors, in whom pure reason hardly existed,* if at all, and whose mind, so far as it can have had any function, would appear to have been an organ for adapting their movements to the impressions received from the environment, so as to escape the better from destruction. *Consciousness* would thus seem in the first instance to be nothing of a sort of *super-added biological perfection,*—useless unless it prompted to *useful* conduct, and inexplicable apart from that consideration. *Deep in our own nature the biological foundations of our consciousness persist,* undisguised and undiminished. Our sensations are here to attract us and to deter us.... Whatever of transmundane metaphysical insight or of practically inapplicable aesthetic perception or ethical sentiment we may carry in our interiors might at this rate be regarded as only part of the *incidental excess of function* that necessarily accompanies the working of every *complex machine.* (pp. 23-24, emphasis added)

James argues against the kind of associationist psychology built around the idea of *faculties,* as per Locke. He explains the difference around how one would understand *memory*: "if by faculty, you mean *a principle of explanation of our general power* to recall, your psychology is empty. The associationist psychology, on the other hand, gives an explanation of the general faculty" (p. 117, emphasis added). As such, the laws of association govern all trains of thinking: "Whatever appears in the mind must be introduced; and, when introduced, it is as the associate of something already there. This is as true of what you are recollecting as it is of everything else you think of" (pp. 118-119). Memory is indissociable from *thinking*: "the art of remembering is the art of *thinking*; and ... when we wish to fix a new thing in either our own mind or a pupil's, our conscious effort should not be so much to *impress* and *retain* it as to *connect* it with something else already there. The connecting *is* the thinking; and if we attend clearly to the connection, the connected thing will certainly be likely to remain within recall" (p. 169). He explains the ramifications of such theories for teachers: early psychologists considered all deeds in terms of will, with everything going through the "intermediation of this superior agent." This doctrine had been exploded by discovery of the reflex action.

> The fact is that there is no sort of consciousness whatever, be it sensation, feeling, or idea, which does not directly and of itself tend to discharge into some motor effect. The motor effect need not always be an outward stroke of behavior. It may be only an alteration of the heart-beats or breathing, or a modification of the distribution of blood, such as blushing or pale, tears etc. But in any case it is there in some shape when any consciousness is there; and a belief as fundamental as any in modern psychology is the belief at last attained that conscious processes of any sort, conscious processes merely as such, *must* pass over into motion, open or concealed. (pp. 170–171)

Ideas and feelings arising internally, such as out of memories, can constitute a "sensible impression" as much as externally arising sensations, such as touching a cold surface with the fingers. This is important for the theory of association overall; the "inner" and the "outer" provide raw data that become associated in consciousness, an argument that is naturalized in James but was subjected to vociferous debate amid the early 1800 dissections of the brain and nervous system (Richardson, 2001). The point is that, by the time James wrote, inside and outside could "both" play significant roles in terms of conditions of proof. The new relationship between body (as both observable behavior and interior physiology) and mind (consciousness-as-thoughts in a sequence or associative chain) positions body and physiological measures as the legible surface and final arbiter in the early phases of child development for conscious processes *must* pass over into motion-as-change.

Consciousness is always already going on: "Now the *immediate* fact which psychology, the science of mind, has to study is also the most general fact. It is the fact that in each of us, when awake (and often when asleep), *some kind of consciousness is always going on*. There is a stream, a succession of states, or waves, or fields (or whatever you please to call them), of knowledge, of feeling, of desire, of deliberation, etc., that constantly pass and repass, and that constitute our inner life" (James, 1899/1915, p. 15). The "first general fact" is "We thus have *fields of consciousness*" and the "second general fact" is "that the concrete fields are always complex" (p. 17). Consciousness is understood through the dynamics of proximity-impression and focus/margin. Because consciousness *is always going on* the proximity of any thing, it can leave impressions and get "in" there even if one remains unaware that they "got in."

Following the stream of consciousness discussion in *Talks*, a focus/margin distinction is raised. James uses focus and center synonymously, the former more frequently, to depict how consciousness shifts. He takes this as so evident that the terms focal object and marginal object "require no further explanation" (p. 17). Consciousness *is not possible without sensation* and accompanies it for the most part: "In most of our fields of consciousness there is a core of sensation that is very pronounced" (p. 17). The theory of consciousness cannot survive without an appeal to sensation *and* to a focus/margin distinction. The recombinatorial tendencies of focus/margin *are native to humans*, that is, humans *as* and *having* associational constitutions are preprogrammed for a focus/margin distinction and for the relation between them to shift in numerous but not infinite ways.

The sequence of human–biologic–associational constitution–sensation–memory-consciousness-thought–focus/margin is rounded out by the theory of substitution-inhibition. James provides a specific audit trail for how to teach an infant a desired behavior over the top of an already-existing unwanted one. The biology of adaptation makes substitution possible and helps to redefine education as reaction: "Man is an organism for reacting on impressions: his mind is there to help determine his reactions, and the purpose of his education is to make them numerous and perfect. *Our education means, in short, little more than a mass of possibilities of reaction*, acquired at home, at school, or in the training of affairs. The teacher's task is that of supervising the acquiring process" (p. 37). Governing the entire activity of teaching is this principle: "*Every acquired reaction is, as a rule, either a complication grafted on a native reaction, or a substitute for a native reaction, which the same object originally tended to provoke. The teacher's art consists in bringing about the substitution or complication, and success in the art presupposes a sympathetic acquaintance with the reactive tendencies natively there*" (p. 37, italics in original).

It is in the shift from a broader associationist and sensationist psychology into fine-grained elaboration of modes of substitution that the complex relation between Jamesian philosophical psychology and the contours of processes suggestive of the colonizing and/or the imperialist arise. James uses the example of how to teach an infant to beg for a toy instead of snatching as an instance of substitution. The native (child) has to come to you for something desirous. Then you have "knowledge of" them, construed, and this is a key leap, as *control*, and the educative process can begin, but not without some biological struts: "Now, if the child had no memory, the process would not be educative." Memory allows elimination of the intermediary steps; it permits substitution of nice begging for snatching, inhibits the snatch response, and redirects the infant to obtain the toy through the adult's authority. Inhibition is tied to a notion of memory-as-efficiency. A series of brain diagrams illustrate how centers of memory and will facilitate the final substitution in the process inscribing the infant's ontology with the key couplets of becoming governable before school is begun: see-snatch; slap-cry; listen-beg; get-smile (p. 40).

The posteducation inhibition and efficiency of response achieved is key to the determination of success: the child will always beg the adult for the thing desired rather than go through the above couplets each time. "The first thing, then, for the teacher to understand is the native reactive tendencies—the impulses and instincts of childhood—so as to be able to substitute one for another, and turn them on to artificial objects" (p. 43). The native reactions of fear, love, curiosity, imitation, ambition, pugnacity, pride, ownership, constructiveness are dual-edged, both necessary for the supplement that education is and a site of danger if left unabated: "acquired reactions must be made habitual whenever they are appropriate" (p. 63), suggesting the significance of mechanism of habit, association, apperception, interest, attention, memory, and especially will, and giving meaning to what James calls "superior reasoning power." What demarcates Man from animal turns on the relation between "the higher functions" that permit substitution, memory, and reproduction of a begging action rather than snatching. If these higher functions are absent or deemed compromised, the lower instincts take over.

In sum, *Talks* extends and rearranges somewhat the Cartesian sequence reflected in post-Herbartianist and post-Darwinian debates over Being: To be human = having an associational constitution = to be educable = organizing tendencies as habits of behavior = apperceiving = naming things = detecting possible conflicts/tensions between new and old things named = needing an act of will to decide the outcome = enlarging of practical mind = basis from which higher psychic faculties may then spring. In the innocuous sounding description of children, "I cannot but think to apperceive your pupil as a little sensitive, impulsive, associative, and reactive organism, partly fated and partly free, will lead to better intelligence of all his ways. Understand him, then, as such a subtle little piece of machinery. And if, in addition, you can also see him *sub specie boni*, and love him as well, you will be in the best possible position for becoming perfect teachers" (p. 190) were formed new horizons dedicated to perfection of organismic status, including introspective states and control of perceived external flux.

Native Informant/s: That-Which and Who-That

To disentangle how the principles and limits of toleration might be understood in relation to the above, to the (re)inscription of the human and the elevation of the practical as apex of maturity, the "laws of operation" that had to be in place before the "laws of association" could ever be named as such are important to distill. The pluralist, apparently open, and flexible cosmology for which James is famous, prefigured in his "outward tolerance for whatever is not itself intolerant" and in his critiques of imperialism, science, the Absolute, and monism, relied for their appeal to heteronomy, second-order normativity, and introspection upon the operation of textual dependencies that Gayatri Chakravorty Spivak refers to as "native informant/s" (that is not "real interviewees," but projections). Spivak (2000) argues that in Kant, Hegel, and Marx, in various ways, a projection of native informant(s)[5] operates unacknowledged as a site of unlisted traces:

> Increasingly, there is the self-marginalizing or self-consolidating migrant or postcolonial masquerading as a "native informant." ... The texts I read are not ethnographic and therefore do not celebrate this figure. They take for granted that the "European" is the human norm and offer us descriptions and/or prescriptions. And yet, even here, the native informant is needed and foreclosed. In Kant he is needed as the example for the heteronomy of the determinant, to set off the autonomy of the reflexive judgment, which allows freedom for the rational will; in Hegel as evidence for the spirit's movement from the unconscious to the consciousness; in Marx as that which bestows normativity upon the narrative of the modes of production. These moves, in various guises, still inhabit our attempts to overcome the limitations imposed on us by the newest division of the world, to the extent that, as the North continues ostensibly to "aid" the South—as formerly imperialism "civilized" the New World—the South's crucial assistance to the North in keeping up its resource-hungry lifestyle is forever foreclosed... . To steer ourselves through the Scylla of cultural relativism and the Charybdis of nativist culturalism regarding this period, we need a commitment not only to narrative and counternarrative, but also to the rendering (im)possible of (another) narrative. (p. 6)

The normativity, heteronomy-indeterminacy, and movements between conscious and unconscious that appear within an associationist system can be traced through an *epistrophé* carried on the back of projected characters (Sells, 1994)[6]—the emanation-return of native informant/s projected and coming back with messages and/or tasks performed. At least two such projections can be outlined here: native informant/s projected as Natives (that-which make the subject possible) and as feeble intellects (who-that lend solidity and capability to the subject).

The projections of Nativity that lent whiteness a rarefied organismic status are encrypted in the evolutionary theory, securing caste formation in regard to educability. They become present as whispers, shaping political horizons through the text's turns around what constitutes biology and reason, operating as that-which enables a series to be recognized *as* a series. The assumption of developmental levels bequeathed by processes of evolution and presumed embodied, the gradients between the levels and their sequencing, the appeal to inborn nature and that which is fixed, speak the unspoken raciology (Gilroy, 2001). The emanation that *is* the return becomes apparent where and when such "characters" are placed to the negative side of that which they are used to construct. Moreover, such projected native informant/s seem to return as though from an exterior, as though outside, traveling back across the borders established between the eye and the world, only to blur what is inner and outer. "Infra-human ancestors" are to be understood via evolutionary theory as characters reminiscent of a previous age and residing in "everyone's" growth and development as the primordial stage. "They" operate implicitly as both outside objects of perception, commonsensically visible on the street and in textbooks, and inside as incitement to progress for those whose programming allowed for it. Such native informant/s became un-subjects with four main roles: help establish the poles that sequence evolution; position sensation as the primordial site of knowledge-production; turn the practical (biologically conceived as ability to sense and evade environmental crisis and hence survive) into the apex of educatedness; and make the origins of consciousness appear unclear/invisible by visibly occupying the origin of human evolution as the clearly marked "dark" and "exotic" body.

The overt naming of feeblemindedness, which included both feeble intellects and lunacy, brings reworked racializing distinctions into a new relation with dis/ability and nation formation.[7] Native informant/s cast as feebleminded generate instability, between being raced and beyond race, between dependence and independence, troubling the neatness of racializing binaries. The liminality arises in that awkward form, the feeble intellect—not so mad as to be mad, not so sane as to be left completely alone—a native informant whose naming marks a crossover point between the coining of the term eugenics in 1888 (Galton) and the major international eugenics conferences of the first decade of the new century. James' *Talks* is written in the middle of this period, the invention and "working out" of the "menace of the feebleminded"

(Trent, 1994). Such native informant/s bear double movements: the feeble-minded as belonging to the race as sickly whiteness and subject of welfare, and the mad as beyond race, as altogether irredeemable and unclassifiable beyond the designation of madness.

> In law courts no *tertium quid* is recognized between insanity and sanity. If sane, a man is punished: if insane, he is acquitted; and it is seldom hard to find two experts who will take opposite views of his case. All the while, nature is more subtle than our doctors. Just as a room is neither dark nor light absolutely, but might be dark for a watchmaker's uses, and yet light enough to eat in or play in, so a man may be sane for some purposes and insane for others,—sane enough to be left at large, yet not sane enough to take care of his financial affairs. The foreign terms "disequilibré," "hereditary degenerate," and "psychopathic" subject, have arisen in response to the same need. (James, 1899/1915, p. 164)

The heredity degenerate, fully-fledged as a lower kind of human in the text, announces what the first consideration of child development—efficiency—means (i.e., doing what one is "fitted for"). This can only be done where it is understood that full development is secured via *memory plus philosophical mind*. The nativity of mind, its always already being something appointed or endowed with a seed that limits the extent of development possible at birth, not only recreates castes of educability, but also enables the feeble intellect to shape recognition of the normal especially in regard to *memory*. Feeble intellects are "found in those who have almost no desultory memory at all. If they are also deficient in logical and systematizing power, we call them simply feeble intellects; and no more need to be said about them here. Their brain-matter, we may imagine, is like a fluid jelly, in which impressions may be easily made, but are soon closed over again, so that the brain reverts to its original indifferent state" (p. 122). James returns to such intellects several times in *Talks*, never quite able to leave them behind. The depth of their work becomes clearer as the microphysics of memory is elaborated. It appears most evident in the definition of education. Education consists "in organizing of *resources* in the human being, of powers of conduct which shall fit him to his social and physical world" and "An 'uneducated' person is one who is nonplussed by all but the most habitual situations. On the contrary, one who is educated is able practically to *extricate* himself, by means of the examples with which his *memory* is stored and of the *abstract* conceptions which he has acquired, from *circumstances in which he never was placed before*. Education, in short, cannot be better described than by calling it *the organization of acquired habits of conduct and tendencies to behavior*" (p. 29; emphasis added). The process can only take place under propitious circumstances; the gap between the subject as such and the child can only be bridged by "culture" where "nature" has allowed. Nature needs culture, but cannot be produced by it. Production lies with what Spivak (2000, p. 15) calls the "empirico-psychological reflexes" of lesser-than-subjects who-that constitute the internal divisions of educatedness and "mess up" the polar racializing ones, who reveal the limits of culture and purify the realm of nature precisely via their "pollutive" presence.

Finally, the couplets that hold up the strata existing in castes of educability are reasserted through the term *practical*. Without sensation, the ability to know the rest of the world is compromised: "No one believes more strongly than I do that what our senses know as 'this world' is only one portion of our mind's total environment and object. Yet, because it is the primal portion, it is the *sine qua non* of all the rest" (p. 25). The native informant/s projected as feebleminded return to occupy the negative side of that which they help *routinize within the series*. Such informant/s thus perform three main roles: troubling the passage of linear time as meaning progressive improvement; messing up the neatness of racializing binaries; and illustrating how the mechanical system of mind formation and perception operate as routinized by becoming its failure.

In sum, whereas the native informant/s projected as Native establish the poles upon which a series can be identified as a series, the informant/s projected as feebleminded indicate how the series works by interrupting it, as wayward and sometimes even worse as morbid. The former native informant/s set historic time, while the latter erupt as untimely, as too early reminders of mortality, as perturbations that threaten the ordering of the future. As Spivak (2000) notes, this invocation of linear time is crucial to resecuring the exclusivity of the narrator, of who can occupy the location of theory-builder: "Time often emerges as an implicit Graph only miscaught by those immersed in the process of timing" (p. 38).

From Association to Colonization?: The Limits and Possibilities of Toleration and Anti-Imperialist Discourse

A modified associationist psychology and the labor of native informant/s together lend specificity to the possibilities for being human, for how "differences" are perceived at all, and for the conceptualization/enactment of toleration. The sympathy for "external" (international) forms of injustice that James attends to, such as in the Preface quoted above where he admonishes the U.S. invasion of the Philippines, is in part made possible by the acceptance and obfuscation of "internal" (domestic) forms. The onto-epistemological lens normalizes so that the biological, practical, self-governing human thought invaded by other nations remains built upon gradations accepted at home.

Insofar as James (1899/1915) asserts that "variety in unity being the secret of all interesting talk and thought" (p. 112), one might argue that specific strategies of foundation operate at the site of production of associationist claims to pluralism, indeterminacy, and variety. This is precisely the double-edged sword that difference as configured through appeals to a universal "raw man," as Spivak (2000) puts it, would suggest. The second-order normativity around raw man and the role of native informant/s in shaping His humanity discourages questioning of the racializing and ableizing foundations of master narratives, such as Social Darwinistic evolutionary theory, even as one, such as James, critiques its impact elsewhere on Protestant beliefs. His "I invite you to seek with me some principle to make our tolerance less chaotic" (James, 1899/1915, p. 268) means that such an associationism can never realize a strident critique of the Philippine invasion, of noninterference with others, because the theory of mind-body that grounds the philosophy of character formation has already determined what an other is in order for "it" to be recognizable as such (i.e., new can only be recognized in terms of old). The others of external nations, the "Orientals" in this case, have been interfered with, so to speak, by the liberal pluralist and humanist structure of the complaint, by cutting off the possibility of *not having to say "No!," of not having to engage at all* in refuting the normativities embedded in appeals to human practicality, democratic self-governance, *and* critiques of their transgression that organizations such as the Anti-imperialism League leveled.

There is in James, though, a different possibility that exceeds the liberalist dilemmas often pointed out around his work. It is not the well-worn argument that a self knows what it is by what it is not. Nor is it that the self is constituted by projecting an other who it then uses to reconstitute its self, the standard critique of mainstream anthropology that Spivak (2000) turns on its head and redeploys. While both aspects swirl through his writing, there is something else in James that has to do with the idea that self is a *collective* concept (Latour, 2006). The by-now familiar critiques of self/other relations and hierarchical formations indexical of critical work become more difficult to apply on two grounds. First, James provides a theory for how a self/other divide could even come into being, how it could arise in the first place, how such a distinction could be drawn *at all*. Decades later, a self/other dichotomy would be a major conceptual strut of "postcolonial critique." Second, when James' theory of self-formation as *imitative* and *emulative* in the early phases of life is considered, the process of subjectivity formation becomes chicken and egg. The "self" is a collective concept in that it is formed through imitating those around us, we can only know "self" through patterns that form through imitation of other patterns, and patterns are what (normal) people are born being able to form. "Self" is not easily reducible to individual. James notes the circularity when he asserts that individuality presupposes and proposes. Through education built upon *rivalry*, the self of a developing child will become dissociated from those around who are being imitated and coalesce later as a distinctive mind. How the differences between minds form amid the larger process of "I" formation, James argued, is a continued mystery that psychology had not come close to explaining.

In this version of associationism, the presence of any "difference" leaves an impression that in the future will come to matter, come to fruition in unpredictable ways. So if you do not want to lose the solidity of the "I," at least that which is an acquired habit by adulthood, the wider self-as-cultured-nature ought to be replicated, unwittingly providing a philosophical rationale for colony formation. It will ensure that the impressions being received from "the outside" can be assimilated within existing foundations of the self-as-cultured-nature, not rocking the boat, but traveling back to the perceiver as nice exotic twists, not so different as to disturb but a just-noticeable-difference (Fechner's term) so as to titillate or enlarge the mind. The instantiation of the subject's Ego with the ability to project an individualized "worldview" (the many cognizers needed to view the facts and worths of life for James), and the assumed solidity and validity attributed to "exterior" objects reinforces the synergy between scientific rationality, realism, and colonialism even in accounts that might contest the third term. The collusion is not avoided by appeals to pluralism, perspectivalism, or multiculturalism. Normalization and individuation were twin processes of "American" nation-building, and mainstream education and psychology were guided by broad-based Protestant commitments. The standardization of models of "mind" and "method" (e.g., appeals to pragmatism and the elevation of practice, instrumentality, and social utility) become in the United States generally and in James specifically the new site of a unification sought (yet never achieved) among "populations" divided by enormous historical insults and injuries and with different conceptions of Being, life, death, and awareness, cosmologies irreducible to human-centrism or to belief in such a thing as a discrete mind.

Conclusion

It is through the paradoxes of such logic that the limits of the discourse on toleration come fully into view and their provincialism exposed. It is a form of toleration that can only be granted by the reassertion of a specific human nature and orientation to character formation, a form that circumscribes reflection on "the political," the international, or the imperialist by ascribing to the human and to nature a restricted and essential foundation.

As such, the potential for logocentrism to find its home in the object formations of the social sciences, and not just the biophysical or medical sciences as Anderson's and Abraham's foci and elisions imply, is unleashed: the slash between inner and outer realms that was constituted to give the play of difference, to make it seem that a psychological system could be affected by environment and environment by system, dissipates into one continuous and foundational reference point that can never be disturbed or substituted (system-closure), forging the deep sense of homogeneity, entrapment, and/or circularity that comes from instantiation of second-order norms around figuration of the practical human perceiver. The rewriting of nation-building as human development and perfection of capacities, with education (as "organized tendencies") as the instrument, subsequently establishes limits not only to what toleration can tolerate, but also to what can arise as a violation or complaint, contouring in advance what counts as moral character, ethical relations, or (anti-)imperialism between "humans" living in one "nation" or another. The paradox bequeathed rather than resolved, which exceeds James and the genuine concern for injustice, and interpenetrates the formation of social sciences such as education and psychology, is the cementing of a standard mode of criticism of imperialism that relies upon a subtle, deeply colonizing, and not-so-open response to the question of the human and its seemingly irrefutable surface-depth link that leaves body and mind as objects unavailable to external accountability regarding "their" existence and the value systems this instantiates.

Notes

1. This is quoted in Zinn (2003). The term nation should not be understood as a geopolitical entity that speaks for itself (Abraham, 2006). Names of nations have to be understood as suspended, as both said and unsaid. I have elaborated this saying and unsaying elsewhere as a performatively apophatic one (Baker, 2001, 2006). I thank the editors of the *International Journal of Educational Policy, Research, and Practice*, 8 (2007), to reprint and modify parts of my essay.

2. This is a broader problematic that concepts of matter, spirit, language, rationality, critique, and culture help produce and thus is not reducible to (post)humanism debates.

3. I begin with a "specter" of the imperialist and/or the colonizing as involving elements of *continuous linking and/or sequencing* that presences the dilemma of system-closure (e.g., the new can only be seen in terms of normativities established in the old) and of *substitution* that when applied to relations of "power" can involve a range of "hard" (invasion-eradication) and "soft" (education-conversion) strategies recognized as colonizing or imperialist. I have illustrated elsewhere how this delimitation becomes part of the problem being critiqued (Baker, 2006). I do not claim to be outside the historical vestige of theories of perception or to not be deploying a particular kind. My analysis remains both vehicle and effect of that which it historicizes.

4. Associationism does not mean associating something randomly with something else or just making links between things. In *Talks* it means that something cannot be noticed as "new" without relating it back to an already-existing apperceptive mass in the mind. The "old" categories determine, thus things that come up for notice cannot be entirely new.

5. I use the slash ("native informant/s") and not the parentheses of Spivak's "native informant(s)" to signal the multiple and differential roles played by that-which and who-that kinds. The back and forth between group and singular in such projections suggests something more significant to the argument about limits of "human" that the slash represents.

6. *Epistrophé* is like a projection from within, an apparent movement or an emanation and its coming back, where the emanation *is* the return, for example, that which you thought was "outside" is understood as a projection from "inside" that you see coming back at you as though from across a border and thereby labeled as "outer," "exterior," "foreign," or "external." The effect is labrynthian, a confusion or nonclarity over what or whether there is an inner and outer. It can incite even greater efforts to demarcate and classify. I have appropriated this concept from Sells (1994). Spivak speaks differently, drawing on Lacan, of *foreclosure*.

7. I have discussed elsewhere the implications of race-sexuality, eugenics, heteronormativity, and the shift of ableization from poverty to neurophysiology in psychological discourses in the late nineteenth century (Baker, 2001, 2006).

References

Abraham, I. (2006). The contradictory spaces of postcolonial techno-science. *Economic and Political Weekly*, 210-217.
Anderson, W. (2002). Postcolonial techno-science. *Social Studies of Science, 32*, 643-658.
Baker, B. (2001). *In perpetual motion: Theories of power, educational history, and the child.* New York: Peter Lang.
Baker, B. (2006, November). William James, the dilemma of psychical science, and conditions of proof: A postcolonial reading. Paper presented at the Social Studies of Science and Society annual meeting, Vancouver, Canada.
Baker, B. (2007). The limits of toleration. *International Journal of Educational Policy, Research, and Practice, 8*, 165-180.
Carrette, J. (2007). *Religion and critical psychology: The ethics of not-knowing in the knowledge economy.* New York: Routledge.
Chakrabarty, D. (2000). *Provincializing Europe: Postcolonial thought and historical difference.* Princeton, NJ: Princeton University Press.
Crary, J. (2001). *Suspensions of perception: Attention, spectacle, and modern culture.* Cambridge, MA:

MIT Press.

Gilroy, P. (2001). *Against race: Imagining political culture beyond the color line.* Cambridge, MA: Harvard University Press.

James, W. (1899/1915). *Talks to teachers on psychology and to students on some of life's ideals.* New York: H. Holt.

Latour, B. (2006, October). Knowledge as a mode of existence: A textbook case revisited. Paper presented to Holtz Center for Social Studies of Science and Technology, University of Wisconsin-Madison, USA.

Richardson, A. (2001). *British romanticism and the science of the mind.* Cambridge: Cambridge University Press.

Sells, M. (1994). *The mystical languages of unsaying.* Chicago, IL: University of Chicago Press.

Spivak, G. C. (2000). *A critique of postcolonial reason: Toward a history of the vanishing present.* Cambridge, MA: Harvard University Press.

Tavares, H. (2009). Disrupting the look: Reflections on postcolonial criticism as politicizing curriculum practice. In B. Baker (Ed.), *New curriculum history* (pp. 169-184). Rotterdam: Sense.

Trent, J. (1994). *Inventing the feeble mind: A history of mental retardation in the United States.* Berkeley: University of California Press.

Zinn, H. (2003). *A people's history of the United States, 1492-present.* New York: Perennial Classics.

CHAPTER 18

The Contradictions of Negotiating Legitimacy at Home/Field

BINAYA SUBEDI

Abu-Lughod (1991) uses the term "halfie" to describe the identities and experiences of researchers "whose national or cultural identity is mixed by virtue of migration, overseas education, [and] parentage" (p. 137). To negotiate halfie identity is to come to terms with its fluidity, heterogeneity, and process of "becoming as well as being" (Hall, 1990, p. 225). Abu-Lughod (1991) explores the dilemmas faced by halfie researchers within the context of anthropology:

> As anthropologists, they write for other anthropologists, mostly western. Identified also with communities outside the West, or subcultures within it, they are called to account by educated members of those communities. More importantly, not just because they position themselves with reference to two communities but because when they present the Other they are presenting themselves, they speak with a complex awareness of and investment in reception. Both halfie and feminist anthropologists are forced to confront squarely the politics and ethics of their representations. There are no easy solutions to their dilemmas. (p. 142)

For Abu-Lughod, the ethical issues faced by halfie researchers are complex since they write for and have to answer to multiple communities. Because of the misconceptions within Western societies about the non-Western Other, halfie researchers face the difficult task of undertaking their work. In other words, their "in-between" status requires that they be more accountable to how they have researched and written about the people with whom they affiliate.

My halfie status derives from living in two different countries, Nepal and the United States. This chapter documents the use of rigorous reflexivity in the international aspect of fieldwork, especially when neither the researcher nor the researched is white. Similar to Daza (2008), I ask: "How do researchers negotiate competing narratives presented by research and local community norms that vary across contexts, particularly when research is transnational?" (p. 73). I build upon the work of *native* researchers who have explored the ethical and political context of researching in non-Western societies, particularly in regard to negotiating gender, race, and ethnic identities (Amadiume, 1993; Williams, 1996).[1] I begin by describing my insider and outsider subject positions in Nepal and examine the halfie dimensions of identity within transnational research. Then I explore how the participants in my research problematized my desire to seek legitimacy in the everyday aspect of fieldwork and how my desire to be seen as a "local" was unsettled.

The chapter is part of a larger research project that explored the contemporary interpretation of citizenship education in Nepali schools within broader discussions of globalization and neocolonialism. The data for the study was collected by interviewing four teachers (two women and two men) who worked in three urban high schools.[2] The chapter does not review the overall findings of the study; rather it traces my interactions with the teachers. The teachers' schools were considered academically low performing because a vast majority of the students did not pass the required national high school exam in subjects such as math, science, social studies, and English.[3] The schools enrolled a large number of low-income students from local neighborhoods as well as students who had recently migrated from rural areas.

The Use of Rigorous Reflexivity

Within postpositivist traditions, reflexivity calls for the need to be more open and accountable to how one has participated in research and how knowledge is produced. Concerned with ethical practices, it critiques the role of the researcher as the all-knowing subject, and calls for the need to formulate accountable practices. While reflexivity enables researchers to reexamine their subjectivities, it also asks questions about how researchers have met the needs and concerns of participants. Jackson (2004) suggests that researchers make a distinction between mechanical and rigorous approaches to reflexivity. The former stands for self-serving "empty autobiographical gestures" and does not contribute to dismantling societal structures that perpetuate oppression (p. 37). The latter, which Jackson terms rigorous reflexivity, asks that the "I" be used in a more honest, vulnerable way in order to be attentive to "how we see—and how others see us seeing them" (p. 40).

Scholars who practice a rigorous approach to reflexivity argue that the self ought to be always present in the act of researching and writing (Brayboy, 2000; Chaudhry, 2000). However, mainstream researchers often resist recognizing how reflexive accounts can provide a critical lens to theorize social discourses. Rigorously reflexive accounts of research continue to be labeled as being ego-driven, solipsistic, and narcissistic (Facio, 1993). Behar (1996) observes that researchers cannot avoid how "a personal voice, when creatively used, can lead the reader, not into miniature bubbles of navel-grazing, but into the enormous sea of serious social issues" (p. 14). When women and people of color incorporate personal experiences as a way to theorize issues of difference, their narratives are often interpreted as being of less scientific value and lacking in objectivity (Motzafi-Haller, 1997).

Rigorous approaches to reflexivity question what and how one knows and how one is accountable to practices of representations. Representations, according to Said (1989), "bear as much on the representer's world as on who or what is represented" (p. 224). Rosaldo (1989) argues that researchers ought to question what they can and cannot know: "Because researchers are necessarily both somewhat impartial and somewhat partisan, somewhat innocent and somewhat complicit, their readers should be as informed as possible about what the observer was in a position to know or not know" (p. 69). Reflexivity involves working through messy texts since such approaches "insist on an open-endedness, an incompleteness, and an uncertainty about how to draw a text/analysis to a close" (Marcus, 1994, p. 567). By asking researchers to be explicit about their positionalities, Abu-Lughod (1991) maintains that rigorous interpretation of reflexivity makes "it clear that every view is a view from somewhere and every act of speaking a speaking from somewhere" (p. 141).

There is considerable debate over what constitutes rigorous reflexivity since not all approaches to writing about the self are transformative (Escobar, 1993). According to Pillow (2003), reflexivity that "pushes towards an unfamiliar, towards the uncomfortable, cannot be a simple story of subjects, subjectivity, and transcendence of self-indulgent tellings" (p. 192). To be accountable in their practices, researchers need to be introspective without indulging in "vanity ethnography" (Van Maanen, 1988, p. 93). By questioning neither the uneven power dynamics in fieldwork nor the agency of marginalized subjects, the uncritical adoption of reflexivity can situate the Western self as the creator and the bearer of knowledge. For Fabian (1990), there is no "guarantee that oppressors will be less oppressive just because they become self-conscious" (p. 768). A rigorous mode of reflexivity has the potential to link the personal to the social in order to decolonize the dominant politics of knowledge. As Smith (2005) argues, decolonization is more than a matter of methods or techniques;

it is a "purposeful agenda for transforming the institution of research, the deep underlying structures and taken-for-granted ways of organizing, conducting, and disseminating research and knowledge" (p. 88).

The Field as Home: Locating the Halfie Self in Transnational Spaces

Researchers like me who are positioned in Western academia and who return home to undertake fieldwork establish different kinds of legitimacy or trust in the field. Because of cultural ties and one's lived experiences that go beyond narrow academic interests, the issues that halfie researchers face can be daunting since oftentimes there are no prescribed methods of research to fall back on. If the notion of field as home produces a sense of comfort and has emotional or cultural appeal for halfie researchers, the return is almost certain to be a journey of unlearning. The process of going home and writing return narratives involves rethinking how one had learned to conduct research through one's training. Professionalized in Western academia to pursue white-on-white or white-on-non-white research, halfie researchers have to rethink the politics of how they have been taught to research and write. Therefore, the possibility of misrepresentation can consume halfie researchers for an extended period of time. Halfie researchers often struggle with how to write their research findings and to disclose their experiences to mainstream academia.

The topic of researchers of color investigating the communities they culturally affiliate with is not new, yet it remains marginalized as a serious topic of inquiry in educational research. Although questions of rigor or ethics are important in all research endeavors, the methodological discussions operate on a different level when one is doing research on transnational settings. For instance, the ethical and political issues that halfie researchers may face when researching their cultural communities may be quite different than what European American investigators may encounter when researching in a similar setting. The questions halfie researchers may ask have the radical potential to "[disrupt] notions of power and difference that are typical of debates about Self and Other in traditional ethnographies wherein the Self is the White, Western academic" (Parameswaran, 2001, p. 72). Halfies are "positioned (and not always by choice) in opposition to dominant discourses and structures of power" and similarly are "moved by different sets of questions concerning power, domination, and representation" (Visweswaran, 1994, p. 140). Due to ethnic, linguistic, and gender differences, halfie researchers embody multiple identities, and must interrogate their sense of place in contemporary world systems and ask how "people like ourselves could be engaged in anthropological studies of people like those" (Abu-Lughod, 1991, p. 148). Out of the movement between cultures, they "share the burden and privilege of certain kinds of colonized and racialized subjectivities that allow us to speak as both insiders and outsiders, as transnational intellectuals and as representatives of specific national and/or local constituencies" (Juluri, 1998, p. 86; cited in Parameswaran, 2001, p. 72).

My halfie status is connected to the neocolonial legacy of education. Since the 1960s, the Western approach to education in Nepal has been widely institutionalized to "develop" the country from its traditional and "backward" existence. I studied in an academically rigorous Jesuit school, established by U.S. missionaries in the 1950s as a way to cultivate Nepali children. My parents, who had completed tenth-grade education and had never attended college, believed that the Jesuit school offered opportunities to access college education. Due to the prestige attributed to Western knowledge, schools established by Europeans or European Americans, such as the one I attended, were (and are) viewed as academically superior. Due to their emphasis on the Western curriculum of science, math, and literature, students like me often found ourselves becoming disconnected from local traditions and customs. Hence, from childhood it was not uncommon for students like me to internalize Western cultures as being somewhat more legitimate in the global context. The smooth transition I made into U.S. higher education as a college student was due to my schooling in Nepal.

John (1989) explains the politics of getting a privileged form of education in third world societies:

> Formal education is, after all, also a process by which we learn to avow and remember certain knowledges and devalue and forget others. We grow up repudiating the local and the personal in favor of what will get us ahead and away—thus coming of age within an intellectual field that, by no means arbitrarily, creates disinterest and oversight in some areas and directs desire elsewhere. It is within such an interlocking mechanism for the production of knowledges and "sanctioned ignorances" that our subjectivities are forged. This apparatus makes our transition to first-world institutions, especially in the United States, quite possibly among the smoothest within the third-world system. (p. 11)[4]

What John argues is that we ought to consider the structural context in which the discourses of education operate and the kinds of global mobility and access they provide to those who are educationally privileged. John's analysis of the politics of knowledge is also a critique of the elite education systems in non-Western societies that often privilege Western knowledge, thereby marginalizing indigenous ways of knowing. Thus, halfie researchers like me with third world identifications, who are also educated and socialized in the West, embark on a long journey of self-critique. We come to recognize the politics of our education in our countries of birth, which led us to migrate to the West in the first place. My comfortable schooling, which is undoubtedly a privileged experience in Nepal, did not trigger radical consciousness on issues of social class, ethnicity, sexuality, and gender. And I often took for granted my privileged Jesuit school experience. My own sense of critical awareness about social differences, inequalities, and oppression came about because of my own experiences as an immigrant of color in U.S. society. Because of personal experiences with U.S. "racial formations" (Omi & Winant, 1986), I became aware of the politics of my arrival in the United States and began to view the place of my birth and the global politics of education more critically (Rhee, 2003; Subreenduth, 2008).

Those of us who return to simultaneously visit family members and undertake academic research find a certain comfort in doing research in our "field of choice" (Dillard, 2006), in places that are familiar. This sense of comfort or belonging can also be problematic considering how one may be viewed as an outsider and/or an insider when conducting "home" research. For instance, certain aspects of my life were considered "foreign" during my everyday interactions in Nepal because I have lived for more than 15 years in the United States. Even though I desired to be seen as an authentic local, I was often told that, although I looked Nepali and spoke Nepali, my ways of speaking, body language, and demeanor decidedly included *bedeshi*, or aspects of *Amerikaness*.[5]

My subject position in Nepal needs to be understood in relation to how Western discourses, including those from the United States, are visible in non-Western societies (Shrestha, 1997). In school curriculum, the United States is often represented very favorably because of the economic aid it has provided to the country. Along with Australia and Europe, the United States remains one of the most desired areas to immigrate to for Nepali people. U.S. influence in Nepal and in the world is a reflection of its economic and political power that, in turn, is reflected in the presence of U.S. military, corporate, and cultural entities worldwide (Enloe, 1989). Because of the complex ways that Western discourses continue to be present in Nepal, Western-affiliated researchers, including individuals like me who are returning, cannot avoid how research is connected to global discourses of power and hegemony.

Desire, Legitimacy, and Ethics

How can rigorous approaches to reflexivity help researchers examine issues of desire and legitimacy in fieldwork? Because the dynamics of international power have favored European and North American nation-states, Western researchers have often researched under the illusion that they can be less explicit about their racial or national identity when conducting fieldwork in international contexts. The lack of knowledge of structural discourses reinforces unequal power dynamics in research in which the relationship between personal-cultural and economic-political is left unanswered. For instance, U.S.-based researchers' identities are often mis/read in fieldwork, even being perceived as U.S. government agents, spies, or missionaries (Abu-Lughod, 1988; Coloma, 2008). Although being forthright about one's identification with participants (e.g., via gender or ethnic similarities) is a useful way to come clean of one's investments, a researcher also can examine how cultural differences can make collective identifications contested. Even though all researchers must negotiate legitimacy in the field, halfie researchers cannot assume that their cultural backgrounds will position them as insiders or give them "carte blanche status in the field" (Jacobs-Huey, 2002, p. 793). Delgado-Gaitan (1993) argues for the need to critique assumed notions of community since "sharing the same ethnic background as the participants does not necessarily make the researcher more knowledgeable about the meanings of the participants' feelings, values and practices" (p. 391). For halfie researchers, the process of gaining legitimacy or trust as "insiders" may include demonstrating their language competency, knowledge of community histories or experiences, and commitment to meaningfully address community needs. Despite sharing the same racial, ethnic, or cultural backgrounds, halfie researchers may fail to prove or convince participants of their identities as legitimate (i.e., committed, credible, trustworthy) researchers. The act of negotiating legitimacy is a significant issue for (halfie) researchers since it demonstrates the extent to which participants may perceive them as reliable subjects who can be trusted with the knowledge shared in the research process.

During my research, I often self-identified as a partial insider since I had lived in a nearby neighborhood until my departure for college in the United States. I also embodied a partial insider identity since I speak and write Nepali fluently and I am culturally affiliated with Nepali customs and traditions. Because of family connections, I was able to negotiate initial entry into the schools. In two schools, I was introduced to the teachers by a relative who had once taught there. In another school, the access was negotiated by my father, who, during the first day of my visit, asked me to follow him to the school, where he introduced me to the principal whom he had known for a number of years. I could not help but recognize how family relationships can help researchers; in my case, they helped me gain certain credibility or legitimacy. However, I soon came to realize that my sense of legitimacy with the participants needed to be renegotiated. Because of my father's and relative's assistance, I thought that I would be accepted as an "insider." Yet I discovered that my status of insider-ness was conditional and unstable. My outsider status became evident when I was asked, as one male teacher put it, how I had "suddenly appeared to do research." Similarly, I was asked by a female teacher why I had stayed in *Amerika* for an extended period of time "since your parents are still here." In fact, both teachers often asked questions concerning issues of family separation. The logic of living separately was an oddity for the participants, who often suggested how such an arrangement, as one female teacher put it, was "not a good idea for parents who did not see their family a lot." The same teacher felt that because of migration "the separation of family was becoming more common when younger people moved overseas."

The comment about living arrangements needs to be understood within the context of the Nepali conception of family in which extended families quite often live together and the elderly are cared for by their children. Some of the teachers perceived that I had adopted Western values since I had exempted myself from the responsibility of caring for my parents. Their questions raised a host of issues that were not only about my length of stay overseas and the lack of timely return, but also related to the kinds of responsibility that the people who go "there" should have in relation to people who live "here." I was well aware of the criticism leveled against expatriates who returned only for family visits and who did not make meaningful commitments or contributions to Nepali society. Because of continuous migration to the United States, Europe, Middle East, and within Asia, the social, political, and economic implications of the "brain-drain" is a much debated topic in Nepal (Battachan, 1999). Those who return, particularly if their only interest is for research only, are criticized for remaining indifferent to local struggles. The larger issue of contribution, whether taken up by local people or by expatriates, has particular implications in economically underprivileged nation-states such as Nepal.

Discomforts with Double Consciousness

Scholars who investigate communities they culturally affiliate with face unique challenges in the research and writing process (Alridge, 2003). For example, when undertaking international research, researchers of color from the United

States have explored how they have faced challenges in explaining their "Americaness" as well as their hyphenated identities. Kondo (1990), a Japanese American researching in Japan, writes of her collapse of identity as a way to describe how she came to rethink her "American" identity and to reject how she had become "Japanese." She notes how her informants attempted to make her "native" since participants wondered "How could someone who *looked* Japanese not be *Japanese?*" Harrison (1991), an African American doing research in Jamaica, describes how she had to clarify that she was not affiliated with the U.S. government and that she was opposed to the U.S. intervention in Central and South American affairs. She writes about how she had to explain her African American identity since her participants had limited knowledge about Black experiences in the United States.

In interaction with participants, researchers may resist being open about the multiple identities they embody. During the early stages of my research, I found a certain comfort in masking my double consciousness (Du Bois, 1989) that had emerged out of living in Nepal and the United States. I rationalized that by not revealing the U.S. aspects of my life, I would be taken more seriously as an "insider." Fearing that I would be considered an outsider, I hoped that participants would ask me about my experiences in Nepal since I was seeking legitimacy as an authentic local. The longing to be affirmed as a local had much to do with my own experiences in the United States, where immigrants like me are not considered legitimate residents and where the openly hostile anti-immigrant political climate makes any claims to U.S. citizenship tenuous. Although problematic, my wish to be taken seriously as an insider had much to do with my attempts to belong in Nepal.

My intention of claiming an unproblematic local status was also self-serving. As the research progressed, I became partially open about my identities to secure my credibility with the participants. I often shared stories that attempted to elicit interest from the participants that, in subsequent reflection, I realized was a questionable research practice. I described my U.S. college experiences, particularly my struggles to connect with the humanities and social science curriculum that was by and large Eurocentric. I also shared how in the past five years I had begun to think in English, and when I became accustomed to life in Nepal, my ways of thinking would switch to Nepali, the official (and the dominant) language of Nepal. Yet, upon returning to the United States, it would gradually revert back to English. The teachers were sympathetic to my ordeals, yet the sharing of personal dilemmas did not seem to alter my status as an outsider on some levels.

It appeared that even when I began to recognize my hybrid identity, which was my form of identification in the United States, I often sought to claim a generic Nepali-only identity and resisted the label of *Amerikanized*-Nepali. Not surprisingly, because of my U.S. affiliations, I was often read as a person embodying a hyphenated identity through comments such as "You look like and think like *Amerikanized* man." The perception of my embodying an *Amerikan* appearance and sense of manhood were in sharp contrast to how Asian men like me are represented in the United States. People of Asian descent are often seen only as foreigners despite being born or having lived in the United States for decades (Lee, 1999). Men of Asian descent in the United States are often represented in dominant outlets as being less masculine in comparison to European American men (Eng, 2001). Fearing that I would be read as an illegitimate native, I found myself explaining to participants that I had lived in the neighborhood for close to 17 years.

My generic use of Nepali identity was further complicated when one male teacher who came from an underrepresented ethnic group asked that I consider ethnic issues in my research "since you come from a majority ethnic group." A female teacher similarly spoke about how I ought to look into gender issues within my research since women have historically received less attention in the schooling process. Most of the teachers seemed to agree that discourses of difference were more prominent in society because of the tensions brought by the Maoist insurgency.[6] It seemed that my unproblematic use of a generic Nepali identification subsumed the significance of ethnic and gender differences in doing "home" research.[7] Even when I was committed to working against gender, sexual, racial, and social class aspects of oppression in the United States, I seemed less concerned to trouble my/participants' ethnic and gender identities in Nepal. My longing for a "home" identity sought a selective attachment to nationalist discourses, which have historically privileged male, heterosexual, and certain ethnic identifications in imagining a national identity and citizenship. Similar to Coloma (2008), "I had to come to terms with the idea that the power of essentialism was simultaneously its allure and downfall: it offered both a badge of belonging and definition as well as a shackle of rigidity and constraint" (p. 24).

The Ethics of Speaking about the Self

In spite of being partially open about my identities, I often found myself being evasive when responding to questions the teachers raised, especially related to my personal background or topics about Nepali politics. Because of my lack of in-depth knowledge about local political events, I felt that by being open about my responses, I might be viewed as a less legitimate researcher. I was aware of how the unevenness in the exchange of knowledge was making me complicit in exploitive research practices. Western-educated researchers are rarely trained to talk about themselves in fieldwork, and self-other binaries are reinforced because of the researchers' inability or unwillingness to share their backgrounds and viewpoints. Examining the political context of fieldwork in Afghanistan, Shahrani (1994) argues that researchers who return to their places of birth often find it difficult to explain their "new" identities. Returning researchers may hold different perspectives on social issues and, as Shahrani points out, may fear alienating their participants by sharing their views. Describing her fieldwork in Egypt, Abu-Lughod (1988) explores the difficulties she faced in explaining her identities and her avoidance in speaking about her personal life. She writes about explaining her father's Muslim and Arab background to her informants, yet she did not reveal her U.S. affiliations since for many Bedouin "to have become associated with Americans, as a woman, would not have meant being modern, wealthy, or power, but immoral and 'fallen'" (p. 149). Abu-Lughod explains:

> I was asking them to be honest and was trying to find out what their lives were like, but was unwilling to reveal much about myself. I was presenting them with a persona. They knew nothing of my life in the U.S.—my friends, family, university, apartment—in short, much of what I considered part of my identity. I felt compelled to lie to them about some aspects of this life, simply because they could not have helped judging it and me in their own terms. In that scheme, my reputation as a young woman would have suffered. So I doctored my descriptions, and changed the subject when they asked about me, but I felt uncomfortable doing so. (p. 148)

What Abu-Lughod argues is that researchers consider the complex nature of ethical dilemmas they face in fieldwork and the ways they respond may influence their relationship with participants. The ethical issues raised by Abu-Lughod speak of how participants may interpret the nature of knowledge, including sensitive information, that researchers share in research. Undoubtedly researchers have to make decisions about what to share and what not to share without compromising the ethics of research. When asked to share my experiences in the United States, I wondered how I should respond. I often feared that I would be misunderstood if I were to provide candid responses. The following exchange with a male teacher reveals the nature of questions researchers may be asked and consequently the kinds of challenges researchers face in regard to being open and honest about their responses.

> Teacher: Do you live in an apartment in *Amerika*? You probably have to drive?
> Binaya: We bought a house. My wife has a car, and I have one.
> Teacher: You should give one to your parents. They don't have one. You must be rich.
> Binaya: It is all credit in *Amerika*.
> Teacher: Well, you are still rich. Does your family have a lot of Nepali people near you?
> Binaya: Some. Not many. But I have contacts with a few families.
> Teacher: Then how do you raise your kids?
> Binaya: It is hard, and I speak to them in Nepali often.
> Teacher: I would not be able to live where you are. So you have a lot of American friends from work?
> Binaya: Yes. All kinds of people.
> Teacher: What do you mean?
> Binaya: Some are Nepali. Some are White. Many are Black or Asian or people of different backgrounds. And I connect with Nepali people.

My inability and unwillingness to come clean about my socioeconomic background, as reflected in my response of "it is all credit," speaks to how I was economically positioned in Nepal. The interaction speaks to how researchers cannot avoid highlighting the economic context in which they do fieldwork. Because of the kinds of economic privilege they embody, it is not uncommon for European or European American researchers to be perceived as the face of neocolonialism when they research within third world contexts (Lather, 2004). D'Amico-Samuels (1991) maintains that European American researchers have benefited from local-global conditions that allow them easy access to the "field." In general, Western researchers, because of their privileged positions, often feel that there is no need to reflect on how their personal and professional identities are connected to larger sociopolitical discourses.

Similarly, I have come to recognize that my openness to discussing my connections to Nepali families in the United States and the distinctions I make among racial-ethnic categories mostly came about because of my fear of being perceived as culturally "White." In Nepal as well as in the global context, people often interpret "American" as being White. When one is perceived as being an *Amerikan*, this implies that one is culturally and economically White. As a brown person of Nepali birth who is fluent in Nepali, the participants certainly did not think I was racially White. However, I displayed the cultural aspect of *Amerikaness*. Rosaldo (1989) argues that researchers need to move away from the perspective that participants are the only ones who express and embody cultures. He asks, "What are the analytical consequences of making 'our' cultural selves invisible?" (p. 198). For Rosaldo, the practice of "them" having cultures (meaning they are exotic and "primitive") and us being without cultures implies that we have become modernized and presumably "postcultural." He asks that we not mask our cultural selves in the research process but be open and accountable about our identities and practices.

Conclusion

Halfie approaches to research contribute to our understanding about the complexities of negotiating insider and outsider identities in transnational fieldwork. In our research practices, we need to be honest with the participants about our positionalities since the desire to maintain an image of being on the "inside" can be problematic. Even though I was an insider in many ways, the participants identified certain outsider aspects of my identity, and maintaining the image of insider-only was unethical. My desire to claim an authentic local identity was fraught with problems. I sought a local identity, and my longing for a narrow version of "home-identity" was idealistic since it did not take into consideration my partial outsider status. Often I did not critically reflect on why I was reluctant to share what was asked from me. The contradictory moves I made to avoid my hybrid identity, which I claimed in the United States, speaks of the problematic nature in which we may claim legitimacy in research that in my case operated with the assumption that I would somehow "fit in" despite differences. In other words, halfie researchers can be "natives," yet they can also be "outsiders" on some levels.

Halfie insights into rigorous research practices can enable possibilities to rethink the meaning of field, which has historically been constructed as a dichotomy between local and global as well as between "home" and "field." Traditionally, as Jackson (2004) notes, the idea of "field" has been spoken as an exotic place where Western researchers traveled "to master the life-ways of specific cultures so thoroughly and completely as to understand those cultures as though one were looking through the natives' own eyes" (p. 33). Home, on the other hand, has been defined as a safe and detached place where researchers returned to write their field accounts. Likewise, halfie interpretation of research suggests the need to look at local-global connections since researchers cannot ignore how contemporary global conditions influence the changing ideas of fieldwork. We need to consider how "global flows in trade, politics, and the media stimulate greater interpenetration between cultures" (Narayan,

1993, p. 682). Thus, (halfie) researchers conducting international fieldwork may benefit by situating their research within structural contexts since the "field" they have traveled into is connected to global sociopolitical discourses.

Researchers will benefit by examining how, despite good intentions, they might be complicit in marginalizing participants' ways of knowing and being. For Villenas (2000), researchers who culturally affiliate with communities they are researching need to question how their home and professional training may make them complicit in the research process. Although researchers often claim of "knowing" and may identify themselves as the "knower" of the "discovered" knowledge, in reality the information gained through research on a particular topic is rather limited, considering what a community already knows and the knowledge a community may not share with researchers. By being open about our identities and experiences, we move toward developing ethical relationships in fieldwork. As I learned in my experiences, we are often unable to answer the questions that are posed to us, which can be attributed to our lack of knowledge about specific topics. Researchers who identify with specific cultural communities or those who have established long-term relationships are expected to already have some knowledge about local issues.

When conducting research in non-Western societies, investigators may benefit by examining writings that have been published within the country, including in local languages. This helps researchers understand the complex ways local communities have approached educational discourses. I have come to recognize that academic journals published in Nepal, whether they are written in Nepali or in English, rarely circulate in U.S. academic institutions. It is common to find research studies conducted in Nepal to be published in the English language as opposed to the local languages. Too often, Western academic researchers believe that they can get by without consulting "native" sources that are often deemed as less rigorous and less credible, yet indigenous researchers often feel the pressure to consult Western sources in order to be considered legitimate scholars.

While the scholarly literature on reflexivity calls for researchers to be open about their identities, my experiences suggest that one can be complicit in the act of being open. Perhaps because of the contradictory identities I expressed, I found the notion of being open in fieldwork to be a messy process. Despite my best intentions, I struggled to navigate through the ways of conducting research since I embodied complicit as well as resistant identities. It was the incongruities that I encountered as a halfie researcher that helped me look into how fieldwork can be a messy practice. By looking at the gaps and uncertainties in our research, we can better understand the complexities of theorizing reflexivity, including how we may be open and accountable yet complicit at the same time.

Notes

1. Native research is a body of scholarship produced by researchers whose communities have historically been the object of Western research (Jackson, 2004; Medicine, 2001).
2. This portion of the data was collected in 2000 and 2004.
3. Students who start their formal schooling in the rural regions, where the teaching of English is not emphasized due to the lack of school facilities and qualified teachers, face formidable challenges in their plight to graduate from high school.
4. As John notes, the term "sanctioned ignorance" is coined by Spivak (1988).
5. *Bedeshi* means foreign(er) in Nepali, and the term *Amerika* is often used to speak about the United States.
6. Contemporary political problems in Nepal, including the Maoist insurgency, which had spread to close to one-third of the country during the time of the research, can be attributed to the country's economic conditions in which approximately 42 percent of the population is estimated to live in poverty. The average per capita income in Nepal is less than U.S. $300 per year, and close to 80 percent of the population makes a living in agricultural sectors. In the city of Kathmandu, where I conducted the research, the political effects of the conflict were felt by everyone. Everyday conversations, whether in schools or community events, centered on Maoist-Government conflicts. The Maoist party won the general elections in 2008.
7. For analysis of the marginalization of gender and ethnicity issues in the Nepali educational context, see Luitel (1992) and Koirala (1998).

References

Abu-Lughod, L. (1991). Writing against culture. In R. Fox (Ed.), *Recapturing anthropology: Working in the present* (pp. 137–162). Santa Fe, NM: School of American Research Press.

Abu-Lughod, L. (1988). Fieldwork of a dutiful daughter. In S. Altorki & C. F. El-Solh (Eds.), *Arab women in the field: Studying your own society* (pp. 139–161). Syracuse, NY: Syracuse University Press.

Alridge, D. P. (2003). The dilemmas, challenges, and duality of an African-American educational historian. *Educational Researcher, 32*(9), 25–34.

Amadiume, I. (1993). The mouth that spoke a falsehood will later speak the truth: Going home to the field in Eastern Africa. In D. Bell, P. Caplan, & W. J. Karim (Eds.), *Gendered fields: Women, men and ethnography* (pp. 182–198). New York: Routledge.

Battachan, K. B. (1999). Globalization and its impact on Nepalese society and culture. In M. K. Dahal (Ed.), *Impact of globalization in Nepal* (pp. 80–102). Kathmandu: Nepal Foundations for Advanced Studies.

Behar, R. (1996). *The vulnerable observer: Anthropology that breaks your heart.* Boston, MA: Bacon.

Brayboy, B. (2000). The Indian and the researcher: Tales from the field. *International Journal of Qualitative Studies in Education, 13*(4), 415–426.

Chaudhry, L. N. (2000). Researching "my people," researching myself: Fragments of a reflexive tale. In E. St. Pierre & W. Pillow (Eds.), *Working the ruins: Feminist post-structural research and practice in education* (pp. 96-113). New York: Routledge.

Coloma, R. S. (2008). Border crossing subjectivities and research: Through the prism of feminists of color. *Race Ethnicity and Education, 11*(1), 11-27.

D'Amico-Samuels, D. (1991). Undoing fieldwork: Personal, political, theoretical and methodological implications. In F. Harrison (Ed.), *Decolonizing anthropology: Moving further toward an anthropology of liberation* (pp. 68-87). Washington: American Anthropological Association.

Daza, S. L. (2008). Decolonizing researcher authenticity. *Race Ethnicity and Education, 11*(1), 71-85.

Delgado-Gaitan, C. (1993). Researching change and changing the researcher. *Harvard Education Review, 64*(4), 389-411.

Dillard, C. B. (2006). *On spiritual strivings: Transforming an African American woman's academic life.* Albany: State University of New York Press.

Du Bois, W. E. B. (1989). *The soul of black folk.* New York: Bantam.

Eng, D. (2001). *Racial castration: Managing masculinity in Asian America.* Durham, NC: Duke University Press.

Enloe, C. (1989). *Making feminist sense of international politics.* Berkeley: University of California Press.

Escobar, A. (1993). The limits of reflexivity: Politics in anthropology's post-writing culture era. *Journal of Anthropological Research, 49*(4), 377-391.

Fabian, J. (1990). Presence and representation: The Other and anthropological writing. *Critical Inquiry, 16,* 753-772.

Facio, E. (1993). Ethnography as personal experience. In J. H. Stanfield II & R. M. Dennis (Eds.), *Race and ethnicity in research methods* (pp. 75-91). Newbury Park, CA: Sage.

Hall, S. (1990). Cultural identity and diaspora. In J. Rutherford (Ed.), *Identity, community, culture, difference* (pp. 222-237). London: Lawrence and Wishart.

Harrison, F. D. (Ed.). (1991). *Decolonizing anthropology: Moving further toward an anthropology of liberation.* Washington, DC: American Anthropological Association.

Jackson, Jr., J. L. (2004). An ethnographic *flimflam*: Giving gifts, doing research, and videotaping the native subject/object. *American Anthropologist, 106*(1), 32-42.

Jacobs-Huey, L. (2002). The natives are grazing and talking back: Reviewing the problematics of positionality, voice, and accountability among "native" anthropologists. *American Anthropologist, 104*(3), 791-804.

John, M. E. (1989). *Discrepant dislocations: Feminism, theory and postcolonial histories.* Berkeley: University of California Press.

Juluri, V. (1998). Globalizing audience studies: The audience and its landscape and living room wars. *Critical Studies in Mass Communication, 15,* 85-90.

Koirala, B. N. (1998). *Participatory approach to education for Dalits in Nepal.* Kathmandu: CERID.

Kondo, D. (1990). *Crafting selves: Power, gender, and discourses of identity in a Japanese workplace.* Chicago, IL: University of Chicago Press.

Lather, P. (2004). Ethics now: White woman goes to Africa and loses her voice. Paper presented at the American Educational Research Association. San Diego, CA.

Lee, R. G. (1999). *Orientals: Asian American in popular culture.* Philadelphia, PA: Temple University Press.

Luitel, S. (1992). *Women in development.* Nayabazar, Nepal: Karnali.

Marcus, G. E. (1994). What comes (just) after "post"?. In N. K. Denzin & Y. S. Lincoln (Eds.),

Handbook of qualitative research (pp. 563-574). Thousand Oaks, CA: Sage.
Medicine, B. (2001). *Learning to be an anthropologist and remaining "native."* Chicago, IL: University of Illinois Press.
Motzafi-Haller, P. (1997). Writing birthright: On native anthropologists and the politics of representation. In D. E. Reed-Danahhay (Ed.), *Auto/ethnography: Rewriting the self and the social* (pp. 195-222). Oxford, UK: Berg.
Narayan, K. (1993). How native is a "native anthropologist"? *American Anthropologist, 95,* 671-685.
Omi, M., & Winant, H. (1986). *Racial formations in the United States.* New York: Routledge.
Parameswaran, R. (2001). Feminist media ethnography in India: Exploring power, gender and culture in the field. *Qualitative Inquiry, 7*(1), 69-103.
Pillow, W. (2003). Confession, catharsis, or cure?: Rethinking the uses of reflexivity as methodological power in qualitative research. *International Journal of Qualitative Studies in Education, 16*(2), 175-196.
Rhee, J. (2003). Traveling through our stuck places: Race, gender and cultural citizenship. *Inquiry: Critical Thinking Across the Disciplines, 22*(2), 45-56.
Rosaldo, R. (1989). *Culture and truth: The remaking of social analysis.* Boston, MA: Beacon.
Said, E. (1989). Representing the colonized: Anthropology's interlocutors. *Critical Inquiry, 14,* 205-225.
Shahrani, M. N. (1994). Honored guest and marginal man: Long-term field research and predicaments of a native anthropologist. In D. Fowler & D. Hardesty (Eds.), *Others knowing others: Perspectives on ethnographic careers* (pp. 15-67). London, UK: Smithsonian Institution.
Shrestha, N. P. (1997). *In the name of development: A reflection on Nepal.* Lanham, MD: University Press of America.
Smith, L. T. (2005). On tricky ground: Researching the native in the age of uncertainty. In N. Denzin & Y. S. Lincoln (Eds.), *Handbook of qualitative research* (pp. 85-107). Thousand Oaks, CA: Sage.
Spivak, G. C. (1988). Can the subaltern speak? In C. Nelson & L. Grossberg (Eds.), *Marxism and the interpretation of culture* (pp. 271-313). Urbana: University of Illinois Press.
Subreenduth, S. (2008). Deconstructing the politics of a differently colored transnational identity. *Race Ethnicity and Education, 11*(1), 41-55.
Van Maanen, J. (1988). *The tales of the field: On writing ethnography.* Cambridge, MA: Harvard University Press.
Villenas, S. (2000). This ethnography called my back: Writings of the exotic gaze, "Othering" Latina, and recuperating Xicanisma. In E. St. Pierre & W. Pillow (Eds.), *Working the ruins: Feminist post-structural research and practice in education* (pp. 74-95). New York: Routledge.
Visweswaran, K. (1994). *Fictions of feminist ethnography.* Minneapolis: University of Minnesota Press.
Williams, B. F. (1996). Skinfolk, not kinfolk: Comparative reflections on the identity of participant-observation in two field situations. In D. Wolf (Ed.), *Feminist dilemmas in fieldwork* (pp. 72-95). New York: Westview.

CHAPTER 19

The Noninnocence of Recognition: Subjects and Agency in Education

STEPHANIE LYNN DAZA

> Postcolonial critique bears witness to those countries and communities [and subjects]–in the North and the South, urban and rural–constituted, if I may coin a phrase, "otherwise than modernity." Such cultures [and subjects] of postcolonial *contra-modernity* may be contingent to modernity, discontinuous or in contention with it, resistant to its oppressive, assimilationist technologies; but they also deploy the cultural hybridity of their borderline conditions to "translate," and therefore reinscribe, the social imaginary.
>
> — Bhabha, 1994, p. 6

How is a nonunitary, discursively constituted subject, a subject constituted "otherwise than modernity," not disempowered in its impurity, deviance, and complicity, but rather linked with agency, not through essentialism, but through its ability to, echoing Bhabha above, deploy the cultural hybridity of borderline conditions in order to reinscribe the social imaginary? How is this subject (mis)recognized? My interest in subjectification, the production of subjects and subject authenticity, is deeply autobiographical. As a light-brown, feminine-looking queer woman, born in the United States and adopted by a racially prejudiced, homophobic, working-class white family in the Midwest, my construction of who I am and how others have constructed me are often different and complicated. After years of hearing my family's slurs based on race and skin color, I asked, "Don't you realize you are talking about me?" To which they responded, "You aren't that dark." I left my "home" and "family" in the Midwest in search of a "real" identity and a "real" home, settling in San Diego at the U.S.-Mexican border, and then living in Bolivia as a Peace Corps volunteer, where I hoped to learn and did learn Spanish as a second language. My journey and desire to speak *and live* Spanish was wrapped up in my search for legitimacy as a brown person of color and, of course, my presumption, grounded deep in humanist ideals, of what an authentic brown subject ought to be. In hindsight, my adopted family did recognize me; indeed, I'm not that dark. I am a light-skinned Brown person and a dark-complexioned White one, but recognition is more complicated than that.

Can/do we "make" our selves legitimate, as Yoshino (2006) suggests, by covering some traits and playing up others? Rather than the need to uncover the self, as if a true self exists, do we need to uncover the idea of the "true self" as an effect of a humanistic discourse of authenticity and recognition? Does the possibility of being more human ironically lie in the hope of posthumanism, in decolonizing our investments in being human outside of discursive narratives within which we are shaped? Rather than giving up on recognition, might we reimagine recognition as less innocent and more complicated?

This chapter focuses on the noninnocence of recognition as part and parcel of the process of subjectification. It discusses the constitution of subjects to delineate the implications of staying in the ruins of foundationalism in order to decolonize our investments in humanist conceptions of subject authenticity. Drawing on postcolonial and psychoanalytic frameworks, the chapter complicates ideas of subject authenticity presented in my previously published article, "Decolonizing Researcher Authenticity" (Daza, 2008). It takes to task the theoretical underpinnings of that article, specifically Yoshino's (2006) use of object relations scholar D. W. Winnicott (1896-1971). The chapter's purpose is threefold: (1) to provide an overview of the theoretical perspectives on subject and recognition; (2) to unpack the humanist discourses in the conceptualization of my article "Decolonizing Researcher Authenticity" (hereto referred as DRA); and (3) to explore the implications of theorizing subjects using the noninnocence of recognition as a relevant perspective for rethinking subject production and agency in education.

Subject Matters

This section offers theoretical perspectives on the "subject" by examining its formation within three frameworks: Humanism, the Post, and Postcolonial.

Humanism

In its Enlightenment guise, the self is conceptualized as a stable, coherent, rational, and knowable entity, and "becomes the basis for a mode of knowing that is considered 'scientific' [and] ... deemed to be both 'true' and 'objective'"

(Peters & Burbules, 2004, p. 40). Humanism is a grand theory that "has produced a diverse range of knowledge projects since man (a specific Western, Enlightened male) first began to believe that he, as well as God, could, through the right use of reason, produce truth and knowledge" (St. Pierre & Pillow, 2000, p. 5). The same humanist discourse that constitutes the knowing subject as sovereign also constitutes an object of study, which the knowing subject can understand, categorize, and even "help" (e.g., as analyst, warden, teacher, and researcher) (Foucault, 1965/1988, 1966/1994). With the power to define legitimate power as neutral and disinterested, the humanist hope is that the knowing subject can utilize knowledge for freedom and socially beneficial progress (Flax, 1991).

Humanism has been used by various groups "to color and to justify the conceptions of man to which it is, after all, obliged to take recourse" (Foucault, 1997, p. 314).[1] Examples include the Nazis' desire to "cleanse" society of Jews, Israel's delegitimization of Palestine, and the Catholic mission to "civilize" indigenous peoples. The effects of humanism for people "on the wrong side of humanism's subject/object binaries—male/female, white/black, rich/poor, heterosexual/homosexual, healthy/ill, and so on" have been devastating (St. Pierre & Pillow, 2000, p. 5). Questions of the limits of such foundations have emerged from conditions of demographic and social changes and have led to the production of oppositional knowledge (Fanon, 1967/1951; Freire, 1970; Lorde, 1984).

Foucault (1997) draws a distinction between humanism (reoccurring value-laden themes) and the Enlightenment (events and historical processes). The simultaneous interrogation of "man's relation to the present, man's historical mode of being, and the constitution of the self as an autonomous subject" has roots in the Enlightenment (p. 312). Thus, it is in the ruins of the Enlightenment where we find ways to work through humanism, but against its limits; or rather, "the critique of what we are is at one and the same time the historical analysis of the limits imposed on us and an experiment with the possibility of going beyond them" (p. 319).

The Post

Many theoretical trajectories contribute to what can now be referred to as a prolific "post" period (St. Pierre & Pillow, 2000). By "post," I mean the various turns in social science that have worked within and against humanism to denaturalize it as foundational, but not replace it with another grand narrative. Foucault (1997) writes, "we must try to proceed with the analysis of ourselves as beings who are historically determined, to a certain extent, by the Enlightenment" (p. 313). The choice is not "either accept the Enlightenment and remain within the tradition of its rationalism... [or] criticize [it] and then try to escape from its principles of rationality... [or even to] determine what good and bad elements there may have been" (ibid.). The interest of the post "lies in the awareness that the epistemological 'limits' of those ethnocentric ideas are also the enunciative boundaries of a range of other dissonant, even dissident histories and voices.... It is in this sense that the boundary becomes a place from which something begins its presencing" (Bhabha, 1994, pp. 4-5). Herein is the idea of "working the ruins" of humanism (Lather, 1997) by staying in the ruins of foundationalism rather than replacing it. For "recognition," a core concept of humanism, this is where a noninnocent recognition may emerge as useful.

One of the key turns of the post period is central to understanding what Yoshino theorizes as covering, or coerced assimilation. He argues that "what society comes to imagine as 'normal' and 'mainstream' are myths that limit us by forcing us to highlight privileged traits and hide disadvantaged ones in order to fit in" (Daza, 2008, p. 72). In other words, mainstream discourses about identity shape subjects. According to Foucault (1972), discourses "systematically form the objects about which they speak" (p. 49).

> [T]he set of rules which at a given period and for a given society define: the limits and forms of the *sayable*. What is it possible to speak of? .... What utterances does everyone recognize as valid, or debatable, or definitely invalid? .... What individuals, what groups or classes have access to a particular kind of discourse? .... the relationship institutionalized between the discourse, speakers and its destined audience [and] .... How is struggle for control of discourses conducted between classes, nations, linguistic, cultural or ethnic collectivities? (Foucault, 1968/1991, pp. 59-60)

While humanism is "subject-centered" and assumes that the knowing subject can trace social processes and understand experience, the ruins of foundationalism are "subject-constructed" and question the role of the subject (researcher) as knower and the subject's ability to know outside of the effects of, and the knowledge produced by, discourse that also constitutes, legitimizes, and authorizes the subject as knower (Foucault, 1966/1994). Likewise, the object is constituted within discourse and by the knowing subject. Coloma (2008) defines the process of subjectification as "an ongoing and situated negotiation of self-naming and being named by others that relies on visible and non-visible markers of difference and is implicated in power relations" (p. 20). In DRA, I provided an example of this process, showing how researcher authenticity was constituted by various discourses. This chapter explores the process of subject recognition, not subjectification. How are subjects recognized in the process of subjectification and/or as a result of it?

One of the most salient criticisms of post ideas is the lack of (or limited) agency that a subject constituted by discourse has and how this limits the possibility of social justice work. While power works through "coherent regulatory fictions" (Butler, 1999/1990), according to post ideas, discourse is not static. "Paradoxically," Butler (1999/1990) notes that "the reconceptualization of identity as an *effect*, that is, as *produced* or *generated*, opens up possibilities of 'agency' that are insidiously foreclosed by positions that take identity categories as foundational and fixed. For an identity to be an effect means that it is neither fatally determined nor fully artificial and arbitrary" (p. 187). Staying in the ruins of foundationalism indicates that subjects both produce discourse and are produced by discourse. Unfixing the subject, a posthumanist idea of the subject, or what Coloma (2008) calls "constituted subjectivity," keeps open the possibility for different dynamics because it frees up the subject from being fixed (as either privileged or oppressed) and interrupts the subject/object binary.

When taken-for-granted truths and knowing subjects become the effects, and not the original cause, of discourses, new possibilities emerge for thinking about subjects (researchers), objects of study (participants and things studied), knowledge production (research, truths, data, policy, and so on), and the relationship among subjects, objects, and knowledge. For example, Proctor's study of teachers' responses to the No Child Left Behind Act illustrates how knowledge production is not one directional, but is shaped by participants when teachers are repositioned as actors in shaping policy (Proctor & Demerath, 2008).

Despite the proliferation of post perspectives, there has been a reassertion of humanist themes, or the "(re)privileging of positivism" in science (Lather, 2007). Such (re)privileging is a reaction to the post period: "When it seems that science is becoming unmoored, when too many odd people claim to be scientists, when multiple forms of valid knowledge proliferate, reaction formations are inevitable" (St. Pierre & Roulston, 2006, p. 678). It also is a result of "a worldwide audit culture with its governmental demands for evidence-based practices" (Lather, 2007, p. 3).

Postcolonial

In "The Possibilities of Postcolonial Praxis in Education," Subedi and I state that a primary concern of postcolonial studies is the critique of imperialism and its legacies. This includes "the severe limitation of claiming universal notions of history, experiences, and/or culture that subsumes differences" (Subedi & Daza, 2008, p. 2). One of the postcolonial challenges for education, then, is the work of decolonizing. Decolonizing work is staying in the ruins by simultaneously referencing intelligible forms and working their limits to interrupt their legitimacy and authenticity (Muñoz, 1999). Therefore, the discursive production of a nonunitary subject is not disempowered in its impurity, but rather is linked with agency through its ability to deploy hybridity that taps into and reinscribes subject authenticity. Following Anzaldúa's (1999/1987) concepts of "mestiza" and "borderlands/la frontera" that refuse either/or identities for self or home, and would rather negotiate the in-between-ness of subjects and places constructed as unitary, the effect of a postcolonial theoretical perspective on subject authenticity and recognition is more about sustaining contradictions and ambivalence, rather than unified coherence. Thus (mis)recognition, an effect of the process of subjectification—and the pleasure and pain of being hailed by others as the subject that one sometimes ascribes and refuses for oneself—is acknowledged in post and postcolonial frameworks (Benjamin, 2006).

Research in the post and education has begun to take seriously the constitution of subjects but, with a few exceptions, post research has not fully addressed the concept of recognition (Butler, 2004; Benjamin, 2006). Recognition has implications for interpretations, even if interpretation may not end in recognition. To misread or misrecognize presupposes knowing, recognition, or, in short, *a* reading. Whether fixed or constituted, how are subjects and their agency recognized or misrecognized?

Theoretical Perspectives of Recognition

> Now, we can begin to see why the threat of the (mis)translation..., among the ... peoples who pick through the refuse, is a constant reminder to the postimperial West, of the hybridity of its mother tongue, and the heterogeneity of its national space. (Bhabha, 1994, p. 60)

Bhabha (1994) notes that in the ruins of foundationalism when dispossessed subjects "pick through the refuse" (the loss of unitary, coherent, and knowable subjects that were possible under humanism in its Enlightenment guise), the threat of (mis)translation is the possibility of recognition. In the rejection of a humanist subject/object, the edge of identification emerges: "otherness has left its traumatic mark" and is recognized (p. 62). However, difference—not similarity—has been at the crux of post analyses, including my own (Daza, 2008). Bhabha (1994) even argues that "what is theoretically innovative, and politically crucial, is the need to think beyond narratives of originary and initial subjectivities and to focus on those moments or processes that are produced in the articulation of cultural differences" (p. 1).

What work is done when recognition, not difference, is the focus? How is being recognized as one positions oneself as similar and different to being hailed in ways that one does not position oneself? Is this recognition? How is complicating recognition as less innocent and less certain useful to understanding subject production? How do we know if/when we are recognized and misrecognized? In the DRA article, I focused on how the same referent could be read differently in different contexts and by different people, and argued that the ambivalence inherent in imagining and inscribing subjects unfixes the subject and provides productive gaps for new narratives of researcher authenticity to emerge. I was interested in decolonizing research's investment in nondiscursive subjects through difference, rather than through recognition. At the beginning of the chapter, I chart my investment in subject agency and authenticity though difference, accustomed to being positioned in ways that are different from how I position myself. However fleeting and superficial, there are times when my subject of desire seems to be either affirmed by others or at least not misrecognized. Below I analyze two situations to think about the process of recognition.

My first example took place at a Bikram yoga class that I take in Dallas, Texas. A classmate, assuming that my mother only spoke Spanish, stated that it might be hard for her to take the yoga class since it is in English. My classmate recognized me as having a Spanish-speaking family. Although my husband and I speak to each other and to our son in Spanish, my white adoptive mother from the Midwest is a monolingual English speaker. Some kind of interpretation, perhaps part misrecognition and part recognition, happened, but recognition is more complicated than the humanistic notion that my classmate knows me or my family for who I/we "really" am/are.

My second example also illustrates a less innocent notion of recognition. At a Dallas raw food gathering that I attended with my son in May 2008, I was asked if I had a partner, not a husband. In almost every other situation where my son and I were together, I was misrecognized as heterosexual (Daza, 2008). That I was asked if I had a partner, rather than assuming that either I was a single mother or I had a husband, opened up different subject positions for me as a self-identified queer woman. Recognition is not so much about naming or knowing a subject as this or that, but about leaving open the possibility to be otherwise.

Situating Recognition

From Hegel to Butler (2004) and Benjamin (2006), "recognition" has been an important concept in understanding subject authenticity that gets lost in the prevailing discussions about difference. It could be argued that difference is predicated on recognition or rather the lack of recognition and its limits. The articulation of and encounter with cultural differences are only intelligible in light of the possibility of likes. The degree to which difference is valued over likes or likes over difference might be situated along a spectrum between two polarities: Habermasian verses post theories (Passerin d'Entrèves, 1997).

Habermas prefers to see the project of modernity as flawed and unfinished, but is hopeful in its rational potential for emancipation and Enlightenment. Unlike the post, Habermas does not focus on difference, ambiguity, or the linguistic turn. According to Williams (1997), "Habermas favors an inclusive paradigm, [which is] an alternative to subject-centered reason ... [and an escape from] the subject-object paradigm, objectification, Foucauldian dividing practices, and the like" (p. 15). In an inclusive paradigm, "participants in interaction and institutions are no longer originators who master others and situations but are members and products of traditions in which they stand and solidarity groups to which they belong" (ibid.).

One of the main concerns of post theorists with respect to Habermasian theory is its simplistic accounting of recognition. As Butler (2004) explains, "Recognition is not the simple presentation of a subject for another that facilitates the recognition of that self-presenting subject by the Other" (pp. 131-132). Recognition is a complicated process where the subject-other are reflected in one another but where neither collapses. "Mutual recognition only becomes possible in the context of a shared orientation.... [E]ach recognizes the other in virtue of the form each gives to the world... True subjectivities come to flourish only in communities that provide for reciprocal recognition, for we do not come to ourselves ... alone, but through the acknowledging look of the Other who confirms us" (Butler, 1987, p. 57). For the post, recognition is "a site of power by which the human is differentially produced" (Butler, 2004, p. 2). Butler explains that "the terms by which we are recognized as human are socially articulated and changeable." Conferring "humanness" on some and depriving others of it presents "the problem of who qualifies as recognizably human and who does not"; "it is only through the experience of recognition that any of us becomes constituted as socially viable beings" (ibid.).

Benjamin (2006), drawing on Winnicott (examined in the next section), stakes out a middle ground along the spectrum. With simple harmony on one end and complete disorientation on the other, Benjamin follows Butler with the caveat of the possibility of recognition, albeit not permanent or with any regularity. She theorizes what she calls "thirdness" as a space that is possible when recognition is a two-way street. Benjamin's focus is on "the process of creating thirdness, that is, on how we build relational systems and how we develop the intersubjectivity capacities for such co-creation" (p. 119). She explains that "co-creation gives rise to a radically different notion of third ... as the principle of respect and activity on the part of both sides, even the side traditionally defined as passive" (ibid.). This shows the fragility of the two-way cocreated third space and "its susceptibility to a kind of breakdown in which the patter of 'doer and done to' predominates" (p. 19). In such a breakdown, with the collapse of thirdness or recognition, Benjamin argues that the dominance of subject-object opposition and one-way direction of effects are more clearly visible and that the subjects are coparticipants in the creation of the thirdness or in its breakdown.

The Ruin of Humanism in Yoshino and Winnicott

In the "Decolonizing Researcher Authenticity" (DRA) article, I draw on Kenji Yoshino's (2006) notion of covering as a theoretical framework to unpack subject authenticity. As the process of writing DRA came to a close, I regretted not providing more analysis of what I came to read as a humanistic discourse of authenticity in Yoshino's work. Left unexplored was Yoshino's use of Winnicott's theory of True and False Selves that inspired his uncovered and covered selves, respectively. That humanistic discourses inform covering is not surprising since "we are always speaking within the language of humanism" (St. Pierre & Pillow, 2000, p. 4). My aim is not to dismiss Yoshino's work for its humanist discourse, but to provide a more complex understanding of it and its uses for understanding subject authenticity and recognition. This is not a story about moving from, or out of, humanism to posthumanism: "the reason there is no story to be told is that none of these stories are the past; these stories are continuing to happen in simultaneous and overlapping ways as we tell them" (Butler, 2004, p. 4).

Yoshino. Yoshino's writing about humanity and authenticity is grounded in humanism. He argues that authenticity is being who we fully are: "individuals cannot articulate what authenticity is, but know an existence lived outside its imperative would be a substitute for life" (Yoshino, 2006, p. 186). Yoshino seems to believe that there is a possibility of "full humanity," but argues that "*the mainstream is a myth*" (p. 25; italics in the original). On the one hand, by viewing the mainstream as a myth, he recognizes that narratives produce subjects. On the other, when he talks about a "universal project of human flourishing" and "the virtue of inhabiting a more authentic self that one is simultaneously more alive and inert," he presumes that we can get outside of discursive narratives to become and unveil a true self (pp. 25, 72). Yoshino's hope is that subjects will be able to assert their true selves and that the law will recognize them. My purpose is to address the fluctuation in Yoshino's logic to illustrate the importance of theorizing recognition, not just performance and subjectification.

Yoshino (2006, pp. 186–187) explains the concept of "authenticity" with an example from Carol Gilligan's work with children. He claims that children have an authentic voice that is lost when they are forced to cover as they spend more time navigating and needing to fit into society. While children may increasingly cover to fit norms, or perhaps become more savvy at performing identities, why would this suggest that they were "real" before? Butler (1999/1990), following Foucault, explains that the body is not "real" in any significant sense prior to its determination within a discourse through which it becomes invested with an "idea" of what is "real." Authenticity, like being "sexed," "gendered," and "raced," "is an historically specific organization of power, discourse, bodies, and affectivity" (p. 117). As such, the innocent use of authenticity produces a "real authentic self" only as a concept of the discourses that disguise the power relations responsible for its genesis.[2]

Yoshino (2006) maintains "that this quest for authenticity is universal" and that the "project of self-elaboration [is] emblematic of the search for authenticity all of us engage in as human beings" (pp. 27, 184). While I agree that the desire for authenticity is strong, whether we all search for it is not my interest, but rather the nature of "authenticity" as innocent or noninnocent is. What does it mean to search for authenticity outside of discursive narratives in light of posthumanist assumptions?

Yoshino (2006) offers that his "ultimate commitment is to autonomy as a means of achieving authenticity, rather than to a fixed conception of what authenticity might be" (p. 190). Thus, while authenticity might not be fixed, it would be married to the idea of an autonomous subject. Although he does not exactly explain what he means by "autonomy," he reinforces the ideas of a sovereign subject and noninnocent authenticity when he suggests that subjects decide what authentic would be for them, rather than the law, the state, or the employer. Butler (2004) notes that while groups may desire more autonomy, "what precisely autonomy means, however, is complicated ... since it turns out that choosing one's own body invariably means navigating among norms that are laid out in advance and prior to one's choice or are being articulated in concert by other minority agencies" (p. 7). She further argues that autonomy, one's sense of one's own subjectivity and ability to determine it, is itself constituted by what is outside of it:

> self-determination becomes a plausible concept only in the context of a social world that supports and enables that exercise of agency and that one only determines "one's own" sense of [subject] to the extent that social norms exist that support and enable that act of claiming [such subject] for oneself. One is dependent on this "outside" to lay claim to what is one's own. The self must, in this way, be dispossessed in sociality in order to take possession of itself. (Butler, 2004, p. 7)

While much of what is outlined above suggests that Yoshino wants us to search for our authentic self outside of the power relations responsible for it, further probing into his use of Winnicott's True Self suggests otherwise. In my DRA article, I posited that Yoshino, much like post theorists, maintains that subjectivity is negotiated between a person's own construction and outside demands. When Yoshino (2006) states that "the True Self is the self that gives an individual the *feeling* of being real" (p. 185, italics added), is this the idea that "feeling real" might be wrought from within discursive narratives of power? What kind of agency, then, might be produced—a free market, consumer agent?—"where consumption is seen as an automatic license of autonomy and pleasure" (Latham, 2002, p. 55)?

While Yoshino (2006) spends fewer than five pages discussing Winnicott's work (1965, 1971), Winnicott's ideas provide the underpinning for his concept of covering. Much of what Yoshino says about the True and False Self seems to present a foundationalist notion of the subject. He argues that the role of the False Self is to hide and protect the True Self by complying with outside demands, such as the demand to cover or assimilate. The False Self "gives an individual a sense of being unreal, a sense of futility, [but] it mediates the relationship between the True Self and the world" (p. 185). According to Yoshino's use of Winnicott, in a healthy individual, the fully realized True Self can strategically use the False Self as a tool in navigating outside demands. In an unhealthy individual, "the False Self completely obscures the True Self, perhaps even from the individual herself. In a less extreme case, the False Self permits the True Self 'a secret life'" (ibid.). Such thinking not only seems to present a humanist notion of the subject, but other problems are unresolved. Why is the True Self the "real" self, especially if the individual believes that the False Self is the real self?

Winnicott. Winnicott's object relations theory has made significant contributions to the development of theories of the subject. As Flax (1991) notes, "certain aspects of Winnicott's [1975] object relations theory, especially the rejection of Enlightenment notions of reason and knowledge and the emphasis on the importance of mothering in the constitution of a self, are particularly compatible and complementary to postmodernist projects and feminist theorizing" (p. 108). He emphasizes the relational work between theory and practice, between analyst and patient, and between mother and child. Like other object relations theorists, he claims that humans require the subject-object relationships (Flax, 1991, p. 111). In contrast to Lacan who "posits an irreducible gap between analyst as the one who 'ought to know' and the desire of the patient," Winnicott "exemplifies the extent to which psychoanalysis *is* a form of relational work" (ibid.). Might Winnicott's work help show the extent to which research is also a form of relational work?

Whereas the True Self enters into and thrives in reciprocal relations with others, the False Self, in Flax's (1991) reading, "is likely to be plagued by feelings of deadness, futility, unreality, rigidity, and an inability to enter into and enjoy reciprocal relations with others" (p. 113). Flax argues that Winnicott's "'false' self ... *is* overly rigid, intellectualized, and controlling an alternate, 'true' one that has many of the characteristics of the postmodernist 'decentered' one" (pp. 110–111). For the most part, Yoshino (2006, p. 185) keeps with this understanding, describing the False Self in its complicity with outside demands and, in so-called healthy individuals, the True Self as partially constituted by the False one.

According to Winnicott (1971/1991) the space of relations between the subject and the object creates "a world of shared reality ... in which the subject can use and which can feed back other-than-me substance into the subject" (p. 94). This is Winnicott's notion of the "transitional space" (e.g., third space) that, according to Flax (1991), is "one of his most important contributions to (possible) post-Enlightenment thinking" by "break[ing] decisively with Enlightenment values in identifying the capacities to play and to 'make use of' and 'relate to' objects, rather than reason, as the qualities most characteristic of human 'being'" (p. 118). The transitional space bridges the gap between subject and object, and in the process, the object is destroyed in the subject-object hierarchical dynamic. Using the examples of parent-baby and analyst-patient, Winnicott (1971/1991) contends that through this destruction the object is no longer an object of the subject-object relationship, but is also a subject. Rather than conceptualizing subjectification as the subject's gaze constructing the object or as the return of such gaze, he offers the possibility of a subject seeing a subject seeing her/his subject.

Winnicott's idea of the subject, particularly as constructed "in and out of relations with others," runs alongside the conditions from which poststructuralist and postcolonial notions of complicity and ambivalence have emerged. Yet, his work remains mired in foundationalism, both deeply invested in and breaking with humanism. First, Winnicott's ideas do not give up the language or desire for a subject outside of discourses that constitute meaning. He offers "strong arguments for the importance of a stable, 'core self'" (Flax, 1991, pp. 110-111). Second, the True Self and the idea of subject/object relations are posited in isolation from other social relations, such as class, gender, and sexuality (p. 161). While subjects both shape and are shaped by relations with others, the "worlding" of the third space is not considered. Following Spivak (1985), I use "worlding" to mean that the imperialism of the third space, with its investment in concepts and thinking that compartmentalize relations and conceal power, such as the hierarchies in binaries, to disguise their workings as natural and legitimate, is not being decolonized. Third, Winnicott does not argue that everything exists within the context of the third space, unlike many post theorists who suggest that everything exists within discursive epistemes. He does not believe that what is produced in the third space is equivalent to or inclusive of external reality, or should be made to conform to outside demands (Winnicott, 1971/1991; Flax, 1991). We see this idea in Yoshino's project of working against forced covering.

Recognition in Yoshino's Covering

How performances are read is implied in Yoshino's work, but his focus is on the subject's performance of playing up and downplaying traits, rather than problematizing how performances and traits are recognized or interpreted. Yoshino argues against covering or playing up traits to fit norms, whether mainstream norms or group-based identity norms. That is, the demand to "act black" or "act gay" by playing up traits (stereotypes) that are associated with such referents infringes upon the subject's authenticity in the same way as the demand to "act white" or "act straight" does. Through his colleague's words, Yoshino troubles his own project and begins to look at the role of recognition or interpretation.

> [As his colleague notes, Yoshino's] commitment is to help people "be themselves" —to resist demands to conform that take away their ability to be the individuals that they are. But the covering idea could perpetuate the stereotypes [it] seeks to eliminate. One way minorities break stereotypes is by acting against them. If every time they do so, people assume they are covering some essential stereotypical identity, the stereotypes will never go away. (Yoshino, 2006, p. 190)

Here we begin to see how the recognition or reading of performances is important to Yoshino's argument. Readers, in part, decide what norms and stereotypes are, if people and their actions affirm or break with mainstream or group identity norms, and to what extent.

Yoshino (2006, pp. 189-190) shares two examples that help illustrate the role of recognition. If a woman does something stereotypically masculine, like fix her bike, Yoshino suggests that she could be read as downplaying feminine traits and playing up masculine ones, rather than simply fixing her bike because it is broken. If an African American academic is studying German Romantic poetry, s/he could be read as trying to cover her/his African American identity, rather than simply studying what s/he was interested in. A reader could not read these examples as covering unless the reader had certain presuppositions about female and African American identities. Subject recognition is not just about how subjects perform, but also how their performances are read by others and how such interpretations are embedded in discourses of power. Meaning rests in the "interplay between the text, author, and reader" (Voithofer, 2005, p. 3).

In the DRA article, I partially explore the need to examine the conditions of possibility for recognition in order to look at the ways in which recognition is discursively produced. That is, certain readings of subjects are rendered (im)possible given certain histories, contexts, readers, and so on. Two examples from DRA are (1) I am rendered intelligible as heterosexual, despite considering myself queer; and (2) when reactions to a family photo labeled my son lucky to have light skin and my nephew unlucky to be darker, the hegemony of the everyday norm that values lighter skin over darker made any response futile and unintelligible. As Butler (2004) aptly puts it, "I may feel that without some recognizability I cannot live. But I may also feel that the terms by which I am recognized make life unlivable" (p. 4).

The tensions described above call for a more complex interrogation of recognition, of the terms by which subjects are constrained and exceeded, in order to open possibilities of living more "authentically," which is what I hope Yoshino (2006) means when he talks about a "universal project of human flourishing" and "the virtue of inhabiting a more authentic self that one is simultaneously more alive and inert" (pp. 25, 72). This is "not to celebrate difference as such but to establish more inclusive conditions for sheltering and maintaining life that resists models of assimilation" (Butler, 2004, p. 4). Covering would be one such model of assimilation. The recognition example that I describe, where I am asked if I have a partner, not a husband, illustrates a way of establishing more inclusive conditions and human flourishing, at least from my point of view.

To Be or Not To Be: Noninnocent Recognition

Working the ruins of narrow, essentializing, imperialist, and mastery knowledge, postoriented education theorists and researchers have been reimagining knowledge and subject production (Kumashiro, 2008; Lather, 2007; Rhee & Subreenduth, 2006; Subedi & Daza, 2008). Since the scholarly literature in education has focused on difference, research on recognition has been limited. This is surprising considering the implications of theorizing recognition for agency and the importance of agency in educational research. Agency is a paradox requiring both recognition and distancing. Butler (2004) explains:

> The "I" that I am finds itself at once constituted by norms and dependent on them but also endeavors to live in ways that maintain a critical and transformative relation to them. This is not easy, because the "I" becomes, to a certain extent unknowable, threatened with unviability, with becoming undone altogether, when it no longer incorporates the norm in such a way that makes this "I" fully recognizable. There is a certain departure from the human that takes place in order to start the process of remaking the human.... The critical relation depends [on] articulat[ing] an alternative, minority version of sustaining norms or ideals that enable me to act. If I am someone who cannot *be* without *doing*, then the conditions of my doing are, in part, the conditions of my existence. If my doing is dependent on what is done to me or, rather, the ways in which I am done by norms, then the possibility of my persistence as an "I" depends upon my being able to do something with what is done with me. (pp. 3-4)

In other words, "to be" means both to be and to not be recognizable. Agency paradoxically rests in the noninnocence of recognition.

Given that Butler (2004) provides counterarguments to the advantages of remaining less than intelligible, some kind of recognition is implied and not abandoned. If (mis)recognition within loathsome norms is unbearable, then it follows that "survival depends upon escaping the clutch of those norms by which recognition is conferred [even if] it may well be that [a] sense of social belonging is impaired by the distance. Estrangement is preferable to gaining a sense of intelligibility by virtue of norms that will only do [one] in from another direction" (Butler, 2004, p. 3). Even if there is a desire to be recognized and intelligible, the capacity to refuse to be (mis)recognized within a set of norms, albeit with consequences, presupposes a distance from them and a lack of need for such norms, but not necessarily a lack of desire to be recognized. Despite my (mis)recognition as a not-so-dark person of color, "estrangement" is a fitting term to describe my relationship with my adopted family.

The postcolonial challenge for education that the chapter presents is the noninnocence of recognition as an aspect of subject authenticity. My adopted family's (mis)recognition of me points to a more complicated, noninnocent recognition. In my yoga class example in which my colleague (mis)recognizes me and my family within the context of language, recognition is the effect of ruins or Bhabha's (1994) threat of (mis)translation from picking through the refuse. Finally, the example of being asked if I have partner, instead of a husband, shows the noninnocence of recognition as a recognition that is not so sure of itself.

Foregrounding the noninnocence of recognition is to foreground complexities, uncertainties, and the effects of the ruins of recognition. The noninnocence of recognition as an aspect of subject authenticity is when the subject loses her/his desire for certainty and intelligibility. It is an awkward position that is not about losing one's sense of subjectivity in light of norms and hailed interpellations, but about the subject (as both who we think we are and how we are imagined to be) that cannot be simple, innocent, or sure of itself. According to Lather (2007), "accepting loss [of innocence of recognition, of who we thought we are] becomes the very force of learning, and what one loves when lovely knowledge is lost in the promise of thinking and doing otherwise" (p. 13). This is recognition in a more complicated, made from refuse, and uncertain way. "If we make a division between 'lovely knowledge' [in the case of subjects, who we think we are as agents/subjects and who others think we are] and giving that up, and if we can hold in tension our preferences for what we want with what we find [in the case of subjects, who we imagine our self to be in tension with who we are imagined to be]," Pitt and Britzman (2003) argue that "we also see that a working distinction between belief and knowledge opens one to accept the losses that compose the force of learning.... [D]ifficult knowledge is what one makes from the ruins of one's lovely knowledge" (p. 766).

Whereas Lather, Pitt, and Britzman ask for a recapitulation of lovely knowledge for difficult knowledge, I am interested in a difficult subject that emerges from the ruins of one's lovely ideas, what I call humanist constructs of both difference and recognition. When recognition is noninnocent, we learn to accept the loss of who we think we are, thought we were, want to be, and the subject we are imagined to be. The loss of innocence in being recognized and in recognizing is the promise of being and becoming otherwise.

Notes

I would like to thank Roland Sintos Coloma for his detailed feedback on early versions of the chapter that helped shape its final direction, nx Jeong-eun Rhee for taking her time to read it and ask such thought-provoking questions.

1. I could have changed the references of "man" to "human," but have decided to keep the original form to reflect the meaning in light of humanism and the Enlightenment.

2. Here, I am borrowing from Butler (1990/1999, pp. 117, 142) by replacing her concepts of "sex" and "gender" with "authenticity."

References

Anzaldúa, G. (1999/1987). *Borderlands/la frontera: The new mestiza* (2nd ed.). San Francisco, CA: Aunt Lute.
Benjamin, J. (2006). Two-way streets: Recognition of difference and the intersubjective third. *Differences, 17*(1), 116-147.
Bhabha, H. K. (1994). *The location of culture.* London and New York: Routledge.
Butler, J. (1987). *Subjects of desire: Hegelian reflections in twentieth-century France.* New York: Columbia University Press.
Butler, J. (1990/1999). *Gender trouble: Feminism and the subversion of identity.* New York: Routledge.
Butler, J. (2004). *Undoing gender.* New York: Routledge.
Coloma, R. S. (2008). Border crossing subjectivities and research: Through the prism of feminists of color. *Race Ethnicity and Education, 11*(1), 11-28.
Daza, S. (2008). Decolonizing researcher authenticity. *Race Ethnicity and Education, 11*(1), 71-85.
Fanon, F. (1967/1951). *Black skin, white masks.* New York: Grove.
Flax, J. (1991). *Thinking fragments: Psychoanalysis, feminism, and postmodernism in the contemporary West.* Berkeley: University of California Press.
Foucault, M. (1965/1988). *Madness and civilization.* New York: Vintage.
Foucault, M. (1966/1994). *The order of things.* New York: Vintage.
Foucault, M. (1968/1991). *The Foucault effect: Studies in governmentality* (G. Burchell, C. Gordon, & P. Miller, eds.). Chicago, IL: University of Chicago Press.

Foucault, M. (1972). *The archaeology of knowledge.* New York: Pantheon.
Foucault, M. (1997). *Ethics: Subjectivity and truth.* New York: New Press.
Freire, P. (1970). *Pedagogy of the oppressed.* New York: Herder and Herder.
Kumashiro, K. K. (2008). *The seduction of common sense: How the right has framed the debate on America's schools.* New York: Teachers College Press.
Latham, R. (2002). *Consuming youth: Vampires, cyborgs, and the culture of consumption.* Chicago, IL: University of Chicago Press.
Lather, P. (1997). Drawing the line at angels: Working the ruins of feminist ethnography. *International Journal of Qualitative Studies in Education, 10*(3), 285-304.
Lather, P. (2007). *Getting lost: Feminist efforts toward a double(d) science.* Albany: State University of New York Press.
Lorde, A. (1984). *Sister outsider: Essays and speeches.* Freedom, CA: Crossing.
Muñoz, J. E. (1999). *Disidentifications: Queers of color and the performance of politics.* Minneapolis: University of Minnesota Press.
Passerin d'Entrèves, M. (1997). *Habermas and the unfinished project of modernity: Critical essays on the Philosophical Discourse of Modernity.* Cambridge, MA: MIT Press.
Peters, M. A., & Burbules, N. C. (2004). *Poststructuralism and educational research.* Lanham, MD: Rowman and Littlefield.
Pitt, A., & Britzman, D. P. (2003). Speculations on qualities of difficult knowledge in teaching and learning: An experiment in psychoanalytic research. *International Journal of Qualitative Studies in Education, 16*(6), 755-776.
Proctor, M. J., & Demerath, P. (2008). Building the realism bridge: Shaping policy through collective research. *Language Arts, 86*(1), 42-51.
Rhee, J., & Subreenduth, S. (Eds.). (2006). Special issue: De/colonizing education: Examining transnational localities. *International Journal of Qualitative Studies in Education, 19*(5), 545-672.
St. Pierre, E. A., & Pillow, W. S. (Eds.). (2000). *Working the ruins: Feminist poststructural theory and methods in education.* New York: Routledge.
St. Pierre, E. A., & Roulston, K. (2006). The state of qualitative inquiry: A contested science. *International Journal of Qualitative Studies in Education, 19*(6), 673-684.
Spivak, G. C. (1985). Three women's texts and a critique of imperialism. *Critical Inquiry: Race, Writing, and Difference, 12*(1), 243-261.
Subedi, B., & Daza, S. (2008). The possibilities of postcolonial praxis in education. *Race Ethnicity and Education, 11*(1), 1-10.
Voithofer, R. (2005). Designing new media education research: The materiality of data, representation, and dissemination. *Educational Researcher, 34*(9), 3-14.
Williams, R. R. (1997). *Hegel's ethics of recognition.* Berkeley: University of California Press.
Winnicott, D. W. (1965). *The maturational processes and the facilitating environment.* New York: International Universities Press.
Winnicott, D. W. (1971/1991). *Playing and reality.* New York: Basic Books.
Winnicott, D. W. (1975). Mind and its relation to the psyche-soma. In *Through pediatrics to psycho-analysis: Collected papers* (pp. 243-254). New York: Basic Books.
Yoshino, K. (2006). *Covering: The hidden assault on our civil rights.* New York: Random House.

CHAPTER 20

Mediating Globalization: The Non-resident Indian Student in an Era of "India Poised"

ALIYA RAHMAN

Introduction:
Of Tata, Takeovers, and "Time's Great Precipice"

On January 31, 2007, representatives of India's Tata Group conglomerate submitted a final bid over e-mail to purchase the Anglo-Dutch steel producer Corus for what amounted to US$12.04 billion. The bidding war between Tata and the Brazilian steel producer Companhia Siderurgica Nacional had lasted for three months, and the result was (and remains) the biggest acquisition by any Indian company to date.

From the earliest whisperings of Tata's intent to buy in October 2006, the Corus takeover had been painted as high drama by Indian and international news media that spoke regularly of colonialism and empire. After all, not only was an Indian company seeking to buy a descendant of British Steel, but Tata Group had always been regarded as something of an anticolonial hero in Indian business lore. As the story goes, founder Jamshedji Tata studied in England and returned to India to establish cotton, iron, and steel mills that rivaled those of the British Empire. He built Mumbai's Taj Mahal Hotel in 1903 because most of the city's large hotels, which were European-owned, would not accommodate Indians. Tata Group, which grew by acquiring firms from hydroelectric power to K-12 textbook publication, made headlines in 2000 for its purchase of Tetley, Britain's largest tea bag company, a move that the British *Times Magazine* named as an act of "reverse colonization" (Whitworth, 2006).

When the final Corus purchase was announced, India's *Economic Times* included on its front page a large drawing of what New York's Times Square might look like after a few more seasons of Indian-led takeovers (Giridharadas, 2007). On the Square's billboards were Videocon and Tata, rather than Budweiser and Baby Phat. The British *Observer*'s headline read: "Empire Strikes Back" (Wachman, 2006). The *Times of India*, which recently had become the world's largest selling English broadsheet newspaper (TOI, 2005), described the event as the "arrival of India as a big player in the globalisation game, one that looks upon companies and markets of the world as its playground" (BBC, 2007). The *Times* had assembled a more elaborate multimedia response, a nod not only to Tata's maneuver but also to the arrival of 2007 as India's sixtieth year of independence. On the homepage of the *Times*' "India Poised" campaign, users could post messages describing their roles in "the Global Indian Takeover" (TOI, 2007b). In a January 2007 television ad for the campaign, which aired on domestic and international channels, megastar actor Amitabh Bachchan walks alone on a foggy dock, a new oversea highway rising behind him,[1] and recites an anthem penned by veteran Indian lyricist Gulzar, entitled "India v/s India":

> There are two Indias in this country. One India is straining at the leash, eager to spring forth and live up to all the adjectives that the world has been recently showering upon us. The other India is the leash. One India says, "Give me a chance and I'll prove myself." The other says, "Prove yourself first and maybe then you'll have a chance."
>
> One India lives in the optimism of our hearts. The other India lurks in the skepticism of our minds. One India wants. The other India hopes. One India leads. The other India follows. These conversions are on the rise. With each passing day, more and more people from the other India are coming over to this side. And quietly, while the world is not looking, a pulsating, dynamic new India is emerging. An India whose faith in success is far greater than its fear of failure. An India that no longer boycotts foreign-made goods, but buys out the companies that make them instead.
>
> History, they say, is a bad motorist. It rarely ever signals its intentions when it's taking a turn. This is that "rarely ever" moment. History is turning a page. For over half a century, our nation has sprung, stumbled, run, fallen, rolled over, got up and dusted herself, and cantered, sometimes lurched on.
>
> But now, in our sixtieth year as a free nation, the ride has brought us to the edge of time's great precipice. And one India, a tiny little voice at the back of the head, is looking down at the bottom of the ravine and hesitating. The other India is looking up at the sky and saying, "It's time to fly." (Gulzar, 2007)

The references to a history of oppression under colonialism are neither explicit nor unmistakable. India in an era of globalization[2] is poised at a juncture where identity and temporality dictate the terms of material survival. For those at the bottom, we see in the metaphor of the precipice a crystallization of what Arjun Appadurai (2006) calls a double-edged sword of globalization: "fear of inclusion, on draconian terms, and fear of exclusion, for this seems like exclusion from history itself" (p. 35). The Indians on "this side" of the precipice *want* to crawl out from under the boot of colonialism, embrace market liberalization, and ride into a prosperous future in a vehicle called globalization, eliminating, if they must, those who do not support their mission of freedom. Those on "the other side" are barred access to that future, perhaps even to modernity itself, by their fears of losing the globalization game. They find themselves left behind to stagnate and starve in an isolationist past where they are not free, but still strain at the end of the colonial leash. Having provided the only speakable answer, the anthem poses a question of identity that is vital to the nation's survival in an age of globalization: "What kind of Indian are *you*?"

I use small-scale qualitative research to explore "non-resident Indian" (NRI) as a culturally available category that produces and is produced by the large-scale global political and economic circumstances that shape the geography of Gulzar's precipice. I first provide a brief history of the NRI category, beginning in the 1970s and leading up to the first Pravasi Bharatiya Divas ("Non-resident Indian Days") of the twenty-first century. Next, I discuss my interviews with four students who fit the state definition of NRI and who were attending university in the United States, by focusing on how they understood their own nationalities and roles as non-resident Indians. My purpose is to argue that as the Indian state stretches out to eclipse both its former colonial masters and the world's current superpowers in the very capitalist economic terms by which it was declared a "developing" nation, a space emerges for a class of cultural mediators, in this case, non-resident Indians. In their state-mandated roles as sentinels of Indian freedom and purveyors of economic liberalization, such mediators must navigate the territory between supporting projects of national liberation and global dominance.[3] The mechanisms by which students manage these projects simultaneously serve as central points for the chapter.

As currently defined by the Indian government, an NRI is either (1) an Indian citizen living outside of India or (2) a Person of Indian Origin (PIO), where a PIO is a citizen of any country (except Bangladesh or Pakistan) who has held an Indian passport at any time, has at least one grandparent who was an Indian citizen at some point after 1955, or is married to one of these previous two types of people (MOIA, 2005). Yet, in the 1970s, the state definition of NRI referred only to an Indian citizen who had been living outside of India for 183 days or more. By the earlier definition, two of the students interviewed (Rishi and Jaswant) would be classified as NRIs, while the others (Shreya and Ambica) would fall outside of the category due to their United States citizenship. By the current definition, all of them fit into the NRI category. However, the students embraced *and* rejected the NRI label due to cultural, financial, and career implications that I shall discuss in the body of the chapter.

On Rationale and Methodology

The study emerged out of a general interest in globalization and a specific interest in the much-hyped rise of former colonial economies and the people who participate in them to positions of dominance in the global capitalist economy. Having lived in Bangladesh during the 1980s and 1990s, I had a great deal of contact with India through people, entertainment, goods, policies, and ideas that passed between the two nations. Yet, as an American-Bangladeshi researcher with a U.S. passport, my relationship to India and the NRI students in the study was complicated by 60 years of shifting military loyalties and alliances, contested water-sharing treaties and trade agreements, linguistic and religious divisions and wars, and border conflicts.

I chose to do qualitative research into the lives of students in higher education as a means of defining a micro-scale site of inquiry for looking at so large-scale and fast-moving a phenomenon as globalization or, as Appadurai (2006) explains, to "slow down the whirl of the global and its seeming largeness of reach is by holding it still, and making it small" (p. 47) in the body of the individual. I wanted to explore an overarching question particularly relevant to the NRI case: how did students negotiate the tension between the two projects of national liberation and global domination in the state rhetoric on the role of the NRI? Implicit in the question are three others: First, how did students connect their identities as Indians and/or NRIs to their own subalternity or emancipation?[4] Second, to broaden from nationality as an independent category of analysis, how were students' racial, sexual, gender, and class identities implicated in their negotiation of their roles as Indians or NRIs? And finally, did students see themselves as the Ministry of Overseas Indian Affairs saw NRIs as former colonial subjects approaching emancipation at the helm of India's rise to economic preeminence in the world?

Through snowball sampling (Creswell, 1998), I recruited four students who (1) identified as Indian in any sense, (2) had attended the same large Midwestern research university in the United States between 2005 and 2007, (3) had spent at least three years cumulatively in the United States, and (4) were willing to work with me for three separate one- to two-hour recorded interviews. Students completed a short, open-ended background information questionnaire that allowed them to describe their race, nationality, and gender, and that asked them to indicate whether the university classified them as an international or domestic student. They also participated in a series of interviews based on Irving Seidman's (2006) three-interview structure, which progresses from a "focused life history" to a session on the "details of the experience" (in this case, the interviewee's time as an Indian student at the university), and finally a "reflection on the meaning" (the meanings of "NRI" and "Indian" for the students). The interviews were completed between May and July 2007, and my transcripts and notes were member-checked by the students the following October.

The Emergence of the NRI: A Brief History

Ample scholarship on globalization supports the idea that increased transnational movement (physical, financial, and imaginative) and new forms of wealth generated by electronic finance markets have complicated projects of building and maintaining national economies, and that states experience anxiety over losing sovereignty to globalization as a result (Ong, 2005; Saxenian, 2006). Appadurai proposes that one way for states to mediate anxiety is through the production of minority categories, where the minority itself is a construct enabled by the democratic revolutions of the eighteenth century. When the minorities are poor in both financial and cultural capital, "they are convenient symbols of the failure of many forms of development and welfare. When they are wealthy, they raise the spectre of globalization, working as its pariah mediators" (Appadurai, 2006, p. 43). The NRI can be viewed as an example of a wealthy mediator whose production both reflects and channels the Indian state's anxiety in an era of "India Poised."

The late 1970s through early 1990s saw uses of the phrase "non-resident Indian" by the Indian government in granting tax breaks to citizens residing outside of India for over 183 days. During that period when new economic policies brought about profound market liberalization to a formerly protectionist national economy (Bagchi, 1991), the Indian government aggressively sought capital after the financial crisis of 1991 and removed barriers that had limited NRI investment. Consequently, NRI investors were marked as a distinct group to be courted, and the Indian economy became increasingly dependent on their capital. This was evident during the building of the Narmada River hydroelectric dams, in which India found itself unable to meet the World Bank's payment schedule and considered floating NRI bonds for Gujaratis living abroad as a viable option for bailing itself out (Wood, 1993). That currency speculation and the consequent withdrawal of capital from the Indian market by NRIs contributed greatly to the nation's 1991 financial crisis remains a topic rarely discussed (Dash, 1999). The promotion of consumer-driven globalization also emerged as a state strategy during this period. As Satish Deshpande (2003) argues, "while the consumption of Indian goods and the rejection of foreign products in the pre-1991 period era were associated with patriotism and anti-colonialism, consumption in the current wave of globalization is linked to India's potency in the global marketplace" (p. 10). Nowhere was this potency illustrated more clearly than in the NRI lifestyle and its personification in the young, cosmopolitan head of state, Rajiv Gandhi (Lukose, 2005).

Public and private sector efforts of the twenty-first century, such as the India Poised campaign, Citibank's NRI Rupee Checking Account, and the opening of the Ministry of Non-Resident Indian Affairs (renamed as Ministry of Overseas Indian Affairs [MOIA] in 2005) have continued to promote a reliance on NRIs to steer globalization in India's favor. At the opening of the MOIA, President Manmohan Singh marked the potential of NRIs' proglobalization values: "Indians abroad have not only been successful in many walks of life, but have also been a source of inspiration for their brethren back home. The new Ministry of Overseas Indian Affairs, which reflects our recognition of their values, will tap their potential of contributing to our economic growth" (MOIA, 2005).

On January 9, 2003, the Ministry held its first annual Pravasi Bharatiya Divas (PBD), marking the day in 1915 when Mahatma Gandhi returned from South Africa (Rediff, 2003). Each year's PBD program has included high-profile speakers (such as Fijian Prime Minister Mahendra Chaudhury and musician Ravi Shankar), award ceremonies for notable NRIs and PIOs, and fora for airing grievances about home countries (e.g., a 2008 session on the French turban ban preceding President Nicolas Sarkozy's visit to India). Public reaction to the PBDs has been mixed, with resistance centering on the government's courting of NRIs at the expense of domestic Indians. For example, A. K. Bhattacharya's (2003) coverage of the PBDs remarked: "A government that is yet to ensure free access to drinking water and primary education for all its people living in the country is set to splurge Rs. 11 crore (Rs. 110 million) on a three-day show to understand the sentiments of those who chose not to live in this country" (p. 1).

Indeed, state attitudes toward NRIs and globalization do not reflect beliefs shared by all Indians. However, the government's decades-long effort to engage with NRIs has seen returns not only in the private sector but also in government treasuries. For example, NRI bank accounts and financial schemes in the state of Kerala have accounted for 25 percent of the state domestic product since 1970 (Lukose, 2005, p. 918). Consequently, technologies such as the overseas Indian citizenship (OIC) card, introduced in 2007 to grant additional voting and investment rights to PIOs worldwide, continue to emerge. Through the state's awarding of economic and political privileges to Indians abroad and the efforts of Indians to expand their privileges, the NRI category emerged as a signifier of wealth, mobility, and competitive success. At the same time, NRIs became implicated in the twinned roles of leading India to freedom and securing global dominance.

Negotiating Roles: Liberation, Domination, and the NRI Student

Jaswant

Jaswant was born in New Delhi into a Punjabi family that he described as descendant from royalty and whose transnational real estate and construction firms had built many of the "colonies" (residential communities) surrounding their home city. He lived with his mother in California until the age of 10, and upon moving back to his original home in New Delhi enrolled in a school that catered primarily to affluent Indians who saw themselves as current or future NRIs. Jaswant recalls his school accepting payment in U.S. dollars only, providing students with new Mercedez-Benz buses and an air-conditioned soccer field, and requiring laptops instead of notebooks. Although he believed that the school was not academically rigorous, he felt that it excelled in its mission of connecting internationally mobile future leaders to each other.

During high school, Jaswant completed two of what he called "world tours" with his sister and parents, several-month long international vacations for which he took time off from school. He described the trips' purpose as edification and preparation for life through seeing the world, the very same idea that underlied the "grand tours" popular among sons of the Western European aristocracies of the 1800s (Hoffa, 2007). After high school, Jaswant took two years to work as a model for international fashion labels, act in small parts in the Tamil and Hindi film industries, and attend a six-month yoga retreat. He described the retreat as a source of profound spiritual and physical transformation that inspired him to plan for a second career path to complement his ownership of the family business.

> *Jaswant:* I want to open up a huge yoga studio. Like yoga is like the second largest, um, industry under the sports category, you know.... So, yoga is coming up in a really big way now. And I want to do yoga, you know? I want to, I want to—people are opening up yoga in their own homes over here, studios. And what they teach is nothing what is compared to, uh, old ancient yoga in India, where it actually originates from. And it's completely changed now. They have *pool* yoga, and doing yoga inside a swimming pool, and you know that's *bullshit*, you know? Complete bullshit. You know? If you want to do yoga, just teach yoga properly, and all the different asanas, you know?

After high school and in college, Jaswant deliberately dated non-Indian women. It was important to him to "have an Italian girlfriend, have a German girlfriend for a change," so that he would be prepared to interact closely with people from different countries. He interacted with other Indians, but avoided spending time with working-class Indians "who come up as clowns," as he did not want Americans to "relate [him] to them." In 2005, Jaswant enrolled in a U.S. university that offered a hybrid construction engineering and management program, which aligned well with his future plans.

> *Jaswant:* India's a growing economy of course, you know? And as an Indian I think I also want to contribute to it, you know? Personally. My father's construction company's already in India, so once I get my experience around here I'm going to go back to India and start — start not only working on my own firm and my father's firm and growing it, but also contribute a major part of it to the Indian growing economy, you know? And since real estate in India is also growing in a big way, I think if I establish a name over there in a big way, then I will help India grow in a certain way, in a certain industry.

Although he saw himself as initially living and working in various European and North American countries, he expressed that because he was an Indian who called India home, he would eventually settle in New Delhi. His understanding of the significance of being an NRI aligned more closely with the Indian state's rhetoric compared to the other students in the study. He saw himself and his family as successful Indians and NRIs who played a vital role in the development and internationalization of the Indian market, though he did not frame this in emancipatory terms. In his interviews, he recounted statistics about the growth of the national economy and stories about business happenings as important personal pieces of information. From a young age, Jaswant had been taught skills that allowed him to travel and work internationally, and his family's well-established assets in the United States and India allowed him to move himself and his finance capital across borders easily.

Shreya

Shreya was born in Hyderabad, Andhra Pradesh, into a Hindu farming-caste family that she described as "really poor." In India, she lived with her brother, two cousins, and mother, who worked in a factory manufacturing Halls lozenges. While she recalled that some of the children in her family went to school with no food for lunch, Shreya did not connect being poor with having an unhappy childhood. She remembered being "pretty cool" in her school in India, and was aware at a young age that she could influence other people to do what she asked. "I remember especially this girl who was new to the class," she told me. "Maybe I was jealous of her. I always made everybody hate her.... I think maybe she was better at running than I was."

Sponsored by relatives in the United States, Shreya moved with her family to Seattle, Washington, at the age of 10, although she admitted that she often told people "seven, to sound cooler." In Seattle, her mother took a catering job and her father, an engineer, began to live with the family after many years away. Shortly after their arrival in the United States, Shreya's brother and cousin were killed in a car accident, an event that made her feel that she would need to be independent and successful to support herself and her parents.

Her father's job took the family to Indiana, where she attended middle school, high school, and university, and where she interacted with Indians outside of her family for the first time in the United States. As an undergraduate, Shreya realized that she, "like every single gal, [wanted] to live in New York" so that she could work, be independent, and "be sophisticated," an idea that she developed from watching the television show *Sex and the City*. Shreya explained that while she had wanted to be an actress, the loss of her brother and her interactions with NRIs pushed her to choose an undergraduate degree in chemistry that she felt carried promises of success and mobility, and that would prepare her for medical or physical therapy school.

> *Aliya:* What do you remember learning, while you were growing up, about what it means to be a non-resident Indian?

Shreya: Oh my god. This is my favorite topic. Um, to be a very successful – like, successful person. Pretty much to be better than everybody else. You know? Like in *looks*, and in being *smart*. Actually, it's basically being rich. Indian people are superficial! Like I said, all they care about is *money*. And looks. But more so money.

Aliya: Money and looks. Anything else that goes into being the best? Other stuff about your life?

Shreya: Yeah, respect! Prestige.

Aliya: Ok, how do you get that?

Shreya: Highly educated. Like become a doctor [laughter]. If you're not a doctor, you're pretty much a loser! You know? Like, you know, a PhD or something, very highly educated. And that's how you get the rest of it.

Shreya described herself as "a generic kind of girl" with respect to her plans for life and marriage. She wanted to marry and begin having children before she was 26 (she was 22 years old at the time of the interview), and wanted to own a physical therapy practice at a young age so that she could send money to her parents when they retired in India and could secure the kind of prestige that she felt was demanded of her as an Indian in the United States. She explained, "I want everyone to be like, 'You need a p.t.? Go to Shreya!'" In summer of 2007, she had completed a one-year master's program in basic medical sciences, and in March 2008, she was accepted into a physical therapy program.

Shreya used her identity as an NRI to help navigate the spaces between different groups of South Asians. She talked frequently of "FOBs" and "ABCDs," acronyms that students used to label "Fresh Off the Boat" students who had recently arrived in the United States from India and "American Born Confused Desis" where "desi" refers to people or things from the nations of the Indian subcontinent. Shreya resisted embracing either label, and instead identified as an NRI who could be branded neither as a socially awkward "traditional Indian" nor as a culturally conflicted Indian American immigrant. From the NRI position, she could manage her identities through fashion choices, knowledge of popular culture, and decisions about how to discuss her gender and sex. For example, she said, "Indians in India wouldn't know who the hell [the singer] Amy Winehouse is, you know? It's something like … [the television show] *Everybody Loves Raymond*! I'm *sure* they don't watch that in India! Maybe they do, but, you know, that's what doesn't make me a FOB." When explaining why being sex-positive granted her insider status with some women but marked her as anti-Indian to others, she said, "I feel like if Indian

FOBs see me sleeping around with everybody, they're not going to be like 'God, what a slutty girl.' They're going to be like 'What a slutty *Indian* girl.'" For Shreya, college was a place where she could learn to negotiate gender, sexuality, and nationality in ways that would validate her status as a "good" Indian woman and help her to be a successful competitor in the United States.

Rishi

Rishi's parents left Tamil Nadu in the 1970s to work in the Middle East, living first in Saudi Arabia and later in Dubai. Rishi grew up in Dubai, where he attended a school that was administered by India's State Board of Education. He explained that because Dubai's Indian community was physically, legally, and culturally separated from the rest of the emirate, he had only known one Arab closely. Identifying with the behavioral codes that he associated with his parents' Brahmin morals, Rishi did not want to date, drink, or visit bars during high school, and spent his social time at the homes of friends who behaved similarly. Upon arriving in college, Rishi was surprised to find public places, dating, and alcohol at the center of undergraduate social life. Although he did not want to drink regularly or date extensively before marriage, he recognized that he was socially isolated from his peers because he "didn't party." Because he saw this as a potential roadblock to being able to socialize with colleagues and employers, he began systematically researching bar culture.

> *Rishi:* I started learning about the culture more. Uh, you know, people apparently they have common topics. That's what I realized. They talk about partying. They talk about drinks. You know, the different alcohols, and you know, like the imported ones. And I had *no* idea. I didn't even know what a "Jack Daniel" was, I didn't know like there's something like beer and stuff like that. But I was a very gullible and a very naïve person, you know, to be honest. So I was like a bachcha [child]. Ok? Then I kind of developed a lot and started learning a lot. You know? God bless the Internet .... [things] that can enhance your interpersonal skills, you know? So stuff like that. Just pick out a common topic and just research upon that. You don't have to try it if you don't want to, but you just research it. Make people think that "Oh, you're also part of the group."

Rishi never discussed his classes, but talked at length about the cultural knowledge that he learned as a college student outside of class. His university education allowed him to gain cultural competency by practicing activities that he did not enjoy or approve of, echoing his vegetarian parents' decision to eat meat at their Saudi employers' social functions for the sake of employment. It was a decision that he saw as neither hypocritical nor something that he could afford to forego if he was to secure employment and be successful abroad.

When I interviewed Rishi, he was working under-the-table as the night shift clerk at a local motel and had one semester left in his undergraduate electrical engineering program. Upon graduation, he planned to apply for jobs "abroad" that, he explained, meant not in Asia or the Middle East. Rishi called Dubai home, but said that he could never own a business there nor return except on a tourist visa due to the United Arab Emirates' policies for guest workers that make up the majority of its population. He explained that because Dubai "gives more of preference and more benefit to Arabs," there were better business opportunities for him in the United States or Canada. The geography of his current and past experiences gave rise to a complex narration of nationality and citizenship. In describing this, he explained:

> *Rishi:* Ok, the thing is uh, I'm – the nationality, I do say Indian. I don't ask questions. Because I know that I'm from India. My parents are from India, and I'm an Indian. I have Indian blood running through my system. That makes me an Indian. And um, for say the country of residence, I can't say India because I haven't been in – I haven't stayed in India for a significant portion of time. I was brought up in Dubai, all right? And currently I'm in, studying in America. So now *that* creates a twist on the whole story and where, you know? Because majorly [sic] I've spent my life in Dubai so I mostly write down Dubai. But I don't really have a residence visa there because of the rules and regulations. Um, so I mean, if you ask me I *am* a citizen of India because I hold an Indian passport, and since I have Indian blood running through my system that makes me an Indian. And the only difference is that I was brought up in a different place. So I'm an NRI. Non-resident Indian.

When I asked Rishi how his national identity impacted his future plans, he told me that he did not want to live or work in India after completing his education: leaving India was a marker of upward mobility and was a desirable thing to do. The NRI category meant to Rishi something compatible yet very different in purpose from the MOIA's mobilization of the term. Rishi's responses were consistent with the rhetoric employed in MOIA President Manmohan Singh's speech that described living and working abroad as an important part of being a successful Indian, but also indicated that normative understandings of citizenship and nationality were inadequate for explaining his life. Thus, the NRI category allowed him to reject binary identity constructions and the expectations that came with them so that he could work and live abroad in ways that did not threaten his identity as an Indian.

Ambica

Ambica was born in Waterloo, Iowa, to Telugu-speaking parents who left Andhra Pradesh in the 1970s. As a toddler, Ambica moved with her family to a small town in Indiana, where her parents opened a psychiatric practice. She did not have close relationships with other Indians outside of her family during her school years, having spent her entire life in Midwestern communities where there was no visible South Asian community. She learned about Indian culture from her parents and two older brothers who left home in the 1990s to study medicine (one in the United States and one in India) and from family trips to India during her childhood. As a teenager, she worked as a clerical assistant at the family clinic. Ambica believed that she and her brothers, like many Indian children, generally did better in school than Americans and would move on to middle class or elite jobs in the United States because their parents placed more emphasis and effort on learning. She began learning to play the violin when she was three years old, performed in a piano recital at Carnegie Hall as a child, and spent a brief period during high school in a rock band with her two brothers.

In high school, she decided that she ultimately wanted to open a branch of her family's clinic in New York City, where she believed she would be challenged because "if you make it there, that means you're *really* something." Working for someone other than her family after medical school was not an option for her, nor was working in India, a geographical move that she regarded as indicating failure for doctors. She saw her family's position as "already up here," and found "no reason to start down here; it doesn't make any sense."

In college, Ambica's core social group was comprised for the first time of South Asian students. She studied with other desis in her basic medical sciences program, but resisted participating in student organizations or discussing romantic relationships with them because this resulted in "too much drama," particularly around issues of being a "good Indian girl." While Ambica wanted to be as successful a doctor as her mother, father, and two brothers, she learned during college that her family was unaccepting of her desire to date women because they believed that it would make it impossible for her to include her chosen family in her public life as a successful Indian doctor. She was sure that her mother did not want their family clinic to be "run by a lesbian" because she considered it anti-Indian to have a partner of the same sex. Consequently, she avoided discussing or disclosing her sexual orientation around Indians, though she openly dated women in other contexts, and she rejected her family's disapproval after spending extensive time searching Hindu texts for homophobic doctrine and finding none (this, she said, was one reason why she liked Hinduism). Ambica asked me if I could research the topic. She was happy to see that Ruth Vanita (2002) had extensively documented instances of same-sex love in Hindu texts, but drew no peace of mind from Suparna Bhaskaran's (2004) work on the roots of homophobia in modern India. Bhaskaran argues that, in India's rise to preeminence in a global capitalist economy, there is a need for aggressive heterosexual female consumers as epitomized by India's stockpile of Bollywood starlets and Miss Worlds. Hence, being a lesbian is contrary to state interests. Ambica threw out this argument, proposing instead that Indian homophobia was more likely of "the colonists."

At the time of our interview, Ambica had just completed the same one-year master's program that Shreya had attended. She also had been accepted to medical school, after which she planned to live and work in the United States, which she called home, for the rest of her life. For Ambica, NRI was not a category with which she identified except to explain to others why she behaved differently than people who had been born and raised in India in terms of her sexuality or future plans, as it allowed her to do this without recounting her Indian nationality. For example, when asked what "NRI" meant to her, she explained:

> *Ambica:* When I went to India everybody's like, automatically, because I was Indian, they were like, um, "Oh, so are you going to move here?" And I'm like "No, why would I?" And they were like "Well, you know, because you're Indian." And I'm like "No, because my home is America." Period. Like, and then I actually switched the question and asked them, I'm like "Are you going to move to America any time soon?" And they were like "Why would I do that?" I'm like "Exactly. Why would I do this?" And I'm like "You would never move, because India's your home. Period.".... I'm American, but I think I'm equally Indian in the sense that I'm proud of who I am. I have no issues. I have no identity *crisis* of what I am.

On her background information questionnaire, she wrote of her nationality: "American, but I am of Indian origin." She explained that she told people she was "Indian, but born and raised in the U.S." because "people tie 'American' with being white. That's why I guess I say I'm Indian but I was born and raised here." Ambica's reluctance to call herself American, despite her U.S. citizenship and her history of living in the country, is as much a reflection of other people's inability to understand complex national identities as it is an effect of racialized nationality. To deal with both, Ambica mobilized the NRI category in circumstances where others were unable to understand her valid understandings of home and how she understood her obligations to India (none) and Indian culture (some).

Research Questions: A Discussion

I return to address the three questions posed in the introduction of the chapter. First, how did students connect their identities as Indians and/or NRIs to their own subalternity or emancipation? While they felt pressured by responsibilities that they saw as part of being Indians abroad, students saw themselves as having a great deal of agency and believed that this was both a reason for and a result of being an Indian whose family had left India. Because they located the Indians they knew in the United States as members of the U.S. middle or international elite class, the students saw Indians in the United States as upwardly mobile people and placed themselves within this narrative. From Ambica's insistence that the people who "really make it" do so in New York (as she intended to do) to Rishi's explanation that the right path for him as an NRI did *not* include returning to India, students saw themselves as part of an emancipated group of Indians abroad. However, this was contingent on far more than nationality.

Gayatri Spivak (1999) sets forth three points on the movement of subalternity toward hegemony, the first two of which are particularly relevant to this discussion. First, she states, "simply by being postcolonial or the member of an ethnic minority, we are not 'subaltern.' That word is reserved for the sheer heterogeneity of decolonized space" (p. 310). Second, she explains:

> When a line of communication is established between a member of subaltern groups and the circuits of citizenship or institutionality, the subaltern has been inserted into the long road to hegemony. Unless we want to be romantic purists or primitivists about "preserving subalternity"—a contradiction in terms—this is absolutely to be desired.... Remembering this allows us to take pride in our work without making missionary claims. (p. 310)

So, while attempting to preserve subalternity by policing the borders of who is considered a "true Indian" would be counterproductive to the project of emancipation, it *is* important to acknowledge that there is heterogeneity within the category of "Indian" that results in differing degrees of access to the circuits of institutionality. It is useful to explore how heterogeneity impacts who considers themselves obligated to or embedded in the project of national liberation. As Spivak indicates, being Indian does not imply subalternity. Many other factors come into play, which returns me to my second question.

How were students' racial, sexual, gender, and class identities implicated in their negotiation of their roles as NRIs? As Ambica explained in her first interview, nationality might "have nothing to do with citizenship" and regulatory technologies like passports or green cards might be negotiated by shifts in taste or other areas of identity (Dolby, 2000). Ambica's regulation of how publicly she affirmed same-sex romantic relationships and Shreya's movements between a "sophisticated," sex-positive woman and a sheltered, abstinent "good girl" reflected conscious and unconscious shifts in national identity and/or presentation. The emergence of such details from questions about the meaning of "Indian" and "NRI" indicates an intense interdependency between nationality and other spheres of identity. Such interdependency affected how students understood their relationship to India's global economic positioning, which brings me to my third question.

Did the students see themselves as key players in the project of Indian liberation? Not necessarily. While all saw the successful, well-educated business owner as a model NRIs should aspire to become, the students' complicated insider/outsider relationships with India served to disconnect their goals from national economy or nation-building projects. Shreya and Rishi identified their nationality as "Indian" and saw a clear line of geographic, academic, and financial progress from their grandparents' generation to their own, narrating themselves as positive outcomes of generations of diligent study. Yet, they thought that moving to India would interrupt the positive trend, and did not feel obligated to send money to India except to support their parents in retirement. Ambica expressed similar fears of regressing from her family's current position ("up here") and described herself as American and under no obligation to India when it came to discussing what kinds of career, family, and sexual options were available to her. Jaswant was the only student who explicitly stated that he wanted to be part of an India that was "coming up in a big way," but saw his role as further propelling an India that had come into its own, rather than as someone involved in national liberation.

I return at this point to the chapter's overarching question: how did students negotiate their roles in the state's twin projects of national liberation and global domination? Simply put, it seems that the NRI students in the study did not find any difficulty in this task, because none saw themselves as key players in the first project and most did not situate their own life goals with the second. They narrated the drive to be competitive and successful as something that was central to their lives and connected to being Indian, but (except in Jaswant's case) they did not see this as working for *India's* benefit. Although some of the students spoke of Britain's control over India in the past, none located *themselves* within a history of colonial oppression. Although Jaswant wanted to be part of India "coming up in a big way," he stated that his royal lineage had always placed his family above other Indians. Shreya, who vividly remembered living in poverty in Hyderabad, believed that she had a widened range of life choices open to her as a result of emigrating, and believed that she would own her business if she exercised her agency and stayed in the United States. Rishi, who acknowledged that he had grown up with few legal rights in Dubai and that his parents had left India for economic survival, believed that his choices would lead him through an immigration track and to entrepreneurial success in a future that did not include investing in India. Ambica, who acknowledged that her queer sexual identity barred her from acceptance in both the Indian and U.S. mainstream, wanted above all else to "make it" in what she saw as the world's most competitive and cosmopolitan city, something that she believed she would achieve because her Indian parents had prioritized well in raising her.

But such a conclusion raises new questions. Students did not see themselves in state projects of global domination or national liberation, but does this mean that they are not, indeed, players in those processes? Might students *have to* reject participating in both projects because they are inherently contradictory? Since we have already established that these students cannot be considered subaltern in the sense that Spivak employs the term, does this mean that students cannot, by virtue of their emancipation, even attempt to participate in projects of liberation as they move through the spaces of higher education? To all three queries, I would say no. Not only would such proposals be theoretically unsound, but they would foreclose the possibility that those who are deeply embedded in structures of institutionality, such as NRIs and/or academics, can still unhypocritically do postcolonial and anticolonial work. Supporting the belief that this is possible is, to me, the central postcolonial challenge in education.

Epilogue:
NRI Students and the Postcolonial Challenge in Education

Tata's global expansion made headlines again when its US$2.3 billion decision to purchase the automobile brands Jaguar and Land Rover from the Ford Motor Company was finalized on May 26, 2008 (*Economist*, 2008). The purchase came a week before the state government of Maharashtra announced that it would allocate 193 million rupees (US$4.5 million) to build a statue of the warrior-king Chhatrapati Shivaji, an icon embraced by the Hindu nationalist Shiv Sena ("Army of Shiva") party and associated with anticolonial guerilla combat tactics, on an off-shore site near Mumbai (Pinglay, 2008). Erected along the coast of India's financial and film capital, the statue would stand at a height of 93.5 meters, 0.8 meters taller than New York's Statue of Liberty. The India Poised campaign, too, has lived on. Its homepage displays a welcome message: "Please take the time to read the note alongside. It is a peek into our intentions when we return to launch the next phase of 'India Poised.'" That note appears below.

> D.O.
> Two modest alphabets.
> Placed side by side however, they form a word potent enough to turn a seething mass of people into a nation.
> Do.
> The last time we decided to Do or Die, it changed the map of the world. Today the eyes of the world are upon us again.
> What are we going to do?
> Are we going to turn from a land of philosophers into a nation of do-ers? Or are we going to keep thinking about what we should be doing instead of doing something about what we're thinking?
> Are we going to continue talking about our infrastructure and our potholes and our property and our health care? Or are we going to use that telephone, that shovel, the PIL, that ballot paper and do something to make it happen?
> The truth is this.
> Thinking can only happen from an armchair but doing must happen on your feet. Thinking may be a great way to get things started but doing is the only way to get things done.
> And let's face it, you're never really caught in a traffic jam, you are the traffic jam.
> So let's stop basking in our glorious past or day dreaming about our magnificent future. Let's do something about dominating today.
> And domination starts with Do. (TOI, 2007a)

We see here an argument for contemporary domination worldwide as a means of escaping historical colonial domination. On one hand, because the MOIA rhetoric portrays global domination not as contradictory to but as a mechanism for national liberation, it legitimizes the former project in ways that may do nothing for the latter and that reinscribe the very ideologies that necessitate liberation movements in the first place. This is precisely one way in which the insertion of the subaltern can be "manipulated to legitimate globalization" (Spivak, 1999, p. 310). That is, the argument that Indian dominance in the global economy is evidence of the subaltern speaking and thus a thing only to be desired glosses over the possibility that such dominance may never benefit subaltern groups, if it is evidence of the already emancipated becoming more wealthy (e.g., if Jaswant, a member of the Indian elite who has long had access to the circuits of institutionality, opens his yoga studio).

Such a twinned strategy is also not without emancipatory possibility. At its core, the MOIA strategy centers on a tripartite import scheme of internationally acquired though not necessarily "foreign" *currency, expertise, and stories* into the Indian economy to counterdeficit in the public and private sectors. It is a strategy that founders over poor distribution of inflow, but is not inherently problematic except in an extreme isolationist view of international relations. It depends not only on willing NRI investors and returning graduates to provide the first two commodities, but also on a network of visible Indians living willingly abroad, like the students in the study, to provide the last, as their stories are told as positive examples of globalization. While currency and expertise are appropriated by the already enfranchised, stories and narratives are renewable resources that are more difficult to control in terms of whom they may reach or benefit. The dissolution of subalternity begins, as Spivak says, with the establishment of communication between the subaltern and the circuits of institutionality. If representations of emancipated Indians flowing into India can validate the possibility and indicate the mechanics of such a communication, then NRI students participate in projects of liberation by moving daily and visibly through the spaces in and around higher education, regardless of their consciousness of such projects.

Notes

1. I am indebted to Sheetal Mehta-Karia at the Ontario Institute for Studies in Education of the University of Toronto for providing me with valuable background information regarding the significance of this image.

2. I understand "globalization" to mean "a growing magnitude or intensity of global flows such that states and societies become increasingly enmeshed in worldwide systems and networks of interaction" (Held & McGrew, 2003, p. 3).

3. I use "national liberation" to refer to ongoing projects of strengthening the sovereignty of the Indian state. The Indian independence movement of the 1940s can be considered a significant step in this process, but should not be considered the *only* step. I understand more recent attempts to decrease the hold of foreign governments and multinational organizations such as the World Bank and the International Monetary Fund over the Indian economy as

additional projects of national liberation. It is important to remember that victories on the level of the nation-state, such as "the event of political independence" (Spivak, 1993, p. 48), cannot be assumed to give rise to the liberation of all people living in the nation-state. "Global dominance," which I use to refer to projects of strengthening the dominance of the Indian state/market over other national governments/economies, is a similarly nuanced term. The rise of the Indian state and market to positions of dominance in the global political and economic arenas should not be understood to imply a rise to dominance of Indian people over citizens of other nations, many of whom remain disenfranchised both within India and in the host nations of the Indian diaspora.

4. I use "subalternity" as employed by Spivak (1988, 1993, 1999) in her attempt to move away from Gramsci (1992) whose understanding of the term she believes has been complicated by imperialism. For Gramsci, the term refers to the condition of being structurally written out of the circuits of power through which the dominant regime maintains its position. For Spivak, this understanding has given rise to a native informant class that is produced by and works in the service of the colonizer, rather than the colonized. She understands the subaltern instead as that which is defined by what it is not. On the flip side, "emancipation" refers in the Gramscian sense to a condition of having access to circuits of power employed by the dominant regime. In this study, that group is a transnational capitalist bourgeoisie, within which affluent NRIs most certainly belong. However, Spivak's move (with which I align here) suggests that emancipation, like subalternity, becomes a matter of representation, such that the emancipated can be understood as the referential subject against which the subaltern is defined.

References

Appadurai, A. (2006). *Fear of small numbers*. Durham, NC: Duke University Press.
Bagchi, A. (1991). Reflections on the nature of the Indian bourgeoisie. *Social Scientist, 9*(3), 3-18.
Bhaskaran, S. (2004). *Made in India: Decolonizations, queer sexualities, trans/national projects*. New York: Palgrave Macmillan.
Bhattacharya, A. K. (2003, January 8). The importance of being an NRI. *Rediff.com*. Retrieved January 11, 2008, from http://www.rediff.com/money/2003/jan/08spec.htm
British Broadcasting Corporation (BBC) (2007, February 1). India media upbeat on Tata's win. *BBC*. Retrieved June 1, 2007, from http://news.bbc.co.uk/2/hi/south_asia/6319481.stm
Creswell, J. (1998). *Qualitative inquiry and research design: Choosing among five traditions*. Thousand Oaks, CA: Sage.
Dash, K. C. (1999). India's international monetary fund loans: Finessing win-set negotiations within domestic and international politics. *Asian Survey, 39*(6), 884-907.
Deshpande, S. (2003). *Contemporary India: A sociological view*. New Delhi: Viking.
Dolby, N. (2000). The shifting ground of race: The role of taste in youth's production of identities. *Race Ethnicity and Education, 3*(1), 7-23.
Economist (2008, May 26). Tata, Jaguar, and Land Rover: A used-car bargain? *Economist Online*. Retrieved May 26, 2008, from http://www.economist.com/business
Giridharadas, A. (2007, February 5). India is reveling in being the buyer. *The New York Times Online*. Retrieved April 26, 2008, from http://www.nytimes.com/2007/02/06/business/worldbusiness/06rupee.html
Gramsci, A. (1992). *Prison notebooks* (J. A. Buttigieg & A. Callari, trans.). New York: Columbia

University Press.

Gulzar. (2007). India v/s India. Transcribed February 20, 2007, from http://www.indiapoised.com/video2.htm

Held, D., & McGrew, A. (Eds.). (2003). *The global transformations reader: An introduction to the globalization debate* (2nd ed.). Cambridge: Polity.

Hoffa, W. (2007). A history of U.S. study abroad: Beginnings to 1965. *Frontiers, 15,* 1-314.

Lukose, R. (2005). Consuming globalization: Youth and gender in Kerala, India. *Journal of Social History, 38*(4), 915-935.

Ministry of Overseas Indian Affairs (MOIA) (2005). Information required under section four of the RTI Act. *Ministry of Overseas Indian Affairs.* Retrieved March 3, 2007, from http://moia.gov.in/shared/linkimages/138.doc

Ong, A. (2005). Ecologies of expertise: Assembling flows, managing citizenship. In A. Ong & S. J. Collier (Eds.), *Global assemblages: Technology, politics, and ethics as anthropological problems* (pp. 337-353). Carlton: Blackwell.

Pinglay, P. (2008, June 3). India plans huge "liberty statue." *BBC Online.* Retrieved June 3, 2008, from http://www.news.bbc.co.uk/2/hi/south_asia/7433486.stm

Rediff India Abroad (2003, January 5). 1,200 NRIs to attend Pravasi Bharatiya Divas. *Rediff India Abroad.* Retrieved January 11, 2008, from http://www.rediff.com/news/

Saxenian, A. (2006). *The new Argonauts: Regional advantage in a global economy.* Cambridge, MA: Harvard University Press.

Seidman, I. (2006). *Interviewing as qualitative research.* New York: Teachers College Press.

Spivak, G. (1988). Can the subaltern speak? In C. Nelson & L. Grossberg (Eds.), *Marxism and the interpretation of culture* (pp. 271-313). Urbana: University of Illinois Press.

Spivak, G. (1993). *Outside in the teaching machine.* New York: Routledge.

Spivak, G. (1999). *A critique of postcolonial reason.* Cambridge, MA: Harvard University Press.

Times of India (TOI) (2005, June 26). Times now masthead of the world. *Times of India.* Retrieved May 20, 2007, from http://timesofindia.indiatimes.com/articleshow/1152489.cms

Times of India (TOI) (2007a). D.O. India poised. Retrieved March 20, 2008, from http://www.indiapoised.com/

Times of India (TOI) (2007b). Take on the world. *India poised.* Retrieved January 20, 2008, from http://www.indiapoised.com/

Vanita, R. (Ed.) (2002). *Queering India: Same sex love and eroticism in Indian culture and society.* London: Routledge.

Wachman, R. (2006, October 22). Empire strikes back: India forges new steel alliance. *The Observer.* Retrieved May 20, 2007, from http://www.guardian.co.uk

Whitworth, D. (2006, May 27). The empire strikes back. *Times Magazine.* Retrieved October 20, 2007, from http://www.tata.com/tata_sons/media/20060527.htm

Wood, J. R. (1993). India's Narmada River dams. *Asian Survey, 33*(10), 968-984.

AFTERWORD

Southern Theory and Its Dynamics for Postcolonial Education

ANNE HICKLING-HUDSON

An important recent book in the field of postcolonial education is not about education, but about significant texts in the development of social theory in the world shaped by colonialism. In this Afterword, I will discuss how the ideas of Raewyn Connell's excellent study, *Southern Theory: The Global Dynamics of Knowledge in Social Science* (2007), can help dynamize postcolonial education with its exploration of various philosophical contexts.

Postcolonial theory resonates with Connell's work because it argues for the vital necessity of knowledge on a planetary scale to forge an understanding of and solutions to the devastating problems of global society. It challenges and seeks to counter the harm done by prevailing models of social thought which have been shaped, and picture the world as having been shaped, almost exclusively "by men, by capitalists, by the educated and the affluent" (Connell, 2007, p. i), especially by those in the global metropoles of Europe and the United States. For most of modern history, the majority world of the global "South" as well as oppressed communities within the global "North" have been forced into a peripheral position in relation to elites whose power, wealth, and advancement rested to a great extent on the exploitation of the South. As Connell points out, the social sciences have used this deliberately underdeveloped world (Rodney, 1972) of the "periphery" mainly as a mine for data that are interpreted through the lens of minority-rich world theories. Education as part of the social sciences has, in my view, been very much a part of this process.

Postcolonial theory helps to uncover and rebuild the autonomous yet hybrid identity of those dispossessed by imperialist dominance, its exploration and probing of indigenous, local, and creole or blended knowledges. It challenges, counters, and can reshape political structures that have their roots in colonialism and imperialism. Connell does not categorize or name her theory-building as "postcolonial," and only occasionally deploys the term in its temporal and philosophical usages when she talks of the postcolonial state (p. 188), postcolonial society (p. 215), postcolonial knowledge (p. 96), and postcolonial studies (p. 167). Whether or not her book could be said to be located within the contested paradigms of postcolonial theory, it contributes dynamically to it because of its detailed exploration of the agendas and philosophies of texts that relate to colonialism, decolonization, imperialism, and forging new ideas in the global South, taking these studies "seriously as theory—as texts to learn from, not just about" (p. x).

Although Connell states that her study is not a history of social thought, it does function as a critical historiography of selected social texts and their contexts. It starts by showing how the social sciences took their modern institutional form in the second half of the nineteenth century at the high tide of European imperialism. Sociology grew out of the racist colonial assumption that societies progressed according to "laws" of social evolution in which the "primitive" was inexorably displaced by the "civilized." Its methods sought to demonstrate this, as shown in the chapter on "Empire and the Creation of a Social Science" (pp. 3-25). Other scholars have similarly shown the imperialist basis of other academic disciplines, for example, Brian Hudson in his pathbreaking 1974 article "The New Geography and the New Imperialism," followed later by geographers who extended this field of study and applied a postcolonial style of analysis in different locations (Smith & Godlewska, 1994), and Helen Tiffin (2004) discussing the "benev(i)olence" of English literature education in the Caribbean and other British colonies.

By the second half of the twentieth century, the overt, evolutionary racism in colonial social thought had been rejected by revisionist streams of social science, including functionalist sociology, modernization theory, and neoclassical economics. However, these later traditions were themselves neocolonial: "formed ... on ethnocentric assumptions that amounted to a gigantic lie—that modernity created itself within the North Atlantic world, independent of the rest of humanity" (Connell, 2007, p. x). Connell provides a very useful outline of later attempts to correct these distortions, including Marxist theories of imperialism from Hobson and Lenin onwards, and the "world system" approach developed by Wallerstein and his colleagues to name patterns of domination, oppression, and enforced dependency. But Connell points out that, in spite of inspirational ideas in these theories, they continue to "work through categories produced in the metropole, and does not dialogue with the ideas produced by the colonized world" (p. xi). She argues that such a pattern continues in the updated streams of social science thought, including those of Habermas and Foucault, Giddens and Bourdieu, queer theory, economic modeling, evolutionary psychology, and most of the literature on globalization.

Thus, even late modernist and postmodern social sciences, with their assumptions of universality and/or their techniques of exclusion and erasure of global majorities, continue to be hegemonic, shored up by the weight of metropolitan wealth and power. Alternative ways of thinking about the world are marginalized, intellectually discredited, relegated to outdated historical thinking, or appropriated. The erasure of global thinking is similar, suggests Connell, to the Australian experience of "terra nullius," the brutal invasion and colonization of timeless cultures in an ancient land said by the British to be occupied by nobody. Her use of this metaphor is striking:

> *Terra nullius*, the coloniser's dream, is a sinister presupposition for social science. It is invoked every time we try to theorise the formation of social institutions and systems from scratch, in a blank space. Whenever we see the words "building block" in a treatise of social theory, we should be asking who used to occupy the land.
>
> Can we have social theory that does not claim universality for a metropolitan point of view, does not read from only one direction, does not exclude the experience and social thought of most of humanity, and is not constructed on *terra nullius*? (Connell, 2007, p. 47)

In my experience as an academic in education, Connell's thoughts are appropriate to much of the research and writing on education. Scholarship informed by postcolonial education theory is rare and perhaps even unique in its commitment to dialogue with ideas and issues in the colonized and postcolonial world. Such commitment is illustrated by the books and edited collections produced in the postcolonial education field. Roland Sintos Coloma's collection follows earlier works, such as John Willinsky's groundbreaking book *Learning to Divide the World: Education at Empire's End* (1998), the volume *Disrupting Preconceptions: Postcolonialism and Education* edited by Hickling-Hudson, Matthews, and Woods (2004), and special editions of journals including *Discourse: Studies in the Cultural Politics of Education* (2002) and *Pedagogy, Culture and Society* (2006). This is only a start, however, and needs to be taken much further. Aparna Mishra Tarc, in this collection, makes the point that "Postcolonial studies are slow to come to education, in part, because postcolonial studies threaten to undo education, to unravel the passionately held-onto thought and knowledge of the modern Western-educated student and scholar" (p. 195). Connell's *Southern Theory*, with its lucid discussions of the intellectual power and insights of social thought in societies marginalized by the imperialist system, provides a rich context and resource for this observation.

Postcolonial theory, with its epistemological shifts that challenge modernist Western knowledge construction, representation, and truth claims (Hickling-Hudson, Matthews, & Woods, 2004, p. 4), engages not only with the complexities of decolonization, but also with globalization's consequences in recent decades (Tikly, 2004a, 2004b). It is particularly apt for exploring the implications of educational colonialism, decolonization, and experimentation, not only for the former colonies, but also for the former colonial powers. It explores multiple ways of knowing the world, and enables us to refine the goals of emancipatory social action in ways that take the needs, aspirations, and practices of specific cultures into account. As Fazal Rizvi points out in Coloma's volume, postcolonial theories can perform a valuable role, not least because they draw attention to the false universalism of globalization and show how contemporary social, political, economic, and cultural practices continue to be located within processes of cultural domination through the imposition of imperialist structures of power.

The key argument of Connell's book is that "colonised and peripheral societies produce social thought *about the modern world* which has as much intellectual power as metropolitan social thought and more political relevance" (p. xii, italics in original). The book closely examines selected texts in the context of Africa, Iran, India, Latin America, and Australia, as a contribution to the work that needs to be done "to develop the connection, as well as the contrasts, between these bodies of thought and those of the metropole" (p. xii). This position is extremely important to education not only because education scholarship draws heavily on social science theory and assumptions, but also because it has its own trajectory that needs to be analyzed in the framework of a critical historiography of educational knowledge. Thus, a task similar to that undertaken by Connell, a close analysis of texts, debates, and trends of thought in specific contexts that have been ignored or distorted by the metropolitan gaze, needs to be mapped out and implemented in the education field.

I outline below points from Connell's discussions that struck me, a Caribbean-born and educated scholar teaching in an Australian university, as being particularly valuable for the philosophy of education both in "Northern" and

"Southern" contexts.

Connell discusses African texts within the context of anticolonial intellectual movements that constituted an epistemological break with Eurocentrism. An important influence in the thrust for decolonization, these movements included the new African historiography, the artistic and intellectual productions of negritude, ethnophilosophy, and ethnoscience, and the political thought of the African struggle for independence. That the potential of this intellectual ferment was disappointingly not developed in the latter half of the twentieth century was due partly to internal disagreements and partly to the weak position of many African intellectuals and universities that were squeezed out of commissioned research and national influence by the imperialist global economy and its allies. The difficult terrain for decolonization stems from the thoroughness of the cultural work done by the "colonising structure," as African historian Valentine Mudimbe calls the apparatus of colonial rule which "undertook the domination of space, the integration of local economies into the capitalist system, and the re-forming of the natives' minds" (Connell, 2007, p. 97). Connell outlines the current South African-led thrust for an African "renaissance" to revalidate indigenous thought and culture in the search for sustainable and authentic development. At the same time, she points out the concern of some African scholars about the dangers of drifting toward racial essentialism in this search, with the possible consequence of marginalizing or excluding progressive and committed groups in the population.

The intellectuals in modernizing Iran cited by Connell are those who challenge the thought and hegemonic influence of the "West." One of these scholars, Jalal Al e Ahmad, uses a vivid and thought-provoking term that can be roughly translated as "Westoxication" or "Westafflictedness" or "Plagued by the West" (Connell, 2007, p. 118). They challenge the oppressive strictures of current conservative Islamic governance in many locations. Particularly interesting is the revolutionary thought of Ali Shariati, an Iranian scholar whose work in the 1970s and 1980s promoted banned ideas about the radical ethos of the original message of Islam. It includes analyzing the implications of believing in the unity of all men and women in one God, discussing the meaning of the imperative for these believers to commit themselves to social equality, and examining the vulnerability of systems of domination and the permanent possibility of agency, opposition, and change (pp. 118–137).

One of the striking images from the book's section on Indian social thought is the pain and disruption caused by colonialism. Connell discusses how the psychological pain connected to imperialism was probed by Ashis

Nandy in his 1983 text *The Intimate Enemy: Loss and Recovery of Self under Colonialism*. For India, this pain was experienced in the family, in education, and in the limits of attempted resolutions through political and later cult-like mysticism (Connell, 2007, p. 186). For Britain, the empire inflicted psychological damage in its glorification of violence and masculine valor, contempt for the feminine, fear of cultural complexity and the Orientalized "other," and promotion of the myth of the homogeneous "British race." These dispositions also induced lasting psychological damage to the colonies of settlement to which they were exported, such as Australia, New Zealand, and Canada (p. 184). Connell analyzes Mohandas Gandhi as the one who most successfully cracked the code of British imperialism by stepping outside of its norms. His deployment of the Hindu folk technique of nonviolent resistance forced the system of British rule to reveal its violence and failure, and ultimately rendered India ungovernable by the invaders. Connell also discusses the importance of the Indian intellectual movement, initiated in the 1980s by Ranajit Guha and encapsulated in the journal *Subaltern Studies*, to counter the traditional focus on the state and the struggles around it, with a focus on the politics of the people (pp. 166–168).

A school of development studies that has key significance for understanding majority-world society in the context of imperialist dominance grew in Latin America, as Connell shows by analyzing important themes from the work of Argentinean economist Raul Prebisch in the 1950s, and in the 1970s, the pathbreaking cultural studies analysis *How to Read Donald Duck* by Ariel Dorfmann and Armand Mattelart, and the radical historical sociology of development, *Dependency and Development in Latin America*, by Fernando Cardoso and Enzo Faletto. This latter text did the vital work of mapping how Latin American political economies changed, but always within the context of dependency, during the nineteenth and twentieth centuries. Connell notes that one of the most important theoretical analyses of Cardoso and Faletto was that "development" is not the opposite of "dependence," as modernization theory would have us believe. Instead, "Development can occur in a way that maintains dependence; new forms of dependence emerge historically, and this process is still going on" (Connell, 2007, p. 147). This analysis is, in my view, of crucial significance for illuminating entrenched dilemmas in the decolonizing world and its education systems.

In Connell's view, the carefully thought out method of Cardoso and Faletto for the analysis of transnational social processes "is far more sophisticated than most of the metropolitan literature on 'globalisation' that appeared 25 years later" (p. 148). Yet she goes on to show that this kind of Marxist-oriented social science thinking lost credibility in the last two decades of the twentieth century, with the victory of neoliberalism in Latin America and throughout the world, bringing a crisis of impotence for popular politics and the social sciences. As public enterprises and the welfare state were dismantled and income even further distributed toward enriching the already wealthy, Chilean social scientist Martin Hopenhayn utilizes "postmodern themes of complexity, indeterminacy, and the local in understanding contemporary society, and in justifying social science's new interest in everyday life rather than large structures" (Connell, 2007, p. 154). Nestor Garcia Canclini, analyzing Latin America's mega cities, points to deep fissures between internationally oriented elites and local communities of survival, yet argues that old models of hierarchical domination no longer apply, and power is increasingly hidden from public view. He feels that cultural production (e.g., in popular music and television) provides important possibilities for regional action to defend cultural independence and diversity (pp. 161–162). It seems to me that postmodern Latin American theorists are relevant to helping educators push the boundaries of their understanding of the importance of cultural studies analysis to education.

Connell discusses the scholarship of feminist social scientists from Australia, India, and Latin America. Educators can expand on this work by investigating it as a key source of gender analysis for postcolonial education theory. Australian sociologist Cilla Bulbeck explores the theme discussed in the United Nation's Decade for Women (1975–1985) as to "whether it was possible to have a united international feminism, given the different situations of women in different countries, and resistance to the dominance of white feminism" (p. 85). In India, although some feminists such as Vananda Shiva adopt and expand questionably dichotomous Western models of women as peaceful and men as violent, they also emphasize the importance of women in local leadership, particularly in the green movement (pp. 175–176). Anthropologist Veena Das takes an original path of studying the complexities of gender relations and state power during critical events, such as the British partition in 1947 of India into Hindu and Muslim states and the Union Carbide chemical disaster at Bhopal that killed thousands and injured hundreds of thousands. Her work transcends studies of local communities, showing how the powerful discourses of the state, judges, doctors, and social workers can redefine reality to the detriment of the victims. For example, at Bhopal the long judicial process converted the pain of the victims' mass poisoning and the issue of multinational liability into a scene of multinational charity through a settlement that many thought was radically inadequate (pp.

178-179). Chile's Sonia Montecino stresses how identities change with different socioeconomic circumstances. She explores historical shifts and changes in feminine identities, including tension between maternal and workplace identities, the construction of collective identities for women within the struggles of women's movements as well as the struggles to get men to recognize injustice to women in their habitual practices and to recognize women as legitimate leaders and equal workers in the public sphere (Connell, 2007, pp. 156-158).

Connell's reflections on the social sciences in Australia lead her to a deep unease and rejection of the universalistic, nongrounded generalizations that are based on "the silence of the land" (Chapter 9). She points to dispossession as one of the most undertheorized concepts in modern social thought, and argues that it needs to sink roots in the many kinds of dispossession suffered by Indigenous peoples (p. 206). Aboriginal philosopher Mick Dodson reminds us of the connection between the issues of poverty and social exclusion with the seizure of Indigenous lands, for "the result of not having access to your land is the destruction of culture, language and spirituality" (pp. 202, 195). Connell notes the significance of linking our theory-building to specific places, identifying the placed sites of the globalizing firms and people who make wealth from them: "The wealth acquired by the neoliberal economy ... comes to rest in the pockets of particular suits, covering bodies that sit or lie on particular square metres of the land.... That is why so much effort goes into protecting the places of the rich" (p. 209). New possibilities in Australian social science were flagged by a perspective that saw Australia as a product molded by colonialism. In this context, scholars reinterpreted their connection with colonialism, some rethinking the relationships between settlers and Indigenous peoples, and others providing new directions in studies of gender, migration, and the family (pp. 84-86).

Connell ends by discussing the importance of "Southern theory" for contributing to the development of a global study of socioeconomic patterns (Chapter 10). Such theorizing displaces the prevailing tradition of using what amounts to be ethno-social sciences of Western metropolitan theory and imposing distorted interpretations of global patterns. Metropolitan theory is built on probing social processes and structures in a manner that often does not examine its own assumptions. In leaving out the voices of the global South when talking about the global, it enacts intellectual violence to the experiences of more than three quarters of the world, and thus has no possibility of successfully tackling global problems. As Connell puts it, dominant theory is reluctant, or perhaps lacks the concepts, to talk about "the destruction of social relations, about discontinuity and dispossession, about the bloodshed involved in creating the world in which we currently live" (p. 215). It also rarely examines the social processes of the elites, institutions, interests, and strategies that are implicated in perpetuating these catastrophes.

All of this is of vital importance to postcolonial studies in education. Like Connell, educators need to emphasize strongly the necessity for a countervailing social science to carry out "power structure" research that studies the capacity of the metropole to act as metropole. Such research would study how institutions shape the ruling practices of dominant elites (Connell, Ashenden, Kessler, & Dowsett, 1982; Connell, 1993). It would study the role of the metropolitan state, its technologies, and the cultural institutions, such as museums and research centers implicated in the global dominance that perpetuates and even deepens the inequities of old-style colonialism. It would study the important gender dimension, following the lead of feminist research that currently provides a picture of imperialist masculinities. It would be aware of the conditions underlying the production of knowledge, including the international linkages of the social science workforce and the comparative impoverishment and fragility of the institutional base of scholars in the South. It also would know the implications of the biases of global publishing for influencing the circulation of knowledge (Connell, 2007, pp. 212-220). Such clarification would help to explain the worrying trend that, 40 years after independence, African universities and schools (and to my knowledge those in many other regions) continue to use Western metropolitan models of education with very little Africanization of content and language, an indication of the continuing metropolitan cultural hegemony that produces difficulty in finding ground for new developments in social thought (p. 109).

Postcolonial research in education would continue to stress the importance of the contextualized probing of identity in all of its complexities, contradictions, and strivings, a direction taken up by several contributors to this edited collection. Without a firm hold on this, we cannot clarify our individual and collective roles as citizens, educators, and networkers committed to changing the shape and function of the education still so deeply influenced by colonialism. Heidi Safia Mirza in this volume provides an example of this clarification. In uncovering the erasure of black women's genealogy in British universities, she draws attention to how journeys into the heart of whiteness constitute a place of pain as well as a form of resistance with potential for contributing to transforming the academy. In my experience of teacher education in Australia, it is not only students "of color," but also some white students who experience pain, embarrassment, and rage at the unjust hegemonies of whiteness. It is important for us to interweave education into the cultural tapestry of region and globe, as is done in this volume by Cameron McCarthy's analysis of C. L. R. James' *Beyond a Boundary* on the sociocultural location of cricket, illustrating many layers of Caribbean society including history, empire, schooling, identity, social class, sports organization, and current neoliberal change. We need to deal with the challenges of educating ourselves and our students to unlearn many of our taught perceptions of the world, whether in the global South or the global North (Willinsky, 1998). It is imperative to question the structures of schooling as they relate to society (Hickling-Hudson, 2002; Hickling-Hudson & Ahlquist, 2003; Koh, 2004) and to tease out new dimensions of postcolonial leadership for education.

The wide canvas of postcolonial education thinking helps to put into perspective debates as to whether educational critique and activism should be informed more by what is seen as "post"colonial or "anti"colonial thought and traditions (Rizvi in this collection; Dei & Kempf, 2006). Such a question leads to another: what is the difference, and is it important for education analysis? Proponents of the anticolonial stance, which has been taken up by several Indigenous scholars, claim that it connotes a more activist tradition of resistance to oppression than the postcolonial stance that is seen as more abstract. But it is clear, when we take the long view that Connell's *Southern Theory* takes of global social theory, that activist anticolonialism is embedded in postcolonial education studies and vice versa. An anticolonial perspective is necessarily postcolonial in the sense of contesting colonialism and the modes of domination and dependency that stemmed from it. A postcolonial perspective deconstructs colonialism, neocolonialism, and imperialism not just for the sake of semantics, but in order to challenge, resist, disrupt, and push beyond the implications of these systems to forge new answers. The potential for new vision in current circumstances is deepened and extended by the utilization of "post"techniques and concepts such as discourse, genealogy, and governmentality that are not utilized by older approaches. Stephanie Lynn Daza (in this collection) reminds us of Luke's point, made over ten years ago, that whereas postmodernism responds to modernism and poststructuralism to structuralism, postcolonialism responds to colonialism and not the end of colonialism. Questioning leads to clarification, but at the same time we should consider how to combine our resources rather than fragment ourselves by debates that do not get to the heart of our shared concerns.

References

Connell, R. (2007). *Southern theory: The global dynamics of knowledge in social science.* Crows Nest, Australia: Allen & Unwin.

Connell, R. W. (1993). *Schools and social justice.* Philadelphia, PA: Temple University Press.

Connell, R. W., Ashenden, D. J., Kessler, S., & Dowsett, G. W. (1982). *Making the difference: Schools, families and social division.* Sydney, Australia: Allen & Unwin.

Dei, G. J. S., & Kempf, A. (2006). *Anti-colonialism and education: The politics of resistance.* Rotterdam & Taipei: Sense.

Hickling-Hudson, A. (2002). Re-visioning from the inside: Getting under the skin of the World Bank's education sector strategy. *International Journal of Educational Development, 22*(6), 565–577.

Hickling-Hudson, A., & Ahlquist, R. (2003). Contesting the curriculum in the schooling of indigenous children in Australia and the USA: From Eurocentrism to culturally powerful pedagogies. *Comparative Education Review, 47*(1), 64–89.

Hickling-Hudson, A., Matthews, J., & Woods, A. (2004). Education, postcolonialism and disruptions. In A. Hickling-Hudson, J. Matthews, & A. Woods (Eds.), *Disrupting preconceptions: Postcolonialism and education* (pp. 1–16). Flaxton, Australia: Post Pressed.

Hudson, B. (1974). The new geography and the new imperialism. *Antipode: A Radical Journal of Geography, 9*(2), 12–19.

Koh, A. (2004). The Singapore education system: Postcolonial encounter of the Singaporean kind. In A. Hickling-Hudson, J. Matthews, & A. Woods (Eds.), *Disrupting preconceptions: Postcolonialism and education* (pp. 155–174). Flaxton, Australia: Post Pressed.

Rodney, W. (1972). *How Europe underdeveloped Africa.* London: Bogle L'Ouverture.

Smith, N., & Godlewska, A. (Eds.). (1994). *Geography and empire: Critical studies in the history of geography.* Oxford, UK: Blackwell.

Tiffin, H. (2004). The benev(i)olence of imperial education. In A. Hickling-Hudson, J. Matthews, & A. Woods (Eds.), *Disrupting preconceptions: Postcolonialism and education* (pp. 143–154). Flaxton, Australia: Post Pressed, 143–144.

Tikly, L. (2004a). Education and the new imperialism. *Comparative Education, 40*(2), 173–198.

Tikly, L. (2004b). Globalisation and education in sub-Saharan Africa: A postcolonial analysis. In A. Hickling-Hudson, J. Matthews, & A. Woods (Eds.), *Disrupting preconceptions: Postcolonialism and education* (pp. 109–126). Flaxton, Australia: Post Pressed.

Willinsky, J. (1998). *Learning to divide the world: Education at empire's end.* Minneapolis: University of Minnesota Press.

Acknowledgments

Like all meaningful intellectual, political, and pedagogical projects, this book is a labor of love. It emerged initially from discussions with Stephanie Lynn Daza, Jeong-eun Rhee, Binaya Subedi, and Sharon Subreenduth, whose brilliance has inspired and nurtured me since our graduate school days at The Ohio State University. Its content has been generously supplied and enriched by the contributors in this collection, who share and expand my vision for postcolonial studies in education. My deepest appreciation goes to the authors who accepted my invitation and trusted me with their words and insights. I want to thank Cameron McCarthy and Shirley Steinberg for facilitating the publication of this book, and Kari Dehli for the invaluable gift of time and resources which enabled me to complete a large bulk of the editing during my first term in a new department and country. Alexander Means and Anna Kim provided helpful editorial support. I also want to thank David Warren and the Scarboro Foreign Mission Society for the image of the young Filipino schoolchildren (circa early 1960s) who grace the book's cover. Christopher Myers, Sophie Appel, and Valerie Best of Peter Lang are a pleasure to work with and patiently responded to the questions and concerns of a novice editor.

To my parents Aida and Jesus and to my siblings and in-laws, Bernadette, Edward and Katherine, Desiree and Joe, I am sustained by your unconditional love and support, in spite of my intermittent visits, phone calls, and emails. I am very proud of my niece Helena Isabella and nephew Aidan Josh who live on both sides of the Pacific. To James C. Eslinger, working on this book was a productive distraction and made the distance slightly bearable. I am looking forward to a new chapter of our life together in Canada.

Some of the chapters in this book have been published previously elsewhere, and the respective authors and I thank their original publishers for permitting us to reprint them:

> Coloma, R. S. (2006). Putting queer to work: Examining empire and education. *International Journal of Qualitative Studies in Education*, 19(5), 639–657.
> Kaomea, J. (2006). Nā wāhine mana: A postcolonial reading of classroom discourse on the imperial rescue of oppressed Hawaiian women. *Pedagogy, Culture & Society*, 14(3), 329–348.

Rizvi, F. (2007). Postcolonialism and globalization in education. *Cultural Studies <=> Critical Methodologies, 7*(3), 256-263.

Subedi, B. (2006). Theorizing a 'halfie' researcher's identity in transnational fieldwork. *International Journal of Qualitative Studies in Education, 19*(5), 573-593.

Tikly, L. (2004). Education and the new imperialism. *Comparative Education, 40*(2), 173-198.

Villenas, S. A. (2007). Diaspora and the anthropology of Latino education: Challenges, affinities, and intersections. *Anthropology & Education Quarterly, 38*(4), 419-425.

Viruru, R. (2006). Postcolonial technologies of power: Standardized testing and representing diverse young children. *International Journal of Educational Policy, Research, and Practice, 7*(1), 49-70.

Last but not the least, I am indebted to many intellectuals, activists, and educators, both recognized and unheralded, who have worked and continue to work to challenge the history, legacy, and continuation of imperialism and colonialism. May this book serve as a guide for praxis in solidarity with struggles yet to come. I am because we are.

Contributors

NINA ASHER holds the J. Franklin Bayhi Endowed Professorship, is Associate Professor of Educational Theory, Policy, and Practice, and of Women's and Gender Studies, and is Co-Director of the Curriculum Theory Project, at Louisiana State University, United States. She has published in the areas of postcolonialism and feminism, multiculturalism, and Asian American studies and education.

BERNADETTE BAKER is Professor in the Department of Curriculum and Instruction, the Center for Global Studies, and the Holtz Center for the Social Study of Science and Technology at the University of Wisconsin-Madison, United States, and the University of Turku, Finland. She works within and between the domains of philosophy, history, sociology of knowledge, comparative cosmology, and transnational curriculum inquiry.

ROLAND SINTOS COLOMA is Assistant Professor of Sociology and Equity Studies in Education at the Ontario Institute for Studies in Education, University of Toronto, Canada. His research focuses on transnationalism, empire, and diaspora, theorizing difference and intersectionality, history and cultural studies. He is working on a manuscript regarding the history of the public school system in the Philippines under United States rule in the early twentieth century.

ANTONIA DARDER is Professor of Educational Policy Studies and Latino/a Studies at the University of Illinois, Urbana-Champaign, United States. Her research focuses on issues of racialized inequalities with an emphasis on questions of identity, language, culture, the body, and social class. She is the author of *Culture and Power in the Classroom* (1991), *Reinventing Paulo Freire: A Pedagogy of Love* (2002), and *After Race: Racism After Multiculturalism* (2004).

STEPHANIE LYNN DAZA is Assistant Professor of Curriculum and Instruction at the University of Texas-Arlington, United States. Her research focuses on feminist, postcolonial, and queer theories, research methodologies, globalizing and schooling trends in the Americas, policy, difference, and in/equity. She is the cochair of the Postcolonial Studies in Education special interest group of the American Educational Research Association (2007-2010).

ANNE HICKLING-HUDSON is Associate Professor in the School of Cultural and Language Studies in Education at Queensland University of Technology, Australia. A scholar of postcolonial theory and comparative education, her publications analyze educational policy, national development, teacher education, and curriculum. She is currently researching Cuba's contribution to global education, and educational initiatives to counter the HIV/AIDS pandemic.

JULIE KAOMEA is a Native Hawaiian, Associate Professor in the Department of Curriculum Studies at the University of Hawai'i, United States. Her research focuses on the enduring effects of colonialism in Hawaiian and other "post"-colonial educational communities.

ANNA KIM is a doctoral student in the Department of Sociology and Equity Studies in Education at the Ontario Institute for Studies in Education, University of Toronto, Canada. Her research examines sex trafficking, government policies, and activism.

CAMERON MCCARTHY is Professor of Educational Policy Studies and Research Professor in the Institute of Communications Research at the University of Illinois at Urbana-Champaign, United States. He is the author of *The Uses of Culture: Education and the Limits of Ethnic Affiliation* (1998), and the coauthor of *Reading and Teaching the Postcolonial* (2001). He is working on a new book entitled *The Aftermath of Race*.

ALEXANDER MEANS is a doctoral student in the Department of Sociology and Equity Studies in Education at the Ontario Institute for Studies in Education, University of Toronto, Canada. A former public school teacher, his research interests include educational policy, cultural studies, and urban education.

HEIDI SAFIA MIRZA is Professor of Equalities Studies in Education and Director of the Centre for Equalities, Rights and Social Justice at the Institute of Education, University of London, United Kingdom. She established the Runnymede Collection, an archive documenting the history of the civil rights struggle for a multicultural Britain. She is the author of several books, including *Race, Gender and Educational Desire* (2009).

APARNA MISHRA TARC is Assistant Professor of Urban Education at York University, Canada. Her scholarship explores pedagogies of historical remembrance and psychoanalytic and postcolonial theory in the context of urban teacher education. She is a former elementary school teacher in the Philippines, Vietnam, and Canada.

ALIYA RAHMAN is a doctoral student in the Department of Educational Leadership at Miami University, Ohio, United States. Her research focuses on the political, economic, and cultural significance of study abroad relationships between the United States and the global South. She is currently conducting historical research on the role of study abroad curricula in U.S. colonial and imperialist projects.

JEONG-EUN RHEE is Assistant Professor of Curriculum and Instruction at Long Island University, C.W. Post, United States. Her research interests include postcolonial subjectivity, educational migration, globalization, and de/colonizing research methodologies. She is the cochair of the Postcolonial Studies in Education special interest group of the American Educational Research Association (2007-2010).

FAZAL RIZVI is Professor of Educational Policy Studies at the University of Illinois at Urbana-Champaign, United States, where he directs an online program for teachers around the world in Global Studies in Education. He has written on theories of globalization, educational and cultural policy, and the internationalization of higher education. He is currently researching how Indian universities are engaging with issues of globalization and the knowledge economy.

BINAYA SUBEDI is Assistant Professor in the College of Education and Human Ecology at The Ohio State University, United States. His research interests include postcolonial theory, critical global education, race, globalization, and immigration. His book *Critical Global Perspectives* is forthcoming (Information Age Press). He is working on the educational implications of refugee and working class people's migration from Nepal to Asia, Europe, and North America.

SHARON SUBREENDUTH is Associate Professor of Teaching and Learning at Bowling Green State University, United States, where she serves as project director for an educational and community exchange between South Africa and Ohio, United States. Her scholarship incorporates transnational perspectives in theorizing urban and marginalized schooling, curriculum knowledge, teacher education, and pedagogical practice.

LEON TIKLY is Professor of Education at the University of Bristol, United Kingdom. His research interests include the impact of globalization on education in the postcolonial world and the achievement of Black and minority ethnic students in the UK. He directs a research program consortium looking at implementing education quality in low-income countries (EdQual).

SOFIA A. VILLENAS is Associate Professor of Education and Director of the Latino/a Studies Program at Cornell University, United States. An anthropologist of education, she explores the intersections of culture, language, race, class, gender, and migration. Her scholarship mobilizes theories and knowledge produced by U.S. women of color to examine Latino parents' and specifically Latina mother's experiences and modes of resilience as pedagogy.

RADHIKA VIRURU is Associate Professor and Coordinator of Early Childhood Programs in the College of Education at Qatar University in Doha, Qatar. Her interests include postcolonial theory, its application to international early childhood education, and qualitative research.

RINALDO WALCOTT is Associate Professor of Sociology and Equity Studies in Education at the Ontario Institute for Studies in Education, University of Toronto, Canada. His areas of specialization are cultural studies and cultural theory, queer and gender theory, and transnational and diaspora studies. He is working on a manuscript entitled *Black Diaspora Faggotry: Frames, Readings, Limits*.

LISA WEEMS is Associate Professor of Cultural Studies and Curriculum at Miami University, Ohio, United States. Her scholarship utilizes feminist poststructuralist and postcolonial theories and qualitative research methodologies to examine issues of race, gender, and sexuality. Her current areas of interest focus on transnational popular culture and girlhood studies.

www.ingramcontent.com/pod-product-compliance
Ingram Content Group UK Ltd.
Pitfield, Milton Keynes, MK11 3LW, UK
UKHW022237230426
12048UKWH00018BA/1322